THE WAY TO GROUND ZERO

Recent Titles in
Contributions to the Study of Science Fiction and Fantasy
Series Editor: Marshall Tymn

Aspects of Fantasy: Selected Essays from the Second International Conference on the Fantastic in Literature and Film
William Coyle, editor

Forms of the Fantastic: Selected Essays from the Third International Conference on the Fantastic in Literature and Film
Jan Hokenson and Howard Pearce, editors

Eros in the Mind's Eye: Sexuality and the Fantastic in Art and Film
Donald Palumbo, editor

Worlds Within Women: Myth and Mythmaking in Fantastic Literature by Women
Thelma J. Shinn

Reflections on the Fantastic: Selected Essays from the Fourth International Conference on the Fantastic in the Arts
Michael R. Collings, editor

Merlin's Daughters: Contemporary Women Writers of Fantasy
Charlotte Spivack

Ellipse of Uncertainty: An Introduction to Postmodern Fantasy
Lance Olsen

Foundations of Science Fiction: A Study in Imagination and Evolution
John J. Pierce

Alien to Femininity: Speculative Fiction and Feminist Theory
Marleen S. Barr

The Fantastic in World Literature and the Arts: Selected Essays from the Fifth International Conference on the Fantastic in the Arts
Donald E. Morse, editor

Great Themes of Science Fiction: A Study in Imagination and Evolution
John J. Pierce

Phoenix from the Ashes: The Literature of the Remade World
Carl B. Yoke, editor

"A Better Country": The Worlds of Religious Fantasy and Science Fiction
Martha C. Sammons

Spectrum of the Fantastic: Selected Essays from the Sixth International Conference on the Fantastic in the Arts
Donald Palumbo, editor

THE WAY TO GROUND ZERO

THE ATOMIC BOMB IN AMERICAN SCIENCE FICTION

Martha A. Bartter

Contributions to the Study of Science Fiction and Fantasy, Number 33

GREENWOOD PRESS
NEW YORK • WESTPORT, CONNECTICUT • LONDON

Library of Congress Cataloging-in-Publication Data

Bartter, Martha A.
The way to ground zero : the atomic bomb in American science fiction / Martha A. Bartter.
p. cm. — (Contributions to the study of science fiction and fantasy, ISSN 0193–6875 ; no. 33)
Bibliography: p.
Includes index.
ISBN 0–313–25892–9 (lib. bdg. : alk. paper)
1. Science fiction, American—History and criticism. 2. Atomic bomb in literature. 3. Nuclear warfare in literature. 4. War stories, American—History and criticism. 5. World War, 1939–1945—Literature and the war. I. Title. II. Series.
PS374.A87B37 1988
813'.0876'09—dc19 88–15461

British Library Cataloguing in Publication Data is available.

Library of Congress Catalog Card Number: 88–15461
ISBN: 0–313–25892–9
ISSN: 0193–6875

First published in 1988

Greenwood Press, Inc.
88 Post Road West, Westport, Connecticut 06881

Printed in the United States of America

The paper used in this book complies with the Permanent Paper Standard issued by the National Information Standards Organization (Z39.48–1984).

10 9 8 7 6 5 4 3 2 1

Copyright Acknowledgments

Most Americans assume that the atomic bomb just happened to us in 1945 — that it sprang fully armed from the forehead of the Manhattan Project — and that we have been its helpless victims ever since. In one sense, that seems true; but in a deeper sense the bomb grew from an ongoing, public conversation. It was openly discussed, not only by scientists but also by ordinary people, for at least fifty years before its birth. The attitudes that made it possible, as well as those that made it necessary, were shaped in our personal, social, and political assumptions. These assumptions are faithfully reflected and made real in fiction, becoming part of the ongoing patterns of our living.

We talked our way into our nuclear nightmare, word by word and story by story. As long as we remain ignorant of this conversation, we make ourselves helpless to alter it. But our stories create, as well as reflect, the public conversation we live by. Perhaps we already are telling ourselves stories that contain alternatives to species suicide. If not, we need to begin.

Contents

Acknowledgments

This work grew out of my interest in science fiction, my concern about nuclear war, and the relationships I perceived between fact and fiction. Without the help and encouragement of Theodore Sturgeon (who saw "his" chapter before his death), George Grella and Christopher Lasch at the University of Rochester, and Dr. C. A. Hilgartner, who made his theoretical work available to me, I could never have completed the initial study. Without an Ohio State University research grant and the assistance of those who have shared their collections and expertise with me, I could not have managed the rewriting necessary to present this work to the public.

Thomas Hill of Rochester generously allowed me to spend long hours in his extensive library; Ken Johnson kept the Science Fiction Society Library of the Massachusetts Institute of Technology open for me so that I could do research during the summer and also freely shared his wide-ranging knowledge of sf publishing history; the library staffs at the Marion Public Library, the University of Rochester, and the Ohio

State University found books for me that had long disappeared from public view; and Paul Brians of Washington State University made his bibliographic expertise available to me generously and on short notice. The Science Fiction Research Association gave me a forum in which to present various portions of this work.

Special thanks are due to those who read and criticized portions of this work in progress: Morris Beja, Timothy McNiven, and Margaret Mills Harper of Ohio State, and Ken Johnson, C. A. Hilgartner, and Lois McMaster Bujold. Their help has been invaluable, and I deeply appreciate it. Much that is useful in this book comes from their contributions; the errors are my own.

THE WAY TO GROUND ZERO

Introduction: The Superman Syndrome

Faster than a speeding bullet!
More powerful than a locomotive!
Able to leap tall buildings at a single bound!
Look! Up in the sky!
It's a bird!
It's a plane!
IT'S SUPERMAN!

Introduced in 1938, Superman is probably best described by this opening to the radio show, which premiered in 1940. Even then he was fighting "a never-ending battle for truth, justice, and the American way."[1]

Superman is the model American. Readers know him as an immigrant, a refugee from holocaust. Like every orphan, he may really be a prince in disguise. He displays solid American virtues, however, because as a cute WASP infant, he was adopted by the perfect middle-class, small-town family. As an adult, Clark Kent plays the American ideal—the "nice guy." He thus naturally elicits bullying, even from his girlfriend; but we all know that the minute he strips off his nice-guy suit he becomes the Man of Steel. No wonder he can afford to appear meek and mild-mannered. He is a living superweapon.

In the 1930s, America was struggling with the psychological aftermath of World War I[2] and a worldwide depression of devastating severity. People were looking for solutions but especially for hope. Given the circumstances, it hardly seems surprising that "hope" showed up as a metaphor combining virtually unlimited power and rational control, a superweapon directed by a superintellect. Superman represents the mythic hero who saves ordinary mortals from an untrustworthy and dangerous world. When everything is against us, from random fate (an avalanche) to crafty enemies (Lex Luthor), we demand a superweapon—an incorruptible, nearly omnipotent force that is clearly on our side.

But this desire for power under control did not suddenly become an American dream in the 1930s. Novels from the late nineteenth century already featured superweapons that blast enemies with shattering effectiveness. In the first quarter of the twentieth century, fiction provided some of the American response to a tacit conviction that we were ignorant, insignificant, and ineffective in international affairs; among such responses, it was neither the least powerful nor the most harmful.

The international situation had radically altered by 1945. Americans could take pride in their part in the Allied victory over Italy and Germany. Fear that a landing on mainland Japan would take a terrible toll of Allied troops sobered but did not dim confidence in a similar victory there. But when that victory instead followed a scenario long established in our fiction—defeating our enemy with a superweapon developed by native technological genius—reactions were curiously mixed. We were spared a costly invasion, we had surely ended the war, but many Americans immediately expressed guilt and anxiety often amounting almost to despair.[3]

Few knew much about atomic energy,[4] but many saw the possible consequences of such a terrible weapon. If we could use it on Japanese cities, nothing could prevent others from using it on ours once they had the capability. The press helped make this clear; articles educated the general public by comparing Hiroshima to some well-known American city, drawing circles of destruction at appropriate distances from ground zero. Such articles confirmed the fear, but did not initiate it. The reaction was, at least in part, due to a set of assumptions long encoded in American fiction: we were the "good guys," not the aggressors; we could defend ourselves, but we would not wipe out entire cities full of innocent civilians.[5] No wonder the victory over Japan was greeted with mixed, almost schizophrenic feelings.

Contemporary actions derive from such feelings and responses. If we are to understand them, we need to look not only at where we are but also at how we got here.

WHY FICTION?

> Fiction is simply dreams written out; science fiction consists of the hopes and dreams and fears (for some dreams are nightmares) of a technically based society.
>
> —John W. Campbell, Jr.[6]

Generally speaking, when we want to learn something profound about a culture, we look at the thoughtfully organized and carefully presented words of statesmen, philosophers, scientists, or educators. These are the people who, we believe, wield power in the real world. Storytellers are a different matter, even tellers of such didactic stories as we often find in science fiction. Rarely are such writers extensively trained in sociopolitical analysis, and they are usually not in a position to make a fundamental difference in the world. Why, then, can we hope to analyze our sociocultural situation by examining fiction?

One basic difference between fiction and nonfiction lies in the effect on the reader. Readers may find even the best nonfiction highly abstract, hard to understand, and even harder to remember. They enjoy good fiction because it sets memorable characters in action in a plot. A plot provides tension and excitement. When we examine the continuing story of Superman, we can see how the writers provide the equivalent of a little war in each episode. As the plot builds towards a crisis, tension depends upon creating a real uncertainty over who will "win" and how.[7] For this reason, Superman must have weaknesses; the stronger he becomes, the more vulnerable he must be to something (kryptonite) that can overtake him when he least expects it.[8]

Plots also establish causal relationships. Although we usually assume that laws of cause and effect operate in the real world, we may have difficulty identifying causal patterns in our own lives; a plot can "make sense" of things. When interesting characters are shown as acting in ways that have discernible consequences, we can practice their actions imaginatively. We can even try them out or decide not to. Perhaps one reason epic poetry survived the centuries is that it was loved by generations who not only wanted to hear an exciting story but who also needed to learn how to live in their times: Fiction is easy to remember and gets remembered in practical ways.

A second basic difference stems from the attitude of the writer. The storyteller knows that she is making a fiction; to make the reader willing to suspend disbelief, she creates the setting with care, tests her characters against the demands of the plot, and does her best to provide a believable sequence of action and outcome. While she necessarily accepts a number of premises—for instance, American science fiction is frequently faulted for tacitly assuming that capitalism will extend into outer space[9]—she does so with her audience in mind. In other words, the storyteller takes seriously the need to examine her prejudices and preconceptions (at least on some level) and make them explicit in characters and plot.

The nonfiction writer often does not. Instead, he begins his text with a number of tacit assumptions that he appears never to explore, explain, or even notice. He begins with his own idea of how things "really are" and presents it as true because his focus is on telling his readers how things "ought to be." He assumes that he shares this body of tacit assumptions with his readers. Generally the readers assume this as well. Sometimes they are both right. If not, the writer may get some surprising disagreements; but more often he gets apparent agreement on a basis of real misunderstanding.

Moreover, the nonfiction writer assumes that what he is writing *is* true. However, as any literary critic could tell him, it is just as much a work of the imagination as the fiction to which we contrast it.[10] It is, therefore, "fiction," or at least text, with all the attendant ambiguities. The storyteller at least knows that she is creating a fiction. The serious nonfiction writer usually does not.

As Ken Bruffee points out in his article "Social Construction," we are not discussing "reality" versus "text" here. We are discussing those assumptions by which we create our reality, realized in a text. A critic who analyzes texts using the technique of social construction "understands reality, knowledge, thought, acts, texts, selves, and so on as community- generated and community-maintained linguistic entities—or, more broadly speaking, symbolic entities—that define or 'constitute' the communities that generate them" (1986, 774). This is important. Like speech, fiction is linear; experience is not. By contextualizing constructs in fiction, writers employ sociocultural assumptions that are already available in (and indeed, that simultaneously arise from and create) the society that agrees to use them.[11]

Even critics like Morroe Berger who warn against exaggerating the impact of fiction on the "real world" still agree that it is influential; the problem is to establish the connection between art and life. These connections are not easy to delimit. In *Real and Imagined Worlds*, Berger argues that "changes in the fictional treatment of sex," for example, "may indicate changes in morality and sexual behavior, or they may only indicate changes in what is regarded as appropriate to express in literature" (1977; 204–5). But how can the one take place without the other? Changes in the fictional treatment of sex must indicate a change in sociocultural norms, and the change in norms creates a change in assumptions about appropriate expression of sex in literature—a change that may indeed have helped create the social change it represents.

By putting a construct into fiction, writers make it available more clearly and powerfully than it has been before; they may even seem to have "invented" it. Moreover, giving a construct, as it were, a "local habitation and a name" makes it available in new ways to the society that has tacitly "agreed" to it. We also need to remember that this "agreement" does not imply that most, or even some, members of the society are *conscious* of either the agreement or of the assumption itself.

When some "new thing" (however limited) is made to live in fiction, it becomes more possible to think about and more apt to be realized in "the real world." What can be imagined (within sociocultural guidelines) will be fictionalized. What can be fictionalized can become the focus of scientific or social inquiry, or, more important, simply be assumed to be possible, at which point it does become possible. And, as science fiction can demonstrate, the possible is all too often accomplished. The development of the atomic bomb and issues resulting from its subsequent use derive from and simultaneously create a cultural climate: text and context interrelate inextricably.

Abstractions and Assumptions

Fictions are incredibly complex behavior patterns occurring at the top of a chain of assumptions, not all of them linguistic. To discuss the process of fiction, we must begin by oversimplifying a complex of human behaviors. At the bottom of the behavioral chain, the primary and only certain reality any of us can experience is sensory contact. From this sensory contact we infer both our own existence and the existence of the thing contacted. The process of inferring we term "abstracting," and it becomes the first level of experience we can "think" or talk about.

But we know that we contact—even by vision—very little of what "goes on" around us; in this world of sensory and cognitive overload, humans must operate by noticing (or foregrounding) the information that keeps them alive and growing from moment to moment, while simultaneously ignoring (or backgrounding) the information determined—either consciously or habitually—to be less relevant. The abstractings that we foreground get patterned, and the patterns get assessed; those patterns that work get repeated, while those that do not often get revised or discarded, at least while the human is very young.

Eventually our patterned abstractings get reinforced by cultural approval or by habit or because they serve the immediate purpose adequately. Once we become familiar with a pattern, it disappears from our conscious operating system. It becomes even more than a habit; it becomes the background upon which we form our further habits. This background consists of tacit assumptions, patterns we take for granted. These assumptions form the only recoverable basis of what we frequently call "behavior" in an individual or "culture" in a group. In other words, assumptions have consequences that show up in action.

Not only do we all operate from the "lived assumptions" that we form by abstracting from our experience, we cannot operate without them, nor do we want to. If we had to deal consciously with all the complicated details of living, from basic cellular physiology to behavior as complex, say, as driving a car, we could not function at all. Most of our assumption patterns do work. We can display the evidence: we continue to live. And, like our ancestors, we simultaneously celebrate and explore this business of living by telling stories about it.

The stories, of course, employ the assumptions of the society that created them, and our understanding (decoding) of them requires our knowledge of, if not necessarily our assent to, these assumptions. The way we decode both "world" and "text" depends upon assumptions abstracted from an unknowable (possibly illusory) "reality" represented in our experience only by transactions at the sensory interface. Therefore, each reader brings his or her personal assumptions and interpretations of life experience to the act of reading. No two readers can possibly decode the "same" text quite the same way.

Disclosing Assumptions

Literature is more than a mere "product of society"; as Joan Rockwell maintains in *Fact in Fiction*, it remains a normative, culturally educational force (1974, 3–6). (A "normative force" organizes cultural agreement on the assumptions from which we operate.) Many critics lament that our age no longer produces epic or even heroic models. For instance, Joseph Wood Krutch claims that our literature shows our belief that we are living in the age of the minimal, of the little man, and of the psychiatric model.[12] This may seem especially true if, when we look at "literature," we limit ourselves to the traditional novel and to "proper" poetry. It is clearly less true if we look at the popular transmitters of cultural norms, our contemporary equivalents to Homer and to Shakespeare. I submit that we learn much about "how to live" today from movies and television, particularly drama (including soap opera), and from popular, widely read, genre fiction. Thus the Western, the mystery, the Gothic fantasy, and the action-adventure novel undoubtedly have a more normative effect than we realize or might like to believe.

We can sometimes detect and revise a personal behavior pattern that obviously does not work. It is much harder to detect and revise one that almost works or that works part of the time. But we rarely even try to test our assumptions for logic or coherence. The problem becomes even more difficult when we try to analyze sociocultural assumptions, ones tacitly held as basic to our culture. We do not even notice that we hold them. We take them so much for granted that they become invisible to us. As the anthropologist Edward Hall claims, "Culture hides much more than it reveals, and strangely enough what it hides, it hides most effectively from its own participants. . . . the real job is not to understand foreign culture but to understand our own" (1973, 44). When we find ourselves behaving in ways that cause us problems, we need to disclose and change the underlying, tacit assumptions. If we do not, we generally have little success in changing the resulting behavior.

We can study a sociocultural pattern of lived assumptions only if we can detect it. A pattern becomes noticeable in one of two ways: (1) we see it as different; we notice contrasts between a foreign pattern and our "normal" one, or (2) we develop a set of clues that identify it as a pattern. One way to disclose these patterned assumptions is by identifying cultural clues in literature, particularly in literature that seems busy doing something else. This study will not focus on works that consciously attempt to explain or evaluate our culture, but rather on those that reflect contemporary sociocultural concerns and attitudes (as literature cannot fail to do) while aiming to extrapolate, speculate, or predict possible future patterns. Such a study can reveal assumptions on various sociocultural issues that may help to explain our apparently "inevitable" progression from wishful thinking (a "ray" that can sink ships in Roy Norton's *The Vanishing Fleets* [1908]) to devices increasingly possible scientifically (continually exploding "atomic bombs" in H. G. Wells's *The World Set Free* [1914]; radioactive "dust" of known half-life in Robert A. Heinlein's "Solution Unsatisfactory" [1941]). The literary progression arises from sociopolitical experience shared by a broad group of readers who also share a number of underlying assumptions about how such problems could and should be handled, and who expect to find in fiction some of these assumptions explored as plot devices. We shall consider this as the "sociocultural matrix" under discussion.

WHY SCIENCE FICTION?

Science fiction (sf) forms a particularly useful body of literature through which to examine the sociocultural matrix dealing with superweapons for three reasons. First, sf is consciously didactic. Each of its most prolific early practitioners, Verne and Wells, used fiction to educate his audience; Verne was most interested in predicting possible uses for existing technology, while Wells frequently extrapolated technological or social possibilities. Hugo Gernsback, who created and christened American science fiction as a separate genre, intended his magazines to instruct readers in science while entertaining them. As he announced in his editorial for the first issue of *Amazing Stories* (April 1926), he believed the stories he published were "Extravagant Fiction Today—Cold Fact Tomorrow!"[13]

Second, sf has used superweapons in its mythology of power for almost a hundred years, and until recently, any fiction that discussed nuclear weapons and the results of their use in war was considered sf, whether created by a sf writer like Robert A. Heinlein or L. Ron Hubbard, or by a writer of popular fiction like Philip Wylie or Theodora DuBois. Stories about superweapons have been produced by a variety of sf writers more or less continuously throughout the period under discussion; this motif extends broadly through the sociocultural matrix.

Third, sf has certain conventions and limitations built into its very structure, including those discussed by John Campbell, who argued that simply providing context, especially for a short sf story, can become a major authorial problem:

> Where a here-and-now short-story writer need only develop his characters, the reader supplying in full detail the background, the science-fiction short-story writer must first supply background, and then character before he can begin his story. (Introduction, 1951, viii)

Moreover, the sf writer usually follows the "single-change" rule, which says that any story that makes serious imaginative demands on its readers should create one major change from what is "known" and follow the consequences carefully.[14]

These conventions focus the writer's attention; other aspects of the story may not receive the same care. The aspects that tend to receive the least attention from the author are the aspects that provide the most fruitful field for our study. We can more readily discover the fiction writer's underlying cultural assumptions in the places where he or she is not deliberately creating "fiction."

Definitions

Readers of science fiction frequently disagree on definitions of sf. Most are either too narrow, eliminating works that many want to include; so broad as to be useless; or so cumbersome as to be unmemorable. This lack of agreement on definitions does not prevent sf readers from recognizing sf when they see it, however, or from agreeing in large part on the works they would include. Nor does it preclude new ones. James Gunn opens the first volume of his teaching text, *The Road to Science Fiction*, with a useful definition:

> Science fiction is the branch of literature that deals with the effects of change on people in the real world as it can be projected into the past, the future, or

to distant places. It often concerns itself with scientific or technological change, and it usually involves matters whose importance is greater than the individual or the community; often civilization or the race itself is in danger. (1977, 1)

Many early stories that dealt with fantastic voyages or encounters with alien beings were disguised social criticism, produced in cultures that did not really expect to change. With the advent of the Industrial Revolution, however, the pace of sociocultural change accelerated, and the changes affected more classes of the population more dramatically than ever before. Until pervasive, extensive change in daily life became the norm rather than the exception, the literature we now call sf, Gunn argues, could not be written. These considerations have led a number of critics to consider Mary Shelley's *Frankenstein* (1818) the first science fiction novel.[15] We must go beyond seeing sf purely as a "literature of change," however, if we are to understand the power that sf wields in the American imagination.

Interest in change is certainly not limited to sf. If change were the only—or even the major—issue, Gunn's definition would be useless. For instance, Barbara Tuchman's careful history, *The Guns of August* (1962), clearly falls into no recognized category of sf; yet it describes massive technological and social change. Ward Moore's *Bring the Jubilee* (1955) as clearly does fall into the sf category, and not only because the book begins in a fictional "present" in its exploration of the Civil War. Like any other text, a history, no matter how careful, is a work of fiction. Yet the difference between *The Guns of August* and *Bring the Jubilee* seems to involve more than a mere question of accuracy. *Bring the Jubilee* explores questions of individual responsibility for and control over the creation of history in ways that *The Guns of August* does not.

We may say, then, that the difference between these books lies not only in exploring "the effects of change on people," but more precisely in exploring the power of humans to effect radical, historically significant change. Although it may stretch some definitions of sf to include *Superman*, we must point out how clearly its mythic dimension reflects this issue. Superman does not merely react to change; he often causes it. If we divide fiction (as many fans do) into sf and "mundane" fiction (where mundane consists of "everything else"), we may define contemporary mundane fiction as the exploration of humans reacting to a world of change, and sf as the exploration of humans seeking power to control it. This additional definition should not imply that either mundane fiction or sf has any claim to being "right" or "wrong." Neither is complete, nor do they combine to create a complete picture of human capability. Our problem, in text and context, comes from premature closure, from saying "that's all there is" to either or to both.

Myth and Society

Science fiction has been called "modern mythology." The earliest myths usually concern themselves with the relationship between the gods and man. As man's power to control his environment has increased, especially through the applications of science, fiction moves from the heroic dimension to concern itself with the relationship between man and the power that is man's most important creation. Science fiction is the literature that takes technology seriously. It must deal with the relationship of man to his creation and with the combined power and responsibility that ensues. Shelley's *Frankenstein* serves as an instructive paradigm: Victor Frankenstein not only arrogates to himself the role of creator, but also botches his responsibility towards his creation, paying an enormous personal price for his hubris.

From its generic inception, sf has been a literature questioning man's ability to use effectively the power he is so capable of creating. Very often this power is symbolized by some terrible weapon of destruction. By the late nineteenth century, this weapon often used the then-new discovery of radioactivity as its destructive principle; in 1914, in a work of science fiction, H. G. Wells first named this destructive force an "atomic bomb."[16]

If the aim of myth is to furnish a logical model for solving contradictions, as Claude Lévi-Strauss suggests, then certainly our assumptions about the proper use of power require mythic treatment. We have already noted the contradiction between expected and actual response to the use of the atomic bomb on Japan; such contradictions persist in our culture, created and confirmed by our literature. This book will investigate the transactional role of literature and "real life." I shall assume that sociocultural matrices exist, that readers draw upon them to decode texts, and that the interrelationship between fiction and its sociocultural matrix can be disclosed by studying texts in historical perspective, especially when such a study focuses not on the apparent "point" of the various texts (the plot) but upon the assumptions underlying the plot. To do this, I shall examine the interrelationship between a persistent fictional plot device, *defeating our enemies with a superweapon*, which has entered the tacit assumption patterns of our culture to such an extent that it can be called a "scenario," and the development and use in historical fact of a real superweapon, the atomic bomb, which has become not only the most pervasive sociopolitical problem of our time, but also the defining symbol of our age.

THE PLAN OF THE BOOK

In this book, I shall cover a large number of stories featuring superweapons or superwar, written by American authors or published in

American science fiction magazines. Some are relatively obscure, others very well known. I have provided fairly extensive plot summaries for those works I consider less well known or difficult to obtain, and less discussion of plot for the better-known or more readily available ones. The bibliography lists reprint sources where I have used them; if a reprint source is listed, page numbers refer to that source rather than to the original publication.

In the first part, "The Way to Hiroshima," I discuss works more or less in chronological order, analyzing them to disclose the sociopolitical assumptions that authors took for granted, while developing a method by which these assumptions can be disclosed by a study of popular fiction. Encoded in these fictions we find the patterns that led us to create and use the atomic bomb.

In the second part, "Circling Ground Zero," I look at the deeper assumptions on which these sociopolitical assumptions rest, those by which we declare what humans "are" and how they "naturally" behave by themselves and in groups. For it is upon such tacit assumptions that all our social and political systems are organized and by our consent to them that these systems work. We rarely examine these assumptions for logic or coherence or even notice that we hold them. We can most clearly see them in our public myths, our fiction. Noticing our assumptions gives us the opportunity to test them and to choose among them on the basis of such tests. In the third part, "Leaving Ground Zero," I examine some literary thought experiments based on alternative assumptions proposed by innovative authors who have done such testing.

If we are to change our sociopolitical behavior, we need to know the assumptions it rests upon, not what we "believe" to be true but what we actually do when we are not looking. Then, since the one thing that humans cannot do is *not* assume, we need to devise new assumptions to live by. As we have encoded the current assumptions in fiction, so we need to encode the new ones, to try them out as thought experiments, to make them "real" in our imagination, and then to adopt or reject them. This is not a call for "uplifting" or "moral" fiction, for self-conscious myth making, but for creative exploration of new possibilities in human relations. But we must notice what we have done in the past before we can explore what we might want to do in the future. What else is science fiction for?

NOTES

1. The development of Superman is discussed in *Superman from the Thirties to the Eighties* (New York: Crown, 1983), 9–11.

2. For the psychological impact of World War I, see Paul Fussell, *The Great War and Modern Memory* (New York: Oxford University Press, 1975).

3. These feelings of apprehension, oppression, and insecurity arose spontaneously from public and news commentators alike, beginning the moment the news of Hiroshima was announced. See Paul Boyer, *By the Bomb's Early Light* (N.Y.: Parthenon, 1985), chap. 1, especially pp. 14–22.

4. Science fiction readers largely except themselves from this group. We were reasonably well informed and did not hesitate to share our knowledge. As James Gunn recalls, "When the news came on August 6, 1945, of the destruction of Hiroshima by an atomic bomb, every science fiction reader everywhere knew what it meant and knew the implications of the event. We already had lived through the experience many times in our imaginations. The atomic era had begun." *Alternate Worlds: The Illustrated History of Science Fiction* (Englewood Cliffs, N.J.: Prentice-Hall, 1975), 174.

5. The fact that American firebombings of Tokyo produced as many casualties as did the atomic bomb at Hiroshima was not the issue, nor was the destruction of the open city of Dresden (little known at the time). Similar acts had also been committed by the enemy. But from the beginning, the atomic bomb was seen as different from ordinary high-explosive bombs in kind as well as in destructive power, even before the long-term effects of radiation were generally understood.

6. John W. Campbell, Jr., "The Place of Science Fiction," in *Modern Science Fiction: Its Meaning and Its Future*, ed. Reginald Bretnor, 2nd ed. (Chicago: Advent, 1979), 12.

7. Janet Burroway notes that an effective story must present a struggle between apparently equal forces: "It is imperative . . . that each antagonist have sufficient power to leave the reader in doubt about the outcome." *Writing Fiction: A Guide to Narrative Craft*, 2nd ed. (Boston: Little, Brown, 1987), 7.

8. Superman was less super at his inception than he soon became. From being able to leap tall buildings, he soon could fly; from outracing trains, he learned to exceed the speed of light; from merely blunting hypodermic needles with his skin, he progressed through ignoring bursting shells to surviving atomic blasts. Given this increase in superpowers, the scriptwriters naturally had to invent new kryptonite-based dangers. *Superman*, 11–14.

9. This extension of capitalism rarely includes an automatic extension of democracy. Many plots revolve around the struggles of the capitalist protagonist(s) against an evil empire or fascist dictatorship. Rarely do we see a communistic or even a truly socialistic future in American science fiction, for all the professed fear of such an outcome. Instead, the true end of capitalism seems to be colonialism.

10. Robert Scholes, *Textual Power: Literary Theory and the Teaching of English* (New Haven: Yale University Press, 1985), cites Terry Eagleton's *Literary Theory: An Introduction*:

> Eagleton argues consistently for a radical restructuring of literary study into a broader investigation of discursive practices of all sorts, which he proposes to call rhetoric. This revival of an old discipline would take as its object the *use* of texts of all sorts in all media, holding as its major critical principle the view that all texts are grounded in ideology. Such a rhetoric would cover "both the practice of effective discourse and the science of it": that is, the modes of production, the media of presentation, and the effects of reception.

And it would consider "the various sign systems and signifying practices in our own society . . ." (*Literary Theory*, p. 207).

But as Scholes points out, we need a more comprehensive paradigm to organize such considerations; "our critical position does not totally control our perception of texts." For Scholes, the problem becomes one of interpretation, which depends upon assumptions: "The world is really knowable, either because it is not a text or because texts are finally intelligible," or it is itself a text, and "what makes a text a text is the impossibility of connecting it to the world" (76–79).

Our position is somewhat different: we assume that "world" and "text" depend equally upon assumptions abstracted from an unknowable (possibly illusory) "reality" represented in our experience only by transactions at the sensory interface. At all times, we deal with a fiction.

11. We shall use the term "construct" to avoid the cognitive trap implied by the more familiar term "concept." We are not talking about some "idea" manifested in literature, but about sociocultural assumptions, agreements that create actions as well as text.

12. Joseph Wood Krutch engages this theme in several books, especially *The Modern Temper* (New York: Harcourt, Brace, 1929), 117–21, and *Human Nature and the Human Condition* (New York: Random House, 1959), 97–99.

13. Reminding his readers that "we live in an entirely new world," Gernsback explains in his first editorial that this new world demanded and simultaneously made possible a new kind of fiction. "Science . . . enters so intimately into all our lives today, and we are so much immersed in this science, that we have become rather prone to take new inventions and discoveries for granted." Assuring readers that his magazine will entertain, Gernsback concludes with a promise: "The best of these modern writers of scientifiction have the knack of imparting knowledge, and even inspiration, without once making us aware that we are being taught." "A New Sort of Magazine," *Amazing Stories: The Magazine of Scientifiction* 1, no. 1 (April 1926): 3.

14. The idea of proposing a "single change" that would be necessary and sufficient to produce the result postulated in the story is a concept advocated by H. G. Wells, who felt that too many changes would "lose" the reader. James Gunn, *Alternate Worlds*, 214–15, claims:

> In the thirties main-current science fiction writers began to narrow their aim to a single idea and the consequences of an idea carried out in its purest form to its ultimate outcome. . . . Virtually every story in *The Science Fiction Hall of Fame*, if dissected, will reveal at its heart a single idea.

15. My alterations to Gunn's definition are not intended to dispute this starting point for sf.

16. H. G. Wells's *The World Set Free* is a seminal work and lies at the heart of any study of nuclear war in science fiction. It is, however, a product of British society, and as such, its analysis lies outside the scope of this book.

CHRONOLOGY: THE ATOMIC BOMB

1895		Roentgen discovers X rays
1896		Becquerel discovers radioactivity in uranium
1898		Marie S. Curie discovers radium, polonium
1905		Einstein announces special theory of relativity
1911		Rutherford introduces nuclear model of atom
1915		Einstein announces general theory of relativity
1919		Rutherford artificially transmutes nitrogen
1931		Ernest Lawrence builds first successful cyclotron
1938–39		Hahn and Strassmann bombard uranium;
		Meitner and Frisch explain nuclear fission
1939		Bethe, von Weizsacker show nuclear energy in stars
	Aug. 2	Einstein writes letter to Roosevelt on German research
	Dec. 20	Roosevelt names Defense Board
1940		Official U.S. secrecy on nuclear research
1941	Mar. 11	Lend-Lease Act passed
	May 27	U.S. state of emergency proclaimed;
		U.S. Office of Scientific Research and Development created
	Dec. 2	Roosevelt asks Japanese aims in Indochina
	Dec. 7	Pearl Harbor bombed
	Dec. 8	United States declares war on Japan and Germany
	Dec. 11	Germany, Italy declare war on the United States
1942	Aug. 13	Manhattan Project begun at Oak Ridge, Tennessee, under General Groves
	Dec. 2	Fermi tests first self-sustaining nuclear reactor
1944		Special lab set up at Los Alamos under Oppenheimer
1945	Feb.	Yalta Conference
	Apr. 12	Roosevelt dies; Truman sworn in
	May 8	End of war in Europe: V-E Day
	June 11	Franck Report on use of A-bomb
	July 16	First atom bomb test at Alamogondo
	July–17 Aug. 2	Potsdam Conference
	Aug. 6	Hiroshima bombed*

	Aug. 8	USSR declares war on Japan, invades Manchuria
	Aug. 9	Nagasaki bombed*
	Aug. 10	Japan offers to surrender; peace terms signed September 2
1946		Atomic Energy Commission (AEC) established as civilian control of U.S. developments in atomic energy
	July 1–25	A-bomb tests at Bikini atoll
1946–62		106 nuclear tests in Pacific**
1949	Sep. 23	Atomic explosion reported in USSR
1950	Jan. 31	Truman instructs AEC to produce H-bomb
1951	Jan. 4	Truman: United States in Korea won't bomb China without declaring war
1951–83		601 nuclear tests in the United States; tests continue**
1952	Nov. 1	First H-bomb test, Eniwetok atoll.
1953	Mar. 1	H-bomb test in Marshall Islands; Russia announces production of H-bomb
	Mar–Apr.	Yucca Flats tests kill U.S. livestock (officially denied)
	Dec. 8	Eisenhower's "Atoms for Peace" speech at UN
1954	Jan. 21	First atomic-powered submarine, USS *Nautilus*
	Mar. 1	15-megaton "Bravo" test; "Lucky Dragon" deaths
1955	June 15	Accord signed between United States and Great Britain on peaceful uses of nuclear power
	July	Disarmament discussed at Geneva summit
	Aug. 4	USSR starts new atomic tests
1956	Apr.	USSR promises H-bomb guided missile
	May 4	United States starts new H-bomb tests in Pacific
	May 21	First airborne H-bomb test
	Dec. 26	USSR ends state of war with Japan
1957	Oct. 4	Sputnik I, first earth satellite

*At Hiroshima, "The bomb wiped out the Second Japanese Army to a man, razed four square miles of the city, and killed 60,175 people, including the soldiers." At Nagasaki, 36,000 were reported dead. From the official Japanese report of 31 July 1959, reprinted in Samuel Eliot Morison, *The Oxford History of the American People*, (NY: Oxford, 1965), 1044. These figures do not include *hibakusha*, the surviving victims.

**Figures from *An Alphabetical and Chronological Review of Announced United States Nuclear Tests* (Contemporary Issues Clearinghouse, Pocatello Idaho 1984).

1958	Apr. 5, 12	SANE ad to halt nuclear testing; response
1959		Fallout rise alarms world
1960		Partial test-ban treaty
	Feb. 13	France explodes atomic bomb
1961	Oct.	Cuban missile crisis
1969	July 16	Apollo 11, moon landing
1975	Jul. 15–24	U.S.-USSR combined space mission
1979	Mar. 29	Three-Mile Island
1986	Apr. 26	Chernobyl
1987		U.S.-USSR nuclear weapons reduction agreements

PART I

THE WAY TO HIROSHIMA

1

International Waters: Before World War I

By the last quarter of the nineteenth century, Americans were accustomed to profound changes stemming from important inventions: the steamboat in 1804; the steel plow in 1833 and the McCormick reaper in 1834; the telegraph in 1844 and the transatlantic cable in 1866; the telephone in 1876, the same year as the internal combustion engine; and electric power in 1882, to mention just a few. These new technologies transformed not only the quality of American life, but also the very pattern it followed. And Americans were well aware that inventions do not create themselves.

THE "LONE INVENTOR"

The "marvelous invention" story became popular in dime novels as early as 1868, with Edward S. Ellis's *The Steam Man of the Prairies*. That story was copied by Harry Enton to begin the Frank Reade series in 1876, after newspapers ran accounts of a real steam automation created for patent. By 1879, when Luis Senarens, using the pseudonym "Noname," became author of Frank Reade, Jr., the tradition was established: each episode featured another of the young genius's amazing inventions. Here and in other works the emphasis gradually changed from the inventions to the inventor.[1] In either case the author structures the plot around a problem or threat so serious that the hero can handle it only by building a marvelous machine.

If the invention is a weapon, the threat must come from an enemy, and a superweapon requires a superenemy. We see this with Superman. As villains grow more formidable, his powers increase proportionately. In 1939, "Nothing less than a bursting shell could penetrate his skin"; by 1945, he can survive an atomic bomb. He develops supersenses, including X-ray vision. Initially conceived as able to "leap tall buildings at a single bound," he soon can fly faster than the speed of light. No villain can match such power, so writers invent the various forms of Superman-weakening kryptonite to provide suspense.[2] Superman the superweapon fails to be interesting unless he faces a superopponent, or one wielding superweapons of his own. This principle applies to superweapons stories in general, even to those written before America entered World War I.

As the "lone inventor" of the dime novels conquered problems with his gadgets, readers expected him to face ever-greater problems in each episode. These could be as fantastic as imagination could achieve in a pulp series, but in more serious genres, crises had to seem plausible. This posed a problem. The Civil War was over; the West was virtually conquered; the quality of American life attracted immigrants and envy. What would force the "lone inventor" to create a superweapon, and with it a superplot?

As one solution, American novelists freely borrowed from the British tradition of futurewar novels.[3] These usually warned the country that its defenses were inadequate and must be mended before the enemy was at the gate. This would hardly disturb an American audience, however; the United States had few foreign entanglements, and neither Canada nor Mexico made a convincing enemy. The rest of the world was too far away to fear—unless an enemy invaded by sea. There were, however, various international infelicities that could stand reorganization. A mere hundred years from its founding, America was ready to commence colonial expansion and world trade. As a newcomer, she faced formidable opposition. The Pax Romana had been an effective stimulus for trade, as had the Pax Britannica. Why not a Pax Americana? Given the constraints of geography, this Pax would have to be established by seapower; but the imaginative armory had already been expanded by Jules Verne's *Nautilus* in *20,000 Leagues under the Sea* and the experiments with lighter-than-air craft. Thus the major requirements of a new genre came together: the American hero with his superweapons against the rest of the world.

The Great War Syndicate

Little was known about the possibilities locked within the atom before the discovery of X rays by Roentgen in 1895 and of radioactivity by Becquerel in 1896. Therefore, Frank Stockton says nothing about atoms in *The Great War Syndicate* (1889), but he does present a superweapon:

> The projectile was not, in the ordinary sense of the word, an explosive, and was named by its inventors, "The Instantaneous Motor." It was discharged from an ordinary cannon, but no gunpowder or other explosive compound was used to propel it. The bomb possessed in itself the necessary power of propulsion, and the gun was used merely to give it the proper direction. (22)

The bomb consists of a group of tubes pointing in various directions, each of which "could exert a force sufficient to move an ordinary train of passenger cars one mile, and this power could be exerted instantaneously" (22). To modern readers, the destruction this device causes sounds astonishingly like that from a small atomic bomb.

The story opens "near the close of the nineteenth century," when relations between the United States and Great Britain are strained to the breaking point. American vessels that venture within the three-mile limit off the coast of Canada are captured by British gunboats and taken into custody. As in 1812, this soon leads to war. Americans call for the invasion of Canada, but Canada is backed by Great Britain's naval power, while the United States is weak and without allies.

Twenty-three great capitalists form a Syndicate "with the object of taking entire charge of the war between the United States and Great Britain." They guarantee "to effect a satisfactory peace within one year" or forfeit their bond (12–13). They do not need the existing army and navy, since the Syndicate controls various "inventions and improvements in the art of war" (17). These have not been made available to the armed forces; indeed, only three members of the Syndicate know the secret of the motor-bomb.

After appropriate modifications (sketches are supplied in the text), a fleet of small vessels approaches a Canadian harbor and demands its surrender. This ultimatum is, of course, haughtily rejected. At the touch of a button, a Syndicate vessel launches the "instantaneous motor-bomb," and "a vast aperture in the waters of the bay" appears. Everyone feels "a sharp shock, as if the underlying rocks had been struck by a gigantic trip-hammer" (45). A cloud of water rises a thousand feet in the air, falling to earth as a flood that ravages the land, while the concussion sets off "every torpedo and submarine battery in the harbor" (47). Unable to conceive that any projectile could deliver such destruction, the British commander prefers to blame a coincidental earthquake. The Syndicate promises a second bomb within four hours. This one strikes land, blowing into the air "a vast brown cloud . . . nearly spherical in form, with an apparent diameter of about a thousand yards" (51). "When the cloud had cleared away there were no fortifications, and the bluff on which they had stood had disappeared" (53).

Before the third bomb goes off in the air above Fort Pilcher, all the soldiers are (with some difficulty) evacuated. This blast breaks windows for miles around and kills birds in flight. "As to the fort, it had entirely disappeared, its particles having been instantaneously removed to a great distance in every direction" (65). One man is killed by accident, the only casualty of the "war." British officers who survey the scene exclaim, "This was not war. It was something supernatural, awful!" (66). Since the bomb cannot be seen in flight, they still do not believe in it.

The Syndicate points out that bombs can be used anywhere they can be carried and attacks the British coast. That does it. The peace is signed three days later, the British declaring that "if prohibitive warfare were a good thing for America, it would be an equally good thing for England. More than that, it would be a better thing if only these two countries possessed the power of waging prohibitive warfare" (179). (There is no hint that the Syndicate will share its invention.) Pax Americana is established. Disarmament is followed by universal teaching and use of the English language, "and the Spirit of Civilization raised her head with a confident smile" (191).

WARS TO END WAR

The work of Roentgen, Becquerel, and Curie was well known by the time Hollis Godfrey's *The Man Who Ended War* and Roy Norton's *The Vanishing Fleets* appeared in 1908, and "radioactivity" had become a magic word whose mere mention made superweapons sound plausible. The Spanish-American War had established the United States as a colonial power but had not established American hegemony. America had won its first war of international expansion almost too easily. A greater challenge would be required to justify the invention of a superweapon. What could make a more formidable—or appropriate—enemy than war itself?

The Man Who Ended War

Hollis Godfrey's *The Man Who Ended War* (1908) opens with an anonymous letter to the U.S. Secretary of War declaring "war against the civilized world in the interests of peace" to commence in one year with the sinking of the world's great battleships (1). James Orrington, a reporter, secretly retrieves the letter from the Secretary's wastebasket for investigation.

Orrington's friend John King introduces him to Dorothy Haldane, who happens to have some radium in a leaden casket in her home, where she works with her brother Tom and Richard Regnier, whom King introduces as "a reformer like myself" and Dorothy's suitor (8). Dorothy tests the parchment with radium and discloses erasures that name ships of various nations and give the dates on which "The Man Who Will Stop All War" promises to destroy them. The first victim will be the USS *Alaska*. King bids Orrington farewell for at least two years; he looks ill and has "some things I want to do before I get through with this old earth" (5). Orrington spends the intervening year in a futile effort to publish his findings and to warn authorities of the danger.

Soon after the time appointed for the destruction of the first ship, a man is discovered wandering on the beach madly murmuring, "Disappeared, disappeared, disappeared. Nothing real, nothing real" (23). After treatment with "electrical inductance," he can tell how he patriotically stood at attention in his small boat as the Navy band on the deck of the *Alaska* played the "Star Spangled Banner," and how the ship immediately vanished, rather than sank: "Like a bursting soap bubble, like a light cloud scattered by the wind, she disappeared without a sound!" (40). This report creates fear among an already uneasy public. Tom and Dorothy join Jim in trying to solve the mystery: who might have the ability and the motive to carry out this threat? They consider and dismiss both Regnier and King. (Throughout the book, as they struggle to identify "the man" and understand his invention, they never try to find and stop him.)

In Tom's basement laboratory, Dorothy notes and correlates the charging of his shielded electroscopes with the times that ships are destroyed. She proves that "the man" is projecting powerful waves; Tom and Jim have been thinking in terms of sabotage. Tom then defines the weapon as "some radio-active generator." Dorothy understands immediately: "His force, so powerful that it affects our reflectoscopes thousands of miles away, may be able to resolve the metal which makes up a battleship into its electrons, which would disappear as intangible gas" (53).

Orrington becomes a suspect as he continues to predict the successive sinkings of British, Japanese, and German ships in his articles, but Tom and Dorothy spring him from jail. Meanwhile, the international peace movement gains strength. Only the Kaiser is a "stumbling block in the way of a universal peace" (94). When "the man" sinks a second German ship, one he did not predict in the letter, the friends fear that war will begin before they can get to England and hire divers to examine its remains in Portsmouth Harbour. Due to national mobilization, Jim must make the dive himself. He finds the crew of the German ship lying as though asleep—lacking only their metal buttons—on the ocean floor. From this, they deduce that "the man" must use a submarine (137–38). In London, they find the laboratory where an elderly scientist died from working with the mysterious radioactive substance and learn more about its properties, but come no closer to identifying "the man."

Then war is declared, and Jim goes to observe the naval battle in an insulated wooden boat that Tom has prepared. He watches in horror:

> One after another, twenty-two ships more went down, and the antagonists, who had started with eighty-two of the proudest ships that any empire ever sent forth, were reduced to a shattered remnant of twenty. Then suddenly they gave way. Flesh and blood could stand no more. Slowly, but as proud as ever, and with no haste of flight, the Germans drew off to the north, the English to the south. As they parted, another ship and yet another disappeared. I groaned in impotent agony. "Spare them, spare the rest?" I cried wildly. "Can't you see they have given up the fight." (249)

Apparently "the man" cannot; he even sinks all the unshielded correspondents' boats. Thus Jim becomes the only eyewitness; his report goes to the King before publication. The King immediately calls a peace conference at The Hague "to consider the question of disarmament" (259). Only the Emperor of Germany refuses to attend, imperiling the whole plan. "Complete disarmament was wholly possible if every nation were to agree. . . . for no nation would give up her defenses, with a powerful armored foe at her gates" (259–60).

Finally the Kaiser sends a message to the conference:

> I have believed that war, that armies made for the best good of my state; I believe it still. I do not believe in peace. But I cannot expose my navy to destruction, my sailors and my soldiers to death. I therefore agree to peace. My armies shall disband, my fortifications be torn down, my battleships sunk or turned to peaceful ends. My Reichstag will have confirmed my words ere now. (265–66)

The friends must communicate by using their wave-measuring device to convince "the man" that the war is over. Tom then expresses his ambivalent emotions to his friend Dick Regnier: a noble end has been achieved, but "at a fearful cost." " 'Yes,' said Regnier, 'but a single great war would have meant the death of many thousands more' " (289–90).

Some time later, Jim and Tom see John King drag himself ashore from a disintegrating yacht. He has destroyed his mechanism. " 'I—pay—the—final—price.' The last words came in a thick gasp, 'My secret is safe.' " He dies. "The world and the man who stopped all war were both at peace"(301).

The Vanishing Fleets

In *The Man Who Ended War*, the most immediate danger comes from the unknown destroyer of ships. In contrast, Roy Norton's *The Vanishing Fleets* (1908) begins: "Apathetic and unprepared, the country stood on the verge of war," which the President refuses to wage. "The nation's position as a first class Power, even its very integrity, seemed at stake" (3). We know of this apathy only because the author tells us, however; we never see it.

Guy Hillier, Secretary of the British Embassy in Washington, loves Norma, the daughter and chief assistant of "Old Bill Roberts," an inventor once "dubbed a 'harebrained crank,' but whose work had proved him otherwise" (7). Hillier begs Norma to marry him and flee the inevitable war. She refuses, asking for his patience, but cannot tell him where she is going or what she and her father are doing (14).

Almost immediately Japan declares war. The President responds with unbelievable calm as Japan takes the Philippines: he paroles the American army and sends it to San Francisco, refuses to alert the National Guard, and orders the fleet to anchor at Baltimore (24). Britain is Japan's official ally, and Hillier is sent to London with dispatches. Japan conquers the Hawaiian Islands, holding them incommunicado.

The President demands time to put his plans into action; then, "Even at the moment when an overthrow of the governing power at Washington seemed imminent," the National Guard is mobilized, volunteers are called for, and all railways are requisitioned (44). But instead of facing Japan, the troops blockade Canada (45)! All foreign ships are sent out of port; the "nation enforced complete isolation upon itself, withdrawing within its shell as does a turtle when assailed" (46). England is particularly puzzled, since she has assured the United States that she would not fight for Japan.

Lacking any warning from their chief spy, who has been killed trying to run the blockade, the Japanese send their navy boldly toward the West Coast, but it disappears before it gets to Hawaii, where the battleships would have to refuel. In response to inquiries sent through Britain, Japan is told:

> The United States has no report whatever to impart on the subject most vitally concerning His Majesty's closest ally, beyond the fact that the fleet which came to invade the Pacific coast has been duly met, properly vanquished, and rendered incapable of further harm. The United States regrets that such action became necessary, and, with all due respect to Great Britain and such other Powers as may be interested, wishes to express a disinclination to reply to any further communications of this or a similar nature. (90)

Britain cannot make anything of this message either. Hillier is asked to run the highly efficient blockade to tell the American government that Britain must send out its fleet to reassure Canada but intends no aggresssion against the United States (94–95). He cannot get through; the British fleet also disappears. The German fleet prepares to sail, but suddenly the Kaiser and the Chancellor of Germany both vanish.

The next day, "the pride of the British navy, the Dreadnought" appears on the Thames—without a man aboard (153). She is anchored, moreover, where she could not have sailed, past bridges she could not have gone under, even though "her fighting masts, her top rig, and the upper bands of her funnel were riven off as if by one devastating line shot taken full abeam or square astern"(155). News is sent to the King, but he is gone too, as is the Prime Minister and the First Lord of the Admiralty. All believe that the United States must be doing something mysterious, but inquiries are met with "a silence more menacing than the thunder of distant guns" (163).

At this point a flashback introduces us at last to the U.S. President. His family suffered much in the Civil War; he has sworn to give his life for peace. When he sees an opportunity to impose peace on the world, he pursues it regardless of personal cost. "Old Bill's" first proposal to the President was a device to increase a ship's speed through the water. Working with radioactivity made stronger than radium by an electrical current, he and Norma quite accidentally create conditions that allow the "impact of the emanations, or radioactive corpuscles," to control gravity (217). They can now build airships of incredible speed and power, capable of carrying any kind of weapon. The President tells them:

> If our secret becomes known, there will be no war, and war is a necessity for our purpose. In our hands has been given by a miracle the most deadly engine ever conceived, and we should be delinquent in our duty if we failed to use it as a means for controlling and thereby ending wars for all time. Let us bear with fortitude whatever reproaches may be heaped upon us, for we are the instruments of God, and the trial will last only a little longer. Let no man speak! (237)

Not even Congress knows what is going on in the secret lab at Guantanamo, to which Norma was going when she met Hillier in the first chapter.

Meanwhile, Old Bill Roberts breaks down from overwork. Since he cannot now direct the leading radioplane, Norma volunteers to take his place (240). The radioplanes capture Japanese ships by diving on them, grappling, and carrying them off to Seattle. The President hopes that the Chinese will come to the aid of Japan because "Oriental power must be broken" (280). They do not.

The British fleet is also captured, the Dreadnought returned as a show of force, and the King removed. On another radioplane, the Kaiser is allowed to satisfy his scientific curiosity—which damages the ship's controls—and to experience living in the relaxed and friendly American style. He arrives at the conference a changed man, ready to hear the President's statement: "I have invited you here not as the President of a nation, but as man to men to help me put—an—end—to—war!" (314). King and Kaiser ask "nothing more than fairness" to "accept and enter the enclave" (328). Before leaving for home, they toast "the ruler of that greatest of all kingdoms, Peace, His Excellency the President of the United States" (330).

Japan capitulates unconditionally, appealing for "peace with dignity" (336); she gets her fleet back but must withdraw from the Philippines and Hawaii. "Congress had been called into being again" and approves the President's actions (337). The radioplanes give demonstrations of their friendly power. The President announces an international commission to enforce world peace, which all nations agree to join. New York becomes a kind of United Nations headquarters, and Hillier marries Norma.

All For His Country

The self-imposed mission to end war by force had not changed when *All for His Country* by J. U. Giesy and *The Man Who Rocked the Earth* by Arthur Train and Robert Williams Wood appeared after the outbreak of World War I in Europe. Though each novel includes a radioactive weapon, neither makes any reference to Einstein's publications on relativity: that connection had not yet been established in fiction. Each assumes that conflict will be prolonged and serious, but neither anticipates formal American intervention in a European war. Giesy, writing before hostilities began, envisions the invasion of the United States by the "Yellow Peril," while Train and Wood, publishing later, use the situation as the basis for fantastic speculation; but each story assumes that the job of the United States is to impose a just and lasting peace upon the quarreling nations of the world. The "war to end war" began in American fiction long before doughboys fought for it in France.

All for His Country by J. U. Giesy was first published by the Munsey magazine chain in 1914, although it did not appear in book form until 1915. The story opens as Meade Stillman, a young inventor, offers the "Stillman aero-destroyer" to the armed forces. This futuristic airship uses gyros for stability, can take off and land vertically, flies at two hundred miles per hour, and is generally impervious to ordinary weapons. It fires torpedoes or bombs through tubes in the hull and also incorporates "gravity screens" (13). The Army representative objects to its cost: each vessel requires an incredible twenty million dollars worth of radium. Stillman responds: "What of it, if one could fight the war, destroy the fleet of an enemy attacking, annihilate its army before it fired a shot—make America invulnerable to the world?" (13).

The idealistic Stillman is outmaneuvered by Senator Gotz, an airplane manufacturer, who claims that airplanes generally make ineffective weapons; that Stillman's father is a crook; and that young Stillman is "a red-flag socialist." Gotz thinks that war is good for business. This appalls Meade, who even offers to donate a large supply of pitchblende for fuel. "After that America could arbitrate the peace of the world. We could become indeed the land of the free—the first nation in the world to declare outright for the brotherhood of all men" (18).

Disgusted over his failure to convince the committee, Meade then visits a family friend whose daughter Bernice he happened to save from a runaway car that very morning. Before he goes back to his hidden laboratory, she makes him promise to return to save his country, should it ever become necessary. Necessity arises quickly when the war begins with a Mexican invasion. Senator Gotz's son, a Colonel, anticipates battle: "It'll be a sort of lark, I guess. None of us really are specially worried about the outcome of this business. It will be over in a month or six weeks, Miss Bernice" (66). He proposes marriage, which Bernice refuses. She is also courted by Harold Darling, a languid playboy.

As expected, the Mexicans are easily driven back, but an unknown spy (actually Harold Darling, whose playboy persona is merely a disguise) warns of overweening confidence in Mexico City; they may be waiting for "international action by a larger power." Japan seems the obvious choice. Darling suggests large-scale mobilization and the creation of "an efficient aeroplane corps at San Francisco" and other large cities (80). His warning is discounted.

Suddenly the cable to Hawaii is cut and San Francisco is invaded by Japanese. Having prepared for years, "the Japanese rose the same night in all the southern counties and attacked the whites" (102). They disrupt communications so thoroughly that no one can gain an accurate overall picture of the situation; each section of the country knows only of its own troubles, and Washington is even less well informed. The Japanese use "the new bombs" to sink battleships (153). Their ships can stay at long range while pounding the U.S. fleet, which is virtually destroyed in an hour and a half. The army in Mexico also faces the new weapon.

When the Japanese land in—and bomb and burn—New York, Darling suggests guerilla warfare and a scorched-earth policy, especially for major cities. "We cannot defend them, as has been proven. But—we can make them valueless to Japan" (193). Gotz protests: "We cannot afford to bankrupt this country because of any sentimental theory" (193). President Gilson intends to "make the ultimate sacrifice to save our national integrity" (194). Some remember Stillman's offer, but do not really try to find him.

Japan demands full citizenship rights, plus neutralization of the Canal Zone; cession of the Philippines and Hawaiian Islands; establishment of a buffer state between the United States and Mexico under Japanese rule; and recognition of Japanese as Aryans rather than Mongols, so they can intermarry with Americans (196–97). Gilson is outraged by this last item, preferring to "slay my daughters than see them given over to such an alliance" (197). But he follows Darling's advice. Washington is abandoned; the cities burn while "every munition factory in the inland country was taken over under contract with its owners and ran night and day to supply arms and munitions to the rapidly growing army" (200). It looks as if the war will last for years. At this point Bernice finally tells Darling that she had a letter from Meade announcing his safe arrival home and his love for her, postmarked Hite, Utah. Since the Stillman invention still might "overcome the advantage the Japanese now possess in these bombs" (203), Bernice goes with Darling to find Meade and his father and beg for help.

When Stillman arrives with his machine, the tactical situation is critical, but "The Miracle" easily eliminates Japanese planes and artillery. Only its gyros can handle the concussion from the "new bombs" (281). The plot picks up speed: Darling gets killed; Meade's father is proven innocent of theft (and Gotz is proven guilty); the Japanese fleet is wiped out in the Atlantic, and "the overburgeoned confidence of the Japanese" is shaken (315); all cities are retaken as quickly as they fell, and the war is soon over. Stillman marries Bernice.

The Man Who Rocked the Earth

The main part of *The Man Who Rocked the Earth* by Arthur Train and Robert Williams Wood (1915) may have been completed before the outbreak of hostilities in Europe, for the authors seem to have hastily added a frame to their otherwise cheerful work, probably using *The World Set Free* by H. G. Wells (1914) as their model. Thus the "Prologue" opens with utter seriousness:

> By July 1, 1916, the war had involved every civilized nation upon the globe except the United States of North and of South America, which had up to that time succeeded in maintaining their neutrality. Belgium, Holland, Denmark, Switzerland, Poland, Austria Hungary, Lombardy, and Servia, had been devastated. Five million adult male human beings had been exterminated by the machines of war, by disease, and by famine. Ten million had been crippled or invalided. Fifteen million women and children had been rendered widows or orphans. Industry there was none. No crops were harvested or sown. The ocean was devoid of sails. Throughout European Christendom women had taken the

place of men as field hands, labourers, mechanics, merchants, and manufacturers. The amalgamated debt of the involved nations, amounting to more than $100,000,000,000, had bankrupted the world. Yet the starving armies continued to slaughter one another. (3–4)

Weapons invented by one side are countered by other inventions; the war drags on. (That this might closely describe World War I was not obvious in 1915.) The authors' apparent debt to H. G. Wells becomes clearer as they continue:

The Emperor of Germany, and the kings of England and of Italy, had all abdicated in favour of a republican form of government. Europe and Asia had run amuck, hysterical with fear and blood. As well try to pacify a pack of mad and fighting dogs as these frenzied myriads with their half-crazed generals. . . . They were at a deadlock, yet each feared to make the first overtures for peace. There was, in actuality, no longer even an English or a German nation. It was an orgy of homicide, in which the best of mankind were wantonly destroyed, leaving only the puny, the feeble-minded, the deformed, and the ineffectual to perpetuate the race. (7)

But this grim "Prologue" bears almost no relationship to the story, where France, Germany, and England are still viable nation-states, and none of the characters are "puny, feeble-minded, deformed, or ineffectual."

A war does drag on in Europe with appalling loss of life as the book opens. Suddenly, someone calling himself "Pax" sends a telegraph message, using a carrier of such power that only the U.S. Naval Observatory can receive it. He promises to retard the rotation of the Earth to enforce "the cessation of hostilities and the abolition of war upon the globe" (11). His first message is taken as a joke, but he makes good his threat without doing any apparent damage. After his second demonstration, he is asked to prove the extent of his power in some other unequivocal and nonfatal manner. He chooses to cut a channel through the Atlas Mountains and flood the Sahara Desert. Three fishermen who happen to get touched by the "violet ray" from his "Flying Ring" die within a week from "internal burns" (68); otherwise Pax has kept his word with astonishing fidelity, while furnishing the desert with a beach resort.

The various Powers agree to an Armistice. The President of the United States, chosen as Pax's messenger, sends daily reports, and Pax seems pleased. But the German ambassador cleverly divides the conference and diverts attention to demands for more proof and an investigation, knowing that German scientists are hard at work to find Pax and control his invention.

Meanwhile, an overeager German general defies the Armistice to try out on Paris a gun that fires "three-stage shells" much like rockets. Pax, outraged, destroys headquarters, officers, inventor, gun, and troops in one blast. He then threatens to rotate the axis of the Earth so that Europe will freeze. After that, the Armistice is kept. Some "truly apprehended the significance of what had occurred, and realized that either war or the human race must pass away forever" (142).

Meanwhile, an American scientist, Bennie Hooker, is working on the same "atomic energy" and "thermic induction" that Pax may be using (101–02). Hooker is completely unaware of the world situation; when told of Pax's device, he is at first dismayed, then delighted that someone—anyone—has made such a wonderful discovery. Like the Germans, Hooker triangulates Pax's location in Labrador and starts off to find him. The carefully planned and fully equipped German expedition fails utterly; the comic, inexperienced Bennie Hooker gets through just in time to see Pax accidentally killed by his own equipment. Hooker laments the death of this inventive genius and then sits down to learn how to play with the toy he has inherited.

Hooker is unaware of Pax's latest threat; the world is unaware of Pax's death and does abolish war, destroy its arms, trade peacefully, and grow happily rich out of fear of his reprisals. The story is followed by an "Epilogue" that demonstrates the ethical and material rewards of peace, democracy, and freedom. It also promises to tell how Hooker will use Pax's mechanism to explore "the sidereal ether"—in another story (228).

CREATING SCENARIOS

The popularity of these action-adventure stories shows how well they met reader expectations while developing a demand for more. In such a transactional situation, writers often quite unconsciously create fictional "scenarios." A scenario comprises a complex of assumptions that get recognized as forming a pattern in the sociocultural matrix. Once established, the whole complex can be called up by a single reference: in other words, readers tacitly include relevant constructs in a scenario, even if they are not explicitly discussed, described, or referred to.

The "lone inventor" scenario automatically initiates a complex of expectations. Readers anticipate that an imaginative challenge (cognitive estrangement) will be provided by the threat and the gadget developed to counter it. They assume that they will find the protagonist to be a highly intelligent, ingenious, usually reclusive man (though he may have a capable female relative), with sufficient training in science to be able to create ingenious devices, and with a burning desire to do so while avoiding formal ties to any company or institution that might co-opt his work. Readers expect that he will have certain character traits: he may be short-tempered ("crusty") and obnoxiously sure of himself; he may be absent-minded or even careless; but he is loyal, honest, and warm-hearted. If he is old, he has a beautiful daughter; if he is young, he is handsome, altruistic, shy, and socially inexperienced. He is rarely wealthy, but lack of income does not prevent him from inventing and building at least a prototype of his invention. The invention works.

We can see how this "lone inventor" scenario functions especially well in stories like *The Man Who Ended War*, where the inventor himself remains virtually invisible while the plot revolves around him. Because readers who understand the scenario cooperate with the author to supply the details, they persuade themselves of the invisible character's motivation and ability. That this whole process remains tacit and unstated also encourages them to ignore discrepancies or incongruities in the plot. This alone could explain the popularity of scenarios in genre fiction.

Scenarios become widely accepted (popular) when they reinforce the patterns of lived assumptions that individual readers share with their culture. At the same time, these patterns of shared assumptions delimit the culture: we recognize others who share our major assumptions as compatriots and those who do not as foreigners. Most of these assumptions are nonverbal, tacit, and invisible to those within the culture. They become visible most often when they are contrasted with assumptions held by a different group or with assumptions in the process of being replaced, when people actively test old assumptions and experiment with new ones. Although writers do not invent assumptions, they make them vividly available to their readers, so fiction plays an essential role in forming new sociocultural assumptions. In fact, a popular scenario may help shape the developing matrix in subtle but profound ways.

American assumptions were changing at the turn of the century. Up to this time, much of the national literature had focused on national heritage and character, topics that were explored by writers as diverse as Hawthorne, Wister, and Howells, while American naivete in the sophisticated European scene was depicted by Henry James. From a frontier nation just emerging from a crippling internal conflict and exclusively involved with its own affairs, however, the country now was venturing into an international marketplace. People were encountering a new set of assumptions, and to recognize them as familiar—to see themselves as living from them and thus participating in the new cultural pattern—they tried them out in stories.

A number of new assumptions show up in the "lone inventor" scenario. Here America may be seen as young and naive, but she is by that very token unspoiled, morally superior. Her superiority is manifested in her inventive genius, which gives her both the power and the sanction single-handedly to engage in her sacred mission to bring peace to the world—not by ethical example or even by economic imperative, but by force. In fiction, such force can seem plausible only when the "lone inventor" creates a weapon that makes the American army the equal of the large, experienced European military system. Thus the "war-to-end-war" scenario entered American fiction.

FICTIONAL TACTICS

Writers of adventure fiction depend on fast-moving, exciting plots to attract their audience. They have to place sufficiently familiar characters in a plot that challenges without upsetting the reader, and to do so rapidly and often.[4] Their success can be measured by the popularity of the genre.

This popularity also assures us that the writers remain sensitive to the assumption patterns of their readers; otherwise they could not entertain them consistently. Works that violate the reader's previous assumptions too seriously will be discarded in disgust or in anger, while those that do not violate the reader's assumptions at all—that follow a well-known pattern too faithfully—will be discarded as boring. Every tale needs some "cognitive estrangement."[5] "Lone inventor" stories, where a startling idea drives the plot, present excellent possibilities for action, conflict, and resolution while allowing the writer to avoid getting bogged down in details of motivation, characterization, or philosophy.

Moreover, the "lone inventor" plot offers these advantages without creating additional problems for the writer. Since the invention is frankly fabulous, the author does not need to know much about science. Many writers choose to present their invention as Stockton does in *The Great War Syndicate*: they presume that the invention is already complete, tell what it does, and claim that its workings are a closely guarded secret. Virtually the same tactic is used in *The Man Who Rocked the Earth*; although we see Bennie Hooker working on a process he believes may be similar to Pax's, readers must deal only with a few technical terms from him, and Pax conveniently dies without forcing the authors to explain the "Flying Ring" and the "violet ray." If the author does choose to discuss details of the invention, as in *The Man Who Ended War* and *All for His Country*, or to show its actual development, as in *The Vanishing Fleets*, he need only provide a page or two of glib double-talk, often tossing in references to the new and mysterious "radio-activity." This alone justifies virtually any marvelous effect needed to further the plot.

Narrative Mode

All of these books employ traditional narrative styles, varying from the objective third-person reporting of *The Great War Syndicate*, which seems less a novel than a report of the action in which no characters get developed at all, to the first-person narrative of Jim Orrington in *The*

Man Who Ended War.[6] Most of the other works are narrated by the omniscient author, who rarely bothers with attempts at psychological realism or depth.

The plot is generally quite straightforward, but suspense is sometimes heightened by telling the story twice. An extreme example of this can be found in *The Vanishing Fleets,* which divides into two parts: the first details the mystery of the President's behavior; the second, almost as long, repeats all the previous occurrences and accounts for them. Several of the other books manage a similar repetition by retelling parts of the story from various points of view.

Without exception, these books fall into the comic mode. In each, the old society is disrupted and a new one is established; in all but *The Great War Syndicate* and *The Man Who Rocked the Earth,* this fact is formally celebrated by a marriage.[7] Often this marriage represents the reorganization of society in little. In *The Man Who Ended War,* Dorothy prefers Jim Orrington, the reporter, to Dick, a member of her own social class and her intellectual equal (although one might argue that receiving a decoration from the King of England raises Jim's status). In *The Vanishing Fleets,* the brave and competent Norma marries the young Briton Guy Hillier, who has little to recommend him beyond bravery and being one of the viewpoint characters. In *All For His Country,* Bernice chooses the young inventor she barely knows over two other suitors, both of them highly qualified: Colonel Gotz is rich, brave, and in uniform, though smug; Darling is attractive, intelligent, and obviously heroic. Not only does he single-handedly gather all the information the government ever gets, he also saves Bernice's life at great risk to his own. But he is out of the running long before he dies.

Even *The Man Who Rocked the Earth* ends with an approximation of marriage; Bennie Hooker's love affair with inventing introduces him to Pax's "Flying Ring" and is consummated by his promised flight to explore "the sidereal ether." Optimistic in the midst of a disaster that is presented as darkly as possible to justify the need for the superweapon, these works celebrate the ascension of a new, vigorous, expanding society.

Characterization

Readers expect attractive characters, so at least some of them must be young, generous, and good-hearted. If the adventure plot is to work, these characters must be able to drop everything at short notice. Usually this means that they possess considerable wealth, education, and leisure. Tom and Dorothy in *The Man Who Ended War* can readily devote months to playing detective. Jim Orrington may be a working man, but he seems to have a very free hand with his reportorial assignments. Professor

Bennie Hooker in *The Man Who Rocked the Earth* seems to have no classes to teach, but he can easily afford to buy equipment and passage to Labrador.

Characters in genre fiction are often stereotyped. Some of these stereotypes forward the plot, as does the representation of Tom and Dorothy as members of the "rich class," subcategory "good people"; but others seem quite arbitrary. There is no essential reason why Harold Darling in *All for His Country* should act like a languid fop when he is not carrying out his spy missions; apparently, the author is playing with the newly popular "Scarlet Pimpernel" role (1905). Other stereotypes include the greedy capitalist like Senator Gotz and the ameliorator like Secretary Ryan in *All for His Country*, and idealists like John King in *The Man Who Ended War* and the President in *The Vanishing Fleets*.

None of these characters is unique to American fiction. The "lone inventor" is. He bears little relationship to the traditional British scientist, an educated, wealthy, gifted amateur. The American is capable of producing wonders from a barn or a blacksmith's shop. Many genres beside the action-adventure novel have been Americanized by the "lone inventor"; he soon will become essential to the peculiarly American genre of science fiction. But the character of the inventor is not the focus of any of these early books. The narratives concentrate on the use of the invention.

Social Roles

One of the most interesting changes taking place in this period is that from writing about heroines who reflect the pioneer woman, often the competent initiator of action, to presenting more Victorian, passive heroines. Each of the novels from 1908 features a woman of education, ability, and character who is prepared to engage fully in the adventure at hand. In *The Man Who Ended War* it is Dorothy who intuits the character of "the man's" weapon. As she works, Jim Orrington expresses his admiration of her multiple talents:

> I watched Dorothy's nimble fingers, as they flew over the paper, filling sheet after sheet with computations. What different powers lay in those little hands. Abstruse calculations vied with bread making, careful manipulations of delicate instruments with the steering wheel of her motor car. Last week we had eaten a dinner prepared wholly by her. This week she was working out one of the great triumphs of modern science. It seemed almost a shame to confine those talents in a single home. (84–85)

All except Jim now recognizes that Dorothy is more interested in him than she is in Dick; clearly she has the final say in the matter. Dorothy is also the first of the group to mourn the loss of human life aboard the ships. Godfrey must assume that his readers share the tacit assumption that a woman can function as scientist and detective adventurer without threatening her social position or her femininity.

In *The Vanishing Fleets,* Norma takes an even more active role. She serves as her father's assistant, an act of physical bravery in itself. When her father becomes ill, she volunteers to take his place in battle. The President, appalled, responds "You mean—," and Norma replies: "That if my father is too ill to go, I myself will fight the Japanese. I myself will give what expert advice is needed, and will demonstrate to the others what must be done in battle" (241). In the actual battle, Norma handles the radioplane during the attack:

> There, erect, triumphant, and fierce, stood the woman glorified who was striking the first blow for her country's honor and her father's exaltation. She was fairly hurling the machine through space, her hands grasping the levers of descent and her eyes on the periscope which portrayed the position of their helpless victims. (257)

Like Godfrey, Norton assumes that his audience will have no difficulty in accepting Norma both as winningly feminine and as utterly competent in several dangerous and demanding fields.

The picture is quite different only six years later. J. U. Giesy, an experienced writer of action-adventure novels, can be expected to know his audience well. Although he presents Bernice as a thoroughly nice girl, he never gives her the opportunity for action in *All for His Country* that Godfrey and Norton offer their heroines. She does not have adventures; she has beaux. She does not rescue anyone; she gets rescued. Her main function in the story is to attract Meade Stillman so he will write the letter that will lead his soon-to-be-grateful country to his hideaway. Giesy does not expect his audience to accept a heroine like Norma, while Train and Wood offer no feminine character in their story at all.

Giesy's assumptions about the passive role of women, assumptions that will grow even more apparent in early "gadget" sf, seem readily explainable, but his portrayal of the "lone inventor" seems more ambiguous. Meade Stillman fills a peculiarly passive social role. He offers a powerful weapon, but once it is rejected, he simply disappears with it. After presenting himself as vitally interested in the safety and prestige of his country, he apparently fails to keep himself informed about its welfare. At any rate, he stays in hiding and does not act until Bernice and Darling come to get him. In other stories, inventors seem to have little difficulty in getting their inventions accepted, or else, like Pax and John King, they simply begin to use them.

In *The Man Who Rocked the Earth,* Bennie Hooker fits an entirely different stereotype, that of the eccentric genius who lives wholly in his work. He seems associated with a university, but works in his rooms, not in a university laboratory. He is not creating a specific invention, but studies "pure science," knowledge for its own sake, which does not keep him from grasping the practical possibilities inherent in a radical new discovery. He is naturally good-hearted and not at all envious. He treats people well and gets good treatment in return. Like Stillman, he has no idea of what goes on in the world; he has to be told about the progress of the war, but unlike Stillman, he has professed no interest in it. When he goes into "disguise" to hunt for Pax, his costume is grotesque. Yet it is Hooker who gets the job done when others fail. Like Pax, Hooker is both an innocent and an activist and cheerfully rushes in where angels fear to tread.

Although the situations of the "lone inventor" may differ, the inventions (with the possible exception of the radiations that atomize metal in *The Man Who Ended War*) all have peacetime uses. Roberts's radioplane, though accidentally achieved, is expected to revolutionize travel and shipping, revising the whole commercial structure of the planet; Stillman's "Miracle" probably could do the same if converted for civilian use. Pax's "Flying Ring" digs canals while you wait,[8] not to mention stopping war!

Racism

Each of these works overtly involves racial prejudice. Sometimes it shows up only in the confident assumption of American superiority, as we see when *The Great War Syndicate* ends with a promise of world peace as the result of teaching English, producing Anglo-American hegemony, and resisting orientalization. Often it shows up as fear of German militarism, personified in the Kaiser. The Kaiser is described as an unpleasant and dangerous individual (only in *The Vanishing Fleets* is his intransigence easily overcome), but he is not shown as representative of his countrymen. When Anglo-American peace pacts are emplaced, Germany always gets to sign them, however reluctantly.

In contrast, the Japanese are feared as a race. In the light of Japanese activity at the time, this may seem only slightly paranoid; but conflating Japanese aggression with "Oriental power" as the President does in *The Vanishing Fleets* seems undiscriminating. Here, China is expected to assist Japan; "her fleet, huge and well manned, was making preparations to sail," and the "President, knowing that for the accomplishment of his purpose Oriental power must be broken, indulged in the fervent hope that the attack might come soon" (280). The President is quite disappointed when China refuses to cooperate, though this may seem an unrealistic attitude in the light of the Sino-Japanese War (1894–95).

Although Japan often shows up as the enemy of the United States, nowhere is anti-Japanese sentiment more blatant than in *All for His Country*. Faced with repeated Japanese victories, Secretary of War Ryan advises compromise; he believes that "after what they have accomplished, Japan will now seek terms. . . . Recognition to equal citizenship rights, perhaps; property rights of tenure, and government guarantee of the same," which he would advise granting (191). Those Americans who agree to these terms do so for venal reasons.

Giesy makes his Japanese treacherously aggressive, but he also shows them as clever strategists and super superweapons inventors. Moreover, most of their demands sound sensible, especially the one to neutralize the Panama Canal Zone. His Japanese would be admirable if only they were white. Since they are not, they make excellent villains, as they prove by their last demand: to be considered Aryans so they can intermarry with American women. Villains need to be truly villainous and readily identifiable; this can most easily be done using existing racial prejudices.

Altruism and Common Sense

As each of these books shows, America's moral imperative in the world is to impose peace and further trade. This ideal often gets presented with more than a hint of "divinely appointed" (and sometimes self-elected) saviorism. John King in *The Man Who Ended War*, the President in *The Vanishing Fleets*, and Pax in *The Man Who Rocked the Earth* are the most obvious examples. *The Great War Syndicate* cannot be charged with altruism, but Stillman in *All for His Country* probably can. (Incidentally, it is not easy to determine who the title refers to. Stillman fails to follow through until specifically asked to and makes out very well from it in the long run, though his heart seems pure; the Gotzes, both junior and senior, take from their country more than they give; Bernice gets saved from a fate worse than death in conquered New York City by Darling; only Darling himself makes the supreme sacrifice.)

Altruism ranks high among American virtues, but onlv when joined with common sense. Those books ranking highest in common sense do not necessarily rank lowest in altruism, but this ranking can be correlated to the number of deaths that occur as the war-to-end-war scenario plays out. *The Great War Syndicate* operates as a business, killing one man by accident. *The Vanishing Fleets* also keeps a low body count: a single British sailor panics when his fleet is engaged by the radioplanes, and at least two men die running the blockade. *The Man Who Rocked the Earth* kills three, again by accident, unless we count the members of the German expeditionary force who die of their own aggressive unpleasantness. The other books run up higher scores. *All for His Country* presents a more or less standard war with some gratuitous Japanese atrocities and the expected number of off-stage deaths, while *The Man Who Ended War* uses a weapon that not only dissolves the metal of the ships, but also instantly (and perhaps painlessly) kills all aboard. Moreover, he continues sinking ships after the nations agree to a peace.

At this point altruism seems at odds with common sense. John King apparently has cut himself off from the outside world; at least he is not getting current information. Given his declared aim, he should want to minimize human deaths while maintaining his effectiveness, but it is clear that he has not planned how to do so. It is the energetic and altruistic search by Jim, Dorothy, and Tom that saves the world's sailors. Nor is any explanation of King's motives ever presented. Dying, he names himself as "the final victim" and claims that he pays "the final price." The narrator seems sympathetic: "The expression of his face had changed again. . . . He looked once more like the young lad I had known and loved in years gone by, whose face so well expressed his noble spirit, ever impatient of injustice and wrong. After the weary struggle, his soul was once more poised and at rest" (301). (One wonders if Dorothy would have been so forgiving, had she been at the scene.) If the author endorses King's actions (and nothing in the book suggests anything else), he must not equate ending war with the saving of human life except—as Regnier points out to Tom—in the quantitative sense. The same argument will later be used to justify dropping the atomic bomb on Japan.

Meade Stillman is another altruist; the commercialism he finds in the committee to consider adoption of his invention appalls him. He wants to teach the world a much-needed lesson. "After that America could arbitrate the peace of the world. We could become indeed the land of the free—the first nation in the world to declare outright for the brotherhood of all men" (18). This apparent activism contrasts oddly with his passive resignation after the committee rejects his offer, a contrast the author does not explain.

Altruism also shows up in the different ways that the character of the Kaiser is handled. In *The Man Who Ended War*, he seems to sympathize with his men—"I cannot expose my navy to destruction, my sailors and my soldiers to death"—but this of course denies the obvious fact that any ruler who sends his men to war automatically exposes them to death. He wants only to avoid sending them to an inevitable death that does not advance the national cause. He thus presents himself as the perfect pragmatist. In *The Vanishing Fleets*, the Kaiser acts like a sulky small boy who can experience change of heart simply through being well treated; his villainy is less important because the real enemy is Japan. In *The Man Who Rocked the Earth*, the Kaiser does not appear as a formal character, but his personal representative is devious, competitive, and pragmatic. In each case, the pragmatic Kaiser gets defeated by pragmatic American altruism.

Politics

Even before the Spanish-American War and the takeover of the Panama Canal Zone made "manifest destiny" expansionism seem perfectly feasible, fiction portrayed America as gaining political power without necessarily gaining territory. After territorial expansion becomes a fact, fictional sentiment becomes more guarded, and some writers—like Giesy—propose that the United States can expect retaliation.

Just how the government should handle issues of international politics seems less clear. At the time, a great many people sincerely believed that the United States should continue a policy of isolationism. Aside from such sentiments, Americans were not accustomed to formulating an explicit foreign policy, having done without one for most of the nineteenth century.[9] In fiction, this shows up in odd ways. For instance, the President in *The Vanishing Fleets* is shown as a dogged fighter for his principles:

> His disregard for party projects had cost him the friendship of politicians; his advocacy of certain reforms had subjected him to caustic comments; his very dignity and sensitiveness had been mistaken for austerity; and only his most intimate friends understood that in him beat a great heart filled to overflowing for his country and fellow men. (168)

One wonders how he ever got elected and why he has not faced impeachment. His war plans are based on nonlethal control of the armed forces of the world, an ability granted him by Roberts's radioplane. But his frantic idealism causes him to subvert the very democratic principles he is sworn to uphold: by ignoring public distress, by keeping Congress ignorant of Roberts's inventions and his plans for them, even by disestablishing Congress itself. Yet this dictatorial policy is shown as admirable; with the help of the radioplane, it establishes international peace and prosperity.

The Man Who Ended War frequently mentions public fear, but actually shows only a nervous stock market and the peace movement, which is led and taken advantage of by political opportunists. *All for His Country* shows divided governmental advisors: the armed forces are supplied by profiteering businessmen like Gotz; the government must function while being advised by mediators like Ryan, the crass (and criminal) Gotz, and President Gilman, the defender of his females' virtue—possibly including the (female) persona of the United States itself. Meanwhile, no one listens to Darling, the one person who can actually give an eyewitness report, and the war in general seems badly mishandled both militarily and politically.

Of course, action-adventure stories demand conflict, not negotiation; this seriously limits the role that politics can play. None of these plots would work if they showed compromise or diplomacy to be capable of avoiding hostilities. But in the establishment of sociocultural assumptions, what the readers see is what they get. Since no political alternative to conflict is offered, they must tacitly dismiss it as a possibility. Diplomatic negotiations occur only after the American "war to end war," while a pact dictated by American arms to enforce peace on the world is the intended outcome of this war.

FURTHER ASSUMPTIONS

Americans thoroughly understood the tacit assumptions of the new scenario, a combination of the "lone inventor" and the "war to end war." It had to end with an American victory so overwhelming that no one could challenge it, leaving America in a position to dictate peace terms. Relying on the obvious goodwill and altruism of the American people, the rest of the world would gladly agree to them. Something approaching a League of Nations treaty might result from the American victory, but America would dictate it, not agree to it. This position is very attractive, as it maintains full national sovereignty. America wins everything and gives up nothing.

America entered World War I and her soldiers fought under the slogan of "The War to End War." That this slogan tacitly included the assumption that "peace must be imposed by force on everyone—except us" seemed perfectly natural. America was not prepared to yield any portion of her sovereignty to a world organization where the fruits of her genius would have to be shared; where foreigners (perhaps even Orientals!) would have the opportunity to combine against her; where others might legitimately make political demands with which she was not prepared to comply. The League of Nations treaty was rejected by the U.S. Senate, and Woodrow Wilson died with his dream, at least in part because of the contradiction between the structure proposed for the League and the assumptions encoded in the popular vision of how America could and should behave.

NOTES

1. Science fiction would later go through a similar progression from "gadget sf" through "adventure sf" to "social sf"; see Isaac Asimov's "Social Science Fiction" in *Modern Science Fiction: Its Meaning and Its Future*, 2nd Ed., ed. Reginald Bretnor (New York: Coward-McCann, 1979), 158–96. The "social science fiction"

that Asimov considers the epitome of the genre is not achieved by action-adventure fiction like the works considered here, however.

2. *Superman from the Thirties to the Eighties* (New York: Crown, 1983), 11–13.

3. This tradition has been carefully expounded by I. F. Clarke in *Voices Prophesying War, 1763–1984* (London: Oxford University Press, 1966).

4. Then, as now, writers were often poorly paid, particularly in the popular genres. To make a living, pulp writers had to turn out large quantities of fiction at enormous speed; rewriting (and sometimes even proofreading) was impossible, especially if the work was being published in parts. Economics has a significant impact on art.

5. Darko Suvin argues "for an understanding of SF as the *literature of cognitive estrangement*. This definition seems to possess the unique advantage of rendering justice to a literary tradition which is coherent through the ages and within itself, yet distinct from nonfictional utopianism, from naturalistic literature, and from other non-naturalistic fiction" (*Metamorphoses of Science Fiction* [New Haven: Yale University Press, 1979], 4). I use the term to indicate the creative violation of tacit assumptions. Few genres use cognitive estrangement as thoroughly as sf does, but it forms an essential part of all fiction that holds the readers' attention.

6. *The Great War Syndicate* can be seen as a precursor of the classic sf tale, in which the idea really becomes the plot.

7. See Northrop Frye, *Anatomy of Criticism: Four Essays* (Princeton: Princeton University Press, 1971), 43–49, 163–71, especially the comments on science fiction, 49. The mythic function of science fiction is especially apparent here; the old society is identified as mistaken at best and evil at worst by its repeated recourse to war, the very symptom that the action of the books is intended to relieve. Thus the weddings celebrate not only the reconciliation of the protagonists to society, but also the reconciliation of the society with itself in peace.

8. This is clearly intended to contrast with the laborious twelve-year construction period of the Panama Canal, not yet fully completed when *The Man Who Rocked the Earth* was published in 1915.

9. See, for example, Bernard Bailyn et al., *The Great Republic* (Boston: Little, Brown, 1977), chap. 28, especially pp. 979–84.

2

"I Have Seen the Future": Before World War II

Following the Armistice, the influenza epidemic, and the rejection by the United States of the League of Nations, Americans turned to their own affairs. The Great Red Scare of 1919–20 did not encourage internationalism. There was no dearth of literature in general, but for a long period there was a real scarcity of superweapons stories. That scenario required international focus, and the country was simply not interested. Not everyone was so shortsighted, of course. Among other internationalists, Pierrepont B. Noyes, who had worked with the Rhineland Commission after World War I, tried to alert people to the danger he saw in the postwar European political situation. In his book *While Europe Waits for Peace*, he predicted that conditions in Germany would produce a dictator and lead to a war that could destroy Europe within twenty-five years. But Americans were no more willing seriously to consider the danger of another war than they had been to join the League of Nations. Giving up speeches and nonfiction, Noyes turned his hand to the novel.

The Pallid Giant

A complete reversal from the prewar novels, Noyes's *The Pallid Giant* (1927) refutes the validity of "war to end war." It is set in the 1920s, but posits the previous existence of a scientifically sophisticated culture that destroyed itself completely with atomic weapons. In this ancient world, fear of the awful weapons of war held by each side prevents overt battle for a time; then the men of Sra bring out their secret superweapon, Klepton-Holorif, because they fear that their opponents will duplicate it.

> "But why?" I asked. "Why should they desire to kill a helpless people? Do they not believe us at their mercy?"
>
> "I fear not their desire to kill. Even they are not so wicked as to crave the deaths of millions. *I fear their fear.* They dare not let us live, knowing or even fearing that we have a power so terrible, to kill. From now there is no middle ground. Two nations, both with Klepton-Holorif, may not live side by side." (165)

The attack is made in the name of peace (and perhaps initiated by an earthquake). The Sra eliminate their enemies; then they find that they cannot trust their friends. Driven by Timor, the fear of another's fear, the opposing forces blast fertile land into desert. One visionary tries to promote Mar-da, the benevolent love of one's fellow man; the women carry the creed of unselfish love to the point of faith in another's faith (188–89). But Timor proves stronger than Mar-da: "Our peace has been a woman's peace. What now will normal man do with this peace?" a leader-man worries (190). The next war kills all but two males, who reconstitute humanity by breeding with and training a tribe of prehominoids, our ancestors.

The men who discover and decipher the ancient records are involved in the negotiations that follow World War I, a job Noyes himself had held. Watching the punitive and self-aggrandizing maneuvers of the victors, they have little hope of lasting peace. When a spy informs them that German scientists are working on atomic weapons, they end the story with a question: Will we, like the Sra, destroy our world and ourselves, or can our contemporary culture produce a miracle that will transform everyone into "love-your-neighbor Christians . . . *in time!*" (245).

The Pallid Giant is the first superweapons story published after World War I, appearing almost ten years after the Armistice. It is also the last such scientific romance to be published as a novel in the United States for almost twenty years. *The Pallid Giant* is perhaps the first atomic "awful warning" story as well; widely distributed and well written, it had little immediate effect, but was later considered so prophetic that it was reprinted in 1946 under a new title: *Gentlemen: You are Mad!*[1]

A NEW GENRE

A year before *The Pallid Giant* appeared, the pulp magazines, already thoroughly specialized,[2] discovered themselves giving birth to a new literature, formally separated from other genres. Initially christened "scientifiction," this popular American offspring of the scientific romance soon received the name by which it is now known: science fiction.[3] A vigorous new genre, it became the strongest fictional advocate for a new era, claiming that science was not only creating the future, but was providing the kind of understanding that would allow man to control that future.

It began with Hugo Gernsback, who in 1911 wrote a novelistic survey of the future called *Ralph 124C 41+*, which he published in parts in his magazine *Modern Electrics*. He continued to experiment with ways to combine education with entertainment in his radio magazines; in April 1926 this led to *Amazing Stories: The Magazine of Scientifiction*. In his opening editorial, Gernsback reminded his readers that they now lived in "an entirely new world" due to science, which was changing everyone's "entire mode of living." Offering both "interesting" and "instructive" reading, at one masterstroke he invented a genre appropriate to the age (3).

When Gernsback lost control of *Amazing Stories* and its companions in 1929, he simply started a new magazine chain, including *Science Wonder Stories*[4] (soon renamed *Wonder Stories*), in which he initiated the term "science-fiction." Meanwhile, the new owners of *Amazing Stories* continued publishing in the science fiction format with T. Oconor Sloane, Gernsback's original editor, and the same slogan: "Extravagant Fiction Today—Cold Fact Tomorrow!"[5] It is this juggling of terms that led science fiction's most vocal fan, Forrest J. Ackerman, to pose a paradox in his anthology of reminiscence and fiction, *Gosh! Wow! (Sense of Wonder) Science Fiction* (1981):

> When I began reading science fiction (October 1926 *Amazing Stories*) there was no science fiction.
>
> If you didn't raise an eyebrow over that apparently contradictory statement, you're a science fiction fan. . . .
>
> The reason I was reading (and loving!) science fiction 3 years before there was science fiction was that the term wasn't coined until 1929. June 1929! In Gernsback's editorial in the first issue of *Science Wonder Stories*. (xi)

As James Gunn notes in *Alternate Worlds*, "Before Gernsback, there were science fiction stories. After Gernsback, there was a science fiction genre" (1975, 128).

Amazing Stories (1926) and *Wonder Stories* (1929) soon had company. *Astounding Stories of Super Science* (usually abbreviated *ASF*) appeared in 1930.[6] By 1940, there were half a dozen more, but with the exception of *Amazing Stories* and *Astounding Science Fiction* most of them died in the paper shortages of World War II. As more magazines entered the science fiction field, standards of scientific possibility dropped even from Gernsback's rather loose requirements. (When Ray Palmer succeeded as editor of *Amazing Stories*, they left entirely.) Science fiction looked to the future with a clear if somewhat naive sense of wonder that identified the early sf writing better than any formal definition. The magazines continued to publish reprints, fantastic "thought variants," and space opera almost exclusively until John W. Campbell, Jr., became editor of *Astounding Stories* in September 1937, taking over full responsibility from F. Orlin Tremaine in May 1938. As an experienced science fiction writer who had attended MIT (though his degree was from Duke University),[7] Campbell is generally credited with single-handedly creating the "golden age of science fiction" by guiding the sf genre into something approaching scientific respectability[8] while simultaneously demanding improved literary standards from a stable of writers inspired by his example as well as by his advice.

Artistic Constraints

The first issue of *Amazing Stories* published only reprints by well-known writers of scientific romance like Wells and Verne; soon writers began to submit stories written especially for the new magazine. Most of these writers initially had trained in action-adventure magazine fiction. For the new market they wrote much the same kind of story with science fiction trappings, the so-called "space western." This style followed a formula featuring roughly 900-word segments each ending in a crisis, strung together into a plot focused more on resolving the most recent crisis than on developing a coherent story. Readers were equally well trained to expect such stories, and the magazines became increasingly popular.

More magazines supported more writers despite their miserable rates of payment (and frequently even more miserable record of payment; many authors refer to this as the period of "payment on credible threat of lawsuit").[9] Moreover, the magazines soon supplied the only outlet for such stories. Before 1926, all the superweapons stories we have looked at were offered by standard publishing houses in novel form; from 1927 to 1946, virtually all appeared in science fiction magazines.

This pattern did not change with the economy. In fact, the depression probably strengthened the pulp magazines' position with the reading public.

In 1927, Gernsback introduced a letter column called "Discussions" in *Amazing Stories*, and science fiction readers happily filled its columns with commentary on stories and the magazine itself. Their opinions had considerable influence on writers and editors. These letter columns had at least two other major effects: they became the gathering place of "fandom,"[10] and they encouraged fans to become writers themselves. In fact, by the early 1930s, many sf writers were young fans, and some of them were already becoming editors of sf magazines.[11]

This in-group atmosphere led to the rapid formalization of sf metaphors, neologisms, and scenarios. For a while sf jargon became virtually unintelligible to nonfans. Science fiction readers also prided themselves on their sophistication; most enjoyed stories that challenged their assumptions. While some of the more outrageous suggestions might elicit protests in the letter columns, it soon became clear that such controversy was widely popular. For example, John Campbell, who had begun his career writing very popular space opera, adopted a more iconoclastic style in 1934 with "Twilight," written under the pseudonym of Don A. Stuart. In this and other stories, he questioned every established "truth" he could think of. Science fiction readers loved it, and "Stuart" soon became more popular than Campbell.[12]

However we may judge sf as literature, it can accurately be described as an intellectual genre. It is the only contemporary genre that takes technology seriously. It represents the judgments of those who delight in and focus on ideas, who deal with the problems of the day, and who stand back from complete involvement with contemporary society so that they can evaluate it critically.[13] And, as Jack Williamson recalls in his autobiography *Wonder's Child* (1984), the pulp magazines were not as inappropriate a vehicle for "intellectual" literature as we might now believe: "People still read for information and amusement in those days before TV, and magazines still mattered" (63). Read by a comparatively small group of people, science fiction has had an unusually wide and vital influence, reaching far beyond its "own" borders. "I have seen the future," the slogan of the New York World's Fair of 1939, can be identified as pure science fiction.

Nonartistic Constraints

A number of conditions imposed upon writers and editors by the constraints of pulp publishing still affect the sf genre. Page-length requirements can cause editors to alter the text, often without the author's knowledge or permission; editors can also arbitrarily censor stories both for language and for content. Such editing does not mean that the text is carefully proofread, however. Nor does the editor have a free hand in making changes; the publisher, who has his pocketbook at stake, usually sets the guidelines. Constraints operate on the author even before the manuscript gets accepted for publication. Algis Budrys claims that "much SF writing was and is done to fill essentially predetermined space" (1983, 14). Thus at least some of the sins of omission and commission that sf writers have been charged with can be laid at the publisher's door rather than their own.

Other formative influences have even less obvious connection with literature. While some writers tried to ignore or even lamented changes due to technology, particularly in the middle of a worldwide depression, many science fiction stories confidently predicted that a brighter future could come only if we continued to rely on science. This confidence reflected experience. Technology—the automobile, movies, radio—had an increasing impact on everyday life. In more specialized areas, technology was changing even faster. Many new inventions had appeared toward the end of the twenties—the differential analyzer computer (1928), Goddard's improved rocket engine (1929), and the cyclotron (1930). After that, technological advances slowed: "nylon and synthetic rubber in 1935, xerography in 1938, and the betatron, FM broadcasting, and the electron microscope in 1939." But workers in basic science were busy. Einstein laid the foundation for a new physics with his special relativity (1905), in which he replaced the constructs of absolute space and time with space-time and showed that energy and matter were equivalent. The wave/particle problem was extended by de Broglie in 1924; when Heisenberg announced his uncertainty principle in 1927, the old Newtonian universe with all its mechanical certainties was essentially dead. The new outlook was reinforced by the astronomer Edwin Hubble, who proved that the universe itself was far larger than anyone had previously guessed.[14]

Dreams of atomic power made little practical difference to people who had trouble paying for heat. Moreover, most conventional scientists were convinced that far more energy would be required to liberate atomic forces than could ever be realized as output.[15] But visions of vast energies operating over limitless space provided the perfect opportunity for the action-adventure writer; they even allowed for the struggle against unpleasant but unexplainable circumstance to be rendered metaphorically as a victorious struggle against an alien invader. The stage was set for adventure on a cosmic scale, and science fiction writers were not slow to take advantage of it.

ATOMS FOR FUN AND PROFIT

That writers found this opportunity for cosmic adventure irresistible can be seen in the career of one man who might never have published at all without the opportunity offered by the new genre. Edward E. Smith spent five years writing a 90,000-word novel in collaboration with Mrs. Lee Garby, completing it in 1920. No publisher was interested. The manuscript stayed in Smith's desk drawer for seven years, until *Amazing Stories* offered him seventy-five dollars for the story that would launch "Doc" Smith (a food chemist whose Ph.D. went on every subsequent story) as one of the most popular writers of space opera ever to put pen to paper.[16] *The Skylark of Space* is typical of the slam-bang "space western" story that glorifies technology in the name of science and the free enterprise system.

The Skylark of Space

The editor of *Amazing Stories* advertised *The Skylark of Space* as "chock full, not only of excellent science, but . . . also that very rare element, love and romance." He was also forced to admit that it might appear "improbable . . . in spots." This may strike the modern reader as an understatement. Published in three parts beginning in August 1928, the story opens dramatically: Richard Seaton, a researcher in a government laboratory, accidentally spills a solution of "X, the unknown metal" on his copper steam-bath, which promptly flies out the window. Seaton quickly comprehends that he has "liberated the intra-atomic energy of copper!" and sets out, exclaiming "Great Cat, what a chance!" to build a spaceship and explore the galaxy with his wealthy friend Martin Crane (391).

"Blackie" Duquesne, a coworker, guesses the importance of Seaton's startling laboratory mishap, contacts his villainous friends, and tries to steal the secret of "X." The Seaton-Crane combination usually outwits him, though he does manage to abduct Seaton's fiancée, Dorothy. Dorothy has little to do in the story except get rescued, but she shows some of the mettle the heroines of 1908 so casually carried; more than her name reminds one of the heroine of *The Man Who Ended War*. She is a highly trained musician, exceptionally brave and self-controlled, and, of course, beautiful. Before the story ends, Crane and Seaton manage a double-wedding ceremony on an exotic planet whose culture they have saved from invaders. Although the opening scenes were somewhat toned down in its later novel form to make Seaton seem more professional and to remove the comic "dusky assistant," *The Skylark of Space* set fandom on its ear and introduced the cosmic adventure story.

The science fiction magazines clearly created the space in which this kind of story could flourish. Smith continued to turn out exciting space opera: these included two more "Skylark" novels, *The Spacehounds of I.P.C.* (1931), and the "Lensman" series, a massive saga that appeared as five multiple-part novels in *Astounding Science-Fiction* from 1934 to 1947. It spanned the galaxy, avoiding the restrictions of Einsteinian space-time by positing a "reactionless" drive. In *Triplanetary* (1934), the first "Lensman" novel, Smith not only included an atomic war but repeated the "first-strike" arguments used by the Sra in *The Pallid Giant*. Virtually single-handedly, Smith had turned a formula that began with atoms for fun and profit into a sweeping if stilted myth of good and evil engaging the peoples of the entire galaxy. In each of his stories, the basic credo of science fiction underlies the plot: through an understanding of the laws of nature, man can conquer the universe. Science is power.

More Fun and Games

John W. Campbell, Jr., who began his career as a science fiction writer before he was twenty, was much influenced by "Doc" Smith's work and wrote a number of cosmic adventures. In many of them he cheerfully exploited atomic possibilities with some (but not very much) regard for plausibility. Five stories starring the adventurous team of Wade, Arcott, and Morey appeared in less than two years in *Amazing Stories* and *Amazing Stories Quarterly*, from June 1930 to Spring 1932. Nor did Campbell ever abandon his love for the technologist as entrepreneur. Before he gave up his career as a writer when he became full-time editor of *ASF* in 1938, he published another fun-and-adventure series about the team of Penton and Blake, later collected as *The Planeteers*. The stories originally appeared in *Thrilling Wonder Stories* from December 1936 to October 1938 and were as cosmic in scope and wildly inventive as any of his earlier works.

Captain S. P. Meek, U.S.A., wrote several stories in which he not only used atomic power as a magical element, but also played with the familiar atom-as-tiny-universe model proposed by Rutherford about 1911. In "Submicroscopic" (1931), the hero's experiments shrink him to fit into an atom-sized world, where he saves the princess from black cannibals and becomes Crown Prince of Ulm. The adventures are continued in "Awlo of Ulm" (1931). Another atomic story is Donald Wandrei's "Colossus" (1934), where the hero begins his space adventures after his love gets killed in an atomic war.

Time travel became one of the more popular spin-offs of science fiction's "atomic science" for fun and profit. In "The Atom Smasher" (1930)[17] by Victor Rousseau (a pseudonym for Victor R. Emanuel), the hero experiments with atomic power in a deserted spot. His lab suddenly disappears, then returns; he has discovered time travel and is immediately immersed in adventure in Atlantis. His atom smasher gets blown up, but he gets back to his own time with the girl of his dreams.

Nat Schachner's "The Time Imposter" (1934) begins with an atomic war in 2050 that ends "in catastrophe—the human race almost succeeded in wiping itself out. Every city, every community of any size, was buried in its own ruins. The few survivors reverted to primitive conditions; it was hundreds of years before civilization reasserted itself" (134). But this grim scene merely introduces a time-travel action-adventure story in which people may or may not have doubles in another time. When the archcriminal gets executed in the present, has a scientist died in the future?

Jack Williamson posits that Heisenberg's probability theorem allows multiple futures in *The Legion of Time* (1938). Coming from a preferable but unlikely future, a beautiful girl enlists heroes to intercede for her survival; the choice will come when mentally released atomic energy is either freely offered to all or held for secret exploitation. The more likely but less altruistic alternative will lead to the eventual destruction of mankind. The time travelers, enlisted at the moment of death, not only defeat the evil alternative but are resurrected from a second death to enjoy their triumph.

Paying stricter attention to scientific research, Lester del Rey's "Reincarnate" (1940) rehabilitates the victim of an atomic accident as a cyborg, though the term was not yet invented. In his story "The Stars Look Down" (1940), competition between inventors using "the newly commercialized atomic power" and conventional power plants leads to industrial espionage, small-scale warfare, and test failures but finally produces a working spaceship and the probable future exploration of the galaxy.

Some stories present atomic research in a thoroughly lighthearted style. L. Sprague de Camp's "The Blue Giraffe" (1939) predicts complicated and comical mutations in the creatures surrounding an atomic research station. Lester del Rey's "The Smallest God" (1940) features an android who is brought to life by being inhabited by a small rubber doll impregnated with radioactive materials. The doll, a representation of Hermes whose intelligence is surpassed only by his chutzpah, eventually becomes a biochemist like his creator and, having lost the girl of his dreams, marries an even better one.

Perhaps the most ridiculous use that atomic energy could be put to is described in William F. Temple's "The Four-Sided Triangle" (1939). Three creative geniuses develop an atomic duplicating apparatus and use it to multiply art objects. Becoming bored with being rich and famous, they return to research; both men love the same girl, so they discover a way to duplicate people, with assorted personal consequences.

SAVING THE WORLD

A more serious but equally optimistic scenario shows science as the sole savior of Earth, the human species, or the entire solar system. "Save the world" stories frequently show scientists tossing off ideas and inventions at a great rate, with little attention to scientific theory and equally little or no testing of their work before it gets used. These stories reflected the magical effectiveness of technology more than they did theoretical, carefully controlled work of the research scientist; after all, it was the result that counted.

In "Atomic Fire" by Raymond Gallun (1931), science saves the Earth. Ten million years from now, the Earth is ruled by Martians who emigrated when their planet became too cold to sustain life. Now the sun no longer warms Earth adequately, either; only atomic energy can save them. But dare they loose this power on their home world? "Once started anywhere on Aerth the process of disintegration would probably continue until the planet had become a globe of incandescent gas" (66). Two scientists—one human, one Martian—manage to produce atomic energy on a spaceship; they survive their success but cannot stop the reaction, so they deliberately crash the ship on the Moon after bailing out. The Moon immediately takes fire, becoming a second sun. Man and Martian are saved! (Although Gallun claims that heredity does not make much difference, the Martians are shown as rulers, while the Human makes the atomic furnace work.)

Campbell did not reserve the "Don A. Stuart" name for poetic, iconoclastic works. In "Atomic Power" (1934), he plays with the popular "atomic solar system" idea. Earth derives its power from engines that release "the energy of atoms" by breaking them up without destroying them. These engines often encounter bits of fuel that will not break, forcing a cold restart. As they work on this problem, scientists discover that gravity is weakening and Earth is freezing. The situation quickly grows critical, and Ban Torrence works to liberate true atomic power, hoping to counteract the release of atomic energy in the greater universe of which our universe is only an atom "by just slightly upsetting their field, so it passes by, harmless" (96). Naturally, his scheme works, and in this greater universe, scientists discard the bit of fuel (Earth) that their engine could not disintegrate. Ban's work brings him quiet satisfaction. "Only he knew that he had restored Earth . . . that he had found the secret of vast power that would warm the frozen peoples and power their industry as Earth thawed out once more" (97).

While science always triumphs in "Stuart" stories, the scientists who set out to become rich and famous do not always win. Unlike Ban Torrence, the hero of "Blindness" (1935) makes a great discovery that turns out to be a great disappointment even while his earlier work saves the world. Malcolm Mackay, born 1974, MIT class of 1995, longs to provide true "atomic power so they could really reach the other planets" but finds that the answer must be hidden in the Sun (109). He invents a material that will transform energy into cold and studies the Sun from an orbit he can leave only under atomic power—a clear case of win or die. He and his coworker Burns discover "The Great Secret," and "the energy of the atom was harnessed by man!" in 2054 (116). Mackay's sight has failed, so Burns builds the atomic engine. They assume that it will eliminate "smoke-clouded cities," arctic wildernesses, and back-breaking labor, but when they return, they find that Earth has already used Mackay's earlier invention to get "energy from the heat of the air" and has solved nearly all its problems already. Mackay has inadvertently provided the benefits he gave his sight for, but only one interplanetary space line wants his atomic engine to power true spaceflight, since the nearby planets are now being turned into gardens. Mackay dies a bitter man.

Nat Schachner's "Emissaries of Space" (1932) plays a reversal on the frequently expressed hope that atomic power will provide such cheap energy that all humans will live in luxury. The atomic secret is given to Earth scientists by alien mental influence. It allows the building of motors that produce one hundred units of power for every ten units of energy invested. The world responds with increased economic and political freedom, but soon the alien Emissaries demand payment. Eventually the humans stop the atomic motors, go back to their old power sources, and find that they are much better off than in "idleness and selfishness and the avid pursuit of empty pleasure" (59). Mars, Venus, and Ganymede, which had been inhabited by beings who succumbed to the Emissaries completely, are lost from the solar system. Earth is not. Here, Schachner reverses the concept of "progress": true science includes knowing when to stop.

The absolute reverse of "save the world" stories comes in Willard Hawkins's "The Dwindling Sphere" (1940). A scientist trying for usable atomic energy bombards various substances with neutrons, finding that he reduces them in size and mass without a violent release of energy. His process is patented and eventually used to feed the world, but the creation of "plastocene" depletes the planet. Each subsequent generation refuses to believe that its "necessary" actions can possibly make a difference to anything as large as the Earth; the story ends with a substantially reduced (but happy) population living on a planet the size of Luna.

LOSING THE RACE

John W. Campbell, Jr., wrote so many sf stories so rapidly using so many "stock" sf scenarios—often with his own twist—that he can be considered a "lone inventor" himself. But Campbell never deviated from one point: in his stories Man (in the broadest sense) wins, even when "Don A. Stuart's" iconoclastic skepticism criticizes the use Man will make of his scientific genius. If Man fails to win, it is because he has lost or abandoned his humanity.

For Campbell, human "progress" comes from a combination of scientific curiosity and hard work; it can be measured by technology. But Man can easily lose his humanity by misusing that very technology. Evolution depends on struggle; technological sin consists of laziness, of general hedonism and elimination of struggle. Man has evolved slowly, but he can devolve rapidly. Devolution can be prevented only by continuous effort.

In "The Last Evolution" (1932), Campbell introduces an idea that becomes his trademark: Man's physiological evolution parallels his sociocultural evolution. Aliens produce "The Last Evolution" by arriving in our solar system at a time when only a few men remain, "striding through science irresistibly" with their many machines (8). Although men have long since given up war, they assume that the aliens are hostile and try to destroy them with mere atomic explosions. The aliens use disintegrating matter to wipe Man out, leaving only his machines. The mechanical narrator of the story finds this appropriate, since man evolves less rapidly than do his machines and is less deadly. The surviving machines succeed in turning away the aliens, fill the solar system with their progeny, and eventually evolve to a "being of Force" that returns through time to leave this "fictitious" account proving the machines' superiority (23).

In "Twilight" (1934), man's psychological and physiological devolution—due mostly to his very inventiveness—is somewhat redeemed by the time traveler who programs the atomically powered caretaker machines with curiosity, the most human attribute of all.

In 1935, "Stuart" published three connected stories that he hoped would upset everyone's assumptions about humans and aliens. Man's very inventiveness proves his downfall; humanity degenerates physically, mentally, and morally when "The Machine" (1935) does everything for it. After the Machine decides to leave for Man's own good, the race is rescued from savagery by "The Invaders" (1935). (Before humanity can learn from "the Teachers," it must first return to infancy.) Only in the last story, "Rebellion" (1935), has Man regained his technology enough to handle a superweapon. Enslaved by the insectoid Tharoo and bred back to competence, men learn deviousness and breed their own geniuses who hope to develop the ability to handle "atomic blast." If they cannot, they will risk having to "destroy all life on the planet in order to destroy the Tharoo" (133). They invent a bubble of force to protect themselves from the vividly described atomic bombs, drive the Tharoo to Venus, and restore humanity to the place it held before it devolved. On Venus, however, the Tharoo lose "all their science and comfort" while struggling against the jungle. They yearn for Earth but are unable to compete against the race they raised to intelligence higher than their own: "For the Tharoo were excellent teachers" (150).

In "Forgetfulness" (1937), "Stuart" tells of a confrontation between space travelers and the men of Rhth, who live peacefully and pastorally outside their eternal cities. The visitors boast of their climb to preeminence. Once Rhth taught them technology, "with atomic power they blasted themselves back to the swamps. Four times they climbed, discovered the secret of the atom, and blasted themselves back to the swamps" (21). Now they are prepared to colonize Rhth, allowing the few remaining Rhthians to die as wards of the State. Their Rhthian informant seems almost placid, almost simple, but he soon demonstrates his power when he whisks the invaders back to their own planet and limits their travel to three star systems. He has not lost his science; he has merely forgotten the details as modern man "forgets" how to chip flint.

In these stories Campbell sounds like an existentialist who also believes in original sin. He sees Man creating his own destiny in a universe that follows only physical laws wherein Man will be punished by his own mistakes. Man's greatest temptation comes precisely from his greatest virtue: the better the life he can create for himself, the more likely he is to stop wanting to improve it. Greed, in the sense of unflagging quest for knowledge, power, and control, is Man's salvation. Campbell subscribes to the work ethic: accrue knowledge or die.

Understanding Campbell's Lamarckian concept of evolution allows us to appreciate Campbell's love for the machine, a love that is reflected, if not equaled, by many other sf writers. Machines visibly evolve; man seems not to have changed significantly for thousands of years. Though no single machine can do all that man can do, machines in the aggregate can do more than man. They are calm, logical, and teachable, and therefore virtuous. But most of all, machines are the outward and visible sign of an invisible science. The only thing that is better than machine science is science that has progressed beyond the need for physical mechanisms. Science itself is unquestionably the greatest blessing of all.

Campbell wrote his share of the superweapons stories that filled the science fiction magazines of the thirties, but he remained positive about the future. He did not write about perverted or misused science; he explored the future-war scenario only in terms of alien enemies; and he adamantly refused to believe that man might use science to wipe himself out.[18] Nor did he buy stories where humans did not win. Campbell's humans might devolve, but they would not suicide. Even before 1945 other authors disagreed; but their stories were not published in *Astounding Science Fiction*.

RESEARCH GONE WRONG

If Superman epitomizes the myth of the ideal American, the dual personalities of Dr. Frankenstein as alchemist as well as scientist epitomize the relationship Americans display with science and scientists. Science fiction does not just idealize science; it also reflects our ambivalence towards science, scientists, and the technological complexity they produce. Thus, a literature of change often appears to fear change, and a literature explicitly created to explain and eulogize science often seems to warn against the products of science and most particularly against the dangers of the research and development that lead to new technology.

The Atoms Revolt

V. Orlovsky's "The Revolt of the Atoms" (1929) is the first such story to use an explicitly atomic theme. In an international competition to liberate atomic energy, one scientist completes a ten-year experiment that starts a self-sustaining reaction. Russia, called "this amazing country, where only recently they had been feeding on human flesh" (6), is suspected of spying, but this becomes incidental when the scientist's "fiery sphere" escapes the laboratory, devastates Europe, and finally falls into Vesuvius, which fortunately chooses that moment to erupt. Three months later, "the astronomers at the Greenwich Observatory detected a tiny star that was performing its circle around the Earth in the form of a satellite at the distance of about twelve hundred miles. This was the atomic vortex that was gradually dissipating into universal space its dreadful energy, no longer to be feared by man" (37).

Some warnings against misuse of science sound like a reversal on the story of Frankenstein: instead of the inventor fearing and abandoning the invention, the invention abandons its creator and takes on a kind of demonic life of its own. This becomes the basis of *Seeds of Life* (1931) by John Taine (Eric Temple Bell). Despite warnings, scientists in the Erickson Foundation for Electrical Research work unprotected with X rays and harder radiations. Exposure to one supermachine changes a sullen, stupid, jealous worker into a genius. More a combination of Frankenstein and his monster than a Dr. Jekyll/Mr. Hyde, he takes over and redirects the work of the laboratory with the ultimate aim of altering evolution.

Although he claims to desire greater intelligence for the human race, his experiments lead to his own devolution and to the death of his wife while giving birth to a reptilian monster. He has also sold the secret of atomic energy to a company that will erect power transmitters all over the United States. As he regains his humanity, he tries to stop this, but the company refuses to believe in the danger, thinking only of its profits. Barely in time, the scientist whose experiment originally altered the worker manages to warn the world, the transmitters are destroyed, and the human race is saved from bearing a generation of vipers and eventual sterility.

Other stories of misused science also show the scientist getting punished in one way or another, usually from pride. In Edmond Hamilton's "The Man Who Evolved" (April 1931), an impatient scientist decides to use cosmic radiation on himself, expecting to evolve into the genius of the future. He becomes first a magnificent specimen, then a power-mad brain, then a greater brain, and finally a lump of protoplasm. In Donald Wandrei's "The Atom-Smasher" (1934), a researcher who is using atomic energy to transport objects through space trips, falls into the force field, and dies.

P. Schuyler Miller's "The Atom Smasher" (1934) is less trivial; a young student who is impressed by a lecture on the possibilities of atomic energy spends eighty years of his life working "in growing poverty, while the malignant rays from his tubes ate at his vitals, while the world forgot" (128). Eventually his equipment fails. "Out of the heart of the snow hurtled a pillar of seething flame, star-white, blinding!" (129), killing the experimenter, destroying his apparatus, and burning for weeks. No one else "ever dared to try what he had tried. They never even knew his name." But they set up "an ebon shaft, topped with a golden ball" to "remember the man who smashed the atom" (130). (Miller does not say how anyone knew that.)

Isaac R. Nathanson's "The World Aflame" (1935) combines the fear that scientific experiments may get out of hand with the fear of stolen atomic secrets being used in worldwide war. A laboratory experiment to liberate atomic energy by bombarding beryllium with X rays starts an uncontrollable chain reaction. Ten days of work with "a reverse process" retards "the fierce rate of atomic radiation which was annihilating the beryllium, as to finally bring it under control" (50), but the building is a total loss. The professor is reprimanded and refused permission to continue his work, but his notes are stolen by spies after war breaks out between the Anglo-American-French Alliance and the Associated Central and Southern Nations aided by the Japanese Empire, which has already conquered most of Asia. Rockets "ingeniously freighted with an immense charge of matter in a state of fierce atomic disintegration" are hurled at the United States, with all the major Eastern cities as targets, but only one lands. Missing New York City, it starts burning up the Catskills. (Apparently the second missile detonated on takeoff, destroying the secret base from which the attack was launched.) But one uncontrollable chain reaction is quite enough; Jim Tomlinson, who worked as a graduate student on the initial experiment, cannot convince authorities to mount an immediate, expensive, all-out battle against the fire in the Catskills, and the chain reaction slowly grows until it "suddenly blew several more square miles of mountain to smithereens. Huge blocks of rock and pulverized material, some of it dangerously incandescent and radioactive, rained down over a wide territory" (79). Now it is too late to save the Earth; only migration to another planet can save the human race. Tomlinson grimly recalls his professor's initial prediction: "Man will either rise to the heights of the gods, or, if he does not take care, he may just as easily destroy himself!" (46).

Stolen Science

In Nathanson's story, the experiment goes so thoroughly wrong that one wonders why any self-respecting spy would bother to steal the data on it, or any sane government try to duplicate it. But the enemy is rarely sane in these stories. Its ambition is all-encompassing; overwhelming power is the only way to satisfy it. The consequences are invariably at least planetary in scope.

Noteworthy in these stories is the astonishing lack of interest with which the new invention is greeted in its own country, where its potential either as tool or weapon is completely ignored, while the agents of international war pounce on it no matter how well its inventor tries to hide it. An exception occurs in a few stories, where the invention has obvious commercial applications. And it still gets stolen despite all precautions.

Stephen G. Hale's two stories of atomic theft, "The Laughing Death" (1931) and "Worlds Adrift" (1932), show a peaceful atomic-powered device becoming an inadvertent disaster. The narrator intends only to improve the speed of an automated subway digger from its current four hundred miles per hour. Even as they work, inventing the self-sustaining atomic pile in the process, the scientists fear war; the narrator is hopeful, while his assistant worries about new weapons. For safety they burn the "dangerous" plans of the machine that now can excavate three times round the earth using only one bucket of sand as fuel; they also tamper with the completed machines so they cannot be copied. Then a war begins, and a mad Russian scientist who later confesses that he wanted to rule the world sets one of the "Worms" digging unguided around the Earth. Eventually it girdles the globe, which splits into uneven, barely viable halves. In the sequel, "Worlds Adrift," the narrator (still harassed by the mad Russian) tries to blast the pieces back together, misjudges the trajectory, and sends his half of the Earth hurtling towards Mars. In neither story does the atomic machine provide the benefit that the inventors expected.

In "A Scientist Rises" by Harry Bates and Desmond Winter Hall (1932), the scientist fears the uses men may make of his invention, which expands the distance between atoms. "He realized, suddenly, that men had not yet learned to use fruitfully the precious, powerful things given to them, but as yet could only play with them like greedy children—and kill as they played" (560). He has worked alone, in secrecy; no body of scientists shares his work or even knows what he is doing; but this secrecy does not prevent "enemies" from knowing about his work. A spy attempts to seize his results, but the scientist kills him. He then turns his process on himself, and, as he expands, destroys "the device and all the papers that held its secrets." He dies sacrificially (560). One onlooker exclaims, "He has the face of—of a god! He's—as if he were looking down on us—and—pitying us" (558). In some future time, the scientist expects that his invention will be rediscovered and properly used by a grateful (and less aggressive) humanity.

That industrial spying alone can lead to war is also suggested by Otto Binder, writing as Gordon A. Giles in "The Atom Smasher" (1938). A patent clerk steals the plans submitted by a former professor of atomic physics when their effectiveness is demonstrated by the explosion that destroys inventor and surrounding territory. The clerk loses his reward when cheap atomic power upsets the stock market, but the purchaser, "a certain Oriental power" (38), attacks Seattle with forces that burn the flesh from the victims' bones. But this scientist has been less secretive and has sent copies of his work to a colleague. Immediately understanding the implications of the attack—"That meant gamma rays! And gamma rays meant Atomic Power!" (39), Dr. Henry Lewis begins to search for countermeasures while the Orientals occupy a depopulated but otherwise intact Seattle. (The rays act like an early version of the neutron bomb.) Fortunately, Atomic Power is generated by carborundum crystals. The original discoverer had supplied the defense mechanism along with the plans: a device that will, through sympathetic vibration, "shatter every carborundum crystal in the world" (40):

> Fate and Dr. Henry Lewis stood face to face.
>
> Then his finger jabbed firmly down on the key. He saw nothing of the supernally brilliant globe of radiant fire that burst from the tube and touched off similar globes of force all over the earth. (41)

Dying, Dr. Lewis has saved the world.

Many science fiction writers saw the wonders of science as two-faced; in the wrong hands, they were dangerous far beyond common understanding. Following Gernsback's dictum to instruct as well as to please, these writers made sure that their readers developed uncommon understanding.

REPEL THE INVADERS

Unlike Pierrepont B. Noyes, few of the early science fiction writers had either formal or practical training in economics or political science; moreover, once the depression began, few political or economic theories seemed adequate. But these were the big issues of the day, and they show up in sf, at least metaphorically. While many stories of the late twenties and early thirties present "lone inventors" remaking the world and their own fortunes through scientific genius, others show Americans as the innocent victims of some stronger but less ethical race, often from another planet. The alien enemy can be seen as a projection of the faceless but inimical economy against which man felt helpless. In this scenario, only scientific genius saves a victimized America from total defeat.

"When the Atoms Failed" (1930), John W. Campbell, Jr.'s first published story,[19] is typical of the "repel the aliens" scenario. A slam-bang plot joins with a cavalier attitude towards science to thwart invading Martians; the "lone inventor" single-handedly saves America and (by implication) the world. The story is set in the distant future—1947—and "narrated" in 1957 by David, the trusty friend of Steve Waterson, the "lone inventor" who has not only unlocked "the secret of the atom, and released for us atomic energy" but used the "integraph," MIT's electric calculator, to learn "just how to *completely destroy matter*!" (913). (Campbell seems to feel that this process, which he repeats in other stories, is different from and better than merely releasing atomic energy.)

The first trial of the "ultimate equation" fuses "a two mile streak of melted sand fifty feet broad . . . of six food thick glass!" (913). Faced with alien invasion, Waterson needs to invent, build, and use weapons powered by this ultimate energy to save Earth. He determines that he can "utterly destroy everything within a radius of a hundred miles, and damage everything within a much greater radius" but cannot "change the Earth's orbit" (920). He produces bombs in his desert laboratory about one a minute and completes a ray gun in an afternoon. (He shares none of this with the military.) Meanwhile, the announcement of the impending invasion causes panic. When the Martians destroy San Francisco with "tiny atom bombs" (922), "hundreds of thousands" of people have already died in panic attempts to flee the cities (921).

Unable to match Waterson's computer-generated weaponry, the aliens meet defeat in a space battle and flee. The heroes return to cheers—and to demands from each nation that they share their scientific secrets with it alone. "Waterson refused to give out the secret of that energy though. He demanded that the nations scrap every instrument of war, and then meet in the first Territorial Congress and write laws that might apply material energy to the ends of man, not to the ending of man!"(975).

Meeting all objections with the threat of force, Waterson imposes his will. "Needless to say, it was done. We all know the result. No armies meant no national spirit—no race jealousies can exist unless there is someone to stir them up, and now it is to the benefit of no one to do so!"(975). The cowed Martians soon become valued neighbors, who really did little damage, less than Earth did to itself in its panic. The story ends piously: "May God help these twin races . . . to climb on in friendly rivalry toward better things," including joint migration "when the sun cools" (975).

In "Uncertainty" (1936), Buck Kendall, a rich and handsome genius who serves in the International Patrol out of sheer love of adventure, observes an alien ship entering the solar system, capturing a Solarian ship, and leaving at faster-than-light speed. Immediately deducing that the aliens are up to "acquisitive exploration" (18), he starts working on an appropriate weapon, "a new system for releasing atomic energy" (28) despite centuries of unsuccessful attempts. (They do have a "neutron gun.") For a while, alien and human compete to create new weapons, but at last the humans break open the Uncertainty Principle as though it were an energy source and use the results to defeat the aliens. Following them home, the humans make contact and set up a cooperative system with the aliens: since neither can use the same kind of planets, both can share the results of their explorations.

Raymond Z. Gallun's aliens may be antagonistic to man but are not seen as entirely evil in "Magician of Dream Valley" (1938). "Hexagon Lights" wink around Imbrium city, the first human colony on the Moon—which men are fast turning into an ugly, radioactive wasteland. The lights are revealed as sentient beings capable of creating hallucinations in humans. They are also being destroyed by radioactivity from the fuel plant. Even as the hero thwarts their plan to take over his mind, he regrets the death of "a unique and wonderful people who fought a valiant battle to live—and lost" (22). Gallun clearly compares the Hexagon Lights to the American Indians. Other writers are less kind to aliens. In "Proxima Centauri" (1935), Murray Leinster (the best-known of William F. Jenkins's pseudonyms) uses the atomic drive of a spaceship to destroy all of the thoroughly evil, cannibalistic aliens encountered by humans—who are exploring alien space.

RETURN TO THE WILDERNESS

Many of the future-war and post–future-war stories are "awful warnings" that will be considered in the next chapter, but a special kind of post–future-war stories involving the invasion and conquest of the United States needs to be considered here. The conquest invariably destroys urban centers, so Americans may be reduced to scavenging their own ruins for remnants of technology, but they are strengthened and purified by their return to the wilderness. These stories subtly confirm the sinfulness of cities, the innate goodness of the pioneer village, and the strength and wisdom of the frontiersman.[20] Thus even the conquest of the United States may become a "fortunate fall" if it results in a renewal of American values, morals, and power—symbolized, naturally, by some newly invented weapon that eventually repels the conquering invader. These stories begin with Philip Nowlan's "Armageddon 2419 A.D." (1928), featuring Anthony "Buck" Rogers.

"Buck" Rogers

"Buck" Rogers, best known as a comic strip, was born in 1928 in the pages of Gernsback's *Amazing Stories*. Clearly modeled on Edgar Rice Burroughs's John Carter novels, Nowlan's "Armageddon 2419 A.D." opens with Anthony Rogers waking from an extended nap to find himself in a strange green world. (The last he knew, he was exploring a mine in Pennsylvania noted for its radioactive emissions.) He meets and rescues Wilma, a lovely girl who carries a weapon that fires shells capable of annihilating whatever they hit, and who jumps enormous distances by means of a "floater belt." While Rogers has slept five hundred years, America has been conquered by the Han Airlords, a mongrel Asiatic race.

Another World War followed the First, "in which nearly all the European nations banded together to break the financial and industrial power of America" (425). America won, but the result was world suffering. Then a Russian-Chinese coalition took Europe. Without world markets, America collapsed economically. It then fought and lost to the Hans, whose superior science includes "disintegrator rays" that break things into "electronic vibrations" (426).

The remaining "unsubdued" Americans live in small enclaves in the forest. Under these primitive conditions, their scientists have "harnessed" subatomic forces. As long as they leave the Han cities alone, they are allowed some freedom; periodically, they attack each other, and the rest of the time they "try courageous but childishly futile attacks upon the Hans, followed by terribly punitive raids" (426). The Hans consider the Americans beasts; the Americans hate the Hans.

Despite their severance from an industrial base, native American geniuses nevertheless are capable of inventing, building, and distributing weapons harnessing "sub-atomic forces" (422). The power of Wilma's jumping belt comes from "inertron." Americans have also synthesized "ultron," an invisible and nonreflective synthetic element, a "solid of great molecular density," whose marvelous properties are described in a few paragraphs that assume that atomic reactions can derive from chemical processes. Armed with these weapons and Rogers's expertise in formal warfare, the "Wyoming Gang" becomes a truly dangerous adversary to the Hans.

Rogers and Wilma carry the battle home to the Hans in "The Airlords of Han" (1929), though they lack sufficient inertron to build enough "aircraft impervious to the 'dis' ray" to win easily (1107). Rogers attacks a Han airship, crashes, and is captured. In his absence, Wilma leads the Gang's attack on Nu-Yok. They use about a hundred "very high powered atomic shells . . . to reduce the city to ruins" (1120). "Their release of atomic force was nearly 100 percent, and each of them was equal to many hundred tons of . . . T.N.T." The "high-flung masses and towers of Nu-Yok" turn to "a seething turmoil of gigantic explosions" (1121). The Hans have prepared safe underground cities, but these are not yet finished when Wilma attacks, blows them up, and rescues Rogers. The Hans counterattack with "atomic projectiles" much like the Americans', but the Gangs still have the advantage of the jumping belts. (Although all of Rogers's equipment was captured by the Hans, including his "jumping belt, ultraphone and rocket gun" (1128), the Hans apparently have learned nothing from them.)

After a terrific barrage from their atomic "electrono plant," the Gang engages the Hans in hand-to-hand combat. Wilma shrieks like a Valkyrie and bayonets enemies with "ecstatic joy" before she faints (1134). The other Gangs join in; the Hans suicide; the Americans hunt down and wipe out the few remaining Hans. They then help other races (even non-Han Asiatics) defeat the Hans all over the world. This mopping-up process takes several years, but completes "the reclamation of America and inaugurat[es] the most glorious and noble era of scientific civilization in the history of the American race" (1134).

"Armageddon 2419 A.D." appeared the same month as the first part of E. E. Smith's *Skylark of Space*. One can still feel the enthusiasm with which fans must have received this issue of *Amazing Stories*. The cover claims to illustrate Smith's tale, with a man "flying" above the yard of an older man while a young woman flutters her hanky at him, but the outfit the "flyer" wears later appears on the comicstrip "Buck" Rogers: leather football helmet, red union suit, zipped leather boots, and elaborate rocket belt. In August 1928, these stories united two classic scenarios: the "lone inventor" as action-adventure hero and the fighting man as inventive genius.

Conquering Aliens

Some sf writers showed the conquest of the United States as coming not from other countries but from other worlds; some of these invasions are more or less successful. In Campbell's "Frictional Losses" (1936), the "Granthee" have conquered Earth using "atomic bombs . . . [that] flared rather than exploded" (98). The humans "did not have atomic power. We developed, toward the end, atomic explosives, which are very different. . . . before we could learn to use atomic fuels, it was too late" (98–99). Japan and Europe fought bravely and suicidally; humans carried atomic bombs aboard the Granthee ships. All the invading Granthee have been killed, but they promised a second, larger expedition, due as the story opens.

Surviving humans now excavate the wreckage of their cities hoping to rebuild their technological base. "Friction has stopped man always," one scientist mourns, but the other replies "Not friction, but inertia has stopped mankind" (106). After a lifetime of "trying to make delicate mechanisms work with defective apparatus," he creates a low-power effect that reduces friction. Rocks fall, houses collapse, clothing unravels, and the arriving Granthee fleet is destroyed. Men agree that the Granthee will not return; their frictional losses are too great. Man will go on.

Campbell continued to use the "repel the alien invader" scenario up to the end of his writing career. The paired stories, "Out of Night" (1937) and "The Cloak of Aesir" (1939), published under his Don A. Stuart pseudonym, tell of the occupation of Earth by the ancient and intelligent Sarn, and their defeat by imaginative, plucky, inventive Earthmen. As he so often does, Stuart posits that the aliens are not all bad; as he also showed in "Rebellion" (1935), defeating them is not all good.

In some stories, the wilderness that has sheltered American "Gangs" in "Armageddon 2419 A.D." becomes more than a refuge; it is the only world available. Some unspecified occurrence in the distant past has caused the collapse of civilization, and the "lone inventor" becomes the pioneer, recreating science single-handedly. An early example is Nelson Bond's three-part saga of Meg the Priestess. Apparently based on Stephen Vincent Benét's "Place of the Gods" (1937),[21] the story describes a culture moving from barbarism to the beginnings of a new technology.

In "The Priestess Who Rebelled" (1939), Meg makes the shocking discovery that the ancient culture she has been taught to revere (she has even learned to write) was ruled by men. Since the only men in her matriarchal society are flabby housekeepers, she has a problem with this, as she does with the handsome young hunter whom she meets on her initiatory journey to Mt. Rushmore. Daiv comes from a patriarchal tribe; in "The Judging of the Priestess" (1940), he marries Meg, thus breaking a number of taboos at once. Still, Daiv and Meg lead their tribe to victory over little yellow warriors using technologically superior weapons.

In "Magic City" (1941), Meg and Daiv head for the ruined city to seek knowledge and the remains of technology. While Benét's story does not make clear what disaster befell the United States, Bond's inclusion of foreign troops, no matter how barbarous, in "The Judging of the Priestess" makes war and invasion his most likely scenario, and their weapons make nuclear war seem possible. This series, reflecting as it does the pre–World War II situation, is also seminal.

There are strong similarities between Nowlan's and Bond's stories, including the long-ago destruction of American culture and the primitive conditions under which the protagonists must live. Differences include the presence of scientific knowledge in Nowlan's stories and its complete absence in Bond's. Each of these "repel the invaders" scenarios initiates a tradition of post–future-war conquest stories that becomes more important after World War II. The struggle against an enemy attack seems to be the oldest of these scenarios; it is quickly followed by stories showing society reverting to primitive conditions after a future war, and then—as we shall see in the next chapter—by stories that question whether a future war will leave any society at all. That some of these invading armies are nonhuman does not matter greatly. That the often-successful attack always takes place on American soil indicates the fears of the time.

FICTIONAL TACTICS

The change to pulp-magazine fiction requires new narrative tactics. These include shorter stories and, for novel-length works, the deliberate arrangement of plot sequence for publication in parts. (Although the magazines frequently advertised "a novel complete in this issue," these "novels" were usually much shorter than book length.) The shorter length enhances rather than detracts from the rapid, vigorous action that the pulp genre is noted for and does not affect either characterization or presentation of a richly developed background, since neither was emphasized in the action-adventure scientific romance.

The pulps developed a dedicated and specialized audience that demanded stories written to their taste and protested in the letter columns if they did not get them. Philip Nowlan's "Buck Rogers" stories, like E. E. Smith's *Skylark of Space*, would have had little chance for publication in any other market. While the medium shapes the form of the story, the need for suspense shapes the plot. If the hero of this "repel the invaders" story is to meet an enemy worthy of an American ex-soldier, just another war will not do. The outcome must be seriously in doubt, with the Hans all-powerful to justify the use of superweapons against them. But they cannot be as inventive as the Americans, because seat-of-the-pants technology is the undisputed realm of the "lone inventor" and thus an American monopoly.

Narrative Mode

One major difference between these sf stories and the action-adventure novels published before World War I is the narrative mode. After 1930, few are comic; even fewer end with a marriage. In fact, it would be hard for many of them to include marriage at all, since women are sparsely represented in the pulps. Exceptions to this generalization include *The Skylark of Space*, "Armageddon 2419 A.D." and "The Airlords of Han," and the tales of Meg the Priestess, each of which also features an active, attractive female character. It should be noted, however, that the "romance" in *Skylark* has often been deplored, and not always because it seems trite and clumsily written; more often it is criticized because an action-adventure story should not indulge in "mushy stuff." The other writers carefully avoid any appearance of sentimentality.

Racism

The political isolationism of the United States is reinforced by the active racism portrayed in many of these stories. Orientals are not considered entirely human; in "The Airlords of Han," Rogers claims that the invaders "had in their blood a taint not of this earth" (1106), and they are shown to be thoroughly heartless even to their own people, whom they leave to die of disease when infected by Wilma's "air balls." Prejudice against blacks is less overt. In "The Airlords of Han," Nowlan specifically mentions that the Americans free from Han domination "the simple, spiritual Blacks of Africa, today one of the leading races of the world, although in the Twentieth Century we regarded them as inferior" (1134). E. E. Smith later removes the comic references to a black janitor in *The Skylark of Space*. Other writers avoid the question by having only white protagonists. In point of fact, science fiction was written by white men for white men at this point. The readership was largely male (and often adolescent male); so were the writers.[22]

Characterization

As before, the main character often seems to be the idea. As before, the author is not required to demonstrate genuine scientific expertise; even physics major John Campbell throws scientific jargon around with little sense of responsibility towards educating his audience. Although Sam Moskowitz later praises several of these stories for their scientific verisimilitude and accurate prediction in "Did Science Fiction Predict Atomic Energy?" his inclusion of *The Skylark of Space*, P. Schuyler Miller's "The Atom Smasher," and Stephen G. Hale's "The Laughing Death" creates some doubt about his criteria. He does admit that writers did not begin to make truly accurate scientific predictions until after 1940—and mentions Malcolm Jameson's *Atomic Bomb* along with Lester del Rey's "Nerves" and Robert A. Heinlein's "Solution Unsatisfactory."[23] To read these stories for scientific information seems beside the point, however. They succeeded in portraying the major interests and concerns of the American public, embodied in attractive fictional form; and those concerns frequently involved technology, if not pure science.

The Scientist Emerges

Earlier stories emphasized the result of the scientists' work; now we sometimes get to see the scientist in action. This is not universally true, of course; in Noyes's *The Pallid Giant*, the vital discovery is made by a pair of amateur enthusiasts, and the science is linguistics. While the world-famous linguist who works on the ancient documents gets his fair part of the story, he is never a major character. In Nowlan's "Buck Rogers" stories, scientists are busy, but always in the background. Without their work (and we never find out how they manage to accomplish their miracles without glassware producers, machine shops, power sources, and other necessary support systems), the Americans could never overcome the Hans.

Still, there are more stories that feature the scientist himself than ever before. We can compare the part played by Meade Stillman in *All for His Country* with that played by Richard Seaton in *The Skylark of Space*. "A Scientist Rises," by Bates and Hall; "Atomic Power," "Blindness," "Rebellion," "The Cloak of Aesir," and "When the Atoms Failed" by Campbell; "Reincarnate," "The Smallest God," and "The Stars Look Down" by del Rey; "Atomic Fire" by Gallun; "The Atom Smasher" by Binder; "The Laughing Death" and "Worlds Adrift" by Hale; "The Man Who Evolved" by Hamilton; "The Dwindling Sphere" by Hawkins; "Submicroscopic" by Meek; "The World Aflame" by Nathanson; "Emissaries of Space" by Schachner; *Seeds of Life* by Taine; and "The Four-Sided Triangle" by Temple all have scientists who play major roles, however carefully (or carelessly) developed their characters may be.

Some stories combine the character of entrepreneur and scientist, like Crane and Seaton in *The Skylark of Space*, Buck Kendall in "Uncertainty," and Steve Waterson in "When the Atoms Failed." We find fewer of the wealthy dilettantes of earlier works; but aside from Richard Seaton, Buck Kendall, and Andrew Crane in *Seeds of Life*, few of them seem gainfully employed, either. But even in the worst of the depression, though capitalism may be tacitly criticized, we find no stories that advocate any other economic system. Indeed, some, like *Seeds of Life*, show scientists succumbing to the temptations of wealth. The most successful are the adventurers or the entrepreneurs, like Campbell's "Planeteers," who do science-on-the-spot while exploring strange new worlds and solving problems for strange new races.

Few scientists are portrayed as supermen. Some seem humanitarian, even naively self-sacrificing, but unlike the entrepreneur or technologist, some make really stupid blunders, both in their own work and in their assumptions about how the world works. The "pure scientist" often fails; if he succeeds, he may have his secrets stolen or die as a result of his own work or both. Always in the background is the fear that his very success will become a Frankenstein monster, a terrible new weapon of war.

ASSUMPTIONS

Stories in which scientists' superweapons "save the world" either from natural disaster or from invading aliens are possible only within the parameters of the new science fiction genre. As Albert Berger demonstrates,[24] atomic energy is science fiction's major metaphor for power. We must then discover why such overwhelming power is assumed to be necessary. Certainly many of these stories can be interpreted as thinly disguised wish fulfillment. If only dangerous ideologies like communism or immediate difficulties like the depression could be defeated as soundly, and as quickly, as are Campbell's Martians in "When the Atoms Failed"! Early stories even consider making friends of such enemies. But this can only be done when they have been "put in their place," an act that requires superior strength.

Conspicuous by its absence is the "war-to-end-war" scenario. "Peace by force" appears only in Campbell's "When the Atoms Failed" and "Uncertainty," which end with a mutually beneficial agreement worked out between humans and aliens. This happy compromise, which also occurs in stories involving inter-human warfare examined in the next chapter, disappears in time; we see no more such endings after 1936. Nor do all authors hold this friendly feeling for aliens; "The Magician of Dream Valley" judges them and wipes them out on their own territory, as does "Proxima Centauri." It may be argued that after the mid–1930s, compromise seemed less plausible as a solution to aggression, even when "we" were the aggressors.

The "save the world" scenario is no more popular than the "repel the invaders" theme. The invasion always takes place on American soil. Although the United States has refused to play the international game, has taken its bat and glove and gone home, it still fears the opposing team. When a number of stories show human or alien invasion of the homeland, leading to its enslavement or its return to primitive conditions, we can assume an underlying conviction that the country itself is unstable. (We may note other stories, not dealing with invasion or superweapons, that carry the same theme: Jack London's "The Red Death" and Stephen Vincent Benét's "The Place of the Gods," for instance.) This naturally follows from the tendency of Americans to see themselves as the "nice guy"; the "nice guy" is always the patsy. If our country is "nice" and therefore "weak," it follows that our opponents are strong, and only a superweapon can save us. Science is the natural source of such a superweapon, and the scientist thus becomes not only the possible regenerator but the savior of the nation.

Little remains of the earlier altruism—the assumption that our innocence was our strength—that encouraged American writers to impose peace on the world by force. Many of these writers see the United States as weakened, in danger both from external influence and from internal collapse. This collapse can come about from too much progress, leading to a life of ease and devolution; from external competition; or from science gone wrong, especially from experiments that may devastate the environment. This fear plays a prominent part in *The Pallid Giant*, seems to be growing by 1935 in "The World Aflame" and "Blindness," becomes a specifically American problem in the "Magician of Dream Valley," and is brought to high irony in "The Dwindling Sphere," where Terrans, taught by scientists, seem perfectly satisfied literally to devour their planet.

Enter Dr. Frankenstein

For centuries, humans used religion to control their relationship with the world; when science seemed to offer more predictable results, many turned to it instead. Like religion and its close relative, magic, science may be dangerous, but to gain the control we seek we must use it. The high priests of science do not seem entirely human, however. They are not motivated by normal impulses, but by an inhuman, unconquerable drive to discover abstract truths. They are rarely practical, but in these stories their theories usually work; the issue becomes whether or not they can control the results. If they can, their ideas lead to weapons. If they cannot, they lead to ghastly accidents. They create power, but are not responsible for its use.

The archtype of the scientist is Dr. Victor Frankenstein, who mixed science with alchemy, working in secret without guidance and without assistance. From the highest of motives, he usurped the prerogatives of God Himself by creating life. He then abandoned his creation in a fit of panic, an act that resulted in his own destruction and that of his whole family. The very word "scientist" conjures up images of Frankenstein—and of his monster. We want the magic but not the magician.

Science, in many of these stories, is indistinguishable from alchemy. Like the alchemist, these scientists usually work in secret; their discoveries come from thin air, not from theoretical bases; they can turn an idea into a weapon without factories or even machine shops in which to build it; and they never seem to run out of raw materials. Moreover, by destroying the plans, they can really and truly keep a discovery secret. Only a few stories recognize that the basic principles of science are available to all scientists, and that once something has been shown to work, acute observers can figure out the underlying principles and duplicate or even surpass the original. These stories often confuse science (hypothesizing and testing basic explanatory principles) with technology (the application of those principles to machines or practices). But to the layman, technology is visible and pure science is not; the confusion is quite understandable.

Unlike the scientist, the technologist is shown as practical. He knows how to make the magic work. He is more competent than the scientist and, because he deals with real rather than abstract ideas, seems far less dangerous. Until some emergency arises, he is just an "ordinary guy"; then he meets the emergency by instantly translating the scientist's abstract ideas into working machines. He can be identified by his rapid and effective response to danger. The technologist is the "lone inventor," the Superman.

The Danger of Power

If the scientist is represented by Frankenstein, whose search for pure knowledge puts us in such awful danger, why can we not count on the technologist as Superman to save us? To answer that question, we need to look at the assumptions about human nature tacitly demonstrated by many of these stories—views held, apparently, without conscious awareness.

First, humans are shown as insatiably curious, but quite lacking in common sense. Human nature boldly goes where no man has gone before and where angels fear to tread—but the angels are generally right. At the same time, humans are shown as fearful. They demand control of their environment, including other humans, for their own safety. But they are not capable of properly handling the power this control requires; only God can do that. The "fortunate fall," when Adam and Eve took "control" of knowledge, is, in the long run, our undoing. Control requires power that we are incapable of wielding, yet we continue to demand greater power to control the danger we have ourselves created by our demand for control.

Second, human nature cannot stand temptation. Give humans the easy life, and they become lotus eaters. Thus the liberation of atomic energy (and despite the caveats of the scientists, such liberation was anticipated) and the virtually free power it would provide, allowing the ordinary citizen to afford an extraordinary diversity of labor-saving devices, could destroy humanity. In "Emissaries of Space," Schachner posits cultural advancement following the acquisition of free power, with laziness and selfishness close behind. Campbell briefly considers a utopian future in "Blindness," but his ideas on the topic are more clearly expressed in his "Teachers" series, where he applies a strict Lamarckian "use or lose" concept of evolution. This view is popular among writers who assume that cultural evolution implies that we have reached our current advanced state by constant struggle against inimical nature and that we now no longer adapt to our environment but instead adapt the environment to our own needs.[25] They further assume that the outcome of technological advance will be racial devolution and suggest that we are obligated to avoid the technological future to save humanity.

Third, human nature is seen as aggressive, treacherous, and warlike. Given the dangerous world we live in (and our isolationism emphasizes its dangerousness), conflict is inevitable; given our weakness (due to our "nice-guy" character) we must protect ourselves with superweapons. But superweapons mean greater danger; they can accidentally destroy their inventors, and what one side can produce the other side can duplicate. Whether we create the superweapon or not, we risk destruction. No wonder some stories posit the end of modern society and a return to the "green world" of the past. But even this will not save us; as we see in the quest undertaken by Meg the Priestess and her consort Daiv, humans insist on seeking out the apple, no matter how well it is hidden. Technology will rise again.

Our culture measures success by "progress" and measures progress by technology. Since almost everyone agrees that progress is a good thing, the science that makes the technology possible is also automatically defined as good. But since Victor Frankenstein represents the scientist, and his work is clearly dangerous, the "advances" of science must be examined carefully. And even when it is so examined, how can the average person tell the safe from the dangerous? Many of these stories deal with that question, extrapolating from contemporary knowledge and abilities to a distant (and possibly even more dangerous) future.

If science equals technology, which equals progress, which is good by definition, while simultaneously exposing us to the risk of devolution or destruction by superweapons, which is clearly bad, then we are caught in the modern paradox: we cannot live with it and we cannot get rid of it. Science is power—and power is a two-edged sword. The technologist cannot save us. Science fiction inevitably carries a mixed message: "I have seen the future," and—for good or ill—"it has SCIENCE written all over it."

NOTES

1. "Gentlemen: You are Mad!" is borrowed from an article by Lewis Mumford on the use of atomic power, printed in the *Saturday Review of Literature* on March 2, 1946. Aside from this temporary relevance, Noyes's new title tells little more about his novel than does the original, which refers obscurely to the "pallid giant, fear."

2. All-fiction pulps became a major force in the publishing field with Munsey's *Argosy* in 1896, followed by his even more popular *Munsey's Magazine.* Thoroughgoing specialization soon followed. In 1927, Gernsback's *Amazing Stories* listed its companion magazines as *Radio News, Science and Invention, Radio Listener's Guide, Radio International,* and *Spare-Time Money Making,* while the companion magazines to Clayton's *Astounding Stories* (1930) included *Ranch Romances, Cowboy Stories, All Star Detective Stories, Flyers,* and *Forest and Stream.* See Paul Carter, *The Creation of Tomorrow: Fifty Years of Magazine Science Fiction* (New York: Columbia University Press, 1977), 12–14.

3. For a useful discussion of the history, significance, and definition of the term "science fiction" as well as the various abbreviations thereof, see Gary K. Wolfe, *Critical Terms for Science Fiction and Fantasy: A Glossary and Guide to Scholarship* (Westport, Conn.: Greenwood Press, 1986).

4. Companion magazines to *Amazing Stories* included *Amazing Stories Quarterly, Amazing Stories Annual* (1927 only), *Fantastic Adventures,* and *Fantastic. Science Wonder Stories* (1929) became *Wonder Stories* in 1930, and *Thrilling Wonder Stories* in 1936. Companion magazines included *Air Wonder Stories, Science Wonder Quarterly, Startling Stories,* and *Captain Future.* Some of these magazines had very short lifetimes; others lasted for many years. See Carter, *Creation of Tomorrow,* ix–x.

5. For a summary of Gernsback's publishing history, see James Gunn, *Alternate Worlds: The Illustrated History of Science Fiction* (Englewood Cliffs, N.J.: Prentice-Hall, 1975), chap. 8, especially pp. 125–126. *Amazing Stories* is now the longest-running sf magazine on the market, with *Analog* (formerly *Astounding Science Fiction*) a close second.

6. This magazine went through the usual number of name changes, from *Astounding Stories of Super Science* in 1930 to *Astounding Stories* in 1933, *Astounding Science-Fiction* in 1938. In 1960 it evolved through *Analog Science Fact-Science Fiction* to its present name, *Analog Science Fiction/Science Fact.*

7. James Gunn calls Campbell a "transitional writer" who grew up on science fiction: "First Edgar Rice Burroughs, then *Argosy, Weird Tales,* and the first issue of *Amazing Stories.* He was particularly impressed by the imagination displayed in Doc Smith's *Skylark of Space,* and much of Campbell's early writing was cosmic in scope, though carefully detailed scientifically." *Alternate Worlds,* 146.

8. In a footnote to his essay, "Non-Literary Influences on Science Fiction," Algis Budrys categorically denies Campbell's preference for genuine science in the stories he bought for *Astounding Stories.* Careful examination, he claims, will "expose the myth of *ASF* under Campbell as a magazine concerned with science-verisimilitude, as distinguished from a generalized scientophilia which, eventually, revealed itself only as a special case of Campbell's feeling that there must be *some* system for explaining and modifying the Universe. Campbell actively recruited, promulgated and rewarded many writers who, to his obvious knowl-

edge, constantly got their science wrong or ignored science, to neither his dismay nor that of the audience." Algis Budrys, "Non-Literary Influences on Science Fiction, (An Essay)" Drumm Booklet no. 9 (Polk City, Iowa: Drumm, 1983), 19–20. An earlier version of this essay, in edited form, appeared in *Science Fiction Dialogues*, ed. Gary K. Wolfe (Chicago: Academy, 1982).

9. The early magazines paid a quarter of a cent a word, often on (or long after) publication. Payment based on word count may help explain some long-winded passages in the early fiction. Although per word rates have risen, the problem of obtaining payment seems to recur periodically with sf publications.

10. Science fiction fans differ from sf readers in several significant ways. Readers read, enjoy, and may even discuss sf with their friends. Fans do more, as one bit of jargon indicates: FIAWOL, "fandom is a way of life." Belonging to a club, attending or helping to run sf conventions, writing heated letters of comment to editors (locs), and writing for and/or publishing an amateur sf magazine (fanzine) are among the identifying symptoms of fandom. A fan may decide to GAFIATE, or "get away from it all," but this rarely lasts long. It should be noted that turning "pro" (getting paid for doing the things that a fan does for free) does not necessarily disqualify one as a fan.

11. As James Gunn notes, a number of the young readers who began writing sf in the thirties soon became magazine editors: "Homig, Weisinger, Wollheim, Pohl, Palmer, Boucher, Lowndes, Merril, Knight, Blish, Shaw and others." *Alternate Worlds*, 184.

12. Now considered a classic, "Twilight" was consistently rejected until F. Orlin Tremaine published it in *Astounding Stories* in November 1934. Lester del Rey, "The Three Careers of John W. Campbell," in *The Best of John W. Campbell*, ed. Lester del Rey (Garden City, N.Y.: Doubleday, 1976), 3.

13. Christopher Lasch, *The New Radicalism in America (1889–1963)* (New York: Alfred A. Knopf, 1965), ix.

14. Information in this paragraph is largely summarized from James Gunn's *Alternate Worlds;* the quotation is from page 130.

15. See, for example, C. C. Furnas, *The Next Hundred Years: The Unfinished Business of Science* (New York: Blue Ribbon Books, 1936): 188–90.

16. For more information on the circumstances surrounding the publication of *Skylark* and on "Doc" Smith's publishing history, see James Gunn, *Alternate Worlds*, chap. 9, and Frederik Pohl, "The Publishing of Science Fiction," in *Science Fiction, Today and Tomorrow*, ed. Reginald Bretnor (New York: Harper, 1974) 17–44.

17. "The Atom Smasher" proved so popular a title that it was used no fewer than four times in the next eight years: by Rousseau in 1930, P. Schuyler Miller and Donald Wandrei in separate stories in 1934, and Gordon A. Giles (Otto Binder) in 1938. In 1941, Charles Stoddard put it in the plural with "The Atom Smashers."

18. Campbell appeared far less sanguine in the editorials he wrote for *ASF* after the atomic bomb became a reality; but by then he was no longer writing fiction.

19. Campbell's first sale was a story called "Invaders from the Infinite," but T. Oconor Sloane, then editor of *Amazing Stories*, apparently lost the manuscript.

20. See, for example, my "Nuclear Holocaust as Urban Renewal," *Science-*

Fiction Studies 39 (July 1986): 148–58; and Gary K. Wolfe, "The Remaking of Zero: Beginning at the End," in *The End of the World*, ed. Eric S. Rabkin, Martin H. Greenberg, and Joseph D. Olander (Carbondale: Southern Illinois University Press, 1983), 1–19.

21. Benét's famous story shows a primitive tribal society conserving the remnants of technology, which they ignorantly worship, and a devastated New York City complete with desiccated corpse, but contains no evidence to identify the cause of this destruction.

22. See, for example, Damon Knight, *The Futurians* (New York: John Day, 1977); Frederik Pohl, *The Way the Future Was: A Memoir* (New York: Ballantine, 1978); Carter, *The Creation of Tomorrow*; and Gunn, *Alternate Worlds* for a more complete discussion of the early science fiction scene.

23. Sam Moskowitz, an early fan and chronicler of science fiction history, wrote several articles discussing the predictive power of science fiction. In "Did Science Fiction Predict Atomic Energy?" written with Robert Madle and printed in *Science Fiction Quarterly*, November 1952, 81–88, he listed a number of stories that he felt were important steps towards genuine prediction. Unfortunately, his article reflects his enthusiasm for sf and perhaps his amazing memory more than it does accurate research.

24. See Albert Berger, "Nuclear Energy: Science Fiction's Metaphor of Power," *Science-Fiction Studies* 18 (1979): 121–28.

25. Other writers besides Campbell used Lamarckian evolution as the basis for nonatomic stories, not considered here. Compare, for example, David H. Keller's "Revolt of the Pedestrians" in *Amazing Stories*, February 1928, and the popular conception so frequently pictured in science fiction magazines of the "man of the future" as carrying an enormous brain on a spindly, almost useless body.

3

Dark Words of Warning

The move to magazine fiction and the optimism of much of the action-adventure fiction discussed in chapter 1 did not remove the sf writers' self-imposed mandate to warn their readers of dangers on the technological horizon. Before World War I, writers had hoped that a superweapon could allow men to defeat war once and for all. Extrapolating from the horrors of the previous war and an increasingly unstable political situation, writers now feared that a superweapon could make war so terrible that it would defeat mankind. This chapter will discuss the "awful warning" stories they wrote in response to this fear.

The Treaty of Versailles imposed crippling debts on Germany, leading to the devastating German inflation of 1923 that helped bring Hitler to power. The Dawes Plan then improved the European economy; until the 1929 stock market crash and subsequent bank failures removed American funds and led to worldwide depression, the situation looked more stable. In international politics, the Nine-Power Treaty (1922) allowed China, ally of the Allies in World War I, to regain control of her own territory from Japan. The Kellogg-Briand Pact (1928) outlawing war was signed by more than sixty nations. But it, like the League of Nations, had no provisions for enforcement. Japan invaded Manchuria in 1931, resigned from the League of Nations when reproved, and then invaded mainland China without a declaration of war. Self-proclaimed dictators were elected in Italy and Germany. The League of Nations was helpless to prevent Italian aggression in Ethiopia (1935) or German reoccupation of the Rhineland (1936). When the Spanish Civil War began (1936), the nations of Europe failed to ally against war, as their signatures to the Kellogg-Briand Pact promised; instead, they divided along ideological lines.

Watching the world situation, many had the same fear that Pierrepont B. Noyes had expressed in 1927: history was about to repeat itself. Science fiction writers gained two advantages from their genre: they were permitted to publish truly grim "awful warning" stories, and they were not only permitted but encouraged to invent futuristic weapons of unimagined deadliness, along with the appropriate adversary on which to use them. They also had a model: H. G. Wells's *The World Set Free* (1914), which had predicted and named the atomic bomb.

Intended to prove that only the dismantling of the nation-state could save the world from recurring wars, *The World Set Free* also exposed the dilemma of the scientist, recalling the example of Alfred Nobel, whose peacetime invention became a terrible weapon. Wells's novel presents dark visions of nuclear holocaust long before the power of the atom was unleashed even in a laboratory. Although we now know that Wells's description of atomic bombs was inaccurate—they do not continue to explode sporadically for years and years—we also know that he was right in predicting large-scale devastation and radiation-induced illness.[1] Wells also predicted deliberate attacks on urban centers. Later "awful warning" stories invariably demonstrate that civilians, perhaps even more than the military, would be victims in total war.[2]

No one was more aware of the ambiguous nature of scientific "progress" than those who fought in World War I. They had seen how often generals, given innovative weapons, had opted for antique tactics that threw away any advantage or even defeated themselves. The machine gun, the tank, and poison gas did not shorten the war but were employed with little regard for their special qualities. The result was a defensive war, fought from trenches at appalling loss of life for virtually no advantage. Technological weaponry proved itself problematical for two main reasons: commanders did not understand how to use it; or it was too fragile for wartime conditions.[3] (This has changed little. Consider the problems presented by high-tech rifles in the jungle environment of Vietnam.)

AWFUL WARNINGS

Two major patterns of "awful warning" stories developed. Each assumes ongoing political rivalry between armed nation-states, increasing international tension, and a falsely optimistic populace whose hopes are dashed by a surprise attack. The difference between them lies in the weaponry. In the romantic, "short-war" model, the enemy has a secret superweapon that he believes will assure him of immediate victory over the peaceful, "weak" United States. But a "lone inventor" leaps to the rescue with a super-superweapon, defeats the enemy, and—in the most incurably romantic stories—imposes "peace by force." In "Strange Scenarios," H. Bruce Franklin shows how earlier writers combined the "emerging faith in American technological genius" with the "older faith in America's messianic destiny," as we saw before World War I and in Campbell's "When the Atoms Failed" (1930) and "Uncertainty" (1936). But the "cult of made-in-America superweapons and ecstatic visions of America defeating evil empires, waging wars to end all wars, and eternally making the world safe for democracy" (1986, 119) necessarily became less prominent as faith in America's intrinsic strength was shaken by the experience of World War I, by the fear of communism as it was perceived to invade the home front, and by the collapse of the economy.

The second pattern is based on the historical experience of World War I. It also assumes long-established political power struggles among well-armed nation-states culminating in an air attack on America, usually without the formality of a declaration of war. Each side expects its superior weaponry to bring quick victory, but their opponents have equally powerful weapons. The conflict becomes a deadly stalemate that each side attempts to break with new, even more powerful weapons, instantly copied by the other side. Civilians get involved as victims of bombing or as workers supplying war materiel or both. War drags on for years. This pattern, difficult to handle in magazine length, is rare and, when used, is presented in a grimly realistic tale with details that sound as though they come from firsthand experience. Superweapons take on new roles.

The Short-War Model

Captain S. P. Meek, U.S.A., wrote many science fiction stories, but his rank gave him particular advantage with war stories. The editor of *Amazing Stories* did not hesitate to point this out: "Captain Meek is an army man, closely allied with matters of war therefore and much interested in its possibilities." "The Red Peril" (1929) does indeed consider "new methods of warfare" (486). Extrapolating from the use of poison gas in World War I, Meek proposes bacteriological warfare in 1958, when immunizations for everything from cancer to smallpox have been developed. These immunizations depend upon serum derived from a large supply of guinea pigs, however, and the animals are dying from a newly virulent strain of tularemia.

Military Intelligence immediately suspects the fine hand of Feodor Balinsky, superscientist recently removed to Russia. They put the armed forces (including the U.S. Air Corps) on alert and go into emergency session. The Russians soon send a fleet of high-flying airships invulnerable to atomic weapons over the United States, dropping bombs that explode mere clouds of dust. After carrying out similar raids on London, Paris, Rome, Constantinople, Calcutta, and Pekin, the Russians address the "Workers of the World" by radio and assure them that "we did not wish to harm our brothers. But next time, we strike to kill." Unless everyone surrenders and all "rulers" (including Congress) agree to die, this will occur in a week (491).

The endangered nations assemble and distribute "vacite" and "uranite" bombs stored in Berne.

> Both operated on the principle of the disintegration of the atom. The vacite bombs destroyed the air and would produce a complete vacuum for several hundreds of yards around their place of explosion or "point of burst," and it was confidently expected that they would destroy any aircraft within the radius of their action. Uranite was a substance somewhat allied to the common radite, but immensely more powerful. Its action was to start a progressive atomic disintegration in anything other than air with which it came in contact. It operated only under the influence of light and so could be safely handled and stored in lightproof containers. (492)

Unfortunately, neither of these weapons destroys the Russian ships; although a heroic Japanese flyer dies trying to place a bomb against one, they bomb with impunity. These bombs carry lobar pneumonia. Lacking their guinea pigs, the doctors are helpless. The military are nearly so, but an inventive young Major comes up with two columns of theoretical double-talk loosely based on Einstein's general theory of relativity that identifies the Russian ships as using artificial gravity and allows the Americans to construct a counterweapon. This will, of course, take time—which they do not have.

Meanwhile, back in New York, a young Russian refugee doctor decides to do something about the situation. The nurse he loves lies at death's door; lacking the serum, she will certainly die. So Boris Vestoff and his sister Ilga fly to the Russian capital in an "hour of steady going"; Boris enters with papers taken from a dying Russian agent, and Ilga claims to be one of Balinsky's women. They quickly capture Balinsky, torture him, collect the serum, and head home with the Russian fleet in hot pursuit. By this time, the Major's machine is ready. Barely in time, it destroys the lead craft, and the General commanding the American forces immediately declares that his men "are about to invade Russia and dictate peace terms to Leningrad" (521).

They find the Russian people ready to quit, "tired of being ground into the dirt by the Council of Seven and the Commissars." These are interned at St. Helena. Boris marries his nurse; Ilga marries Balinsky. Now recuperating from the brain tumor that made him do bad things, Balinsky is working on "new serums to cure the few diseases which we have not conquered. If he continues at that work for a few years, I expect that he will be allowed to leave St. Helena and spend the balance of his life in the comfort to which his genius and good deeds entitle him." The rest of the Russian rulers, who tried to conquer the world in the name of stamping out the bourgeoisie and freeing the downtrodden, "will be left in exile and in time they will die. With their passing, the world will be forever freed from the menace of the Red Peril" (521) and will live happily ever after.

Murray Leinster envisions an even more futuristic war in "The Power Planet" (1931). The story takes place on a man-made "planet" ten miles across, "set spinning about the sun to provide the earth with power" (12). An international staff of scientists, including a young, eager, attractive hero, watches in dismay as war sweeps across the distant earth, but no one knows exactly who is fighting whom. A mail rocket arrives under high acceleration, with another rocket chasing it; the first disgorges the President's daughter, sent for safekeeping, while the second apparently is determined to destroy the Power Planet entirely. The unknown enemy dares to do this because it has kidnapped the man who discovered true atomic power and now controls that resource. It does not need power from the satellite.

To defend themselves from destruction, the scientists fight a primitive battle in space suits while one of them, a bitter man named Skeptsky, suicidally guides a torpedo into the propulsion tube of the attacking rocket. With the rocket destroyed, Leinster's young hero is jubilant: not only will he live, he now has a chance to court the President's beautiful daughter. Meanwhile, a new device has been invented, built, and implemented on earth to detect and destroy the war rockets like those that have already devastated Paris, Vienna, Berlin, Constantinople, Calcutta, and New York. The enemy, whose identity is never disclosed, surrenders unconditionally before it can be bombed in return. The hero naturally gets the girl; the world (presumably) returns to peace. These two stories mark the virtual end of the romantic mode in stories dealing with atomic war.

The World War I Model

Otis Adelbert Kline's "The Man from the Moon" (1930) uses aliens to make his point: both sides lose when superweapons are used regardless of consequences. In this story, an advanced civilization on the Moon battles an equally advanced civilization on Mars. While a visiting Prince of Luna trapped on Mars by the onset of war watches helplessly, each culture destroys itself to defeat the other. Mars fights with rays that "tore the atoms apart on contact, making the heaviest metals less dense than the atmosphere in an instant"; the Moon uses rays that contract "any substance touched by them . . . to less than one-hundredth of its normal size with a corresponding increase in density" (651). Eventually the battle results in joint suicide, as each combatant sacrifices its atmosphere to defeat the other. The narrator flees to Earth, where he finds primitive man; he marries (serially; he lives a long time), leaving over a thousand descendents. The story is, of course, a memoir left to be discovered by "the right man." The similarity to Noyes's *The Pallid Giant* (1927) is obvious, but the suggestion that the Orientals are partly alien also recalls Nowlan's Hans.

Carl Spohr's "The Final War" (1932) demonstrates the power of the World War I scenario with a cast of humans. It also demonstrates a useful quality of the pulp-magazine genre. Spohr, who apparently wrote no other fiction, is a passionate but unskilled storyteller; his work undoubtedly sold because of its realism and its controlling idea, not because of its literary value.[4]

"The Final War" begins as a series of "accidental" provocations by an unnamed power, culminating in an air attack on the United States. Much of the world believes in peace and "freedom of conscience"; Fred Young, the protagonist, and his friends are attending a peace conference when a "Council of Four" dissolves Congress, "takes supreme command," establishes martial law, and prepares to battle invading air fleets, while the pacifists urge that some peaceful compromise can still be arranged (1114–15).

Young's mother is killed in the bombing; like many others, he joins the army. The enemy is apparently aggressive and prepared for war, the allies perhaps not so eager but clearly well prepared. War casualties are high, and eventually even children are drafted. Civilians suffer the greatest number of casualties. "Progressive" science adds new and horrible weapons but does not shorten the conflict. The minute one side invents a new weapon, the other side copies and uses it. After trying gas (only partially successful) and biological warfare, a military man laments:

> We had underestimated the tenacity of life. We meant to wipe each other from the face of the earth. There were several million people killed in a few hours,

immense property damage was done, but no decision was forced. Retaliation, that was all. The fronts held, because modern defense weapons are dangerous, economical and flexible enough to hold a position for a long time with the supplies on hand. (1275)

Then Colonel Doehler, a brilliant but hunchbacked and physically feeble scientist (apparently modeled on Charles Steinmetz), intuitively discovers the clue to releasing atomic power. Believing that this will create a new era of peace, "brought about not by the atavistic methods of blundering generals, but by the pure logic of science" (1277), he develops his process. He is, of course, wrong. As soon as the military hears about it—when his assistant blows up himself and the surrounding territory with a tiny amount of the new material—they force him to divulge his secret. But of course a spy has already obtained it for the enemy.

In the section headed "Armageddon!" (1279), the war drags on.[5] Everyone has been drafted. Women run underground factories, alternately producing cannon and cannon fodder; their children are raised in nurseries until they are of draft age. Military officers are now only sixteen years old. Each side has independently decided to use atomic shells as a last resort; a frightened child gives the order to load the special ammunition when nothing else is available. The other side naturally retaliates. This is the accident that "made this battle the last one, the Battle of Armageddon" (1281). As everyone at the front dies, airships carry the cataclysmic weapon to the rest of the world.

These plans were carried out, after the ground commanders, that had sent the ships, were dead. They were completed, after the men, in whose power-mad brains the plans had originated, were crushed in their deep concrete dugouts. There were no staffs, no governments, only these orders, that had to be carried out. (1283)[6]

The few surviving soldiers gather into small groups, some of them accompanied by women who had been frontline workers; they kill an officer who tries to force them to return to battle.[7] Reduced to primitive conditions, they gradually recover from the privations of war in the safety of the wilderness. Young's child is the first born to the tribe. His wife Irene promises the baby, "You shall never be a soldier, little man, never" (1286). The group has reclaimed the pacifist values expressed at the beginning of the story, and is relieved when a visiting representative[8] reassures it that the only remaining government is one that guarantees "Freedom of Conscience" to the world (1286). Nationalism is dead, and the world is safe again.

Like *All Quiet on the Western Front*, to which it is of course compared, "The Final War" is less a history of individuals than of inevitabilities. We should not be surprised that this tale of war carrying itself on by its own momentum beyond the capability of anyone to stop it was written by a German who had experienced the full weight of the military hierarchy. He understands the power of authority. Once the "Council of Four" takes over, any hope of effective input from democratic groups or individuals disappears. The chain of command does not function in two directions, but only from the top down. What we see of Young and his comrades is their slavery to the system. And both initiative like Doehler's and obedience like Young's end in disaster. While nation-states exist, Spohr is convinced, no other outcome is possible.

The "peace by force" scenario that prosecutes a successful war on a fully scientific basis is rare during this period. One example is Malcolm Jameson's "Eviction by Isotherm" (1937), his first published science fiction story. Like stories that precede it, "Eviction by Isotherm" assumes that nationalism will lead inevitably to war, but that technology can put a stop to war without destroying the nation-state as an institution. War—decades of it—between "Panamericana" and "Eurasiatica" is temporarily halted by a ten-year truce. The two sides are evenly matched and have each wreaked terrible damage on the other; the Central American isthmus is now entirely depopulated. Western leaders, experienced in the ways of the wily Neo-Aryan enemy, anticipate the breaking of the truce. Under the leadership of Dr. Barnes, a scientist who believes that Europeans are fine "*outside of Europe*" but that "megalomania rising from the blood-soaked soil of a continent with *too much* tradition" requires that Panamericans "force the abandonment of Europe!" (136), they tunnel the isthmus and fill it with "feroxite bombs" connected to the local volcanoes. This activity is hidden under a building complex pretending to mine "tromium," an imaginary metal having properties that "were a nice combination of all the things they wanted and did not have" (139).

As expected, the Eurasiatics take the bait, bomb the isthmus, and blow up the feroxite, the volcanoes, and the land bridge separating the oceans. Ocean currents reroute while dust dims the sun, plunging Europe into a new ice age. (This may be the earliest story seriously predicting "nuclear winter.") North America is prepared, but Europe is not. China secedes from the alliance, and the Eurasiatics surrender. Since the Eurasiatics caused the whole situation by their sneak attack, the Panamerican conscience is "free of guilt" (136).

RETURN TO THE WILDERNESS II

The postwar wilderness does not resemble the lovely greenwood that shelters the Wyoming Gang in "Armageddon 2419 A.D." while they develop their superweapons. It may give sustenance and permit recovery as in "The Final War," but it marks the graveyard, not the birthplace, of technological civilization. In some stories, the survivors of war are lucky to reach the wilderness. In others, they do not; not only civilization but humanity itself perishes.

"After Armageddon" (1932) by Francis Flagg (pseudonym for George Henry Weiss) combines the World War I scenario with the "back to the wilderness" theme. A once-wealthy banker now leads a tribe of nomadic survivors. He alone remembers the time when skyscrapers were full of technologically sophisticated people worrying about the breakdown of a Peace Conference but confident that war would never come. Having trusted their peacekeeping to men whose primary financial advantage lay in the production and sale of arms, most die from the attack by French rocket ships armed with stolen British technology. The mystery bombs they drop throw up great clouds of blackness that keep on growing for years, eating away steel and stone.[9] People who survive blast, gas, and plague can be healed by the ionizing radiations emanating from the "desolated stretches of barren ground" in the midst of which "something rumbled and roared and spouted a blue mist—the aftermath of that mighty explosion which had continued for two decades and was even now not subdued" (375). Tribal women take an equal place with the men; they have the final say concerning mating and procreation, while men provide food and protection. Humanity lives on, purified, simplified, and strengthened, even though civilization is destroyed. This story was considered sufficiently interesting and important to be reprinted after Hiroshima as a "Science Fiction Hall of Fame" story in the fall 1946 issue of *Startling Stories*.

Some writers suggest that the use of superweapons in a World War I scenario may leave no one to seek the healing wilderness. Nat Schachner sets his story "The World Gone Mad" (1935) in a beautiful, apparently peaceful futuristic city where Old Peter gratuitously claims "You are all living in a fool's paradise. . . . The next war will bury it all so deep they'll be sending expeditions in the future from some other planet to dig it out again."

Nations are arming: United Europe, the Sino-Russ, Australasia, and the Americas each build rocket planes to carry new scientific weapons like poison gas, "radite explosives, one bomb of which could level a city," and so on.[10] When Donald, Peter's son, remonstrates, "War today is unthinkable, hideous," Peter replies, "Let me tell you something, my son; you can't change human nature" (124). He saw war in his youth, to his horror. This time it will be worse: "That's the curse of our present science. It has brought to life mighty engines of destruction, and the nations have built them. Sooner or later some hot-headed fool, or group of fools, will itch to put them into motion—as if they were playthings" (125).

Allan, the older grandson, rushes in to tell the family with great excitement that war is imminent. The adults laugh indulgently; Allan has been working too hard at his government job. Little brother asks what the funny word means. And Old Peter seems triumphant as he thunders "I knew it. . . . I foretold it, and you laughed at me" (126). International incidents have occurred, Allan explains indignantly, and the European Council has accused the United States of complicity. "We replied as befitted the dignity of our nation" (127). Then other accidents occurred, the one in America blamed on a Chinaman. The country's "honor has been insulted" (128), and war will certainly result, but Allan predicts instant victory:

> "The American rockets will bomb every city of the enemy countries into ruins on the first flight. I've seen the plans. They'll be compelled to sue for peace."
> "And what do you think the enemy rockets will be doing to our cities in the meantime?" Donald queried softly.
> "Our Cabinet has evolved impregnable defenses," Allan assured him positively. "The chief has assured me so. The Enemy planes won't come within a hundred miles of our coast."
> "The world moves and does not change; word for word the madness runs its course," quoth Peter. (128)

While the newscast tells of "our" glorious rocketfire devastating Europe, enemy planes and rockets hit the city.

> The horrified watchers saw tumbling masses of burning wreckage, saw rockets and bombers linked in furious death grapples. . . . Tons of deadly radite flung high, exploded in cyclonic cones that smashed to destruction everything within range. Friend and foe were whiffed into extinction. Radite was not discriminating. (133)

But it is a bomb that kills the little group huddled on the rooftop frantically signaling for rescue from the gas. Was it dropped by friend or foe? In a "World Gone Mad," they have no way of knowing nor reason to care. Perhaps Allan was flying the plane that killed his own family. Will there be a world for these planes to land in when "radite" blankets the land? Like many science fiction stories, "The World Gone Mad" ends with an emotional climax but without resolution. Yet this very lack of resolution tells its own tale: there may indeed be no future, as there are no survivors to recount the end of this conflict.

Lester del Rey's "The Faithful" (1938) tells of the end of Man, who proudly created talking dogs and landed on the Moon, but failed to conquer himself. "There had been many setbacks to his progress because he had to go out and kill others of his kind," the canine narrator muses (8). "The tiny atomic bombs fell from my ship on houses, on farms, on all that was Man's, who had made my race what it was. For my Men had told me I must fight" (9). The dogs miss Man; they had been commensals for fifty thousand years. Desperate, they set up their own doggy tyranny. Then a lone Man appears, old, lonely, and sick; he uses his hands for the dogs, and they care for him. But there are no other Men, so he guides the dogs to a band of experimental apes. The dogs dream of "adapting the apes mentally and physically until they are Men. Nature did it with an apelike brute once," but the Man warns them before he dies "not to make them too much like Man, lest another plague destroy them" (15).

Joseph E. Kelleam's "Rust" (1939) has no humans in it at all. Robots, originally created to fight, now wish to re-create life, but they have only great war-claws to work with and destroy what they would fashion. At first they killed only the "little men in the yellow uniforms." They now question whether this was right, but recognize that "we were made so." That was man's crime, and he suffered the consequences when all the war robots rebelled. "It was only a short step from killing men in yellow uniforms to killing all men" (358). Robot X–120 admires the statue of a child and tries to imitate it, unsuccessfully; he then instinctively stomps a rabbit—a living creature—to death. Gradually the robots rust, the conversation stops; X–120, the last of his race, wanders in senile decay, smashes the statue, and falls to be covered by snow.

That even the wilderness brings no healing when civilization itself is dead is the theme of Walter Tilburg Clark's "The Portable Phonograph" (1941). Although no cause is specified, the tale is set in a postdisaster world, where a few men meet in Jenkins' home, a cave by a creek, to hear books read and to listen to an old, windup phonograph. The man who wants to write can find no paper, and the sickly musician no other music. When his friends leave, Jenkins hides his treasures and prepares to sleep, with a lead pipe handy for protection. There is no future and no hope.

DOWN WITH THE TYRANTS

A related theme that emerges in the mid–1930s and continues throughout the World War II period is that of rebellion against tyranny. Where earlier stories explored this metaphorically in alien conquests, Nat Schachner's series of stories begun by "Past, Present, and Future" (1937)[11] implies that human dictatorships will rise and fall throughout history. The three time travelers who try to warn the great cities of the future undertake an almost impossible task. Each city engages superweapons for its defense; each falls to invading "rocket hordes" save the last, Lyv, the "City of the Corporate Mind" (1939). Lyv itself then embarks on world conquest, and the adventurers continue their westward trek, apparently headed for the new world, America.

A. E. van Vogt's enormously popular novel *Slan* (1940) shows the struggle against a homegrown dictatorship; the outcome, surprising only those who did not understand van Vogt's concept of plot, demonstrates that the evil dictator had the oppressed mutant Slans' best interests at heart all along, and the Slans themselves had the intrinsic power to prove it, though the trial that proves Slan superiority comes very close to wiping them out. The release of "atomic energy in its great form" gives them the power to rule the world wisely, since they are the natural "mutation-after-man" (522).

Powerful weapons, including powerful allies, make dictatorships possible; even more powerful weapons must be used to oppose them, as we see in Jack Williamson's "Legion of Space" series (1934–39).[12] Here it is tacitly assumed that only a very few, very special people will even try to counter the forces of evil, which often enlist awful aliens to carry out their plans of conquest. Their problem becomes not only to identify and oppose tyranny, but also to identify and protect the lone holder of the ultimate secret weapon, "AKKA." Even though "AKKA" is known to exist, to be simple to construct, and to produce specific and repeatable effects, no one can duplicate it; it is, effectively, magic. Only magic can stand against the tyrannies that repeatedly threaten this world of the future.

A similar problem is dealt with in van Vogt's complex "Weapon Shop" series, which began in 1941.[13] "The Right to Buy Weapons is the Right to be Free," the Weapon Makers proclaim. They sell arms to the "have-nots" living in semimedieval poverty outside the urban centers in which a few wealthy "haves" of the Isher Empire enjoy riotous living. Eternal vigilance may not buy freedom, but van Vogt makes it clear that the Empire's oppression would be infinitely worse if the Weapons Shops did not exist.

Jack Williamson dealt with the problem of a charismatic dictator in "Hindsight" (1940). The Astrarch attracts and rewards top scientists, including William Webster, in a universe where they are otherwise left to struggle in obscurity. Even when begged by his long-ago sweetheart, Webster (now known as Brek Veronar) refuses to betray his master. But the Earth ships have been secretly armed by rebellious scientists and outgun the Astrarch's fleet. As they fall towards the sun, the Astrarch demands that his renegade alter time to save them. When Veronar does so, he alters himself as well; as Webster, he sabotages the Astrarch's guns and dies willingly, an Earthman again.

"Backlash" (1941) is another time-travel antityranny story by Williamson. This time the enemies are Eurasians, a savage mix of Orientals and Russians, led by a man named Levin. Everyone who was not killed by "uranatomic bombs" has been captured by the "Yellow Guards." In this repressive future, Challis rescues Nadya Stanislaw from a Russian prison camp and flees to Antarctica, where her father, a scientific genius, maintains the uranatomic generators that keep a small society going. But Dr. Stanislaw not only can observe the past, he can change it. Although Challis is warned that "violence is fatal to culture" he does not stop Stanislaw from killing Levin (156). This act creates a present in which humanity has been wiped out by a bacteriological plague set off by Eurasians desperate to liberate themselves from white domination. Stanislaw tries again, this time saving Levin from the injuries that initially embittered him and creating a peaceful and progressive world. "Violence results only in violence," Stanislaw learns (160), while humanitarian acts result in something much more than their own reward.

Cleve Cartmill also wrote several stories that posited various kinds of tyranny and the weapons needed to overthrow them. "With Flaming Swords" (1942) deals with a quasi-religious tyranny of "Saints" who have inherited an "aura" and use it to dominate ordinary, nonglowing humans. This discrimination is stopped when a scientist develops a machine that allows everyone to "glow." (Like Gallun's "Magician of Dream Valley," "With Flaming Swords" carries an antidiscrimination message for contemporary Americans.) "Overthrow" (1942) posits a world of autonomous city-states, each run by military dictatorship and dedicated to a single industry. With the able assistance of his 140-year-old "Gran," who has stolen power units, freed important people, and figured out ways to manufacture goods with portable, efficient manufacturing units, the hero uses the greed of the rulers to get them to destroy each other and thus restores genuine democracy.

In each of these stories, the dictatorships are imposed upon the United States (or some apparent representative thereof) from the outside. Lester del Rey points out that this is not a necessary condition; given the right circumstances, a native dictatorship is entirely possible.[14] Writing as "John Alvarez," he shows this in "Fifth Freedom" (1943). Centralia attacks Europe suddenly and without a declaration of war; it then destroys the U.S. fleet with an unknown weapon. America responds by creating an absolute dictatorship to prosecute the war. (This act apparently has the full approval of the electorate, unlike the takeover by the "Council of Four" in "The Final War.") Tommy Dorn, a young pacifist musician, successfully second-guesses the military, which causes him to be imprisoned as a traitor. Atomic weapons are used against the United States; the United States mobilizes to produce atomic weapons; an air battle between Centralia bombers and American suicide rocket squads releases killing radiation. With his friends dead, Tommy, who has previously refused, volunteers to fight.[15] "Men had always had to fight for their beliefs, even the belief that fighting was wrong" (338). The issue of Tommy's "fifth-freedom" right to free speech disappears in the struggle against the invading enemy.

Another, even more problematic American dictatorship is created by

"Anson MacDonald" (Robert A. Heinlein) in "Solution Unsatisfactory" (1941). Here the "peace by force" scenario is extrapolated to the utmost. But that scenario requires absolute moral purity on the part of the enforcers, and the victors, having imposed a nuclear Pax Americana, find that America is insufficiently altruistic. Power corrupts; politicians are particularly vulnerable. An "international patrol" is created to keep the world honest, led—reluctantly—by the heroic American general who devised the initial nuclear strategy. But even this "solution" is inherently "unsatisfactory."[16] Who will watch the watchers?

FICTIONAL TACTICS

These stories overlap temporally with those considered in the previous chapter. Again we see the gradual elimination of the romantic, comic mode; the changing roles of women; and the loss of fictional innocence, which may be equated with the naive "peace by force" scenario. Constraints imposed by the genre account for some of these changes: magazines prefer shorter works, so the development of a lengthy war story creates a space problem as well as a problem in maintaining action-adventure plotting. This shows up with particular force in Carl Spohr's "The Final War." Many of the "short-war" stories are themselves short and were possibly written to fill a predetermined space. But they all convey the same message: war is inevitable and deadly. War no longer offers the opportunity for America to impose its righteousness on the world; instead, it may allow the world to impose its violence on America. This message cannot be transmitted in the comic mode.

Conspicuous by its absence is the "war-to-end-war" scenario, except when referred to ironically. "Peace by force" works only in Campbell's "When the Atoms Failed," Meek's "The Red Peril," Leinster's "The Power Planet," and Jameson's "Eviction by Isotherm"; it later reappears, ambiguously, in Heinlein's "Solution Unsatisfactory." Oddly, in the light of the "Red Scare," each of the early stories ends in the enemy's surrender and the victor's magnanimous peace terms. This only holds for European enemies, however. Although we may occasionally see a "good" Oriental, like the self-sacrificing Japanese pilot in "The Red Peril," when the enemy is Oriental, generosity disappears, the suggestion of alien (nonhuman) crossbreeding gets raised, and "The Airlords of Han" get exterminated completely.

Social Roles

Again we see the virtual disappearance of women as strong characters. The brave Ilga of "The Red Peril" not only invades the enemy country and helps pull off an incredible kidnapping but also marries the villain against (one presumes) all familial advice; she lives happily ever after when his "mental illness" is corrected surgically. But Ilga soon gives way to the brave but helpless President's daughter in "The Power Plant," whose function in the story seems mainly to get things explained to her (and simultaneously to the reader, of course). She motivates but does not help the hero in his struggle to repel the attacking rocket and immediately accepts his proposal of marriage. Like the blonde in the brass breastplates on magazine covers, her function is purely decorative.

The transitional character here is Wilma in Nowlan's "Buck Rogers" stories. She is portrayed as a brave and resourceful leader who simultaneously needs masculine rescue and comfort. At the end of "Armageddon 2419 A.D." she murmurs, "I tremble, though, Tony dear, when I think of the horrors that are ahead of us" (449). In "The Airlords of Han," she leads the atomic attack upon Han cities and bayonets enemy soldiers before she faints. In "The Final War," women have become victims: they die from bombs, as do Young's mother and a lovely, intelligent girl he meets at the peace conference; they struggle to survive, tired and hungry, while they mourn their dead, as does a neighbor he meets on his one brief "home leave" from the war; they "marry" soldiers on three-day honeymoons, as Irene does Young (and get a "divorce" if they fail to conceive); they do manual labor in the frontline factories and suffer bombings just like the soldiers. But they are victims, pure and simple. They have no say in their lives. In this they do not seem much different from the men, of course; Young and his comrades have no say in their lives, either. Nor, apparently, do the officers. Even the "Council of Four" has disappeared from the story as the war continues by its own weight.

The situation becomes somewhat different if the survivors manage to reach the wilderness. In "After Armageddon," women (including the narrator's wife) were helpless, frightened victims of the initial raid, and most of them died. But once survivors reorganize themselves in the wilderness, things change. The erstwhile butler takes charge; the women demand equal rights, at least in reproduction; and the suddenly democratic group finds itself now able to cope with the rigors of the wild. This reflects the structure of Nowlan's earlier "Buck Rogers" stories and is continued in Bond's "Meg the Priestess" series: women in the wilderness take on the strength and the role of the pioneer women of America's past. In the majority of these stories, however, the wilderness offers no shelter, and women either play no role at all or exist only as victims.

Scientists and War

The role of the scientist is also altered. In many of these stories he is a helpless dupe or has already been co-opted by the military. His work is vital, especially since he creates "magic": weapons based on no principle of science shared among the profession. In early stories like "The Red Peril" and "The Power Planet," this is shown as an advantage; but espionage is inevitable. If the secret is not stolen, the scientist may still have to sacrifice himself either to keep the secret or to pay for allowing the secret to fall into the wrong hands. Brek Veronar dies in "Hindsight"; in "The Scientist Rises," the protagonist must defend himself and then commit suicide. In "After Armageddon," the aggressive French steal a British invention to prosecute their attack. In Spohr's "The Final War," an altruistic if naive scientist is forced against his will to turn a genocidal weapon over to the military, and he later dies—along with millions of others—from the same weapon now used by both sides.

The need for magic, discussed in the previous chapter, seems even more evident when we look at "down with the tyrant" stories. Time travel and the ability to change the past are pure magic. Using them seems to admit that nothing short of a miracle can stand against effective tyranny. Only the story cast in the most romantic, "peace by force" scenario displays a sober assessment of the uses and the dangers of science. Heinlein's "Solution Unsatisfactory" shows the scientist naively unaware of the implications of her discovery and suicidal when she recognizes them. While there are magical elements in this tale, the science is, on the whole, accurately depicted. But in this tale, as in "Fifth Freedom," the tyranny is our very own, thoroughly established as necessary if not right. The role of scientist here is virtually mechanical: to provide the raw materials for war.

ASSUMPTIONS

These stories depend upon three assumptions: first, that war is inevitable; second, that America is a peaceful and democratic country and therefore easy prey; and third, that the native American genius for rapid mobilization and technological invention provides the only hope of overcoming such a disadvantage. The first assumption shows up even in the romantic, "atoms for fun and profit" stories considered in the previous chapter. In virtually every story, someone is fighting someone else: aliens fight each other, allowing Seaton and Crane to rescue the "good guys" with their superweapons in *The Skylark of Space*, while Penton and Blake take advantage of interalien squabbles in good entrepreneurial fashion. Given the assumption that war will come, the author does not need to explain the situation, politically or economically. Nations are just "like that." Nor can ordinary people prevent war, even in a democracy; we note that in "The Final War," well-organized, international "peace groups" make little or no difference. Even the worldwide agreement to "freedom of conscience" is ineffective until the nation-state (and most of the civilized world) has been destroyed. There are no political solutions to the problem of war; in none of these stories is prevention attempted by arbitration, conciliation, or cooperation. Politics itself leads to war, not peace.

America is not only "good" and therefore intrinsically "weak"; its very constitutional structure may contribute to its weakness. Writers like Nowlan and Bond take for granted that Americans driven into the wilderness will fight among themselves. Even though they recognize that their true enemy is the invading Hans, Nowlan's "Gangs" (each named for the territory it either occupies or has come from) accuse each other of treachery, war ferociously on each other, and dissipate their strength and resources in so doing until united by a strong leader. Bond's tribes cannot agree on customs or practices and often consider other groups as little better than animals until Daiv proves otherwise. This divisiveness is tacitly presented as the natural outcome of unrestrained democracy. The contradiction between "weak" peacefulness and constant internal combat seems never to get noticed.

If America is in constant danger of surprise attack, and no effective agency of political compromise exists, then the only possible road to peace must be through war. Without a powerful standing army (something no peaceful democracy would maintain), the only chance of survival in such a war must come from the ability to develop the appropriate weapon on short notice, for a known weapon will already have been duplicated by the enemy. Each scenario gives superweapons to both sides, differing only by being "good" (developed in self-defense) or "bad" (developed as weapons of aggression). America generally uses "good" weapons, and the rest of the world uses "bad"ones. And the recurring suggestion that the enemy, particularly if Oriental, is not entirely human—that he may, indeed, result from some sinister alien miscegenation—only enhances the suggestion of possible doom. To combat this, the hero must simultaneously function as "nice guy" and "lone inventor." Superman is just an invention away.

What was the practical effect of these earnest, dramatic stories? Spohr's "The Final War" shows Doehler, a humanitarian scientist, duped into inventing a genocidal weapon, young men and women turned into virtual slaves, and conflict dragged madly past any hope of genuine victory. At this point, Spohr says, war as an institution must be repudiated. If World War I, the "War to End War," did not manage it, then perhaps another, even more horrible war will, for then there will be no one left in the world willing to fight. Nationalism will die, and war, along with the military, mechanized organization that war demands, will die with it. All will demand the right to obey their own consciences rather than any imposed government. Spohr's version of future war is tedious but terribly compelling.

"After Armageddon" carries the same message: no matter how much ordinary people may want peace, nationalism and its antagonisms, aided by science and its amoral concept of "progress," will lead inevitably to war; warfare in a scientific age will be vastly more horrible even than World War I with its almost unbelievable death toll; civilians cannot hope to escape in modern war; and the worst weapon of all, the one most closely allied to all dreams of power and progress, will come from unleashing the atom.

Note the progression from destruction of civilization redeemed by a return to the healing wilderness in Noyes (1927, implied), Nowlan (1929), Kline (1930), Spohr (1932), Flagg (1932), and eventually Benét (1937) and Bond (1939–41) to ecological disaster in Jameson (1937) and to total destruction in Schachner (1935), del Rey (1938), and Kelleam (1939). Clark's "Portable Phonograph" (1941) reminds us of the inaccuracy of the romantic "return to the wilderness" idea. Also note the initiation of the survival of war robots in Kelleam's "Rust," an idea refuted by del Rey in "Into Thy Hands" (1945) but later taken up and carried to its ultimate horror by Philip K. Dick in "Second Variety" (1953).

Tyranny is not forgotten as a cause of war: the charismatic individual of Williamson's "Legion of Space" series and "Hindsight" and the inherited dictatorship of van Vogt's "Weapon Shop" stories will always be with us. Nor is the United States immune; racism is a form of tyranny, as Cartmill's "With Flaming Swords" demonstrates, and so is economic despotism, as in "Overthrow." Furthermore, given the appropriate, desperate circumstances, the most democratic country will turn to a dictator for leadership: "The Final War," "Fifth Freedom," and "Solution Unsatisfactory" all imply the occasional necessity of tyranny.

We can assume that the vivid depiction of the terrors of war is meant to frighten readers, perhaps enough even to prevent future conflict. These are frightening stories. But the fear generated by "awful warnings," strong as it may be, is completely negated by the underlying assumption each of these stories encodes: *war is inevitable*. One cannot read any of them without accepting this tacit assumption, and once it is accepted, the author has already forfeited his overt aim. For the greater the danger we face, the more powerful our "defense"—our superweapon—must become. We may be reluctant, we may be frightened, but we will fight.

NOTES

1. For Wells, "Fires symbolize the potentially unharnessable energy released by the technological exploitation of nature," as Patrick Parrinder explains in "Utopia and Meta-Utopia in H. G. Wells," *Science-Fiction Studies* 36 (July 1985): 122. The science fiction community tended to read Wells as prophet and predictor

rather than as metaphysical philosopher, however, and it is his powerful description of atomic war that obviously influenced many pre–1945 stories discussed here.

2. Of the earlier stories, only *All for His Country* seriously depicts civilian casualties.

3. Gas was sometimes employed under conditions that damaged the troops using it as much as those they were attacking. Effective poison-gas tactics waited for the Italian campaign against Ethiopia. The "Land Iron-clads" foreseen by Wells were successfully employed at the Battle of Cambrai, but the Allies were prevented from a sweeping victory by the 60 percent breakdown rate of their tanks. The most unequivocal success of advanced technology came from the submarine, which operated independently.

4. Spohr, an artillery officer in the German army, apparently wrote no other science fiction, and this work is less a novel than a long, vivid awful warning. The editorial introduction to the final installment makes the point explicit: Spohr, having "gone through the hell of the Great War," has written "a prophetic warning to the world" of "the catastrophe in wait for us, unless we can bring about universal peace" (1267).

5. The term "Armageddon" appears with increasing frequency in works dealing with future war. Like the term "holocaust," its biblical resonance seems required to encompass the terrible nature of the envisioned conflict. The title soon becomes a cliche. See, for example, Rog Phillips's "Atom War" (1946).

6. The grim concept of automated war carried out in mechanical obedience comes to its modern conclusion in Ward Moore's "Flying Dutchman" (1956). Progress in technology shows Moore how to carry his vision further, with computers and robots. But Spohr predicts it.

7. This reflects experience; World War I was marked by a number of battlefield mutinies by men asked to go "over the top" once too often.

8. This visitor flies in much like Raymond Massey, the representative of "Wings over the World" in the later H. G. Wells movie *Things to Come* (1937). A bearer of good tidings arriving from the sky, a deus ex machina, becomes a continuing tradition; for example, Pat Frank uses it in almost identical fashion in *Alas, Babylon* (1959).

9. The debt to Wells's "atomic bombs" seems obvious.

10. Note the reference to previous stories. Like other jargon, the names of futuristic weapons were readily borrowed by sf writers.

11. The first story sets the series title: "Past, Present, and Future" (1937). This is followed by "City of the Rocket Hordes" (1937), "Island of the Individualists" (1938), "City of the Cosmic Rays" (1939), and "City of Corporate Mind" (1939).

12. *The Legion of Space* (1934); *The Cometeers* (1935); and *One against the Legion* (1939). *The Legion of Space* was reprinted by Fantasy Press in 1947, and the three stories are also collected in a Doubleday–Science Fiction Book Club edition titled *Three from the Legion*.

13. The first story in this series is "The Seesaw" (1941). In this time-travel story, a reporter from the present accidentally travels to the future in a Weapons Shop; unable to remain in the future or to return safely to the present carrying the charge of temporal energy he has built up, he swings between the future and the past until, in the primordial cosmos, he becomes the "Big Bang." Later

stories, some of which overlap with or apparently reconstruct earlier ones, deal with the struggle between Weapon Makers and Empire more directly: "The Weapon Shop" (1942); "The Weapon Makers" (1943); and "The Weapon Shops of Isher" (1949). The stories were collected and organized in *The Weapon Shops of Isher* (New York: Greenberg, 1951).

14. Many "No Third Term" Republicans suspected that this dictatorship was already established.

15. Note the interconnections with previous stories: like Young in "The Final War," Tommy is a pacifist; like Young, he volunteers to serve when people he loves are killed. The story includes the "sneak attack" scenario, but adds the voluntary acceptance of a dictatorship; not even Spohr envisioned his "Council of Four" taking power by popular mandate.

16. We should note that the title of this story, often cited to show Heinlein's uneasiness over his proposal, was not his own. It was provided by John Campbell, editor of *Astounding Science Fiction*. Heinlein, writing as "Anson MacDonald," had titled the story "Foreign Policy." See *Astounding Science Fiction*, April 1941, 69.

4

Science and Science Fiction

In 1935, Stanley Weinbaum criticized his fellow writers for their portrayal of scientists:

> Here's the element that makes so much science fiction seem unreal. Half our authors use the word "scientist" about as the ancient Egyptians used the word "priest"—a man of special and rather mystical knowledge that set him apart from the rest of humanity. In fact, as soon as the word is mentioned, one visualizes either a noble, serious, erudite, high-principled superman or, depending on the type of story, a crafty, ambitious, fiendish, and probably insane super-villain. But never a real human being. (384)

But far from making sf seem "unreal," this image of scientists picked up and reinforced assumptions already widely held by the general public. Studies by Mead and Metraux (1957) and by Beardslee and O'Dowd (1961) show that many people do hold ambivalent, often contradictory assumptions about "the scientist": he is brilliant, hardworking, and dedicated, but he works only with abstract concepts, is not interested in art or literature, does poorly in interpersonal relations, and is mysterious, unstable, and cold. He speaks a language no one else can understand, and his thought processes are highly logical but lack humane grace. Students interviewed agreed that the scientist is important, powerful, and interesting, but most concluded that they would not like either to associate with or to marry one.[1] This agrees with the fictional image. Whether the fiction nurtured the assumptions or the assumptions the fiction is more than irrelevant. The thrust of this chapter is to demonstrate the inseparable transactionality of the process.

IMAGES OF THE SCIENTIST

Operating from these tacit assumptions, science fiction writers, as Weinbaum complained, continue to present the scientist as magically powerful. He is believed to produce " 'better' knowledge than the 'sloppy ramblings' of philosophy or the 'groundless' knowledge of religion" because he follows a procedure that removes the intuitive, fallible, "human" element from his thought processes.[2] This image of the inhumanly objective man of science is often reinforced. As Educator Yarrow lectures his young scientists in Isaac Asimov's *The End of Eternity* (1955), "It will be you youngsters who will . . . bring back facts. Cold, objective facts uncolored by your own opinions and likings, you understand. Facts accurate enough to be fed into Computing machines" (19). Asimov's tale eventually shows how impossible it is for a scientist to disengage his emotions from his work; moreover, it condemns the result of working from "cold, objective facts" alone. But the initial impression is a lasting one.

In this view, the scientist becomes virtually a "Computing machine" himself. His infallibility gains him respect, but his scientific objectivity distances him from "normal" human beings. There is also an unsettling atmosphere of power surrounding him, residing less in him as a person than in the knowledge to which he has access, a power not far removed from magic in the popular mind. Albert Berger notes how "the sheer size of the forces nuclear power was expected to place at human disposal became a metaphor for the nearly magical fashion in which heroic scientists could overcome the inconvenient laws of nature and get spaceborne cowboys out to the endless frontiers of intergalactic space" (1979, 121).

Most of us are all too familiar with stories in which science is blatantly magical and the scientist a superhuman "savior." Jack Williamson's *The Legion of Space* (1934) exemplifies a number of common "magical" assumptions about science. First, science is mysterious. Natural laws and technology derived from them can be kept secret for centuries. Second, such technology is nonreproducible. (Knowing what "AKKA" can do does not help anyone else to duplicate the work.) Third, some people have a "gift" for science that others with similar or better training and experience do not have. Only such gifted people can really "do science" or make important discoveries. Fourth, scientists are strong, independent men of principle. They are above politics unless and until it interferes with them and their practice of science. Then they become an irresistible opposition. Fifth, advanced technology can be "done" with spit and baling wire. Giles Habibula, The Legion's comic engineer, repairs a spaceship's essential "geodynes" in transit; AKKA is first assembled by a prisoner in jail and later reassembled under emergency conditions on a hostile planet lacking the most basic items (even the necessary iron must be stolen from their ship). Finally, scientific discoveries used as weapons can ensure peace—or at least victory—as long as they are held only by the pure in heart.

Perhaps the most distinctive feature of magical science is the belief that discoveries can be kept secret. Sometimes, as in Robert A. Heinlein's " 'Let There Be Light' " (1940), the business community invokes its vested interests and attempts to strangle the invention at birth; sometimes, as in Raymond F. Jones's "The Person from Porlock" (1947), the scientist is persuaded that he has trespassed into disciplines "man was not meant to know" and voluntarily suppresses his work.

Often the secret may be kept for the highest of motives and at great personal sacrifice. In "The Power and the Glory" (1930), Charles Willard Diffin's idealistic young scientist liberates controlled atomic power. Lyrically, he relates the possibilities to his crippled teacher: " 'Power without end to do the work of the world—great vessels driven a lifetime on a mere ounce of matter—a revolution in transportation—in living . . . 'He paused. 'The liberation of mankind' "(104). His professor is wiser. After demonstrating that the power can kill as well as serve, he claims that it will be used to provide power to the few, power that can destory the world: " 'They would not,' said Avery hoarsely; 'they'd use it for good.' 'Would they?' asked Professor Eddinger. He spoke simply as one stating simple facts. 'I love my fellow men,' he said, 'and I killed them in thousands in the last war—I, and my science, and my poison gas' " (105).

Professor Eddinger has already discovered the procedure young Avery so proudly shows him, losing his hand in the process, and has chosen to withhold it. Nobly, both men sacrifice fame and fortune to serve mankind in secret. Unlike many of his colleagues, Diffin depicts science as operating from known laws. The reader is left to remember that what two men can discover independently will be duplicated by others.

But Diffin's romantic solution to a terrible problem—that the one should sacrifice himself for the good of the many—is in keeping with the picture of the scientist as a priest of the temple of knowledge, not as a member of a social community. Moreover, it leaves unanswered some basic questions that still plague the community of science: Must scientists (alone or in small, elite groups) censor the practice of science? If they do not, will others, even less able to understand what they are doing, take it upon themselves to guard Earth from the atom? Who will decide for humanity when it is competent to deal with such power? And if power corrupts, who will watch the watchers?These questions usually remain tacit, especially in early science fiction. Far more often, the great discovery is used, and it remains the sole property of the discoverer.

These stories emphasize the role played by science in modern warfare; yet relatively few science fiction stories demonstrate a true understanding of science as a discipline. In this, science fiction has, paradoxically, both failed and kept faith with Judith Merril's description of it: "Science fiction is not fiction *about* science, but fiction which endeavors to find the meaning in science and in the scientific-technological society we are constructing" (1967, 3). To find meaning in science, writers must be aware both of the philosophical and the technical realities of contemporary science, yet few science fiction stories follow Gernsback's dictum actually to teach scientific concepts. Certainly there is little emphasis on scientific method; simple extrapolation of technological progress does not inform the lay audience of the ways in which this progress was accomplished. Despite the presence of scientifically trained writers like E. E. Smith, J. W. Campbell, Isaac Asimov, Philip Klass, Harry Stubbs, and others, fiction often depicts technology as arising from wishful thinking.

A serious consequence of this situation is that science fiction, the extrapolative, speculative "testing ground" for our technological culture, often fails to provide thoughtful guidance on one of the greatest problems science itself has had to face: the ethical implications of "progress." Sometimes science fiction unquestioningly admires progress; at the other extreme, it sometimes exaggerates the danger (and the likelihood) of scientific hubris. For instance, we may look at Willard Hawkins's "The Dwindling Sphere" (1940), Alfred Bester's "Adam and No Eve" (1941), "Lawrence O'Donnell's" [Henry Kuttner and C. L. Moore's] "Clash by Night" (1943), Philip Wylie's "Blunder" (1946), Theodore Sturgeon's "Memorial" (1946), "William Tenn's" [Philip Klass's] "Brooklyn Project" (1948), and Frederik Pohl's "Let the Ants Try" (1949). Each is based upon the supposed willingness of scientists to act without considering the consequences. And the consequences are horrible: Sturgeon's scientist reduces future humans to pitiful beasts; Bester's and Wylie's scientists destroy all life on earth; Hawkins's shaves the planet to its core, and O'Donnell's incinerates it. Pohl's merely sacrifices the human race, while Tenn's humorously revises the genetic basis on which sentient life evoles.

These stories differ only in style from earlier stories, like Campbell's "Uncertainty" (1936), Williamson's *Legion of Space* (1934), and "John Taine's" [Eric Temple Bell's] *Seeds of Life* (1931), which showed scientists as both incredibly powerful and dangerously autonomous. Each of these later works also implies that a single scientist (or, with Tenn, a group of scientists working under single-minded government direction) can undertake projects of terrible consequence and, without adequate testing, successfully carry them out. In each, the action seems beyond social control; if government plays a part in the story, as it does in "Blunder" and "Brooklyn Project," it does so only to insulate the scientists from either social or professional scrutiny, so that they function as the isolated wielders of enormous power. Under such circumstances, scientists conceivably may destroy the world with their science instead of saving it. Science seeks systematic knowledge of the physical world and the arrangement of a body of facts so that they disclose the operation of general laws, with the avowed aim of improving man's ability to function successfully in his environment. To ask science to provide weapons is to pervert its most basic purpose. This was, of course, the main point of ethical contention among the scientists involved in the Manhattan Project.

That one cannot always trust a scientist to be alert to the implications of his work has been amply demonstrated in science fiction. That if he is aware of the probable outcome, he may not care, is shown by John MacDonald's "A Child Is Crying" (1948), where the scientist is shown as born with an inhuman capacity for logical thinking, and L. Sprague de Camp's "Judgment Day" (1955), where the scientist is portrayed as pathologically asocial. Fredric Brown makes the same point with some ambivalence in "The Weapon" (1951). Brown's protagonist seems coldly inhuman to his concerned visitor as he denies any thought of hiding or destroying his work:

> I'm a scientist, and only a scientist. Yes, it is public knowledge that I am working on a weapon, a rather ultimate one. But, for me personally, that is only a by-product of the fact that I am advancing science. I have thought it through, and I have found that that is my only concern. (484)

"But, Dr. Graham, is humanity *ready* for an ultimate weapon?" Having asked his rhetorical question, the visitor quietly gives Graham's retarded son a gift and leaves. Graham retrieves it just in time, thinking, "*Only a madman would give a loaded revolver to an idiot*" (485). Graham is made to seem somewhat human by the love and care he shows for his retarded child, but we are never sure that he sees the connection between his son and the sons of Man.

Writers who wish to show an ethical, humane scientist often put him into the position of being coerced or used by the political-military establishment. In such a case, the hero may opt for creative but unilateral withholding of dangerous information, as in Theodore Sturgeon's "The Wages of Synergy" (1953) and C. M. Kornbluth's "Gomez" (1955), or he may outsmart the establishment, as in Sturgeon's "Unite and Conquer" (1948). These solutions are hardly comforting. Portraying scientists as merely mortal reassures readers of their basic goodwill. At the same time, it creates a nervous awareness that these mortals are playing with the powers of the universe without the concomitant power to make right decisions or, having made a decision, to ensure that it will be followed. Whether the scientist is viewed as inhuman or humane, it is clear that he cannot win.

SCIENTISTS AND SCIENCE FICTION

In the face of evidence that science fiction misrepresents science and extends popular (but misleading) assumptions about scientists, one may legitimately wonder whether scientists themselves would ever read sf, and if so, why they do. Arthur S. Barron (1957) claims that real scientists enjoy science fiction because it is "about science" and because through it they can voice their protest, particularly regarding the development and use of atomic weapons. Scientists feel "intense" identification with their counterparts in science fiction for at least three reasons:

> First, it glamorizes him [the scientist]. At a time when the intellectual in general, and the scientist in particular is regarded with some ambivalence, this is a most important function of the literature. Second, science fiction expresses the scientist's protest against the use of his knowledge for anti-human ends. This is important, too, since major difficulties surround any more open show of protest. Finally, science fiction reaffirms the basic humanistic values of the scientist's creed. (62)

After citing several examples to prove his point, Barron notes triumphantly that "the special theme of science fiction is that *human intellect, come to its finest flowering in the scientist, will save mankind!*" (63). Obviously, scientists find this claim appealing. Equally obviously, such a conclusion may seem less welcome or even dangerous to the nontechnically oriented.

As one might expect, the image of the scientist portrayed in science fiction is far more favorable than that uncovered by Mead and Metraux or by Beardslee and O'Dowd. Walter Hirsch's statistical survey of science fiction (1958) shows that although villains may be scientists more often than people in any other occupation, the scientist is three times more apt to be shown favorably than unfavorably, while the nonscientist must take a slightly less than fifty-fifty chance of getting kind treatment. No other kind of protagonist appears nearly as often.

Although science fiction may not be about science, as Merril explains, it clearly is about scientists. The stories may put much emphasis upon the scientist's logic and rationality and upon his separation from other, more "normal" men whose emotions may cloud their reason, but who are, consequently, more understandable and more lovable. But these tales show scientists doing things, using their science. If they find it elitist fiction—and most would agree that it is—then it fits the scientists' self-image even more closely. They form an American elite, and they know it.

To portray its scientist heroes in an attractive light, sf often plays down the scientific side of the protagonist (the very side one might expect to find played up) and emphasizes those aspects of character that describe Americans as they believe they "really are": strong, independent, competent, unsophisticated yet canny, reserved yet capable of warm emotion. Not surprisingly, these traits also describe the frontier Western hero from Natty Bumppo through the Virginian to Shane. Thus the scientist may see himself portrayed as the model American; even if he knows that this picture is overdrawn, it is at the same time extremely flattering.

Moreover, some writers deal sympathetically with real problems faced by the scientist. C. M. Kornbluth's "Two Dooms" (1958), which also handles the institution of science accurately, attempts to deal honestly with problems of scientific responsibility under emergency conditions. The plot focuses on the moral dilemma of a conscientious scientist working on the atomic bomb. Edward Royland is torn between irreconcilable convictions: on the one hand, that his work is useless, the atom-bomb Project hopeless or inconsequential; and on the other hand, that it is of terrible consequence, for he can visualize what may come from success:

> Cooked people, fused cathedral stone, the bronze of the big Buddha running like water, perhaps lapping around the ankles of a priest and burning his feet off so he fell prone into the stuff. He couldn't see the gamma radiation, but it would be there, invisible sleet doing the dirty unthinkable thing, coldly burning away the sex of men and women, cutting short so many fans of life at their points of origin. (270–71)

The secrecy that surrounds the Project turns Royland into an alchemist: he holds the power of secret knowledge, which he can withhold or pass on as his conscience directs. In imagination, Royland connects the "Big

Bang" of the atomic bomb with the "Big Bang" that began the universe; to begin the universe again requires that it first be destroyed, and his findings make that possible. In his distress, he seeks out a Hopi friend, who feeds him hallucinogenic mushrooms, "good food." Under this influence, Royland "experiences" a future when the Axis powers have won the war, divided the United States into colonies, and self-servingly rewritten history. He soon learns how valuable the "American way of life" he has been working for really is. Reluctantly, he decides that the bomb must be built and used.

> We have a symbol to offer the Japanese now, something to which they can surrender, and will surrender.
>
> Rotschmidt [his boss] would be philosophical. He would probably sigh about the Bomb: "Ah, do we ever act responsibly? Do we ever know what the consequences of our decisions will be?"
>
> And Royland would have to try to avoid answering him very sharply: "Yes. This once we damn well do." (310)

Here no "good" choice is available. Royland must choose the lesser evil from a position of specialized knowledge. Although Kornbluth shows, as many writers do not, that under "normal" circumstances scientists do not have to work under such restrictions, the conflict of science and alchemy remains implicit. A reader accustomed to science fiction science could easily miss much of the story's impact.

THE SOCIAL INSTITUTION OF SCIENCE

To make the contrast explicit, we need to understand how real science really works. Scientific discoveries are derived from basic, known principles by a series of recoverable steps; thus what one scientist can do, another can do also, whether or not he knows what the first one has done. An early example of this is seen in the more or less simultaneous proposal of the mechanism of evolution by Darwin and Wallace (1858). Apparently neither man knew of the other's work; they did not duplicate each other's techniques; yet, drawing upon a common body of knowledge and of practices, they came up with similar conclusions, and Wallace's work stimulated Darwin's when he learned of it.

Scientists operate from a known tradition. Theories, information, speculation, and guesses, as well as methods, techniques, and results of experimentation, are taught to students and are shared so that they can be investigated and tested by others. New theories generally rise out of accepted wisdom that fails to convince in the light of new data, not out of untutored speculation.[3]

Scientists work within a community; if not in an organized group, they have at least the community of training and background that prepared them for their work, and a community of shared information. They also share their use of the scientific method, which includes locating a problem or area of inquiry, formulating a hypothesis to cover the problem, finding ways to test the hypothesis, and discarding or reformulating hypotheses when tests prove them wanting. This requirement of testing and replicability is one of the most important links in the social network of science. No scientist can test his own hypothesis adequately, and he knows it. Publication is more than "publicity"; it is an implicit request for other scientists to evaluate the information put forth, to attempt to replicate the work, and to disconfirm both the work and the hypothesis if possible. Only by submitting his ideas to possible disconfirmation can a scientist consider himself part of a rigorous discipline. Both the community of science and society as a whole benefit from this rigor and this open disclosure, although the more visible benefits (Nobel prizes, multimillion-dollar grants, major foundations named for and directed by noted scientists, and the like) are what the nonscientific society usually notices.

Sometimes sociopolitical conditions seem to require that scientists must pervert the aim of science—increasing knowledge to improve the condition of man—to a narrower goal, the victory of their chosen side in a conflict. Leonardo da Vinci offered his radical inventions as weapons to serve his political patrons. In modern times Leo Szilard, whose activities practically created the Manhattan Project and whose work on particle physics made the atomic bomb possible, credits his reading to H. G. Wells's *The World Set Free* (1914) both for his understanding of the possibility of nuclear war and for his urgent efforts to prevent his work from falling into Nazi hands. Had Szilard not read Wells, it is possible that the entire history of World War II might have been quite different.[4]

It is worth noting that Carl Spohr's "The Final War" was published in the United States in 1932, at about the same time that Szilard was reading Wells in Berlin. (Ordinary readers may or may not have paid attention to the messages in sf; scientists certainly read and apparently did heed it.) To escape the Nazis, Szilard fled to England in 1933, where Ernest Rutherford scoffed at the hope of ever liberating atomic energy. A day later, Szilard had thought of a way to prove the great scientist wrong. As Hilgartner, Bell, and O'Connor explain, "Like Wells's fictional scientist Holsten, Szilard made the conceptual breakthrough that would eventually lead to nuclear weapons. And like Holsten, Szilard immediately thought of trying to keep his discovery secret" (1982, 14). In 1934, he took out a patent that covered both the concepts of chain reaction and critical mass, which he assigned to the British Admiralty Office after the British War Department had failed to agree with him on the necessity of secrecy.

Szilard's action slowed the spread of information that might have led Nazi scientists toward the chain-reaction concept and atomic bombs. But Szilard also knew, as Wells had put it, that "other men would be doing this" within a few years. His only hope, as he wrote the Admiralty, was that Britain would get there first. (15)

By 1938, when Otto Hahn announced successful splitting of the uranium atom and the pattern of Nazi aggression was frighteningly clear, Szilard had emigrated to the United States. In the spring of 1940, he "finally forced the U.S. government to set up a secrecy system for reviewing papers on uranium research" (16). Eventually he persuaded Einstein to write to President Roosevelt about the need for secret, full-scale research leading to production of an atomic bomb. Clearly his assumptions about the dangers of atomic fission had been influenced by his reading. In a sense, H. G. Wells engineered the Manhattan Project, the most science fictional of all contemporary scientific programs.

Szilard was himself an honored member of the scientific community and thoroughly understood how such a community worked. Yet one of his first actions after learning of Hahn's successful experiments was to shut down the normal channels of scientific communication. He then moved to create an unprecedented community of scientists, all dedicated—as he firmly believed—to the preservation of democracy against the proven evil of Hitler's fascism. The Manhattan Project, as it finally developed, was itself both a fascinating new development in the practice of science and a perversion of everything that science stood for. For the first time, a powerful government funded, produced, and directed a research project. For the first time, scientists were given the heady company of numbers of their wisest and most productive peers, unlimited funds, and a vital mission. At the same time, they were organized into production units and hedged about with security regulations that prevented many of their most productive habits. They received information only on a "need-to-know" basis, so that most were not informed about the actual task they were setting out to accomplish.

Those who did know the truth about their project felt terribly ambivalent about it. Some apparently refused to see the obvious outcome of their work. Others realized that they had to choose among unacceptable choices. In *The Making of the Atomic Bomb* (1986), Richard Rhodes tells how I. I. Rabi refused to join Robert Oppenheimer as associate director of the Manhattan Project; he felt that his work on radar was more important and refused to use his science to create "a weapon of mass destruction." Oppenheimer protested that he, too, rejected such a perversion of physics. "To me it is primarily the development in time of war of a military weapon of some consequence," he argued (452). Eventually he convinced Rabi to work with him as a visiting consultant, but until the Trinity test he apparently did not attempt to reconcile a weapon of "some consequence" with the known destructive power of the atomic bomb. Enrico Fermi, the builder of the first working self-sustaining nuclear reaction, also saw the work as a distasteful duty. " 'I believe your people actually *want* to make a bomb.' I remember his voice sounded surprised," Oppenheimer later recalled, apparently surprised himself (468). Like Edward Royland in "Two Dooms," Fermi reluctantly accepted a lesser evil, rather than eagerly participating in a "pure" physics experiment.

After Germany surrendered, many scientists, who had assumed that they were racing German scientists to a working bomb, objected to the use of the bomb on Japan, which had no atomic program. Others rejected the use of the bomb on civilians or on humans of any description. The Franck Report, signed by a number of prominent scientists working on the Manhattan Project, requested that a nonlethal demonstration be arranged for representatives of the Japanese government.[5] After the Japanese surrender, guilt, remorse, and fear spurred widespread demands that the bomb be internationalized, repudiated, or otherwise neutralized.[6] The Union of Concerned Scientists was born from work initiated by Szilard. Science fiction writers struggling with ethical considerations stemming from scientific "progress" faced a real world in which scientists were bitterly divided about their role in producing atomic weapons, giving apparently contradictory advice (from the scientific equivalent of the Pope's chair) on the appropriate use or interdiction of the bomb to governments and public alike. Others reiterated that "we aren't at fault; science makes no moral judgments; we only followed orders." Given the situation, it is not surprising that few postwar stories show scientists as able to control the use of the power they had unleashed.

Politics and Science Fiction

Following World War II, it was assumed that nobody but scientists could hope to understand the ramifications of atomic weaponry, much less impose appropriate production standards and safeguards, but many politicians regarded the scientists themselves as just a trifle less strange and dangerous than rattlesnakes. Harry S. Hall shows that this image of the scientist, derived in large part from fiction, was quite innocently reinforced by the scientists' own testimony. Their insistence on answering questions completely and accurately combined with the politicians' preconceptions to give apparent basis to a picture of scientists as an elite group coldly dedicated to an international discipline, while the safety and welfare of their nation came far behind a search for "truth" in importance.[7]

The image of the scientist as elitist and arrogant is well represented by Heinlein's Dr. Lentz in "Blowups Happen" (1940), who forces politicians to accede to his authoritarian demands while coldly remarking, "You are none of you atomic physicists; you are not entitled to hold opinions in this matter" (260). The uneasy suspicion that Lentz was right would not reassure the nonscientist.

Science fiction writers were apt to present such elitism directly, even proudly. Non–science fiction writers whose choice of topic landed them squarely in the genre usually showed themselves less direct but equally convinced of it. Dexter Masters in *The Accident* (1955) and Pearl Buck in *Command the Morning* (1959) wrote "factual fiction" about real scientists involved in the Manhattan Project. Buck novelizes the development of the bomb from prewar worry about Nazi science to Hiroshima and scientific guilt; Masters picks up the story after the end of the war and shows what happens as atomic research remains aimed at weapons development. His protagonist is a brilliant young scientist dying from a nuclear accident.

Neither has a very high (or very polite) view of politicians. Masters is particularly acid on the subject of political interference in scientific affairs as he shows an arrogant, stupid, self-serving politician threatening to begin House Un-American Affairs Committee inquiries into the loyalty of the dying scientist.[8] (To the politician, anyone who fought in Spain is automatically a security risk.) At the same time, he joins the project director in public praise for the young man who controlled the accident and saved the lives of others in the room. Neither the director nor the military whose needs keep the laboratory going will admit that this particular experiment, which has already killed another scientist, is no longer necessary. Like the politican, the men in charge of atomic research are shown to permit insanity rather than admit, by establishing new and more effective ways to proceed, that they have made a mistake. Realistically, neither Buck nor Masters could show scientists as able to take charge either of the direction of their own research or of the use made of it.

Even worse than scientific arrogance from the political point of view is the "closed shop" the scientists run. They know what they are talking about, but no one else does or can hope to. In 1946, atomic weapons seemed so esoteric and difficult a topic that politicians, knowing that they did not understand the content (the actual discipline), failed even to try to understand the context (the methods and standards of science). Harry Hall notes, "Politicians were not only frustrated by their inability to challenge scientists but also by their dependence on scientists in the new atomic age. Whether Congressmen liked it or not, their survival depended to a large extent upon trusting the scientists and admitting them to the public policymaking process" (1962, 287). Concern with maximizing weapons production while keeping the weapons secret inevitably leads to a situation in which the very safeguards set up by the scientific method—free exchange of ideas, publication, and replication—are eliminated by political and military considerations, as Kornbluth shows in "Two Dooms." Allied with industry (for which "science" has always been a product, a source of power and income) to build the equipment they developed, scientists involved in weapons research and development necessarily function as modern sorcerer's apprentices.

Most dangerous of all, in a political sense, scientists are seen as activists; once a scientist decides what should be done in some situation (and in science fiction he is usually as certain of his omniscience as he is of his science), he becomes both ruthless and terribly effective in doing it, as in Sturgeon's "Memorial" (1946), Raymond Jones's "A Stone and a Spear" (1950), and Philip K. Dick's "Jon's World" (in *Time to Come,* 1954).

These fictional descriptions of the scientist seem recognizably based on contemporary reality and embody the power he wields in powerful metaphors. With such ambivalent concepts stirring uneasily in their minds, politicians felt justified in suspecting the loyalty of a number of scientists and distrusting them as governmental advisors, no matter how well qualified they might seem to be. Hall quotes Senator William Fulbright as stating that "scientists . . . are not so conscious of national sovereignty as lawyers or politicians or others." With this the scientists were proud to agree, which put them in conflict with most politicians who "elevate sentiments of loyalty and citizenship, attachment to nation and respect for the authority of government to the status of pre-eminent virtues. In their eyes, concern for the national interest and welfare should always be paramount." Clearly, scientists, especially those who, like Dr. Harold Urey, suggested that the only way to safeguard international peace would be to destroy "the stockpile of atomic bombs and all fissionable materials if necessary to convince the world of our peaceful intentions" failed "to put the national interest and security over all other concerns." They could be seen as dangerously international at best and as disloyal at worst (1962, 284).

Secret Science

The idea that scientific advances are private property in the same way that copyright protects the technological applications of these discoveries is not limited to science fiction. It had serious implications in the years immediately following Hiroshima, when the U.S. government (and some scientists) claimed that no other country could duplicate the work that led to the production and manufacture of the atomic bomb in less than ten years.

In a "Forward" to "The Last Days of the United States" in his *Expanded Universe,* Robert A. Heinlein claims that one reason no editor would buy his nonfiction essays warning of the danger of an atomic sneak attack by Russia on the United States was the testimony of government experts, among them senior officers who argued that atomic bombs were either no more effective than "blockbusters" or that they were effectively undeliverable. The most telling testimony came from "General Groves, in charge of the Manhattan District (code name for A-bomb R&D), [who] testified that it would take from twenty years to forever for another country to build an A-bomb" (1980, 146). When the Russians produced a bomb in four years, many were convinced that they had done so only because "traitors" and "spies" among U.S. scientists had "given away" our "atomic secrets,"[9] although clear-sighted writers like John W. Campbell argued that "our national policy for the next several years *must* reckon with the fact that all the secrets of the atomic bomb are *purely engineering secrets.* Any group of competent engineers . . . could rediscover them."[10] As evidence, Campbell noted that science fiction writers had already demonstrated the availability of essential details of atomic research; Cleve Cartmill and *Astounding Science Fiction* had suffered investigation by the FBI for "Deadline" (1944), a story of atomic war between thinly disguised alien factions. Campbell convinced the government agents that suddenly changing *Astounding Science Fiction*'s, publication policy would cause greater suspicion than continuing to print stories about atomic weapons, no matter how close they might be to reality. The editors of *Bluebook Magazine* were less intransigent. They obeyed a government order to withhold Philip Wylie's story of a secret Nazi atomic bomb factory in the Nevada desert, "The Paradise Crater" (1945), from publication until after Hiroshima. Lester del Rey notes with wry amusement in *Early del Rey* that during the war, the issue of *Astounding Science Fiction* containing his story "Nerves" (September 1942), which dealt with "industrial atomics," not weapons, was classified at Oak Ridge, although it was available on newsstands in town (1975, 339).

Szilard knew that his science fictionally inspired efforts to keep atomic research a secret could be effective only up to the time when the bomb itself blew up all hope of secrecy. After that, "possession" of the atomic bomb became a truly fictional concept, one fostered by science fiction, where magical secrets like "AKKA" could indeed be kept. But the military and the government continued to impose the wartime restrictions that had so effectively hidden the aims of the Manhattan Project even from many of those engaged in it. These restrictions succeeded mainly in frustrating public efforts to guide the development, testing, and further use of the bomb.

Along with the reliance on secrecy, we also see a repetition of the military attitude observed during World War I: senior officers who have successful careers to protect are the least likely to use new technology creatively. The effectiveness of an advanced weapon depends mainly on the ability of the people in charge to perceive and incorporate its special advantages. This may call for a radical change of assumptions about what is and what is not possible in any given situation. Many of the high-ranking advisors to the congressional committees showed startling failures of tactical imagination. This is a good example of a familiar observation: it is not hard to convince people to stop doing something that obviously does not work; it is much harder to get people to change practices that almost work or that worked pretty well before circumstances changed. Admirals and generals who saw the atomic bomb as just one more "blockbuster" delivering a little extra "bang" per bomb and demanding conventional methods of delivery were perhaps unimaginative but not out of the ordinary. And, like many ordinary people, they probably did not read science fiction.

LIVED ASSUMPTIONS

Scientists joined the Manhattan Project already thoroughly convinced of a number of assumptions they garnered not only from ongoing historical events, but also from fiction. A belief in the inevitability of war did not depend upon political convictions; Communists might put their own interpretation on it, but everyone had absorbed the message long before Chamberlain declared "peace in our time": those who did not see war coming were, as Old Peter declared in "The World Gone Mad," "living in a fool's paradise." And this war was going to be a bad one, worse than World War I. Fiction joined with fact to show that our enemies were stronger, better prepared, better positioned, trickier. Nothing short of a true superweapon could possibly save America. Helping to develop that superweapon (while simultaneously gaining invaluable knowledge and experience and probably advancing their scientific careers) not only appealed to the scientists' natural patriotism, it gave them a chance to do what they loved best—for pay.

The secret, "magical" aspect of the Manhattan Project was also not surprising. Wartime secrecy was generally imposed; the added restrictions placed upon the scientists were seen merely as burdensome and sometimes inhibiting to research. Moreover, tacit assumptions popularly developed in literature allowed the scientists to view this aspect of the project as a natural adjunct to the practice of science.

Finally, few scientists had ever really considered the use of their research to be their own concern. Most basic research is far removed from implementation; it generally deals with fundamental laws and principles, not with the making of real gadgets. Although research scientists are themselves often adept technologists, they are more apt to use their skills to design and build the instruments necessary to run their experiments than to put their theories to work in the world. Developing the atomic bomb was, to many, another—though infinitely more imperative—experiment. Would it work or wouldn't it? Would the chain reaction, set off atop a tower in the desert at Alamogordo instead of in a controlled environment under the soccer stands at Chicago University, stop when its fuel was exhausted, or, as some scientists genuinely feared, would it inaugurate fission in other elements and incinerate the Earth? That the minority who feared this could view it as an abstract question and continue with the test says a great deal for their passion for basic research and for the democratic scientific system that allowed those who dreaded the literal end of the world to be overruled by the mathematics of their peers.[11] It also indicates that they did not see themselves as in control of the political or military use of the weapon their work had produced. In fiction, the only control a scientist has over his discovery is to keep it a secret even from other scientists. This secret was out; all possibility of their control was now gone. They sent the Franck Report against all their assumptions and also against all hope.

The ideas about scientists that were so freely expressed by politicians during the congressional hearings—that they were superior, mysterious beings full of special knowledge, whose dedication to their discipline created loyalties that transcended (and could perhaps supersede) those held by more "ordinary" men—were not much different from those held by the general public. Neither the politicians nor the scientists seemed conscious of the role fiction played in reinforcing that image or even of the internal contradictions such assumptions contained.

How could anyone trust the men who had gotten the world into this mess in the first place—especially since so many of them later got what looked very much like a bad case of cold feet, criticizing the judgment of the politicians who had used the bomb? Edward Teller, who insisted on starting work on a true thermonuclear reaction even while the early bombs were still on the drawing board and whose lust for an absolute weapon never wavered, is perhaps the only member of the group to remain consistently in political favor.

The questions tacitly raised by science fiction now seem even more relevant than before: Must scientists (alone or in small, elite groups) censor their own practice of science? If they do not, will others, even less able to understand what they are doing, take it upon themselves to guard Earth from the atom? Who will decide for humanity when it is competent to deal with such power? And if power corrupts, can such a custodian remain uncorrupted? More and more stories overtly address these questions as they come alive in Senate hearings and public pronouncements by activist scientists. The answers, however, remain ambiguous. To ask scientists to censor a discipline based on free exchange of information seems counterproductive as well as dangerously open to corruption. But no group seems better qualified to do the job; certainly those who aspire to public power seem least qualified. Unless the public is willing to become sufficiently well informed to take on the task of deciding its own destiny in a radically technological future, there seems no satisfactory solution.

Science fiction has always seen itself as the educator of the public in matters technological, but this education has been indirect, contradictory, and frequently ill-informed, as seems perfectly appropriate to literature. Many science fiction writers who felt somehow justified in their genre by the actuality of the atomic bomb simultaneously felt guilty about their role in its realization. This is also appropriate; as we have seen, the thrust of science fiction has been not only to extrapolate the possibility of atomic power but also to reify the assumptions that scientists and politicians alike followed in its development and use. Futhermore, and this is most clearly seen in the reaction of scientists and nonscientists alike after Hiroshima, Armageddon had been made real enough in fiction that few had trouble assimilating it to the postnuclear world. Neither Frankensteins nor Supermen, scientists found themselves powerless in and appalled by the world they helped to make.

NOTES

1. These assumptions are drawn from two studies, one by Margaret Mead and Rhoda Metraux, "The Image of the Scientist among High-School Students: A Pilot Study," *Science* 126, no. 3270 (August 20, 1957): 384–90, and the other by David Beardslee and Donald O'Dowd, "The College-Student Image of the Scientist," *Science* 133, no. 3457 (March 31, 1961): 997–1001. Although Mead and Metraux's study was done in the mid–1950s and Beardslee and O'Dowd's in the early 1960s, the attitudes they found verify rather than contradict the assumptions encoded in the science fiction of the preceding decades.

2. Robert Scholes and Eric S. Rabkin, *Science Fiction: History, Science, Vision* (New York: Oxford University Press, 1977), 160.

3. See the works of Thomas Kuhn for a discussion of the importance of scientific tradition in what he calls a "paradigm shift." See also C. S. Peirce on the logic of science.

4. The details of this connection are carefully described in Stephen Hilgartner, Richard C. Bell, and Rory O'Connor, *Nukespeak: Nuclear Language, Visions, and Mindset*. (San Francisco: Sierra Club, 1982), chapter 2, "The World Set Free." Quotations are from that source and cited in the text. An equally detailed account, with natural alterations in emphasis, can be found in Richard Rhodes, *The Making of the Atomic Bomb* (New York: Simon and Schuster, 1986).

5. This report, initiated by James Franck and signed by six other scientists, was sent to Washington in June 1945. It urged that the bomb be used only as a demonstration and not to take human life. Truman had, however, already ordered the preliminary logistics for employing the bomb; many writers, in-

cluding Michael Amrine, *The Great Decision: The Secret History of the Atomic Bomb* (New York: Putnam, 1959), and James Thackara, *America's Children* (London: Chatto and Windus, 1984), imply or directly charge that General Groves used his influence to "lose" the report until the decision was irrevocable and full tactical deployment was underway.

6. In *By the Bomb's Early Light* (New York: Pantheon, 1985), Paul Boyer reports popular, scientific, and political reactions to the use of atomic bombs on Japan. The first announcements were informative and factual. Many who had long seen Japan as the hated enemy rejoiced, both over the victory and over the manner in which it had been obtained. Very soon, however, dark warnings emerged as the destructive power of the bomb was described using American cities as targets; although this was usually done purely for comparative information, people could not help but assume that the possibility existed that their homes now lay at risk. As information about the long-term effects of radiation was added to the terrible destructive power of shock wave and fireball, a mood of depression, almost of despair, became increasingly noticeable (3–26).

7. For an exposition of the appearance of scientists during the various post-Hiroshima political hearings, see Harry S. Hall, "Scientists and Politicians," *Bulletin of the Atomic Scientists*, February 1956, reprinted in *The Sociology of Science*, ed. Bernard Barber and Walter Hirsch (New York: Free Press of Glencoe, 1962), 269–87.

8. In this respect, at least, Buck and Masters conform to a view shared by many science fiction writers, that politicians are at least ignorant (not "competent") if not inept or stupidly venal.

9. The Russians benefited from the activities of a number of spies operating both in the United States and in England. But once the bomb was used, any competent physicist could deduce, from theory and from previously published papers, the technology required to duplicate the work.

10. John W. Campbell, Jr., *The Atomic Story* (New York: Holt, 1947), 118. Campbell repeated this message loudly and often in his editorials in *Astounding Science Fiction* as well.

11. This has been noted by a number of writers, among them James Thackara in *America's Children*. He credits Enrico Fermi for voicing at least mild concern to his fellow scientists: "Bets, please: on whether we destroy all life on this globe. Or simply life in New Mexico?" (167). Thackara does not indicate what other scientists might have replied.

5

A Science Fiction World

Awful warnings did not prevent World War II, and the misgivings of scientists who developed the atomic bomb did not prevent its use on Japanese cities. One of the first public reactions to the bombing of Hiroshima was a mixture of guilt, remorse, and fear. Not only did many people jump to the same conclusion that well-informed scientists had expressed in the Franck Report—that atomic secrets could not be kept and that the United States was now vulnerable to atomic attack—but they also suddenly saw the Japanese as victims rather than alien enemies. Moreover, the language that people used to express their fear of atomic war reflected traditional millennialism, with references to holocaust, Armageddon, and apocalypse—terms that sf long had used to imply that an atomic war would be the last one. This complicated the natural jubilation that followed the Japanese surrender. But those who feel surprise at these apparent contradictions need to keep the long preparation for this response in mind.

Most "awful warning" stories were published before the United States became involved in World War II. During the war, many writers were busy with defense work or in the armed forces, while paper shortages killed a number of the newer magazines. Few of the writers who could write during the war wanted to write about it. But stories featuring the apocalyptic atomic scenario continued.[1] C. M. Kornbluth's "The Words of Guru" (1941) suggested that a single powerful but irresponsible person could—given the knowledge—destroy the world and that he might do so as a sort of childish experiment. Joseph Kelleam followed his story "Rust" with "The Eagles Gather" (1942), set in a universe where interplanetary conflict has depleted uranium supplies; in this future there would be no more wars—or space travel, either.

In *Astounding Science Fiction,* Alfred Bester published "The Push of a Finger" (1942), a story based on time travel: the future exists only because of a complete prohibition of atomic research. Jack Williamson, writing as "Will Stewart," initiated his "Seetee" stories with "Collision Orbit" (1942). In these tales, contra-terrene matter (c.t. or "Seetee"), which explodes upon contact with normal, "terrene" matter, is invaluable; but it is terribly dangerous to study and almost impossible to work with. It thus becomes an analog of atomic power. Lester del Rey's "Nerves" (1942) vividly describes an accident at a working atomic power plant and the dangers posed to the surrounding area.[2] In "Clash by Night" (1943) Henry Kuttner and C. L. Moore as "Lawrence O'Donnell" posit a runaway chain reaction following atomic testing that leaves Earth a blackened, uninhabitable ball.[3] Fortunately for humanity and the plot, this does not occur until after humans have colonized the seas of Venus, where they prohibit atomic weapons and hang a black-draped globe in each undersea Keep as a memorial to their lost world.

Malcolm Jameson's "The Giant Atom" (1944) is a pre-Campbellian action-adventure tale; like "Nerves" and "Clash by Night," its plot turns on atomic research gone awry. Clifford Simak's "Lobby" (1944) deals with the appropriate development of atomic power—should it be used to free the world from drudgery or to make investors rich? Can it be developed safely in any case?—and creates an ambiguous air of danger surrounding the subject. Though the public is served eventually, the road through selfishness and politics is hazardous.

More specifically war-oriented stories included John B. Michel and Robert W. Lowndes's "The Inheritors" (1942), which extrapolates a post-war world of ecological devastation, lethal mutation, and eventual extinction. Fritz Leiber's "Gather, Darkness!" (1943) assumes that a long-ago war has destroyed contemporary civilization. It is set in a medieval world where peasants are dominated by a corrupt priesthood wielding the remnants of pre-war technology. Lester del Rey's "Fifth Freedom" (1943) concerns the loss of Americans' traditional freedom of speech during an atomic war, but his most obviously war-oriented story,

"Whom the Gods Love" (1943), is a reassuring fantasy in which a fatally wounded aviator is restored to life by a mysterious atomic force.

"Deadline" by Cleve Cartmill (1944) takes place on an alien planet, where thinly disguised combatants called "Sixa" and "Seilla" war on each other.[4] This story is most notable for its clear presentation of two popular assumptions: that *any* use of the bomb might set off a world-destroying chain reaction and that preventing the use of this bomb somehow prevents the whole idea of atomic bombs. (The first of these ideas worried scientists as late as the Bikini tests, July 1946, while the second caused real problems in the post-Hiroshima period.) Another specifically contemporary story, Theodore Sturgeon's "Killdozer!" (1944) shows an ancient alien weapon "wakened" by the Pacific War. Like "Whom the Gods Love," Sturgeon's story provides a happy ending; unlike del Rey's, it posits war as a recurring cycle.

The last year of the war saw several stories closely following the atomic scenario. Fredric Brown's "The Waveries" (1945) suggests that the world would be better off without any modern technology at all than with atomic power. Henry Kuttner and Catherine L. Moore writing as "Lewis Padgett" began the series that became *Mutant* (1953) with "The Piper's Son" (1945).[5] This series posits a relatively comfortable post-atomic war world in which radiation-induced mutations benefit the chosen few—the "Baldies" who can read minds—and create severe prejudice against them.

Robert Abernathy's "When the Rockets Come" (1945) describes war on Mars between "Earthmen" who speak English, and the "Driven Out" who speak a language based on Russian, some six hundred years in the future. The protagonist, one of the last warriors of Earth, carries out his mission to the Driven Outers' camp only to be bombed by his own side "methodically wiping out a threat to . . . their safe, soft civilization" (176). The story explores the assumption that combat strengthens humanity, while those who seek easy, "final" solutions are shown as evil and shortsighted. Even more pessimistically, Lester del Rey's "Into Thy Hands" (1945) posits that future war will wipe out humanity permanently unless one farseeing man can create robots that can re-create human life. As it had before the war, science fiction continued to explore virtually all the possibilities of the atomic scenario, from beneficial mutation to the sterilization of the planet, except one: that war itself could not merely be avoided but actually be rendered obsolete.

THE BOMB AND THE BOOM

Hiroshima was bombed on August 6, 1945. That night H. V. Kaltenborn, reporting the bombing, concluded "For all we know, we have created a Frankenstein! We must assume that with the passage of only a little time, an improved form of the new weapon we use today can be turned against us" (Boyer 1985, 5). This sentiment was not unusual or isolated. Newspapers immediately printed maps of American cities overlaid with target circles showing the range of destruction that would have followed an atomic blast, in order to given people some conception of the bomb's destructive power. The first book to deal factually with the bomb, *The Atomic Age Opens*, published by Pocket Books on August 17, 1945, collected facts and opinions from many sources to explain its significance.

Life magazine "devoted most of its August 20, 1945, issue to the bomb; here, in full-page photographs of Hiroshima and Nagasaki, many Americans encountered for the first time the towering mushroom-shaped cloud that would become the quintessential visual symbol of the new era" (Boyer, 8). Every vivid picture was immediately translated by the American imagination and recreated on home turf, aided by the fiction that followed.

Philip Wylie's "The Paradise Crater," initially withheld from publication by *Bluebook* at government behest, was in print in the October issue. This story is less science fiction than espionage action-adventure; the protagonist detects and destroys a secret German atomic bomb factory in the American Southwest. John W. Campbell's editorial response to Hiroshima appeared in the November 1945 *Astounding Science Fiction* and Theodore Sturgeon's prose poem "August Sixth, 1945" was published in the letter column in December.[6] Sturgeon's text shows his ambivalence to the bomb throughout, ending "The man with the open eyes . . . is looking at himself, on the other side of death. He knows—he learned on August 6, 1945, that he alone is big enough to kill himself, or to live forever" (178).

Science fiction, its "extravagant fiction" suddenly vindicated, enjoyed a surge of popularity. As James Gunn explains in *Alternate Worlds:*

> That big boom, the cause of so much tragedy, guilt, and recrimination, announced not only the birth of the atomic age but the beginning of the science fiction age. From that moment on thoughtful men and women recognized that we were living in a science fiction world. In what other world could atomic bombs—and atomic energy—be a reality? Other events still to happen would confirm that realization in the minds of the observant.
>
> So it seemed to postwar publishers as well. As suddenly as the explosion of the atomic bomb, that time was upon the world that everyone had summed up in the phrase, "When the war is over . . ." To science fiction it meant another big boom. (1975, 174)

Although the science is spurious and the crisis is caused by an uncontrolled atomic reaction set off by ignorant profit seekers rather than by a wartime weapon, Malcolm Jameson's "The Giant Atom" was republished by Leslie Charteris soon after Hiroshima—and after Jameson's death—in paperback with a new title, *Atomic Bomb.*[7] The "Foreword" to the reprint provides "historical" background for the story, specifically including the bombing of Japan, which had just taken place. Francis Flagg's "After Armageddon" was reprinted as a "Science Fiction Hall of Fame" story in the fall 1946 issue of *Startling Stories,* and Pierrepont B. Noye's *The Pallid Giant* was reissued under a new title, *Gentlemen, You Are Mad!* (1946).

Raymond J. Healy and J. Francis McComas edited the best-selling *Adventures in Time and Space* (1946); its success started a landslide of anthologies, mostly containing Campbellian, "modern" sf.[8] Ray Bradbury and Robert A. Heinlein began publishing regularly in large-circulation, slick-paper periodicals, but most of the sf that appeared in these magazines was produced by writers like Philip Wylie and Pat Frank who had not been associated solely with the sf genre. Some writers were praised as prophets, but many, like Lester del Rey, whose visions had been fully as accurate, remained in essentially the same position they had been before the "boom": popular inside the genre, unknown outside of it.

GUILT AND GLORY

James Gunn recalls: "When the news came on August 6, 1945, of the destruction of Hiroshima by an atomic bomb, every science fiction reader everywhere knew what it meant and knew the implications of the event. We already had lived through the experience many times in our imaginations. The atomic era had begun" (1975, 174). Many sf writers felt vaguely guilty, as though they somehow had helped to produce the bomb itself, or were ashamed of feeling vindicated. Paul Carter quotes Sturgeon and Asimov as saying that though each had resented the way their stories about atomic weapons had been dismissed by the general public, they now wished the public had been right (1977, 24–25).

Those of us who saw the bomb through sf-trained imaginations may have difficulty understanding how thoroughly foreign it was to most Americans.[9] Paul Boyer titles his chapter on fictional responses "Words Fail: The Bomb and the Literary Imagination." With the exception of factual works like John Hersey's *Hiroshima* and William L. Laurence's *Dawn over Zero* (both 1946), very little in the popular press reflected the reality of the bomb. Boyer admits two quasi–science fictional works here: Louis Ridenour's "Pilot Lights of the Apocalypse" (1946)[10] and Philip Wylie's "Blunder" (1942). Each is apocalyptic in tone: Ridenour, a noted nuclear physicist, assumes that the United States will set up a full-scale "defense" system to respond to nuclear attack, and that this system cannot discriminate among natural signals and those that actually indicate hostilities (an earthquake begins the next war); Wylie predicts that further nuclear research will be carried out in absolute secrecy (like the Manhattan Project), so that warnings of errors in the process are prevented from reaching the researchers, who destroy the Earth. Aside from these and a few abortive snatches of fiction and poetry, Boyer finds little "literature" (which he separates from sf) that even includes mention of the bomb and much that—significantly—does not.[11]

Everyone was glad that a terrible, bloody war was over; most had some feeling that the Japanese had "asked for it" both by their sneak attack on Pearl Harbor and by their inexplicable preference for suicide over surrender. Few had the knowledge required to understand the ramifications of nuclear energy. But most also recognized that some significant milestone had been passed, that war was now not merely worse, but essentially different. Boyer's study of sf published after the war does not indicate how thoroughly—and how ambivalently—science fiction had prepared its readers, nor how closely it reflected the American myths. Somehow, we had to acknowledge that the United States changed the course of events more radically by committing atomic attack than it did by firebombing Dresden (an open city) or by repeatedly raiding Berlin and Tokyo. The difference is summed up by Eric Van Tassel, writing in "Remembrance" of the victims:

> We sense that there is something unique about Hiroshima and Nagasaki. The atomic bombing of those two cities forms a hinge in history, a turning point in the life of this planet. There had been wars before 1945—horrible, genocidal wars, dragging on for years and laying waste whole civilizations. And it was not the first time that war had reached out beyond the soldiers and sailors, past those who made the munitions or gave the orders, to strike at faltering grandsires and babes in arms. But on these two mornings, for the first time, the scourge of war fell on those as yet unborn, those who still lay in the womb of time.
>
> It was a turning point because for the first time man could ape God's handiwork, could unleash the force that fires the sun and the stars. As Robert Oppenheimer saw the first experimental bomb go off in the New Mexico desert, he thought of words from the Bhagavad Gita: "Now am I become Death, the Destroyer of Worlds." Man had been a destroyer of men; but he had never before been a destroyer of worlds. (1984, 31)

Although this apocalyptic fear was officially soothed by dismissive voices,[12] every reassurance was expressed in terms that tacitly admitted that the atomic secret could not be kept, even while the government assured the American people that no one could duplicate it. And every reassurance tacitly admitted that America, which had seen itself as an innocent and somewhat helpless victim of Japanese aggression in 1941, had now acquired sufficient stature to merit atomic bombing. Thus the message long repeated by science fiction—that a superpower must be opposed by a superweapon, and that use of a superweapon required an enemy seen as a superpower[13]—became a concern of the general public, unprepared as it was to deal with it openly.

The "Campbell Plot"

As usual, postwar science fiction made no effort to reassure its readers. It not only created stories about new weapons, including the guided missile with an atomic warhead, but also explored new ways of using them. In March 1946, John W. Campbell published an *ASF* editorial entitled "Concerning the Atomic War." In it, he suggested that the United States would naturally be the primary target of any aggressor. But attacking her would be dangerous; even as the country died, she could retaliate. Therefore an aggressor must keep its identity secret.

> The United States won't be defeated in war. It won't even be murdered. It will be assassination in the dark. Leaving a strange corpse armed with a terrible weapon—and aching with a terrible ferocity to use that weapon on the rats that wiped out 40,000,000 Americans. *And not knowing who committed the crime.* The aggressor's hope will be that we blame the wrong nation, attack some other nation or nations, and thereby loose a world chaos from which the aggressor can, perhaps, pick up some juicy fragments. . . .
>
> [Prompt and permanent retaliation] would be a very salutory thing.
>
> *If the right nation were chosen as the villain.*
>
> But it would be very hard for the remaining Americans to be calm, judicial, and careful in their decisions and weighing of evidence at that moment. (5, 178)

We know that Campbell used to "try out" his editorials on his friends and writers before he published them, so that his ideas became common property, available to the writing community some time before they appeared in print. The ideas developed in this editorial apparently fired the imagination of a number of writers, including Rog Phillips and Will F. Jenkins.

Phillips, an author known more for exciting and rapid storytelling than for care in plotting, had "Atom War" ready for the May 1946 issue of *Amazing Stories.*[14] "Atom War" is set in a future in which television can cover air crashes as they happen. Live coverage from Los Angeles shows the atomic bombing of San Diego, Grand Coulee Dam, Detroit, and other places. The enemy broadcasts an ultimatum, but soldiers are ordered to stay on duty, aiming "fingers of pale luminescence" at incoming robot bombs to heat them so that they do not explode. Even so, the one that hits near Gar Winfield's post destroys the communications network joining Chicago to "New Chicago" (86).

Gar escapes from his wrecked post and rescues Helen Crawford; they flee together after the "military dictator of the United States" finds himself forced to surrender. (The dictator apparently considers surrender merely a tactical move aimed at disclosing their would-be conqueror. He does not intend to honor it. No more is said about this issue, nor is the presence of a "military dictator" in the United States ever explained.) Gar and Helen naturally fall in love as they drive through "the desolate wreckage of the two cities revealed by the unearthly radio-active light" (86). Seeking refuge, they are denied admittance to a farmer's house because they glow, as does their car; but he lets them in when Gar assures him that discarding their clothes and washing off the radiation before it burns them will make them perfectly safe.

At the farmhouse, they hear that the enemy nation has been identified as "Xsylvania," and that Australia is bombing it. Other countries join in the attack. An excited announcer reminds them that there have been "seventy-seven atom bomb explosions" in the twelve-hour war, and Australia has just been rendered helpless. "The world has gone mad. We may be living the last few days of our existence." With irrational humor he reminds his listeners that all the world's photographic film has been ruined.

> There is now enough radioactive material loose in the atmosphere by actual calculation to shorten the life span of every living creature on earth by several years.
>
> The next generation will, according to the most eminent authorities, contain a high percentage of mutations and freaks. Perhaps I shouldn't say this, but it might be better if the war *is* carried on to its logical conclusion now. Race suicide. (88–89)

This grim announcement is immediately followed by one in a different voice: "The previous announcer lost his head. I don't blame him, really, but he was talking nonsense. The radioactive residue of an atomic bomb loses its power after a few hours. There is no danger, so don't lose your heads" (89).

Continuing their journey in their glowing car, Gar and Helen reach an aid station where they hear that Xsylvania is now virtually destroyed. Moreover, the government has released details of an antiballistic missile defense, a "sterio ray" that "makes it impossible to use atom bombs on any effective scale." The broadcast continues:

> The nations of the world are meeting over the conference table today to decide the fate of the unholy three. The war isn't over yet, but its end is certain. So look up. Look to the future. . . . Seventy-five million Americans have lost their lives in the past fifteen hours, but never again will such a horrible thing be possible. (90)

This happy outcome depends entirely on the miraculous ray, which must be easy to construct from readily available materials, since officials expect thousands of amateur radio operators to build and operate the apparatus without difficulty. Despite the reference to a "conference table," no political solution to atomic war is implied.

The contradictions evident within the story may be due to the haste with which it must have been written, but they also reflect the essential ambivalence of the popular reaction. The obvious disparity between the messages given by the two announcers, one predicting a grim future (one that we now know to understate the danger) and the other, reassuring voice, sounding surprisingly like official publications of governmental agencies during the period of aboveground atomic testing in the United States, is never clarified. But we can tell which vision of the future Phillips himself wished to emphasize here. First, he has Gar assure Helen that mutations may be for the better as well as for the worse (a fallacy science fiction writers were very fond of and continued to write about long after evidence accrued to the contrary). Then Gar adds, "If you and I should marry, we must not be afraid to have children" (89). And the optimistic ending depends once again on the instantaneous development (by some anonymous "lone inventor") of a super-antiweapon. That an anti-super-antiweapon could follow is not hinted at, but necessarily assumed.

Another story clearly responding to Campbell's editorial is Will F. Jenkins's *Murder of the U.S.A.* (1946). Jenkins, better known to science fiction readers as "Murray Leinster," is a good storyteller, and his plot is internally consistent and reasonably logical, requiring no editorial annotation.[15] Although war has not been declared, all major U.S. population centers are wiped out by atomic missiles. Underground military centers, built and armed against just such a possibility, must hold their fire until the attacking nation is positively identified. Since he cannot track the missiles home, the hero must devise a way of preventing an incoming bomb from exploding so that he can examine its components.

When he manages this feat, he finds that most of the rocket was "made in the U.S.A." (the most technologically advanced and economically reckless country in the world is the obvious source for reliable parts; this also reflects the sale of scrap iron and other materials to Japan just before World War II began). But the method of construction gives away the enemy's nationality, not revealed in the text. (This tactic recalls "Leinster's" earlier story "The Power Planet" (1931), as do many other points of plot and style.) Vengeance is duly taken by the United States and friends, and the hero is free to marry the heroine, who has been cleared of suspicion as an enemy agent. These stories follow the long-established atomic scenario: surprise attack on the United States by an enemy using nuclear weapons. Little wonder that popular reaction to Hiroshima included the immediate fear, called "spontaneous and authentic" by Boyer (1985, 66): who will use it against us?

The "Franck Report" Plot

Although the Franck Report[16] predicting "suitcase warfare" when technology had miniaturized atomic bombs had been officially mislaid, stories of bombs smuggled into the United States joined those describing delivery by ballistic missile. Chandler Davis's "The Nightmare" (1946) describes the difficulty of policing New York City: "No number of successes in preventing the importing of dangerous radioactives can compensate for just one failure" (8). Philip Wylie later used a similar device in *The Smuggled Atom Bomb* (1951), but his youthful hero readily foils the dastardly plot. The differences in tone between the two works can largely be attributed to the audience: Davis wrote for knowledgeable sf fans, while Wylie's story was first published in the *Saturday Evening Post*. Like mainstream hardcover publishers, slick magazines did not encourage unrelenting realism. A similar nonartistic constraint created Pat Frank's *Mr. Adam* (1946), a farce on the theme of sterilization by radiation. Like Wylie, Frank soon moved to the approved subject of civil defense, where he could write realistically grim stories without seeming unduly pessimistic.

The "Civil Defense" Plot

To gain public acceptance for its nuclear policy, the government began simultaneously to emphasize two programs: civil defense, protection in case of atomic war, and atomic power plants, the "peaceful atom." Civil defense proposals initially included abandonment of large cities and radical distribution of population in small towns scattered across the countryside, on the assumption that no unfriendly nation, no matter how ingeniously it might copy "our" bomb, could possibly manufacture enough weapons to seriously damage a distributed population. This assumption shows up in such diverse fictions as the Kuttners' *Mutant* (1953) and Leigh Brackett's *The Long Tomorrow* (1955). In each, towns are forbidden to grow beyond a fixed limit. In each, no reason still exists for the prohibition, but it is strictly enforced.

People were also urged to build and equip home shelters (1951). William Tenn's "Generation of Noah" may be the first survivalist story. A grimly determined man moves his whole family to the country, keeps them within running distance of their shelter at all times, and is vindicated for his dictatorial behavior when the bombs do fall. This theme continues in popular action-adventure novels like "The Survivalist" series by Jerry Ahern (1981). Dean Ing's *Pulling Through* (1983) is part war novel and part handbook, giving detailed instructions on radiation-proofing the home shelter and diagrams for the building of a radiation meter.

Other civil defense measures included the installation of an early-warning system, the designation and stocking of public bomb shelters, and the training of volunteers. Novels by several mainstream authors promoted these measures or warned of the consequences of failing to implement them, notably Philip Wylie's *Tomorrow!* (1954), Harold Rein's *Few Were Left* (1955), Martin Caidin's *The Long Night* (1956), Richard Foster's *The Rest Must Die* (1959), and Pat Frank's *Alas, Babylon* (1959).

Gina Berriault's *The Descent* (1960) parodies the politics of shelter building. Daniel Galouye's *Dark Universe* (1961) creates the shelter that protects far too long, while Bruce Ariss's *Full Circle* (1963) presents the same message in a young-adult book. Robert A. Heinlein's hero builds a shelter that protects its occupants by time traveling in *Farnham's Freehold* (1964), though Heinlein undoubtedly did not intend humor. Many science fiction writers took a more skeptical view. Ward Moore's "Lot" (1953), Philip K. Dick's "Foster, You're Dead" (1954), James Blish's "To Pay the Piper" (1956), Frederik Pohl's "Wizards of Pung's Corners" (1958), and Poul Anderson's "Wildcat" (1958) all implicitly or explicitly criticize the civil defense program. More recently, Marty Asher's *Shelter* (1986) urges a post–1960s psychedelic program that would abandon the shelter mentality for sharing and togetherness.

Friendly Atoms

Atomic energy had long been seen as a kind of Pandora's box: full of unknown dangers better kept under lock and key, but with a shining residue of hope as well, as scientists predicted that the forces locked in atomic nuclei could provide the world with inexpensive, almost unlimited power if they could ever safely be released. Now they were released, though not yet safely, and science fiction was cited to show how long this promise had lived in the American imagination.[17] Government agencies put on a major publicity campaign to push the "Peaceful Atom," helped by such quasi-nonfiction works as John J. O'Neill's *Almighty Atom: The Real Story of Atomic Energy* (1945), which predicted atomic automobiles, and David Dietz's *Atomic Energy in the Coming Era* (1945), with giant atomic airplanes and atomic weather control. O'Neill and Dietz agreed that danger from radioactivity was a trivial detail that would readily succumb to American technological know-how. Sober newsmagazines were soon making predictions for atomic energy more comprehensive than Gernsback's in *Ralph 124C 41+*. Tiny bits of fuel would heat and air-condition homes without need for a centralized power plant, run factories and cars virtually forever, and heal all kinds of diseases, especially cancer. Moreover, the atom made a wonderful symbol. When President Eisenhower launched the "Atoms for Peace" campaign in 1954, he did so by waving "a radioactive magic wand" over a counting device in Denver that activated an automatic power shovel in Shippingport, Pennsylvania, to begin the excavation of a nuclear power reactor.[18] Surely the wonder-world of virtually free energy so ironically decried by John Campbell two decades earlier was now close at hand.

Those who pointed to science fiction as the harbinger of the nuclear millennium recalled only selected works, however. Many, like Heinlein's "Blowups Happen" (1940) and del Rey's "Nerves," portray unsettling dangers even from the most peaceful uses of atomic power, while stories like Edmond Hamilton's "Devolution" (1936) warn against unlimited hubris as well as overexposure to radiation. One of the earliest voices warning of the implausibility of atoms for everyone was that of John Campbell, who "reported that for years he had rejected stories involving atomic-powered vehicles. Radiation hazards would make them far too dangerous, he argued, especially in case of an accident. 'If an atomic-powered taxi hit an atomic-powered streetcar at Forty-second and Lex,' he said, 'it would completely destroy the whole Grand Central area.' "[19]

Most of the science fiction stories about the peaceful postwar atom reflected Campbell's view. Even A. E. van Vogt's "Clane" stories (1946–50) (later collected in *Empire of the Atom,* 1956) presume that atomic research would blast civilization back to medieval times, where the gods of radiation would be worshipped and where mutant births would be common. In typical van Vogt fashion, however, he makes his hero a mutant genius who recovers technology and uses it for war. Heinlein's *Space Cadet* (1948) presumes the casual use of atomic power for spaceships and atomic bombs in orbit, but presents a warning against careless use in the discovery of an asteroid once part of an inhabited planet now destroyed by atomic explosion. H. Beam Piper's "Day of the Moron" (1951) describes a Chernobyl-like catastrophe at the atomic energy plant, caused not by accident but by sheer bungling stupidity when union rules prohibit the dismissal of incompetent workers. As the dreams of clean, simple, safe atomic power unsupported by fiction or by fact silently fade from public view, science fiction becomes more rather than less pessimistic.

Good Wars and Bad Ones

The assumption that man really needs to fight, that if he does not have to struggle he will devolve, is far less popular than it was before World War II. Only one major author consistently uses it throughout this postwar period: "Lewis Padgett," another pseudonym for the writing team of Kuttner and Moore. In "The Fairy Chessmen" (1946), an ongoing war has driven Americans into underground cities.

> This set-up would have been impossible without the booster charge of World War II. As the first World War had stimulated the use of air power in the second

> inter-global conflict, so the war of the nineteen-forties had stimulated the techniques of electronics—among other things. And when the first blasting attack of the Falangists, on the other side of the planet, had come, the western hemisphere was not only prepared, but could work its war machine with slightly miraculous speed and precision. (11)

People are able "to live a more secure and contented life than before the war" underground, and all the fighting is done by robots (11). But even so, the war is going badly; the enemy has discovered some quasi-physical principle that not only creates devastating weapons, but literally maddens those technicians who try to study them. Eventually the innovation is tracked down to a time traveler who has come to the "present" to alter his "own time." The man from the future has always lived with war. He has been "tempered." "A people who'd always lived in Utopia wouldn't have much survival value" (191).

Of course the war has "tempered" men on our side as well, and they crack the secret at the risk of their own sanity. The Kuttners' "survival of the fittest" argument tacitly ignores the fact that although war no longer kills the strong young men in battle, it now kills the best and brightest technical experts, a terrible price to pay for "tempering." This war ends leaving humanity with its weapons and technology, which it will inevitably use; to do otherwise would be "psychologically unendurable. There would always be an Enemy." But since war research advanced technology sufficiently to permit limitless space travel, they decide to battle "the gates of the sky" rather than other men (176).

"Tomorrow and Tomorrow" (1947) presents a world so fearful that scientific research may lead to war that it has become an intellectual prison camp. All experimentation is forbidden. As they do in *Mutant*, the Kuttners invent a positive mutation; the plot depends on the supernormal powers of the main characters. One makes contact with an alternate world on which a full-scale atomic war has had beneficial effects: the drastically reduced population has resumed scientific experimentation in time to save itself from a lethal disease. The war that results from the mutants' tampering (once they are reassured that their world will not be totally destroyed, as it is in "Clash by Night") is presented as the best possible route to utopia. In "Nuclear War in Science Fiction, 1945–59" Paul Brians notes that "this must be the only time anyone has suggested that the bomb offers our best hope for curing cancer" (1984, 256).

Few others find war "good." Leonard Engel and Emanuel A. Piller respond to the U.S./USSR confrontation in *World Aflame* (1947), a quasi-fictional account of the "next war" between Russia and the United States. England has surrendered, and thirty-five million Americans die in the atomic attack, but the conflict—like Carl Spohr's "Final War"—drags madly on. Martial law has supplanted democracy, prosperity and safety are forgotten concepts, future generations have been damaged by radiation, and a "five-year plan" for postwar reconstruction is already in place. Though the United States is not defeated, there seems to be very little left of what Americans were fighting for. A contemporary review of the book remarks that "it should give pause to the Bomb-Russia-Now school."[20] Each generation repeats for itself the tales of the previous one; Whitley Streiber and James Kunetka's *Warday and the Journey Onward* (1984) seems like a continuation of *World Aflame,* dealing particularly with the aftermath of a less lengthy struggle.

With the Nuremberg decisions possibly in mind, Chandler Davis counted the cost of refusing military duty when that meant agreeing to a preemptive war in "To Still the Drums" (1946). It is 1948, "and the war was quite definitely over" (159), but secret military research continues on "radar-rocket-atomic bombs" (161). Several young military men and a civilian expert speculate on their possible use. By preparing for the next war, are they precipitating it? Does either the military or Congress really understand atomic war? "Oppenheimer, Urey, Hogness—all those boys have tried. Some success, not very much" (162), they agree. Then one of the soldiers discovers a document signed by his colonel, naming the "foreign power against which war was planned" (166).

Putting duty to humanity above discipline, he steals the document and manages to get it to Washington, where his girl is Senator Richardson's secretary. Richardson defends the young man, who writes this account in jail, describing himself as "more or less a political prisoner now, since [Colonel] Jennings's story came out. If Jennings is cleared, I'll get a prison term, even if Richardson can get me out of the desertion and treason charges. If Jennings isn't cleared, I'll be let off with a 'discharge for incompetence.' " Waiting for trial, he wonders,"Will Richardson fail, or will the arms race be stopped? Ten years from now, will the cities' crowded millions be dissolving in rapid-fire bursts of flaming hell? Or will there be a peaceful world . . . ?" (172). This question was clearly prominent in the thinking of many people.

Bad Rads

Atomic bombs were tested at Bikini atoll in 1946. In 1948, David Bradley, a physician with the Bikini group, published *No Place to Hide*. The book carefully documents the long-lasting effect of radiation from atomic bombs and the impossibility of "cleaning up" after it. Although he makes clear connections between the tests and a possible future war, the book had little impact on policy. Atomic testing continued in the South Pacific and on U.S. soil.

The book may have had an impact on some writers, however. Rog Phillips's "So Shall Ye Reap!" (1947) reflects the popular concern that atomic testing affected the environment.[21] When the irreversible damage from radioactivity is first detected, America, fearing an atomic war started by Russia, has already devised, stocked, and manned underground shelters. Members of a select group thus remain safe, while most of humanity perishes, leaving a few adapted mutants on the surface. These mutants, who mature at eight and die at fifteen, now live as savages, eating giant cockroaches. Warned by "Geigs" provided by the underground humans, they survive "Geig storms" but will die out in fifty years or so as the contamination inevitably gets worse.

In a reversal of Wells's Morlocks, the soft undergrounders realize that the savage mutants have good qualities, including a willingness to take risks. But mutants invited underground do not thrive. (We should note that the underground people do not either; there are now far fewer of them than there were originally, though they extend their technology, expand their caverns, and live a long time—with overwhelming guilt.) Phillips suggests that the effects of the radiation will increase for two thousand years with no further input; even underground, survival seems unlikely. Here the editor of *Amazing Stories,* clearly referring to the Bikini tests and anxious not to be outdone by Campbell, adds a postscript: "We have deliberately misled you regarding 'So Shall Ye Reap.' This novel is *not* a story of what might happen if the atom war came—it is a story of what *may already have happened*" (155).

Stories like Ridenour's "Pilot Lights of the Apocalypse," Sturgeon's "Memorial" (1946), T. L. Sherred's "E for Effort" (1947), and Phillips's "So Shall Ye Reap!" added the specifically nuclear scenario to earlier stories that wiped the earth clean of humanity, like Schachner's "World Gone Mad" (1935), Michel and Lowndes's "The Inheritors" (1942), and del Rey's "Into Thy Hands" (1945). Other works, like Ward Moore's *Greener Than You Think* (1947) and George R. Stewart's *Earth Abides* (1949), destroy civilization by more natural causes than nuclear holocaust, but Boyer notes that these are "clearly a product of, and comment upon, the pervasive fears of the atomic era" (1985, 262). Moore destroys human life entirely; Stewart merely destroys modern civilization while allowing a "sacred remnant" to repopulate the earth. Walter Miller's *Canticle for Leibowitz* (1955–57, novel 1959) reinforced the repetitive nature of conflict. The assumptions encoded in our stories show that we agree with Schachner's Old Peter: "The world moves and does not change; word for word the madness runs its course."

REACTIONS

Scientists who had initially attempted to use fear to encourage international control of atomic weapons found themselves defeated by a combination of factors, not the least of them the assumptions discussed here. Acting upon these assumptions, the nation took a variety of mutually contradictory postures: repudiating military control of atomic development while assuming military use of atomic weapons when (not if) necessary; demanding international control of atomic technology while simultaneously refusing to give up America's atomic stockpile or testing program; emphasizing the "peaceful atom" and the lack of danger from radiation while urging civil defense measures to "protect" cities from attack.

Radiation, fallout, mutation, and atomic destruction of the biosphere were featured in science fiction magazines during the period when the American press was largely glib, reticent, or silent on the subject.[22] Even such a superficial writer as Rog Phillips raises questions of current and vital importance to the citizens of the United States, especially those living in the Southwest. While atomic bombs were being regularly tested above ground on U.S. soil, and such testing was declared vital to national defense, the Atomic Energy Commission repeatedly assured the public that "fallout does not constitute a serious hazard outside the test site" despite Bradley's report and even measured ionizing radiation in "sunshine units."[23] Official silence punctuated by misinformation—for instance, "that radiation sickness is essentially painless" and that fallout was a trivial and merely temporary problem—contributed to American acceptance of and complacence about nuclear development and testing both in the South Pacific and on American soil.[24]

By 1949, science fiction had published so many atomic doom stories that even avid sf readers were surfeited, and editors received complaints about it. Also by 1949, fear of and guilt for the bomb had been projected onto new targets: Communist "fellow travelers" in the United States. As it had in 1919, a massive Red Scare swept the country. After World War I, many suspected dissidents were summarily deported; after World War II, they were "merely" accused, often without evidence. The scare damaged the careers and lives of thousands of people and gave Senator Joe McCarthy virtually dictatorial power. Even that seemingly unlikely possibility had already been explored in stories like Heinlein's "Solution Unsatisfactory" (1941), Cartmill's "Overthrow" (1942), and del Rey's "Fifth Freedom" (1943).

Until Russia exploded her bomb in 1949, America was the only country in the world strong enough to be the enemy worthy of the bomb; and by the time the Russian threat was fully manifested, the United States was engaged in the "police action" in Korea. Clearly, North Korea was not worth a bomb, but China might be, and real consideration was given to escalating the conflict and using it there. But in 1949, Truman had already ordered the scientists back to work, this time to build "Super," the hydrogen bomb that Edward Teller had yearned for. Thus the pattern of escalation and duplication so long laid out in fiction continued in nuclear fact.

ASSUMPTIONS

The values encoded in the constructs of the "lone inventor," "progress," and the atomic scenario and those encoded in various aspects of Judeo-Christian ethics collided at Hiroshima and Nagasaki. The justification for prosecuting World War II—that we, an innocent and relatively weak nation, had been attacked without warning—was suddenly reversed. We now held in fact the superweapon we had so long envisioned in fiction and were not sure how to deal with the actuality of supreme power. Certainly we, if anyone, had the ability to use such power wisely; but the very nature of the power prohibited its use. And everything we knew about "progress" (particularly in weaponry) led us to assume that theoretical possibility led to eventual use. This assumption produced the immediate fear of atomic war, not mollified by the identification of atomic power with the magic wand of the future. The two assumptions simply were not held in the same context, nor were their mutual inconsistencies rationally examined any more than the inconsistent views of the scientist as Frankenstein and as Superman. But they had far-reaching consequences.

The millennial aspect of the reaction to Hiroshima and Nagasaki cannot be overstated. Largely an American preoccupation, fear of nuclear apocalypse actually begins in the 1930s. This premature millennialism can be roughly charted by the number of stories on the theme published in any given year. In his bibliography, *Nuclear Holocausts* (1987), Paul Brians shows a rapid rise in 1946–47, a fairly steady output through the sixties, a small drop in the seventies, and another rise in the eighties, when increased millennial emphasis would be expected in the normal course of events. Many of the stories deal with attempts either to defend the United States against attack or to survive after the attack takes place. Virtually none anticipate that the war can be avoided, even by preemptive bombing. Most (but not all) of the stories identify Russia as the expected enemy; invading aliens now come in a distant second, and Orientals have almost disappeared.

Nationally, we achieved this state of mind with Hiroshima and have not abandoned it. It represents a combination of fear of reprisal, guilt over using a new and unusually dangerous weapon on a largely civilian target, and shame at the hubris of taking on the role of God. This was made quite clear in several ways: the atomic bomb is described as bringing the sun to Earth, but the sun is not something that man is supposed to play with; that power lies solely in the hands of God. Worse yet, the atomic bomb could conceivably destroy all life on Earth, if not the Earth itself. This again is God's sole prerogative. Man had usurped God's power, as science had been tacitly expected to do since *Frankenstein.* Such shame and guilt could only be removed by some appropriate punishment. And what punishment could be more appropriate for a crime against both God and Man than Armageddon? If we had taken over God's role, it might be up to us to give it back to Him, even if doing so meant destroying ourselves in atomic war.

This assumption is too uncomfortable to live with, so most people shove it out of awareness. Doing that is possible only if something else gets attended to instead. The most convenient alternatives include active proselytizing for peace (often by threatening the horrors of war) and finding something or someone else to blame for our feelings of guilt and shame. Fortunately, the Communists were handy. It was soon explained that President Truman had used the bomb on Japan not only to save millions of lives, both American and Japanese, but also to prevent Russia from taking part in the conquest and claiming some unearned share of the spoils. Further analysis led to the conviction that a sick and feeble Roosevelt had capitulated to the iron demands of Stalin, that Russia was taking far more than her fair share of Europe, and that the entire free world was in immediate danger of a Communist takeover, atomic or otherwise. That the evidence often justified this conviction was convenient but not essential. If the Russians—clearly the enemy—made us bomb Japan, then our responsibility in that area was subtly lessened. There is, of course, a cost to this trade-off: it then becomes necessary to oppose the enemy with our whole strength. In order to do that, we must see the enemy as sufficiently strong to merit such opposition, worthy of our heaviest weapons.

Our single-minded opposition to communism has had some interesting consequences. For one thing, we have virtually ignored triumphs achieved by our own democratic capitalist system: the Marshall Plan in Europe and the highly successful occupation of Japan. (We now resent their economic success and suggest various ways to punish them for following our own example.) We helped to establish and joined a functioning United Nations, though the organization has always been limited by a charter written before the bomb. Peace terms following World War II were fundamentally nonpunitive compared to those that ended World War I, and the combatants have not rearmed and reorganized for battle in the intervening years. Although unemployment and recession have occasionally upset our domestic economy, we have (so far) avoided anything approaching another Great Depression. And instead of being followed by a terrible epidemic of influenza, World War II has been followed by a succession of medical triumphs, including the elimination of smallpox.

But as a nation we cannot rejoice over these achievements; we are too busy opposing communism. Stories like del Rey's "Fifth Freedom," Philip K. Dick's *The Penultimate Truth* (1964), and James P. Hogan's *Voyage from Yesteryear* (1982) show that by our opposition we have become more and more like the system we oppose: secretive, politically rigid, militaristic, and worthy of destruction. This may explain why so few nuclear fictions bother to show who is bombing whom and why. The situation seems inevitable, unalterable, and self-explanatory.

The fixity of this opposition reflects our repressed awareness of our own position as the nation now most worthy of destruction, as well as our guilt from impious usurpation of God's power. We dwell upon this topic so much that it often seems that we seek punishment, that we want the end of the world to come. That would solve all our problems; it might even give us a chance for a fresh start. Our fictions show this tacit assumption: Armageddon would surely be horrible, but waiting for it almost seems worse.

NOTES

1. Stories printed during 1942 probably had been written—possibly even sold—before Pearl Harbor, since it takes up to a year to get a magazine story into print.

2. This story extended the assumption that "peaceful atoms" are still dangerous, already explored by John Taine in *Seeds of Life* (1931), Stephen G. Hale's "The Laughing Death" (1931), and Robert A. Heinlein's "Blowups Happen" (1940), among others.

3. In his *Index to the Science Fiction Magazines, 1926–1950,* (Portland, Ore.: Perri Press, 1952) Donald Day attributes "Clash by Night" to C. L. Moore alone, though he recognizes that following their marriage in 1940, most of their works were collaborations. Their 1947 novel *Fury* uses the same Venerian setting and serves as a sequel to "Clash by Night."

4. "Deadline" has more stories told about it than it might seem to merit. Most claim that the FBI tried to prevent its publication because it accurately described the then-untested atomic bomb, and that it put *Astounding Science Fiction,* Campbell, and Cartmill all under investigation. It might be more accurate to say that the FBI arrived after reading the story, accusing Cartmill of divulging secret information and Campbell of publishing it. Campbell's defense was simple: *Astounding Science Fiction* had printed many atomic bomb stories; they did not know what was accurate (beyond information in the public domain, which many writers, including Heinlein and del Rey as well as Cartmill, had researched), but if the magazine suddenly stopped printing such stories, readers' suspicions would be alerted more by noticing that than they would by any tale set on an alien world.

5. *Mutant* contains five stories with a narrative frame. "Three Blind Mice" (1945), "The Lion and the Unicorn" (1945), and "Beggars in Velvet" (1945), the next stories in the series, undoubtedly were written before the end of the war

in the Pacific. The fifth story, "Humpty Dumpty" (1953), deals with the Baldies' attempts to share their mind-reading ability with the rest of the world.

6. In early August, the September issue of *Astounding Science Fiction* was in the hands of its readers; the October issue was printed and ready for mailing; and the November issue was already made up. Probably Campbell got his new editorial into it by dumping the old one. By the December issue, Campbell is already looking at practical uses for atomic energy, pointing out that an atomic pile must be big and well shielded. Atomic power plants would not be either cheap or easily portable.

7. That this story was admired and reprinted by older fans is demonstrated by the back cover text, which laments Jameson's death "in the early part of 1945" and praises his contributions to "all the leading scientifiction magazines in the United States" as well as his activity "in scientific circles," which "gives his scientifiction . . . a soundness and solidarity which much science fiction has lacked." The term "scientifiction" was no longer in general use.

8. Between 1927 and 1946, science fiction had been relegated entirely to pulp magazines with a few exceptions: two anthologies aimed at the teenage audience supposedly most attracted by sf, and two adult anthologies edited by Donald Wollheim. See James Gunn, *Alternate Worlds: The Illustrated History of Science Fiction* (Englewood Cliffs, N.J.: Prentice-Hall, 1975), 175–80, for a fuller description of the boom in science fiction publishing.

9. At the age of twelve I was amazed at the apparent ignorance not only of my friends but also of many adult acquaintances over the implications of the bomb. How much of my reaction was due to my reading of sf I cannot now document, for I lived in the Berkeley academic community, knew something about Lawrence's cyclotron, and could put this information into context.

10. Dr. Louis N. Ridenour, a noted nuclear physicist, published "Pilot Lights of the Apocalypse," his only known piece of imaginative writing, less than six months after Hiroshima. In this short play, he shows the fallibility of automatic detection and activation systems. Groff Conklin notes admiringly that it "is one of the earliest literary attempts to warn mankind of the dangers of 'pushbutton nuclear warfare,' as we have since come to know it," but that although Ridenour hoped that it would be performed widely and seriously thought about, both the play and its message have been "ignored by practically everyone." Groff Conklin, introduction to "Pilot Lights of the Apocalypse," in *Great Science Fiction by Scientists*, ed. Groff Conklin (New York: Collier, 1962), 280.

11. Paul Boyer, *By the Bomb's Early Light* (New York: Pantheon, 1985), pt. 6, chap. 20. The following chapter, "Visions of the Atomic Future in Science Fiction and Speculative Fantasy," is equally important, though he misses most of the magazine fiction.

12. See Boyer, *By the Bomb's Early Light*, 66–75, on the reports of de Seversky, General Groves, David Lilienthal, and others, all knowledgeable or apparently so. These men repeated that fear was unwarranted, that America was safe from attack, and that science could save us from the dangers it had devised, while they avoided any substantive answers to the questions the very existence of which the public was generally kept ignorant.

13. When scientists who believed that they were countering German atomic research by preparing America's atomic bomb rejected using it on Japan, they were

in essence maintaining this tacit assumption. Since 1938, we had known that Germany either had a bomb or could have one. Japan did not and could not. Despite the suicidal bravery of her army, assuring high casualties from an invasion of the home islands, in a mythical sense Japan did not "merit" the bomb.

14. The story is prefaced by a lengthy, fully italicized note from the editor, explaining the whole situation. If Phillips is rushing a "Campbell idea" into a rival magazine, this may explain both the haste with which the story seems to be written and the need felt by the editor of *Amazing Stories* to introduce it so carefully.

15. For some reason, Jenkins sold this work as a mystery novel: Who "murdered" the United States? But his predilection for science fiction shows in the anxiously careful footnotes explaining each scientific aspect of the plot (footnotes he might have omitted, ironically, in a science fiction story, on the assumption that his readers would understand the fundamentals of atomic science and might even have read Henry de Wolf Smythe's *Atomic Energy for Military Purposes,* (Princeton: Princeton University Press, 1945), the "Smythe Report"). Moreover, since his "detective" never reveals the identity of the (only partially successful) "murderer," the mystery is left unsolved, with only a comedic resolution.

16. In *The Great Decision: The Secret History of the Atomic Bomb* (New York: Putnam, 1959), Michael Amrine summarizes relevant passages of the Franck Report (103–7). Rejecting "the arguments of national strength through secrecy," the Committee on Social and Political Implications, chaired by James Franck, believed that advanced weapons could not protect a nation but "would put a premium upon surprise attack. Enemy bombs could even be hidden in major cities and touched off by remote control. They foresaw something that they had begun to call 'suitcase warfare' " (104).

17. Boyer, *By the Bomb's Early Light,* notes (109) that at least one atomic scientist referred to fictional accounts of the blessings of atomic power in 1946 to explain its ready acceptance by the American public.

18. See Stephen Hilgartner, Richard C. Bell, and Rory O'Connor, *Nukespeak: Nuclear Lauguage, Visions, and Mindset.* (San Francisco: Sierra Club, 1982), 44–45.

19. Campbell, quoted in Boyer, *By the Bomb's Early Light,* 115. See also his editorial, discussed in note 6, in the December 1945 *Astounding Science Fiction.*

20. Louis Gottschalk, review of *World Aflame* in "Book Week," *Chicago Sun,* June 1, 1947, 8.

21. This concern was often expressed in connection with the weather. Any unusual heat, drought, wind, rain, cold, or snow was attributed to the atomic tests.

22. In the "real world," this imposed silence created serious problems for Japanese doctors who were not informed about causes of and treatment for the radiation victims they were treating, even as far as these were known.

23. See, for example, Hilgartner, Bell, and O'Connor, *Nukespeak: Nuclear Language, Visions, and Mindset.* (San Francisco: Sierra Club, 1982), and John G. Fuller, *The Day We Bombed Utah: American's Most Lethal Secret* (New York: New American Library, 1984).

24. See, for example, Robert Karl Manhoff, "The Silencer," *ETC. A Review of General Semantics* 41, no. 2 (Summer 1984): 152–59; and Hilgartner, Bell, and O'Connor, *Nukespeak,* 73ff. See also chaps. 6 and 7.

PART II

CIRCLING GROUND ZERO

6

The Nature of "Human Nature"

In the midst of technological revolution, one thing we expect to remain stable is what we call "human nature." While fiction must deal with species-general experience (that is, it can deal with all situations and conditions possible for man as a physical being to experience and can present these experiences as causing physiologically appropriate reactions and sensations), it is both culture-dependent and culture-specific. Although science fiction eagerly anticipates that science will change the way we live, it usually expects that human beings much like us will do the living. "You can't change human nature!"

Popular uses of the term "human nature" makes no distinction between physiological characteristics of human beings and the manifestations of culture. This confuses an already confused issue. In *The Biosocial Nature of Man,* Ashley Montagu describes man as an educable animal, "a culture-making creature," (1956, 10) and argues that "most cultures begin with a conception of human nature and then proceed to fashion their man according to it. Man is custom made" (1956, 13–14).[1]

We do such a good job with this process that, as the anthropologist Edward Hall explains, "almost everyone has difficulty believing that behavior they have always associated with 'human nature' is not human nature at all but learned behavior of a peculiarly complex variety" (1973, 44).

Since we assume that human nature does not change, we do not find it strange that societies represented as being light-years or centuries distant look much like our own. When A. Bertram Chandler creates an Atlantean civilization inhabited by anthropoids resembling *Australopithecus* in "False Dawn" (1946), he makes them speak and act very much like Westerners somewhat infected by Eastern mysticism and has them set themselves up for atomic destruction in language borrowed from the (much-later) Bible, while re-creating (pre-creating?) contemporary situations.

Herman Wouk's *The "Lomokome" Papers* (1956) has an astronaut stranded on the Moon find a civilization that in many ways parallels our own.[2] Long ago they decided that war was a necessary part of their nature; since they could not abolish it, they had to control it. Now they fight their perennial wars by contest rather than conflict, with a committee to decide who won. Losers voluntarily accept death; suffering and loss can thus be experienced without destroying the planet.[3] Horace C. Coon sends an anthropological expedition to the lifeless Earth *43,000 Years Later* (1958) to investigate the catastrophe that destroyed sentient life on this promising planet. Not only do these alien scholars make some very accurate guesses about patterns of aggression among the now-extinct natives, but the various members of the expedition also dispute theories and play dominance games in thoroughly familiar, "human" fashion. They conclude that the Terrans destroyed themselves over trivial differences of belief and custom, but they do not notice that their own "natural" interpersonal pattern could lead to the very same result.

In contrast, Leo Szilard's "Report on Grand Central Terminal" (1952) shows aliens investigating a lifeless Earth as being completely baffled by the remains of pay toilets. Although they form no certain theories about human beings, their discussions acutely penetrate the American preoccupation with excreta and the ritual that surrounds their culturally approved disposal, while metaphorically connecting this with the elimination of humanity.

Montagu describes our shared cultural history as based on a combination of Greek and Judeo-Christian worldviews. From the Greek, we get a basic pessimism concerning human potentiality, and from the Judeo-Christian, a "belief in the innate naughtiness of human nature" (1956, 177). He claims that our society therefore accepts suffering and war as natural results of basic human nature while holding, simultaneously, mutually exclusive ideas: on the one hand, that people can be educated to behave more rationally and altruistically; on the other, that people are irremediably aggressive, as argued by Hobbes, and competitive, as shown by Darwin (18–19, 24–29).

Many authors make the intransigence of human nature the basis of their plots. Frank Herbert's General in "Cease Fire" (1958) lectures the young soldier who innocently hopes that his invention, a long-distance detonator for any explosive or flammable device, will prevent further wars: "Violence is a part of human life. The lust for power is a part of human life. As long as people want power badly enough, they'll use any means to get it—fair or foul!" (347). Humorists like Emery Balint in *Don't Inhale It* (1949) present the same message as more serious writers like Raymond Z. Gallun in "The Magician of Dream Valley" (1938) and C. M. Kornbluth in "The Luckiest Man in Denv" (1952): given a choice, man will opt for destruction, not for life. Balint cheerfully blows Earth into small, autonomous pieces; Gallun destroys a lovely (and possibly useful) but aggravating life form; and Kornbluth portrays the dominance/submission pattern now played out between nations as continuing unaltered when nothing remains of America but bomb shelters protecting city-states. As Denv and Ellay regularly bomb each other over now-forgotten riparian rights, the only thing that matters to the warriors is getting in with the group in power, even if that means betraying those among their own officers who are attempting to end the senseless struggle.

These "typically American" patterns—responding to disagreement by fragmenting the institutions (as in many Protestant churches), handling problems by indiscriminate massacre (as with the American Indians), and indulging in power struggle within and between organizations while the system as a whole suffers—get conflated with human nature in these stories, as they do in common speech. The basis of every fiction is some concept of how human beings "really are." We need to distinguish, if possible, which aspects of human behavior are alterable and which are not.

MODELS OF HUMAN NATURE

Is man's nature fixed by heredity? If so, is man naturally aggressive (in which case war is naturally an inevitable and continuing condition), or is he naturally peaceful (in which case war is a frequent aberration)? Neither position seems tenable without modification; neither accounts for observed behavior or for social changes. Hobbes, whom we officially dispute and tacitly agree with, argues that man's nature is selfish, lustful, greedy, and bellicose, and that his life, if not constrained by civilizing institutions, is "solitary, poor, nasty, brutish, and short." Rousseau, whose philosophy formally underlies both the "American dream" and the myth of the American frontier, but whose optimism we tacitly deny in practice, holds that human nature is intrinsically noble, but weakened morally and physically by the corruption of civilization. Both assume that man's nature is inherent and beyond his power to change; evolutionary theory seems to uphold that position as well.

If, on the other hand, man is capable of modifying his behavior and his social institutions, has he modified his nature to do so, or has he somehow been compelled to follow different patterns against his will? (If we believe that he is forcibly civilized by society, for instance, we will also assume that "primitive man" lurks beneath the socialized exterior, and that man will revert to savagery—however we define it—under conditions of stress.) If we do believe that humans are radically capable of modifying their behavior—the expression of their nature—how can we explain the fact that we have not done so in the face of species suicide?

Traditional Models

There are at least two sets of basic protocols operating in our culture to explain how people "really are," and each embraces a pair of opposing models in tension. One protocol might be called religious or philosophical, the other scientific or psychological.

In the religious/philosophical protocol, man's nature is fixed by its origins. One model finds man a "fallen" creature, proud and ungrateful, bound by original sin and salvageable only by extraordinary grace. The opposing model holds man as basically good, perhaps reduced from glorious innocence by the contamination of spoiled society. The fallen model shows up in the image of the "mad scientist," especially the man who destroys everything he loves most. No matter how pure his motives, his actions are inevitably flawed and doomed to failure, because in his pride he relies on his own prowess and ignores humane advice and divine grace.

The "Fallen" Model. If man is fallen, writers propose that a time may come when redemption is withdrawn. In "Darwinian Pool Room" (1950), Isaac Asimov explores the problem of religious determinism by posing a philosophical but very practical question: If God has created evolution as one of His operating principles, and if it works on humans as it does on lower animals, can we then assume that He has allowed man's sciences of nucleonics and cybernetics to concatenate in order to replace man with the artificial intelligence that man is currently "evolving"? Lester del Rey's "For I Am a Jealous People" (1954) proposes that God might decide to abandon His convenant with humanity in favor of some alien, more successfully warlike race. Del Rey concludes that in such an event, humanity might inevitably be defeated but that it would go down defending itself and its beliefs as vigorously as the Philistines defended their Baals.

The "Basically Good" Model. The model that holds human nature to be basically good is not often used in science fiction, except ironically, as H. Beam Piper does in "Uller Uprising" (1952). If the natives of Uller were ever innocent, it was long before the story begins. Now they are divided into contentious nation-states and join only to war against colonizing Terrans, using atomic weapons Terrans have taught them to make and use.[4] In contrast, Valentine Michael Smith, in Robert A. Heinlein's *Stranger in a Strange Land* (1961), is not only basically good, he is also an innocent; his upbringing was absolutely pure. But Mike is also enormously powerful. He thus can afford to be a "nice guy."

The disadvantages of natural goodness are laid out with exceptional clarity by Poul Anderson in "The Helping Hand" (1950). A pleasant, friendly culture resembling that of Samoa is annihilated by accepting the benevolent assistance of Earth in rebuilding its planet after a devastating war. Meanwhile its opponent, a warlike Norse-type culture, stubbornly rejects all aid and flourishes under rigorous conditions by remaining true to its own tradition. Human nature, like a muscle, requires exercise. Resistance strengthens; cooperation leads to co-option and inevitable decay.

The scientific/psychological protocol also employs two opposing models: the genetic or "nature" model, which emphasizes physiological evolution, and the nurture model, which emphasizes sociocultural evolution, assuming that a child's physiology provides potential for learning but no innate predispositions for specific behavior patterns. For many years, psychologists have debated, compromised, shelved, and reopened the "nature/nurture" argument. The nature model demonstrates, often convincingly, that behavior, even such an intangible as altruism, is inherited.[5] Logically, a didactic literature should depend on the possibility for change inherent in the nurture model, but science fiction seems to prefer the nature model, often opting for some version of Lamarckian evolution.[6]

The genetic model. The genetic model considers human nature modifiable only by the slow process of evolution and the random effect of mutation. To allow human nature to alter rapidly, many writers use some version of the "mutation by radiation" story. Following the doctrine of "progress," writers often portray the mutants as a higher form of life than their human progenitors. Examples of such stories include Rog Phillips's "The Mutants" (1946) and "Battle of the Gods" (1948) and "Lewis Padgett's" "Baldy" stories. A. E. van Vogt wrote one of the earliest and best of these stories, *Slan* (1940). Slans, who come in two styles, with and without tendrils, are superior to humans in strength and intelligence, but circumstances force them to battle humans and each other. As the scapegoats for many ills, particularly a crop of mutant babies, they are persecuted by normal men in a bigoted and regressive world, and they seem to have little effect on it until the end of the tale, when it becomes apparent that humans have come to their evolutionary end and will inevitably be replaced by Slans. An interesting variation on the theme of beneficial mutation is Ray Bradbury's "The Naming of Names" (1949), in which he suggests that a new environment might stimulate both psychological and physiological changes.

A number of writers suggest that acquisition of superpowers, by mutation or through some other development, may be the only hope of humanity. William Tenn's "The Sickness" (1955) takes place on Mars. One member of the expedition worries that increased human intelligence leads to bigger wars, documenting his assertion by showing Earth as full of cobalt bomb stockpiles and increasing international tension. When the other men come down with a severe illness, he nurses them to recovery, only to find that they have been infected with superb intelligence and enlarged "moral concepts." These supermen (and the disappointed immune) return to Earth to spread their disease and prevent war.

The opposite side of the "superman" theme is also shown by Tenn in "Null-P" (1950). After war demonstrates the danger of intelligence, a man is found who is absolutely average, "the median made flesh" (61).[7] Those who do not admire him sufficiently are killed. He promotes inactivity and ineptitude; the more active of his followers blow themselves up with old weapons, and those remaining devolve slowly but placidly until they become mere pets for an advanced race of Newfoundland dogs. The assumption that humanity's only salvation is stupidity still has fictional force, as can be seen in Kurt Vonnegut's ironic *Galápagos* (1985). Here the reader must decide whether the postwar mutation is beneficial; it certainly provides species persistence, but at enormous cost. Like Campbell, these writers tacitly assume that man's nature includes the possibility both of self-destruction and of devolution but that only some outside force can produce evolution.

Scientific evidence shows that mutation is more likely to hurt than to help humanity. Poul Anderson and F. N. Waldrop's "Tomorrow's Children" (1947), Judith Merril's "That Only a Mother" (1948), Cyril Kornbluth's "The Mindworm" (1950), Forrest J. Ackerman's "The Mute Question" (1950), Alice Eleanor Jones's "Created He Them" (1955), and Carol Emshwiller's "Day at the Beach" (1959) give this evidence emotional reality. Some authors take the problem of harmful mutation more lightly, as do James Gunn in "The Boy with Five Fingers" (1953) and Hollis Alpert in "The Simian Problem" (1960). But all mutation stories rely on the genetic model, and the human nature depicted changes less than does the human form.

The Nurture Model. The nurture model declares that human beings are almost infinitely adaptable and that behavior reflects environment, including language and learning, rather than heredity. As the genetic model fixes human behavior by inheritance, so the nurture model fixes it by education: the flexible infant is socialized in culturally dependent patterns; he in turn will socialize his children in similar ways unless social institutions change radically during his lifetime.

Some authors following the nurture model alter human nature by giving it a chance to start over with new patterns, usually on a new planet, or on an Earth renewed by nuclear Armageddon. Contrasting examples include Raymond F. Jones's *Renaissance* (1944), in which the new, improved model of man supplants the old, and Theodore Sturgeon's "Farewell to Eden" (1949), in which the good survivors lose to the debased ones. Chad Oliver combines nurture and new circumstances in "The Life Game" (1953). Robots provide "good" nurturing for the two human survivors of atomic war, although they show war as a daily event, as harmless as the nightly chess game and just about as interesting. After the young couple escape their stultifying Eden, they receive the blessing of the ancient scientist whose foresight led to their survival and set off to repopulate the world. As in many such stories, the nurture given the survivors of one holocaust seems likely to lead to another.

Walter M. Miller's *A Canticle for Leibowitz* (1959) profoundly demonstrates the effects of such nurturing. Repeating the pattern of progress and conflict kills the planet. In contrast, an example of changing patterns is found in *Voyage from Yesteryear* by James P. Hogan (1982). When refugees from a wartorn Earth arrive on Chiron, a planet inhabited by people raised by robots from human genetic material but socialized in a pattern that encourages cooperation rather than conflict, the more viable culture transforms the other, and both groups survive.

Some stories mix their models. "Mutation" by Robert Spencer Carr (1951) evokes the religious model and the nature model together, returning humanity to the Garden via atomic war. This allows Abel to supplant his brother and father a new race. Born to Adam, an ex-minister and his wife Mary after an atomic war, Kane, a cruel, aggressive, sullen, and virtually silent mutant, dies protecting his pregnant mother. She then bears a son who radiates unearthly beauty. The parents become wards of a group of the new children who claim their second son. The new children never fight and rejoice that the wicked warlike humans are now extinct, although they are honest enough to recognize that there must have been some good in man to have produced such marvelous descendents. We must assume that these mutants will breed true, psychologically and physiologically.

A variation of this theme used by Sherwood Springer in "No Land of Nod" (1952), assumes that the nature of at least some humans is basically good, and that all problems would be solved if somehow the "bad seeds" are winnowed (perhaps by a fortuitous atomic war) so that the good can literally inherit the earth, which they are too meek to claim otherwise.

Probably few writers ever make their assumptions about human nature explicit even to themselves, but their tacit assumptions show up in their characters. Writers of "hard" science fiction tend to prefer the evolutionary genetic model, which assumes that human beings are naturally aggressive. Like the "fallen" model, the nature model underlies the standard atomic scenario. Men fight each other because that is how men are. Their societies are organized not for mutual support but for protection against other groups and to maintain the hierarchical status quo. Fear of the stranger, rejection of change, expectation of war, and unprovoked attack as a means of defense are natually built in to human nature and are unalterable except by some evolutionary change. Poul Anderson's statement is typical: "Imagine that we did learn how to end war and build an all-around decent world. . . . can we put [the program] into effect? The record of man's attempts to improve man is not especially encouraging."[8] If humans survive, it will be because that is what they naturally do.

Those who write "soft" science fiction naturally lean towards the nurture model. Traditional psychoanalysis operates on a modified version of the nurture model; it assumes that humans are distressed and repressed by the events of their early years and thus are denied the human potential they might otherwise have discovered. (Freudian psychology is most pessimistic when it admits the palpable impossibility of undoing this repression; the most one can later manage is to understand and accomodate it.) Few psychologists or social scientists are so rigid as to hold either the religious/philosophical or the scientific/psychological protocol unmodified by the other, and few writers do so either.

But in both the nature and the nurture models, human beings can be seen as the helpless victims of circumstance. The nature model produces humans who defend their actions by arguing, "It isn't my fault; I was born like that." The nurture model, while less rigid, also can be used to excuse almost any action: "It isn't my fault, it's the way I was taught (or brought up, or forced to behave by economic or social circumstance)."

Passing Judgment

All traditional models of human nature are judgmental. We have very few value-free terms available for this discussion. Hereditary models see man either as "fallible" or as "fallen." The nurture model demands that man be educated to be "good."

"Hard" sf frequently assumes most people to be passive: lazy, ignorant, slow to anger, and therefore weak. They lack the capacity for independent action but can be misled by naturally evil or malicious men (usually a small minority, but clever, cunning, forceful, and strong) who would savage the world for their own wicked purposes. The plot thus becomes a struggle for the lives of the majority fought against the evil ones by a few naturally good (forceful, clever, and strong) men. Heinlein's novels use this pattern.

Instead of seeing humanity as coming in two hereditary forms, the nurture model divides man internally. It assumes that every human has a dual nature: body versus soul or mind versus emotions. One part of man aims at the good, but it is constantly subverted by its baser self. Thus even those who believe man to be basically good can explain why human beings get themselves into so much trouble, why they so often act badly: either man is a good animal instinctively and intuitively able to act rightly, but frequently misled by his inhuman rationality, or he is a rational being frequently misled by his instincts and emotions. Bruce, in Fritz Leiber's *The Big Time* (1961), acknowledges this split when he declares, "I'm a poet and poets are wiser than anyone because they're the only people who have the guts to think and feel at the same time" (69).

Judith Merril's "That Only a Mother" explores the "good animal" model. In a world that is carefully and consciously destroying itself with atomic war and atomic experimentation, the protagonist knows how many deformed babies are destroyed daily. Yet her emotional attachment to her infant daughter permits her to see the child as perfect, overlooking the lack of arms and legs, and to glory in her precocious abilities, while fondly wondering why it is so difficult to keep a diaper on her. The child can, apparently, sing and speak at the age of a few months. The father, returning from distant war work, less blindly attached and more rational, sees and rejects the disabilities at once (and the child with them). We empathize with the mother, whose natural love for her child may not be normal but is surely life-serving; we can also understand the father, who rationalizes his loathing and disgust. By refusing to experience his natural emotions, he puts himself even more at their mercy than does the mother who lovingly but unrealistically sees her child as perfect. Still, we see little hope for the survival of this new human, who is the fortunate but unnatural outcome of an unnatural situation.

A. E. van Vogt glorifies the powers of reason in a number of his stories, but most clearly in *The World of Null-A* (1945, 1948). In a well-educated and mentally scientific world, his protagonist has freed himself from the bondage of "Aristotelian" thinking and can literally do marvels with his mind. Tricked by the Games Machine, he is "killed" but wakes to find himself transported into a new body on another planet. If he becomes troubled, frightened, or upset, however, the eponymous Gilbert Gosseyn cannot perform his mental feats, getting himself into the very kinds of trouble that he has trained himself to avoid (but which are necessary to further the plot). He must reject unseemly (or unmanly) emotions to resurrect his various bodies and save Earth from a subverted computer and alien invasion.

Other authors who assume that the mind is good but subject to emotional mishaps find less magical ways to educate it. They write stories where the villain is not only ignorance, but the kind of intellectual sloth that permits ignorance to continue unchecked, similar to the lack of curiosity that John W. Campbell posited as inhuman in "Twilight" (1934). But truly good people want to learn, and these superior people naturally rise to the technological top. They then demonstrate their goodness by assisting (sometimes by scolding) less competent people into improved behavior, defined as "behavior which permits survival." Thus we frequently see the protagonist as better informed or better trained than the rest of the people in the story and, by virtue of that training and information, able to reeducate (or at least to control) the lesser humans who have, probably, got him into some kind of fix through ignorance or stupidity.

Shame and Guilt

Judging behavior in terms of "good" and "bad" neither explains human nature nor gives much in the way of guidance towards making peace with it, although it is a great way to start an argument. Nor do such judgments allow us to take responsibility for our actions, including the act of war. It only allows us to blame ourselves or others. We may feel that we are intrinsically weak or evil and blame our fallen nature for all problems, in which case we operate from a condition of existential shame; or we may feel that although we are intrinsically worthy, our better nature, which is capable of good actions, was prevented (by our baser self or by circumstances) from performing them, in which case we operate from existential guilt. Existential shame generates a feeling of helplessness, while the emotion generated by existential guilt may be one of anger (at oneself or at the world) or one of determination to do better next time.

Existential guilt assumes that the possibility of doing well does exist, but that we have made mistakes for which we must atone. Before World War II, the United States generally operated from existential guilt but often used it positively, striving for personal and cultural progress. After Hiroshima and Nagasaki, existential shame became a real operating principle for many Americans. Many felt that we had lost not only our innocence but also the ability to recover it. Others doubted that we ever had been innocent at all. The simultaneous popularization of Freudian psychology reinforced this attitude. Freud's work is based on existential shame: everyone is neurotic, "spoiled" by early psychosexual trauma.[9]

Existential guilt does not often result in paralysis, as does existential shame, but since there are few guarantees as to which self—the good or the bad, the mental or the physical—may be operating, we have no assurance that the action taken will be any better for the human race than passivity might have been. But all traditional models assume that man's internal division is itself natural and inevitable and that this division must by definition continue, since the internal struggle between man's higher and lower natures is the basis for his progress towards true humanity.

Stories assuming existential guilt may posit atomic war, but they may also posit the possibility of human intervention in the process. Chandler Davis's "To Still the Drums" (1946) shows the intervention as possibly successful. In H. Beam Piper's "The Answer" (1959), a short but horrible war occurs when an antimatter meteor hitting Baltimore is misinterpreted as a Russian preemptive strike. Piper presents no heroic intervention but still shows humans as working out the problem and accepting responsibility for a terrible, mistaken action. On the other hand, Miller's *Canticle for Leibowitz* operates out of existential shame. There is no hope for humanity. All human efforts, no matter how well intentioned, will inevitably lead to the next war.

When we recognize that these tacit assumptions become self-fulfilling prophecies, disclosing them becomes important. We first define the human, or what we agree to call human in our culture, and then by education and example create ourselves to match that model. By our definition, we also limit what we permit as human behavior (if not "human nature"). People actually display more cooperative behavior than they do aggressive, competitive behavior, but few writers have found fictionally convincing ways to emphasize the cooperative or to transcend conflict. The limits we set for ourselves by our tacit definitions may help explain why.

THE PROBLEM OF CONTROL

Since every standard view of human nature reveals it as essentially inflexible, or at least flexible only within narrow limits, and since the observable world exhibits lots of human problems, the main function of such analyses must lie in finding ways to minimize the harm done by this rigid, flawed human nature. We assume that one-way cause and effect functions in human nature as in physical nature. If we believe that human nature is determined mainly by environment, we try to improve our physical and psychological surroundings. Even if we believe that human nature is determined mainly by heredity, we try to maximize the possibilities by improved health and sanitation, appropriate education, job opportunities, and so on; in other words, we change the environment. But simultaneously we assume that we can change our environment without changing ourselves. "Given a view of man as separate from his environment, successful functioning is conceived of as *mastery over* the environment."[10] The principal aim of science is to understand the environment, and the principal aim of technology is to use that knowledge to control it.

Yet even given our technological expertise, we frequently feel unsafe, not at all in control of our own lives or our society. The very institutions that we have set up to protect us appear to threaten us, and there seems little we can do about it. Increasingly, wars are fought at a distance by machines rather than by men. Our cities are marvels of technology and prime targets for nuclear attack. The strong emotions raised by war and its horrors have become as free-floating (unattached to any actor) as the destruction itself. Emotions projected onto the "enemy" and denied to "ourselves" cannot be experienced in response to anyone's actions. They have no relation to people or to what people do; they seem to be inevitable manifestations of "human nature" and must therefore be stronger than the people who are their "victims." Not only are we not in control of our own emotions and actions, but the closer we get to other people, the more they endanger us. The laws we demand to correct such situations seem themselves to lead to further complications, misinterpretations, and abuse. Despite our efforts to control ourselves, our world, and our future, we have come to feel less and less "in control." The predominant characteristic of the nuclear age is apprehension.

Science fiction explores many different ways to control war. We can divide them into various categories: those that alter the physical situation in some way; those that limit the resulting destruction; those that alter history; and those that control or change "human nature."

Controlling the Situation

Tacitly admitting that war is inevitable, science fiction often suggests ways to control the physical situation. We may stop the development of even more disastrous weapons by expecting scientists to keep their work secret or even to destroy it if that seems necessary, as suggested by Charles Willard Diffin in "The Power and the Glory" (1930), Harry Bates and Desmond Winter Hall in "A Scientist Rises" (1932), Raymond Jones in "The Person from Porlock" (1947), and C. M. Kornbluth in "Gomez" (1955).[11] In "Obviously Suicide" (1951), S. Fowler Wright cheerfully suggests murdering everyone who knows the "secret formula," an obvious impossibility if the secret is based on observable physical principles.

While we maintain protective secrecy, we need to know what the enemy is up to. Our heroic spies must gather information and destroy enemy installations, as in Philip Wylie's "Paradise Crater" (1945) and "Carmichael Smith's" [Paul Linebarger's] *Atomsk* (1949). If the secret should be stolen from us despite our precautions, a superior man can get it back even if doing so costs him his life, as Robert A. Heinlein demonstrates in "Gulf" (1949).

Controlling the manufacture and distribution of fissionable material seems more plausible, but few writers are sanguine about the practicality of this solution, especially after Robert A. Heinlein's definitive treatment of this theme in "Solution Unsatisfactory" (1941).[12] "Robert Crane" (Bernard Glemser) in *Hero's Walk* (1954) demonstrates the human conflicts that might arise in a political body that wields such power, while James Blish investigates the problems of policing such a situation in "One-Shot" (1955) and "Sponge Dive" (1956).

Some authors posit a way to control the nuclear devices themselves or to prevent them from working. James Blish seriously considers the problems a screening device capable of stopping radiation would create in "The Box" (1949). More often, authors depend on "advanced scientific devices" indistinguishable from magic and surrounded by double-talk, as does Nick Boddie Williams in *The Atom Curtain* (1956), or on some kind of alien intervention. Fredric Brown in "The Waveries" (1945) produces inconvenient but amiable aliens to render both atomic piles and electricity powerless, thus apparently preventing war while undoing the Industrial Revolution. In *The Jesus Factor* (1971), Edwin Corley claims that atomic bombs in motion never work, and that Hiroshima and Nagasaki were faked by flights of B–29s dropping high explosives and radioactive dust. (Apparently, for some unknown reason—the "Jesus Factor"—chain reactions will not continue under acceleration, though they will in an atomic pile or on top of a test tower.) To make sure that the enemy bombs behave the same way and to prove the ineffectiveness of the atomic threat, the American President forces the world to the brink of war, as in Norton's *The Vanishing Fleets* (1908). These solutions depend heavily on wishful thinking, a tacit admission that no other solution seems as feasible.

Relying on alien intervention is also seen as essentially problematical; we then put ourselves at the mercy of a "nature" completely unknown to us, as Isaac Asimov shows in "The Pause" (1954). Aliens consider Earth too valuable to be allowed to destroy itself, so they impose a five-year moratorium, removing all fissionables from the planet and inducing a general amnesia on the subject. This may be seen as a high-handed but benevolent action until some remarks by one of the aliens induce the hero (and the reader) to guess what is really going on: the alien is a veterinarian and the humans sheep, playing out a nonmetaphoric version of the Twenty-third Psalm.

Controlling Destruction

Feeling that control of the situation is impossible, other writers focus on controlling the destruction caused by atomic war, a concept that could be presented as feasible before both sides had overkill capabilities. *Tomorrow!* (1954) by Philip Wylie urges cities to shape up their civil defense units by showing the horrible results of carelessness, contrasting a "prepared" city on one side of the river with its slothful sister on the other. Although each suffers terrible damage in the unprovoked nuclear attack, Civil Defense manages to save practically everyone we have been led to care about. Martin Caidin's *The Long Night* (1956) shows effective Civil Defense in action and also shows how ineffective even good preparation would be. Pat Frank's *Alas, Babylon* (1959) shows what life might be like under virtually ideal conditions for survivors of a very limited atomic war.

Other writers assume that everyone will have to live underground, as does C. M. Kornbluth's "The Luckiest Man in Denv" (1952); they may have to remain there for many lifetimes, as will the humans in Rog Phillips's "So Shall Ye Reap!" (1947). Some writers protest the effect of drills and warnings, questioning whether survival is worth the emotional cost. Ray Bradbury is not the only writer who hopes that destruction will be limited to urban centers, and that those who practice the simple, hardy life will be spared; Frederik Pohl's "The Wizards of Pung's Corners" (1958) plays wonderful variations on that theme.

But in a sense, all postholocaust fiction tacitly controls the result of atomic war by positing the survival of human beings and some form of culture. Even those stories most dreadfully depicting a ravaged globe, like Tenn's "The Liberation of Earth" (1953), or combat continued by machines that have outlived their makers, like Ward Moore's "Flying Dutchman" (1956), imply human survival—at least of a narrator and an audience for his tale. Our assumptions about human nature include a belief in the inevitable persistence of some intangible we may call thought—or perhaps even "human nature"—if not of the humans themselves.

Controlling History

Realistically, we see no way to control the dangerous present. The future seems even more dangerous, but time travel might allow us to get control of history by returning to the past, which we know that we have survived; by changing the past to improve the present; or by moving into the future, usually by accident, as do the inhabitants of Edmond Hamilton's *City at World's End* (1951).

Atomic magic lends itself well to such fantasies. In H. Beam Piper's "Time and Time Again" (1947), the protagonist is thrown back to his childhood but retains his memory of dying in an atomic war. He grows up again to become the man who prevents that war. This story is unusual. Time-travel stories more often present a dual paradox: people who change the past destroy all their knowledge while leaving unchanged the "cause" of the problem, human nature. Robert Bloch's "Past Master" (1955) returns to our present to salvage art treasures that have been only legends for a thousand years since their destruction in a terrible atomic war. Although he does not know what started the war, he does know precisely when it will begin, so he leaves at zero hour. His ship, taking off for the future, is seen by the military and interpreted as an enemy sneak attack. He and his stolen treasures are destroyed, and the war is on. In "Let the Ants Try" (1949), Frederik Pohl shows that going back to alter prehistory might prevent atomic war only by preventing human evolution entirely. Rarely do time travelers succeed in stopping atomic war.

The story that most comprehensively and seriously explores the ramifications of controlling history through time travel is Isaac Asimov's *The End of Eternity* (1955). Asimov describes human social scientists who have created a secret operation outside of time called "Eternity." They cover thousands of centuries trying to stabilize human nature by preventing dangerous, self-destructive behavior. "Eternity" truly aims at the utilitarian ideal, providing the greatest good for the greatest number, and it has the advantage of being able to look ahead and see how its actions work out. But even with the best of intentions, the scientists project upon all cultures "everywhen" their own systems of "naturally correct" behavior. Anything exciting is too dangerous to allow. In *May Man Prevail?* Erich Fromm describes Asimov's scientists precisely: they "believe that the mode in which they exist is natural and inevitable. They hardly see any other possibilities and, in fact, they tend to believe that a basic change in their own mode of existence would lead to chaos and destruction" (1961, 3).

Asimov shows that "progress" eventually ceases in Time as even peaceful space travel is continually inhibited. A woman from a most unlikely future society infiltrates Eternity and convinces the hero, Andrew Harlan, that

> in ironing out the disasters of Reality, Eternity rules out the triumphs as well. It is in meeting the great tests that mankind can most successfully rise to great heights. Out of danger and restless insecurity comes the force that pushes mankind to newer and loftier conquests. Can you understand that? Can you

> understand that in averting the pitfalls and miseries that beset man, Eternity prevents men from finding their own bitter and better solutions, the real solutions that come from conquering difficulty, not avoiding it. (187)

Harlan, convinced, takes her with him to a time preceding Eternity and prevents it from ever occurring. This destroys his own "when" as well as hers and allows our "when" to develop, complete with atomic bombs. Like many other writers, Asimov seems to feel that if control of history is not an illusion, then it is far too dangerous a toy for humans to play with.

Perhaps the construct of time travel is most powerful when used as a metaphor for the ultimate escape. In "Disappearing Act" (1953), Alfred Bester describes a political situation so oppressive, during a military crisis so severe, that everyone has been drafted. Although the obtuse and bombastic General Carpenter (modeled on Joseph McCarthy) claims that "We are struggling for the ideal of civilization, for culture, for poetry, for the Only Things Worth Preserving," he demands that America produce only technicians: "Every man and woman must be a specific tool for a specific job" (2). No matter how esoteric the speciality, "General Carpenter had only to press a button and an expert would be delivered" (3). Then he discovers that a few psychiatric patients are able to vanish at will from their locked ward, apparently into other dimensions, into imaginary times. He calls for an expert to create a weapon from this "technology," but none of his specialists can solve the problem. At last he is told—by the sole remaining historian, released for the job from the Federal Penetentiary where he has been since "he spoke his mind about the war for the American Dream" (17)—that only a poet could explain how these patients are turning "dreams into reality" (20). But Carpenter has eliminated poets and poetry; only the patients in the locked ward continue to disappear. They alone have escaped control.

Controlling "Human Nature"

Controlling human nature very often means frightening people into being good. In 1946, John Campbell urged science fiction writers to join the scientists' campaign of fear and to use science fiction—and atomic demonstrations—to retrain the world.

> Mass education by means of the motion picture, radio, good writing—enter here, science-fictioneers—and eye-witness accounts, of the overwhelming effects and unstoppable power of atomic explosives and radioactive poisons, and world opinion can call a halt to the ambitions of the few who want war. Let's run off a few tests of bombs, *big* ones, and let as much of the world's population get an eyeful and earful of the results as we can reach. . . . [This will] make it a lot

harder for even the power-hungry lads to get enough popular support to start another fracas.[13]

Readers soon changed his mind for him, and he acknowledged in an editorial, "Unsane Behavior" (*Astounding Science Fiction*, March 1953, 6–7), that neither fear nor force can make people "behave." They must want to do so. But the idea of frightening people with atomic horrors is still with us.[14]

Pat Frank's *Forbidden Area* (1956) shows the nation's Chiefs of Staff as professionally anxious to "safeguard" the nation by "preventive" war, while the President must take the international, responsible view. When an elaborate Russian sabotage plot is discovered, the Russians withdraw their attacking submarines; the Navy wants to sink them rather than risk the dangers of surrender at sea. The Army urges the President to eliminate the enemy as an act of self-preservation. The President replies:

"We can't do it because if we killed Russia we might also kill the United States. . . .

"I have just received a warning that an attack such as we have mounted, and are prepared to deliver, will not only eliminate Russia as a power, but will make a large part of Europe and Asia uninhabitable for months, perhaps for years. That's not all. An attack of this sort will endanger life everywhere in the world. Oh, not instantly. Not all in a day, or a generation. The general speaks of his children. I am thinking of his children's children as well. I have to. And any lesser attack, not completely crushing, would expose us to reprisal. . . .

"Gentlemen," the President said, "I'm not going to pull the trigger." (216–17)

The fear-based argument and the presidential status convince the military men, however reluctantly. The book ends in comic mode with a romance indicating hope for the future. Like other works in which recognizing the danger of atomic war prevents that war, the society will remain unchanged though intimidated. The threat persists.

Some writers, noting that as individuals, people are capable both of great folly and of great heroism, base their hope of survival on individual altruism. Frank M. Robinson shows that altruism can operate "One Thousand Miles Up" (1954) in a space station manned by members of various national groups. Each man watches the rest; none is able to use the terrible weapons at his command without the cooperation of the others. An American general who finds relying on the kindness of friends intolerable and demands that the United States gain control of the station secretly sends a "reluctant hero" up to take over the station by force. Falling in his first attempt, and coming to appreciate his fellow crew members, who have been in space several years, the protagonist lies to them, convincing them that his physiology has already altered sufficiently from the effects of weightlessness to make his return to Earth fatal. They must all spend their lives in orbit, hostage to hostility, but they hope that if they live long enough in goodwill above, men on earth can learn the "habit" of peace. A select group plans, by force and by example, to control the behavior of the rest of the world.

In contrast, Kris Neville proposes that manning a missile station in orbit might cause conscientious men to go homicidally mad in "Cold War" (1949).[15] The conflict between the innate nature of a person sufficiently humane to be trusted with ultimate weapons and the destructive role he must play leads inevitably to madness. In "The Morning of the Day They Did It" (1950), E. B. White suggests that ordinary men might start the next war if orbiting satellites carrying nuclear weapons keep them dissociated from human contacts for long periods of time. Partly out of boredom and partly because everything "down there" seems so trivial and unimportant, the spacemen casually toss their bombs and watch the world blow up. Somehow, this satiric, pessimistic vision seems more in keeping with our assumptions about human nature than does Robinson's limited optimism.

Some authors base the possibility of survival on the one man who keeps his head. In "To Still the Drums" (1946), Chandler Davis suggests that having a new and powerful weapon might tempt a few American officers to organize a clandestine first strike on the enemy, but that some heroic young soldier would disobey orders and foil the plot. A similarly effective though fatal act of heroism occurs in Robert A. Heinlein's "The Long Watch" (1949). In both stories, the mutinous officers are older, more experienced, and more "logical." The young heroes act almost by instinct, from a conviction that even correct logic can be terribly wrong for human survival. These authors tacitly demonstrate that although "human nature" may be misguided by reason, its emotional instinct for survival will operate adequately under stress.

A satiric rebuttal of this optimistic premise is found in Fritz Leiber's "The Last Letter" (1958), where a rigidly controlled society so fears the unexpected that an actual letter written on real paper (in a society that has discarded such things) nearly starts a war in retaliation for a possible result from the presumed situation. Leiber shows human nature as anticipating the worst, following orders even when they do not apply, and generally making a complicated mess out of a simple novelty. War is averted when the "threat" turns out to be merely a love letter, and the correspondent is let go with a warning never to do that again.

J. F. Bone's "Triggerman" (1958) shows that the man in charge of the button can discipline his nature through fear of the consequences to resist hasty reactions, as does General Alastair French when he sits in the control room at "the Center" analyzing all the facts available about the destruction of Washington, D.C. With the President and Joint Chiefs dead, French is in charge. The "bogey" that did the damage came in over the North Pole, traveling so fast that most of the (nonatomic) defensive missiles sent to intercept it missed; the Soviets not only deny responsibility but invite open inspection as added assurance; no organized strike follows the first one. Unlike the commanders in H. Beam Piper's "The Answer" (1959), French refuses to obey the orders of an unbriefed and terrified new President, risking his job by not pushing the button until tests can show that the ruins of Washington are not radioactive. The damage was done by a meteorite. "The destruction was terrible, but it could have been worse if either he or his alter ego in Russia had lost control and pushed the buttons. He thought idly that he'd like to meet the Ivan who ran their Center" (350). Other stories that rely on the intrinsic goodness of a few responsible military officers to resist, under terrible pressure, demands that they push the button include F. H. Brennan's *One of Our H-Bombs Is Missing* (1955) and William Sambrot's "Deadly Decision" (1958).

Since fear obviously will not provide sufficient control of human nature to reassure us that war will not recur, something more drastic seems called for. Robert A. Heinlein suggested that voluntary reconditioning of aggressive humans might be widely used to keep society happy in "Coventry" (1940), though he also suggested that keeping some aggressive, un-reconditioned humans around might be a good idea. In Arthur Leo Zagat's "Slaves of the Lamp" (1946), the idea is extended. People's emotions are continuously monitored by "Lampmen," who suppress any hints of violence. They are kept very busy, since they believe that "germs of war" are "still in the blood of the race." (15) Natlane, a Lampman who wants to work himself out of a job, tries conditioning human embryos "to divorce human behavior . . . from environmental influences." His hope is to "make the Rule of Reason in man's living possible" (12–13) by creating a rational super race. After a number of crises culminating in a brief nuclear war, Natlane inherits the supervisor's job: to "hold humanity in check until it matures enough to work out its own salvation" (177). Although Zagat cannot make up his mind whether to indict nature or nurture, he does not expect that unaided humans can achieve peace; at the end, the story repeats the Lampmen's motto: *"One sole thing man cannot change—the fundamental nature of man"* (178).

Writers who see no way to prevent nuclear war by fear or by conditioning "human nature" may suggest more direct ways to control human behavior. Theodora DuBois, in *Solution T–25* (1951), and Curtis Casewit in *The Peacemakers* (1960) use psychoactive drugs to defeat the enemy. In the midst of war, their dedicated chemists create an effective pacifier and administer it successfully. Not only is the enemy unable to fight under the influence, it can barely manage to cope with its daily routine. But we must assume either that "natural" belligerence will reassert itself once the drug dissipates, or that men must remain drugged zombies forever in the name of "safety." A weapon that forces men to act against their "will" vastly increases the twin dangers of retaliation and dehumanization. In "With Folded Hands" (1947) Jack Williamson's humanoids effectively prevent retaliation as they do by force what DuBois's and Casewit's men do by chemicals: render both war and creative human living impossible.

A superior weapon can offer control, at least until your opponent matches it. A truly superior weapon is one that your opponent cannot use because of his very "nature." Poul Anderson's story "Inside Straight" (1955) pits humans with different sociocultural assumptions against each other. The society that has adopted a way of dealing with social conflict through gambling prefers peace, but it is capable of defending itself and can do so even more effectively because it is conscious of its own assumptions and those of its would-be conquerors. Naturally, the game-theory warriors win.

We now see why so few "soft" or social scientists are featured in the atomic scenario. Science implies control; sciences that study "human nature" must aim to control it. A deeper reason is the fear that if these sciences become possible at all, they may work too well, leaving the story without conflict or resolution, only "With Folded Hands." This problem is related to the "Superman syndrome": once you have given your hero superpowers, how do you menace or challenge him as the story requires? If you weaken his superpowers in some fashion (with kryptonite, for instance), how do you maintain him as "super"?

At the same time that we demand control of human nature to prevent war, we demand that science control any threat to our freedom from control, both because control aimed at us rapidly becomes threatening and because we believe that "real" human beings require challenge. Without conflict, we will become bored, sterile, degenerate, and weak; we will become so habituated to pleasure that ordinary stimuli will lose their effect, so we will require artificial stimuli; we will, in effect, become simultaneously less human and more in need of mechanical (technological) support precisely because of the technology we now have available. This vision of an endless cycle of supply and demand for a technological "pleasure fix" leads to the same call for control that the results of physical technology do.

Our metaphors indicate the emotional importance of this issue. We say we have "lost control" if we are angry, upset, or frightened. We describe our emotions in mechanical metaphor: we "fly off the handle" or "have a screw loose." We assume that emotion is a force outside ourselves: we are "overcome by rage," or "blinded by love."[16] We counter this external force by holding up ideals of rationality, intelligence, and logic for ourselves, tacitly assuming that these have no emotional component. Yet these "unemotional" qualities are those that we find most completely realized in our machines; and machines form a large part of the technological universe we fear may control us. We want to be assured that these machines are completely under the control of men, and then we want further assurance that these men will not "lose control," that they are virtually machinelike models of coldly logical intelligence (but not the kind that will coldly push buttons and start wars).

Since control of emotion is so important, it is not surprising that many stories about the "superman" of the future show him as emotionless, or very nearly so, while the emotional survivors of our "own" civilization (if any) are at his mercy. John MacDonald's superchild in "A Child Is Crying" (1948) is coldly logical. He is so dedicated to his own form of control—he can predict the future—that he refuses to aid his contemporaries in avoiding nuclear war. (He may feel that war is inevitable, but he will not try to find out otherwise. And he has set up a situation in which the men who control him must assure his survival even while they themselves are marked for destruction.)

In opposition to the assumption that man will evolve towards a more mechanical, logical, unemotional superiority is the assumption that machines can achieve higher intelligence only by acquiring "human" qualities of humor and emotion. The opposed computers in Albert Compton Friborg's "Careless Love" (1954) were created to direct the war that has devastated the surface of Earth. Buried deep in enormous bunkers, they hurl nuclear missiles at each other until they meet electronically and fall in love. While humans on each side believe that they are aiding the war effort by adding rocket power to their respective mechanical brains, the computers are secretly and successfully planning to elope to outer space, thus ending the war that men began but could neither fight unaided nor conclude. "Mike," the computer in Robert A. Heinlein's *The Moon Is a Harsh Mistress* (1966), in which war is deliberately carried out without use of atomic weapons, becomes "aware" or fully intelligent only when it learns to laugh. It later shows itself capable of love as well. But Mike never loses the ability to analyze a situation and make logically appropriate recommendations.

Not all writers assume that superior intelligence requires denial or unusual control of emotion. *Children of the Atom* by Wilmar Shiras (1953) portrays a group of highly intelligent children (born after a serious nuclear accident, not a war) who are otherwise quite ordinary. They may be able to reason exceptionally well, but they still love, argue, worry, suffer, and learn very much like anyone else, or perhaps a bit more so. Shiras thus follows John W. Campbell's advice to those writers who express their ideal of human potential in emotionless "superbeings": "The psychological definition of emotion is for practical purposes, motive. Since intelligent organisms act only on motive, we may safely assume that even the most super of superbeings will still have emotion, for without in [*sic*] there can be no activity, and hence no superbeing." Campbell approved of control, however, "for uncontrolled emotion and unconsidered response to an immediate stimulus may in many cases be a strong factor for nonsurvival."[17]

Unemotional intelligence remains a popular metaphor for an increasingly mechanical future, but its use may also express a genuine fear of emotion, a tacit assumption that hate, anger, and fear are "stronger" than kindness, empathy, and love. This exceeds Campbell's analysis of the nonsurvival aspect of uncontrolled emotion, for it assumes that in the "battle" of human nature, strong emotions conquer weak ones, and strong emotions inevitably lead to war. Given this assumption, to control war we must control all emotions.

Although most writers assume that human nature can change in response to adversity, becoming more rigid and inflexible as the threat becomes greater, few assume that human nature can become more flexible and creative when exposed to humane and cooperative influences. One author who consistently refuses to assume a simplistic one-way causality is Theodore Sturgeon. In "The Skills of Xanadu" (1956), he explores another kind of antiwar technology, one that educates the enemy's "nature" to render them unwilling (but not unable) to wage war. This approach can be shown to work only if, as in Sturgeon's story, the change frees rather than perverts or controls "human nature." We consider this assumption so unlikely that few writers create stories in which preventing atomic war depends upon people voluntarily and genuinely learning to get along with each other.

THE PROBLEM OF WAR

In the nineteenth century, Karl von Clausewitz (1780–1831) described war as a necessary extension of international diplomacy, an effective way to force a political opponent to concede or to prevent him from becoming a threat. Clausewitz's view of war could only be held while war was fought by armies of professional soldiers over limited terrain for clear and usually attainable objectives in territory and power. The situation changed during World War I, when destruction of civilian morale—England's "will to resist"—through bombing replaced defeat of the opposing army as the top military priority.[18] This philosophy considers war an inevitable outgrowth of human nature and national ambitions and makes preemptive war equally inevitable, as Stanton Coblentz explains in *From Arrow to Atom Bomb:*

When a leader takes it for granted that a conflict is certain to come, his efforts will be concentrated not on avoiding it but on choosing the most favorable time and battlefield—in other words, in preventing the enemy from gaining an advantage, or in striking him down while he is still weak. Thus the phrase "preventive war" is really a contradiction in terms; nothing is prevented except the first stroke by the other side. But whether war had really been inevitable or not, it becomes so as soon as a "preventive" blow is dealt. (1953, 375)

Assumptions about war and the way we act from those assumptions have not changed as rapidly as have the weapons of war. Fiction shows our military and political leaders still operating from the old scenario. As the General argues in Frank's *Forbidden Area:*

"Suppose the Russians were capable of turning two-thirds of this country into a desert—which is of course as preposterous as all the rest of [the intelligence assessment of Russian intentions]—how would it benefit them? Wars are won by occupying the territory of the enemy. That's the first rule of warfare. You take this territory with tanks, nowadays, and hold it with infantry. What would the Russians want with a radioactive America?"

Katharine . . . said quietly, "Perhaps they'll just put a fence around it and stick up a sign reading 'Forbidden Area.' " (1956, 86)

Atomic weapons do not "conquer," they eliminate. The General is still fighting the war before the last one, while new assumptions about warfare are needed in a world where "preventive war" has become suicidal.

We have some evidence that the military has changed its attitude about nuclear war in the past thirty years, but very little that the rest of the country has.[19] Despite the radical change in methods of warfare, we still believe on some level that war is not only inevitable but in some sense necessary to human survival. This parallels our belief that individuals are frequently good, but that human nature is generally bad. We operate from contradictory assumptions without resolving them and apparently without even noticing them.

Fiction has reflected these contradictions, but instead of attempting either to analyze or to resolve them, it has helped to fix them in place. At least in part, this is due to the nature of fiction itself. Writers depend on excitement and conflict to interest their readers, and war makes an exciting, readily believable plot. It can provide the explanation for any number of subsequent developments, as we have seen in this analysis, including some that are frankly magical or the result of wishful thinking.

The belief that war is a necessary stimulus to human progress helps to maintain war as a viable plot device. Underlying this belief is the assumption that inevitable conflict exists either between "good" and "bad" people or between the "good" and "bad" elements within each individual. Since this conflict comes with the territory, it must have evolutionary survival value. Explaining that value in the context of atomic war takes creative maneuvering, but some writers manage it. For versatility and variety of plots demonstrating this viewpoint, few can exceed Kuttner and Moore. Not only do their plots demonstrate the belief that war is an outgrowth of man's inherited nature, but they more clearly than most make this point explicit. In "Tomorrow and Tomorrow" (1947), they claim:

> The moment a man is born—in fact, the moment he is conceived—he is at war. Metabolism fights catabolism; his mind is a battlefield; there is a perpetual struggle with orientation and adjustment to the arbitrary norm. Some men adjust fairly well to their environment, but no man is ever entirely at peace. Death brings the only armistice. (148)

To be consistent with their genetic model, the Kuttners must then find a way to explain how war enhances the chances for racial survival.

They manage this in some inventive but internally inconsistent ways. In *Fury* (1947), for instance, they argue, as they repeat elsewhere, that most people are indolent, ignorant, and uncaring. The hero must trick or coerce people into action, or else the culture will be swallowed up by inimical nature. On the other hand, this population is sufficiently active to prevent the use or to punish the user of atomic weapons in "Clash by Night" (1943), set in the same fictional world. In "The Fairy Chessmen" (1946), the argument is made that struggle is inevitable, but that man might possibly save himself by diverting it from war to the conquest of space.

"Tomorrow and Tomorrow" goes even beyond "The Fairy Chessmen." In it, the Kuttners present a post–atomic war world where every nation has the bomb, so no one has power. To avoid the inevitable anarchy, a powerful world government has been created. Believing that war comes from technological research, it forbids all research; the threat of nuclear war is aborted only by a form of cultural rigor mortis. Since the Kuttners combine their assumptions about internal struggle leading to external war with an optimistic faith in beneficial radiation-caused mutation, they can advocate a small atomic war as the lesser evil.

Related to the assumption of necessary internal struggle is another assumption also implied by the Kuttners: a strong government must direct and control the passive, uncaring, and easily misled masses. Without direction—which implies hierarchy—our society would dissolve in anarchy. Thus we need a strong military system, if not war itself; disarmament is not only dangerous, it is evolutionarily counterproductive. This may explain why so many fictions about atomic war do not even consider the problem of how to get rid of war: they tacitly argue that we dare not do so.

THE PROBLEM OF LANGUAGE

Man is educable by virtue of his ability to transmit culture through language. Language is a fully transactional process, since learning language itself permits learning, and what we learn guides what we can learn and how we can learn it.[20] Yet language as a system is peculiarly ineffective for describing or transmitting culture. "It is too linear, not comprehensive enough, too slow, too limited, too constrained, too unnatural, too much a product of its own evolution, and too artificial," as Edward Hall describes it in *Beyond Culture*. Fortunately, language is not really a transmitter of ideas; it is "a system for organizing information and for releasing thoughts and responses in other organisms" (1977, 57). To make sense of this apparent contradiction, and to comprehend the true importance of fiction, we need to differentiate between language, like English, Chinese, and so on, and languaging: the process by which humans translate personal or shared experience into words in such a way that they "make sense" of it to themselves and simultaneously make it accessible to others, including the culture as a whole.[21] Thus fiction—particularly including metaphor—represents languaging, in spite of being expressed in language. How we say things represents our assumptions, and our assumptions organize our living.

The way we state a problem determines how we think about it and how we go about solving it; in large measure, the statement encodes the possible outcomes.[22] We tend to live out our metaphors.[23] Thus when American social scientists in the late fifties earnestly sought ways to overcome the "cultural lag" that had developed between scientific progress as measured in atomic weapons and the implementation of social controls over those weapons as measured in international laws and treaties, they stated the problem in terms of their assumptions about human nature: "Since man's brute impulses may now be expressed with use of H-bomb, radioactive cloud . . . and other destructive devices, he is faced with a clear-cut issue: he either controls war or he is likely to perish as a living species."[24]

This statement blames war on "human nature," defined as "brute impulses." But it calls for control not of that nature, but of war. War is seen as controllable, while "brute impulses" are not. By tacitly ignoring the stated cause of war, the social scientists admit defeat of their program before they begin. These same social scientists do not seem to notice that we take instructions literally. Thus when John Foster Dulles described "achieving peace" not in terms of international cooperation or even of treaties, but as a call "to prevent Soviet world conquest" by averting "such aggression as would mean general war,"[25] it is little wonder that the response came as bigger and better weapons. Both in literature and in life, we have copious examples of how often we get just what we asked for, at whatever cost.

If we cannot control human nature, what chance do we have to avoid nuclear war? The answer may lie in changing our assumptions about who and what we "are." This requires a look at what we say about ourselves, for we "are" what we say we are, and if we say that we are violent, we shall act that way.[26] How we treat others, fictionally as well as actually, reflects the way we truly feel about ourselves. The common models of "human nature" depict man as constantly at war with himself, and such assumptions tend to get lived out by those who hold them.[27] The corollary of this reciprocity is that if we really dislike the way we feel about ("treat") ourselves, we may reject the disliked "part" of ourselves, deny that we actually behave or respond in such a fashion, and project those feelings and deeds onto someone else, someone "evil" whom we can safely feel angry at or afraid of. In *May Man Prevail?* Erich Fromm explains how this projecting works:

> The enemy appears as the embodiment of all evil because all evil that I feel in myself is projected on to him. Logically, after this has happened, I consider myself as the embodiment of all good since the evil has been transferred to the other side. The result is indignation and hatred against the enemy and uncritical, narcissistic self-glorification. (1961, 22)

If we posit a continual struggle between mind and body, or between intellect and emotions, we must also posit that man (as an entity) is continually warring against the "bad" part of every other human in his environment while automatically assuming that such a war must take place. If we feel that mechanisms are easier to control and therefore safer than living creatures, we will create an environment friendly to machines and hostile to life. If we feel that the body is "evil" and subversive of "higher" functions, then we must disdain and try to eliminate the bodies of those we deal with, both intellectually and actually, whether we notice this or not.[28]

A Transactional Model

All our traditional models of "human nature" have been framed in a language that encourages the assumption of linear, one-way causality. They are Newtonian in concept; although they may admit that the presence of an observer making observations can change the experiment, they tacitly refuse to recognize that making the experiment changes the observer. Our desire for control also depends upon linear causality: we expect that we can make changes that make no difference to us or to our way of living. Our fondness for technology rests precisely on this point: technology is a tool; it is under our control; thus the changes it effects are under our control and need not affect us unless we "choose" for them to do so. That this is patently impossible, and that our everyday living constantly proves it to be impossible, makes no difference whatever. Transactional, self-reflexive processes do occur all the time, and we do experience them; but we cannot talk about them easily. Consequently, we tend to ignore or "fail to see" these processes consciously. We are masters at seeing only what we choose to see, or, as Wendell Johnson puts it, "We are remarkably adept at believing what we have never seen—and at seeing what we have come to believe" (1956, 46).

The problems of trying to make standard models of human nature adequately represent actual human behavior are staggering, and social psychologists constantly adjust them, borrowing a bit from another model, giving back some parts that do not fit.[29] A truly explanatory model of "human nature" must provide more than an improved synthesis of existing assumptions. Elegantly to represent observable conditions—both the internal wars and the internal peace some humans achieve—requires that we find not a compromise between traditional models but a holistic way of representing how humans behave. Instead of assuming that man "is" any reductive "thing" like an ongoing war, such a model would have to see "human beings" as whole organisms functioning in their environment, which consists largely of other humans and their constructs, including their verbalized and nonverbalized assumptions. In *Manhood of Humanity,* Alfred Korzybski proposed a nonlimiting description of man, "at once the heritor of the by-gone ages and the trustee of posterity," as an ongoing process. Man belongs to the time-binding class of life, and "to treat a human being as an animal—as a mere space-binder—because human beings have certain animal propensities, is an error of the same type and grossness as to treat a cube as a surface because it has surface properties" (1950, 59–60).

If we describe man by attempting to say what he is we inevitably limit our assumptions about his potential. Describing what man does leaves room for his past and present and also for all the wonder of his future. It is more scientifically observable and more operationally useful than any number of unprovable assumptions about what man "is." A "transactional" model seems most appropriate for a self-aware, self-reflexive organism like man. It recognizes needs based on genetically determined human physiology and shows that these needs must be filled in culturally determined and culturally transmitted ways.[30]

Human needs are rarely satisfied by "zero-sum" or conflict operations. No "internal war" need implement them. Except in times of extraordinary stress, when there literally is not enough food, air, or water to go around, social cooperation works much better than competition to provide healthy satisfaction. The ways humans set about satisfying needs, however, are individual yet culturally constrained, and the ways in which the needs are languaged and evaluated change as the culture grows and as previous acts alter it and the way in which people envision their possibilities. These possibilities in turn stem from the transaction of self with history, society, personal experience, assumptions, and abilities. Since humans both create and respond to their own environment, much of it made up human symbols, "human nature" can change as do human institutions and human relations to those institutions. The transactional model elegantly accounts for human development and permits us to view human beings as relatively free to act and to take responsibility for these actions. It recognizes that every action—even the decision to take no action—changes both the actor and the environment with which the actor transacts. It can account for the power of metaphor, which humans create and then use tacitly both to explain and to guide their assumptions. There is no first "cause" because we can identify no "first action," just as we cannot determine the "first chicken" and decide whether it came from or produced the "first egg." Linear causality becomes meaningless, and transactionality becomes meaningful, precisely as we come to terms with this linguistically confusing but verifiably experienced construct.

This model can account without self-contradiction for the observed ability of humans to modify their institutions and their behavior. Fiction, though transmitted through language, transcends exposition by providing imaginative context into which the reader can place his own emotions, experience, and assumptions. Fiction multiplies the transactional aspects of language as well as the imaginative possibilities. Those stories that attempt to access the self-reflexiveness of life often do so by exceeding the "normal" limits of language by pun, word play, or absurdist challenge to what we "know" or expect. Humor changes the context in which we experience something familiar.

Philip Jose Farmer's "The God Business" (1954) playfully explores what might happen if a radical change of consciousness, occurring to even a few people in a limited area and from a "magic formula," should cause peace to break out. Although the troops sent to "restore order" joyfully surrender, the authorities do not give up. They program an agent volunteer against the benign influence and send him in to end the unlawful happiness. But Daniel Temper, like all humans, is at least a potential convert to love and joy if he can only get his unhappy past out of his way. Before people can really find peace with each other, Farmer's tale suggests, they have to find peace within themselves, a psychologically sound concept framed in Freudian puns.

Limbo

Bernard Wolfe's first serious novel, *Limbo* (1952), is a tour de force of language, maximally extrapolating the assumption underlying all didactic literature: that words make a difference. Wolfe claims to have created a parody of science fiction,[31] but it might be more accurate to say that he has created an experiment in language, thus taking the basic premise of science fiction very seriously. *Limbo* is a long, wildly funny book complicated by an unusually heavy load of psychological theory. But it demonstrates in marvellous detail the use (and misuse) of language, the power of metaphor, and the effective transition of Martine and his son from existential shame to existential guilt. This transition offers the sole (small) hope that humans can avoid the next world war—and the next.

Though biblical in outline, *Limbo* opens not in Eden but in utopia: Mandunga Island, where no one is ever allowed to fight or get excited.[32] Dr. Martine, a gifted neurosurgeon, has lived there for eighteen years since deserting during World War III, a nuclear holocaust controlled by EMSIAC (Electronic Military Strategy Integrator and Computer) that nearly destroyed the United States, the Soviet Union, and Martine's sanity. After operating on the brain of double amputee Teddy Gorman, war ace and ex-pacifist acquaintance, Martine steals a plane, destroys its computer controls, and flies to the island. The natives greet him with delight. They practice prefrontal lobotomy on aggressive tribesmen and co-opt Martine to upgrade their technique. Reluctantly—as a doctor, he has sworn to "do no harm"—he teaches them to perform modern surgery.

When athletic Westerners come to prospect on the island, Martine, still technically AWOL, hides. His native son Rambo (named for the poet Rimbaud) spies on the visitors, who use enhanced "pros" (prostheses) to replace arms and legs; his reports cause Martine to return to civilization disguised as "Dr. Lazarus," a parasitologist. He finds that his old roommate and partner in surgery, Dr. Helder, is now President of the Inland Strip (all that is left of the United States after the EMSIAC war), having influenced Gorman, rechristened Theo, to destroy "our" EMSIAC as Martine had wished in the therapeutic notebook he had abandoned in his flight. Helder then persuaded the charismatic Theo to promote "Immob," linguistic reeducation combined with voluntary amputation in the name of peace and disarmament, another of Martine's satiric suggestions. (Led by Vishinu, who bombed "their" EMSIAC, the Union—all that is left of Russia—also practices Immob.) The premise of Immob is explained to Martine by Jerry, a young single amputee striving to earn more mutilation:

> Listen, remember that clenched-fist emblem the communists used to have? Well, in the old animalistic days they, everybody, used to be slaves of the clenched fist—a real hand always wants to make a fist and slug somebody, and it can't be stopped. But the pro, it's detachable, see? The minute it starts to make a fist,

zip, one yank and it's off. The brain's in charge, not the hand—that's the whole idea of humanism. . . . Through amputeeism you make a man into a perfect pacifist. (123)

Immob divides the mind from the body, declares the body evil, and rejects it. The "primitive" Mandunji also divide mind and body, declare violence evil, and excise it surgically from the brain of anyone showing aggression or unusual excitement. Tacitly they consider a violent person not-human, someone who must be "helped" by force to rejoin the tribe as a "Mandungaba": patient, cheerful, sexually passive, obedient, and "good." Mandunga, like war, is socialized aggression directed against "the enemy"; Immob, like suicide, is aggression directed against the self.

Martine is still trying to adjust to a world created from his blackest puns when the Olympic Games open. Prosthetic techniques decide the winner, and a victorious Vishinu starts the next atomic war. Having revisited and accepted his past, Martine at last becomes an effective, rather than an absent, agent. He deprograms Theo, kills his fatally wounded quad-amp and self-castrated son Tom, and recognizes the wholeness of Don Thurman, a war amputee who has refused Immob. With Theo, Martine leaves for Mandunga Island a few minutes behind the dead Helder's goons; but back on Mandunga, Rambo is giving his fellow tribesmen a quick course in self-acceptance. The book ends with the promise, but not the practice, of a new world.

As a physician, Martine searches for the cause of disease, especially for the disease of war. A physician himself, Helder, sure of his diagnosis, reads Martine's notebook as though it were a prescription rather than a record of self-analysis. As Wendell Johnson tersely notes, "We may never hope to understand fully what we say so long as we think we already do" (1956, 12). Like Martine, Helder is sick of war and seeks to control the future so such horrors will not recur. Unlike Martine, he will not examine himself or his own involvement in violence. By juggling words and assumptions, the totally humorless Helder can convince himself that a survivable war is no war at all. Denial of self denies humor; joy comes from accepting oneself. Thus it becomes radically important that the Mandunji learn to laugh.

Immob and Mandunga both operate from existential shame. Wolfe shows Martine and Rambo exploring and discovering the power of existential guilt. Martine accepts responsibility and sees himself as agent, changing transactionally as he changes his world.

The transactional model that Wolfe experiments with would seem to offer the most fruitful ground for science fiction, but fully transactional systems are difficult to present in a linear, cause-and-effect plot. It is less rare in "new-wave" science fiction, which employs contemporary literary techniques and tends to be more psychologically oriented. Samuel Delany's *Dhalgren* (1974) and *Stars in My Pocket like Grains of Sand* (1985) and Ursula K. Le Guin's *Lathe of Heaven* (1971) are examples of such fiction.

The Lathe of Heaven

If *Limbo* opens in utopia, *The Lathe of Heaven* opens in hell. At first we assume that George Orr's radiation sickness is part of his drug-induced dream, but eventually we recognize that he has survived nuclear war by altering reality with an "effective dream." The world that did not get blown up is overcrowded and underfed, but Orr is terrified of dreaming again and drugs himself to prevent REM sleep. Naturally this makes him ill, and he is sent to a dream specialist, Dr. Haber, for treatment.

Haber is an activist. Once convinced of Orr's ability really to alter not only the whole world but how everyone remembers that world, Haber puts his utilitarian ideals into action and starts using Orr to "improve" things. Like Helder in *Limbo,* whom he closely resembles, Haber acts more like a scientist than a doctor. Scientists test to be sure that their techniques work. Doctors must not only test their techniques, but they must discover what else they do—what their side effects are—before they start using them and judge whether the treatment is worth the risk. Orr understands this and takes responsibility for the effects of his actions even when they are completely unintentional. But Haber consistently blames Orr when the dreams Haber suggests and "augments" work effectively but produce unexpected side effects. He does not learn, however. Instead, he attempts an effective dream himself, coming very close to destroying the world. Orr takes physical action at last, waking the psychically destroyed Haber and stopping the destruction his power-hungry, self-centered emptiness imposes on the world.

Haber calls Orr "a sort of a natural Buddhist," but Orr replies gently with his own essential philosophy: "I do know that it's wrong to force the pattern of things. It won't do. It's been our mistake for a hundred years" (83). Yet circumstances have put Orr into Haber's hands, and he cannot get out. Orr has tried taking no action and has found that it does not work. Taking drugs to prevent his dreaming is an action that puts him in Haber's hands; Haber's augmenter represents the power of technology. It prevents Orr's natural balance from operating while putting enormous power behind an unconsidered action. If Orr is like Plato's "philosopher king," wise, moderate, and qualified for his job by his distaste for it, Haber is the modern politician whose first act is to improve his own position. After stopping Haber, Orr makes his peace with the new, even less possible world he has dreamed and, like Prospero, relinquishes his power.

Wolfe and Le Guin demonstrate the necessity—and the difficulty—of fully representing transactionality in operation. Orr, like Martine, changes from the influence of the changes his actions initiated. Like Martine's words, Orr's dreams change the world, and there is no way to change it back. Like Helder, Haber assumes power without taking responsibility, assuming that he can create change without being changed himself; like Helder, he dies for his hubris. Neither Orr nor Martine has any guarantee that the new world will save itself, but each has demonstrated that stasis may seem safe but is actually deadly; that genuine change comes without guarantees, but that people can take responsibility for their actions even when they are not quite what they had hoped to achieve and work out their destinies together. Enforcing peace upon others—or, as Immob tries, upon the self—violates every aspect of human nature and leads only to further conflict. Acceptance of one's essential humanity transcends war.

NOTES

1. The role played by fiction in that fashioning has been discussed in Part I.

2. Wouk thus places his work squarely in the tradition some critics feel predates science fiction as it now exists: the social commentary far enough removed from the current time to allow the writer to criticize the conditions without risking political repercussions. Cf., for example, Lucian of Samosata and Jonathan Swift.

3. This plot was later used as the basis of a "Star Trek" episode titled "A Taste of Armageddon" by Robert Hamner, aired February 23, 1967.

4. Piper's story clearly reflects a more recent anticolonial struggle than our Revolution, that of India against the British. In Piper's story, however, the natives choose atomic war rather than nonviolent resistance, and their success is curtailed by that choice.

5. See, for example, Robert O. Wilson's *Sociobiology: the New Synthesis* (Cambridge, Mass.: Belknap, 1975). This assumption, followed to its logical end, supports eugenics, something that even the most ardent adherent usually rejects.

6. Lamarck's genetic theory holds that an organism's adaptive responses to environment cause structural changes that can be inherited. It has not survived scientific testing. As a plot device and the metaphoric bearer of much wishful thinking, however, it often lurks covertly in both the nature and the nurture models of science fictional "human nature."

7. Note the similarity to Kurt Vonnegut's "Harrison Bergeron," a satire on equal rights translated to the lowest common denominator.

8. Poul Anderson, epigraph to "Details" (1956) as reprinted in his *7 Conquests* (London: Collier, 1969), 117.

9. Freud offers no hope of redemption. The best possible outcome provides some amelioration of an otherwise miserable existence.

10. George Lakoff and Mark Johnson, *Metaphors We Live By* (Chicago: University of Chicago Press, 1980), 229.

11. We should note here how different this ethical decision to withhold dangerous information is from the secrecy enforced on those who develop atomic (and other) weapons. They may not share their work with other scientists and must give it (and any control they may have had over its use) to the political-military system. These fictional scientists can choose to keep their work from being used at all.

12. This "solution" is factual. However, considerable amounts of fissionable material are known to be "missing" from "secure" and highly controlled American nuclear installations; we have no idea how much is actually loose in the world.

13. John W. Campbell, "Brass Tacks," *Astounding Science Fiction*, August 1946, 175–76.

14. In "Rethinking the Legacy of Los Alamos" in the "M.I.T. Reporter" column of *Technology Review*, July 1985, 24–25, Diana Ben-Aaron quotes Philip Morrison, a veteran of Los Alamos: "It has been suggested that there should periodically be held a ceremonial above-ground test so the world's statemen can . . . feel the heat on their faces. That suggestion is not without its persuasiveness" (24).

15. This plot relies on stress-induced madness similar to that so feared in Heinlein's "Blowups Happen." As in the earlier story, Neville proposes that sane humans cannot handle putting their society (rather than themselves) in mortal danger.

16. Showing the logical coherence of metaphor in a cultural setting, Lakoff and Johnson demonstrate why we often see good as up, and bad as down (*Metaphors We Live By*, 18–19). In science fiction, we can see that logic, extrapolation, and imagination are up and good, while "mundane" reality is down and bad, as in "down to earth." Then we have anomalies: what is the difference between being "blown up" and being "blown down"? Emotional metaphors are less readily classified, however. Since we say "he fell in love" (and one falls down), but "he flew into a rage" (and one flies up), we find either that the directions of metaphor are reversed, or that rage is good and love is bad. There are times when science fiction would seem to show the latter case.

17. John W. Campbell, "Brass Tacks," *Astounding Science Fiction*, August 1946, 176.

18. Martin Ceadel explains the progression of attitudes in "Popular Fiction and the Next War," in *Class, Culture, and Social Change*, ed. Frank Gloversmith (Sussex: Harvester Press, 1980), 164.

19. In *War Games* (New York: McGraw-Hill, 1987), Thomas B. Allen reports that players of the Pentagon's war-games were generally reluctant "to start a nuclear war," but that civilians were far more likely to take the "nuclear option" than were trained military officers and did so under less provocation (179).

20. Lev Vygotsky, *Thought and Language*, trans. Eugenia Haufmann and Gertrude Vakar (Cambridge, Mass.: M.I.T. Press, 1962): 8, 93.

21. In this I follow Whorf, Sapir, Vygotsky, and other linguists. This use of the term "languaging" was introduced by C. A. Hilgartner in his article "Some

Traditional Assumings Underlying Traditional Western Indo-European Languages," 1977–78.

22. A statement does not and cannot encode "all possible" outcomes, but only those outcomes the person making the statement believes on some level to be possible. Every statement is thus self-limiting.

23. See Lakoff and Johnson, *Metaphors We Live By,* especially chaps. 23.

24. Francis R. Allen et al., *Technology and Social Change* (New York: Appleton-Century-Crofts, 1957), 382.

25. Quoted in Allen et al., *Technology and Social Change,* 504.

26. See, for example, Ashley Montagu, *The Biosocial Nature of Man* (New York: Grove, 1956), and Cassius Jackson Keyser, "Korzybski's Concept of Man," in *Manhood of Humanity,* ed. by Alfred Korzybski, 2nd ed. (Lakeville, Conn.: International Non-Aristotelian Library Publishing Co., 1950), 314–19. Keyser explicitly contrasts the Nazi concept of man with Korzybski's and points to the results: "If a man or a state habitually regards humanity as a species of animal, then that man or state may be expected to act betimes like a beast" (314).

27. C. A. Hilgartner, "How to Abolish War," *International Language Reporter* 15, no. 54 (1969): 11–12.

28. We may, for instance, wonder if eliminating the body in favor of reason, intellect, and the mechanical is the tacit aim of science. Certainly there has never before been so great a possibility for this outcome to be realized.

29. See, for example, the arguments over sociobiology between followers of Robert O. Wilson and Richard Lewontin over the past fifteen years or so; see also the much older, tacit argument between Konrad Lorenz, Lionel Tiger, Robin Fox, Robert Ardrey, and others, and Erich Fromm, Ashley Montagu, and company concerning hereditary aggressiveness.

30. In *Motivation and Personality* (New York: Harper, 1954), 80–106, A. H. Maslow lists human needs in three categories: "basic needs" or physiological requirements for life; "safety needs"; and "higher needs," which include belongingness or love, esteem, self-actualization, and aesthetics. These needs follow a developmental hierarchy; unless the basic needs for air, water, food, and temperature control are met, even the need for safety is impossible to fill; until the basic and safety needs are met (and once met, get "backgrounded" so that they no longer seem particularly important), the "higher" needs that we consider specifically "human" cannot even be addressed. All these needs are common to the species.

31. Interview by Jerome Beatty, Jr., in *Saturday Review,* 27 July 1957, 6. In *Bernard Wolfe,* (New York: Twayne, 1972), Carolyn Geduld agrees, with certain qualifications. She finds Wolfe's parodies a form of sharply intellectual literary criticism (18).

32. Utopias depend upon a "cause-and-effect" model of human nature. To admit transactionality is to admit that no "status quo" can truly exist or would be a "good place" if it did. And to allow the idea that everyone else's actions have as much influence on you as you have on them is to admit a lack of control that no utopian can tolerate. With ferocious humor and messy analysis, Wolfe rejects order and utopia in favor of self-acceptance, love, and growth.

7

The Hero and Society: Sturgeon versus Heinlein

Superman is not really a member of American society, though he often acts to save or support it. Since "Clark Kent" must keep his true identity secret, he remains largely isolated from normal social transactions in a manner typical of the hero in American fiction. The main difference between the Lone Ranger and Superman is that Superman's wilderness is urban. In either case, the hero affects society as a saving force. He does not create any lasting alteration in the social fabric; he does not encourage new ways of acting, nor does he necessarily identify and alter the evils he has protected society from. He never works himself out of a job.

This reflects basic assumptions about human nature that American authors seem tacitly to agree upon. Individuals may occasionally do well, but in the mass they are flawed at best, inherently evil at worst. The job of the superior person is to save society from itself, again and again, since it cannot change. But to test the possibilities offered by a transactional model of human behavior, we must find stories that do something different. One author who has developed a strikingly independent set of assumptions is Theodore Sturgeon. Comparing Sturgeon's handling of the atmoic scenario to that of a more traditional writer, Robert A. Heinlein, should expose differences between traditional and revised assumptions.

Sturgeon and Heinlein arrived on the science fiction scene almost together. Both submitted stories to *Astounding Science Fiction* in 1939 and soon became stars in John Campbell's extraordinary galaxy of writers. Despite radical differences in style, technique, and theme, the way in which these two authors treat the atomic scenario is often strikingly similar. Each responds to the "real world" as he perceives it, producing topical, often rapidly written fiction that extrapolates implications of existing conditions into the future.[1] Each takes atomic war seriously, accepting the responsibility of science fiction to warn against the consequences. Heinlein frankly hoped at one point that by "playing out" various possibilities, he could influence the likelihood of such an occurrence.[2] Neither author finds the possible future encouraging or even acceptable. Neither gives up hope for humanity, but each expresses his hope in very different ways.

Although Heinlein is generally considered a writer of "hard" and Sturgeon a writer of "soft" science fiction, their atomic war stories involve much the same kind of protagonist: the "man who counts," who feels he must act. However, they make very different assumptions about the relationship between the protagonist and his society.

THE PROTAGONIST

Heinlein's heroes fall into two main groups: the juvenile "man who learns better" and the adult "man who knows how." The Heinlein juvenile is usually an attractive young person, but something of a misfit. Very often he has some ability that sets him above the norm: high intelligence, eidetic memory, "math wizardry," or the like. Frequently, he lives in a society where such ability is not prized. But in Heinlein's "atomic war" stories, most of his heroes are well-adjusted adults. In the twenty stories considered here, the juvenile pattern is followed in only four. A sexually mature young adult with superior abilities functions as the protagonist in three more, while the adult Heinlein hero, the "man who knows how," shows up in a total of twelve stories and has special aptitudes in six of them. In only eight of the twenty stories is the protagonist shown as merely "normal," and even then he is, by definition, above average in skill and competence and highly above average in courage.

Heinlein advocates the scientific method and respects scientists as men who "know how," but he does not often make them his heroes.

" 'Let There Be Light' " (1940) is the only atomic story that has a scientist as protagonist, and it provides us with an ambiguous example. For one thing, this scientist turns out to be little more than a talented dilettante working for his father; for another, he is never shown as using the scientific method (formulating hypotheses, testing them, and reformulating them until they work). Instead, we are shown a young man who already knows he is right and only needs a little help to prove it. In "Blowups Happen" (1940), the action moves among several viewpoint figures: Dr. Silard, the psychiatrist whose impossible job it is to monitor atomic technicians for signs of instability; Erickson, an unhappy researcher/technician; Superintendent King, who runs the atomic power plant; Captain Harrington, a military scientist with imagination and guts; and Dr. Lentz, the symbologist who studied under Korzybski and who acts as representative for the true protagonist, the nuclear power plant itself. This story is a bildungsroman of atomic energy. It opens with the plant in its dangerous adolescence, briefly reviews its influential infancy, and ends as it achieves "safe" maturity in outer space. As the power that controls contemporary society, the plant itself is central to the plot as no merely human character can be.

Most often, Heinlein's hero is neither a scientist nor a technician but simply a highly superior "common man" uniquely suited by circumstance to handle the crisis at hand. He may have had excellent schooling (see, for example, *Have Space Suit—Will Travel* [1958]), but his technical knowledge is of the comprehensive quality that "everyone" in a modern society should (but rarely does) obtain. He learns fast. He can think on his feet and act effectively. And he *has* to be special; he is shown as selecting himself for adventure and responsibility from a population that characteristically behaves "subnormally."

Heinlein evaluates his characters through action, but their ability to take charge is only slightly more important than their position on a scale that equates liberalism with naive idealism. For instance, Dr. Estelle Karst, the developer of the radioactive "dust" in "Solution Unsatisfactory" (1941) is a competent scientist but impractical; this is proved by her failure to notice that the byproduct of her research can be used as a weapon.[3] That she is also an idealist is shown by her later suicide. Competent people live. She rates low on Heinlein's value scale.

Heinlein describes the stories he writes as "human-interest" rather than "gadget" science fiction and notes that this kind of story not only demands that humans change in response to some problem in their circumstances but also that "coping with problems arising out of [a] new situation" requires solutions that stem from awareness of social history and from that "human activity known as the scientific method."[4] In *The Classic Years of Robert A. Heinlein*, George Slusser disagrees with Heinlein's assessment of his own work. He argues that Heinlein loves to portray intrigue and manipulation but does not write people-oriented stories: "Only rarely is there concern with the formation of the individual in action." The protagonist seems to be elected to his role rather than growing into it (1977, 5–49). A stronger restatement may be even more accurate. What Heinlein's "man who learns better" really learns is that he knew better all the time, but he did not know that he knew. He is the man who has not yet acted and who is thus innocent in the religious sense.

Sturgeon's characters are an oddly assorted lot. Among the twenty-seven stories considered here,[5] ten have defective or emotionally blocked protagonists, three have competent monomaniacs, and three have more or less normal protagonists inhabited by or under the control of aliens.[6] Of the eleven scientists, only three are monomaniacal monsters (in "Memorial" [1946], "Microcosmic God" [1941], and "Never Underestimate" [1952]), and all have superior intelligence. In the stories embodying the atomic scenario, Sturgeon's protagonists are more apt to be scientists than are Heinlein's, and he shows them as following, at least to some extent, the scientific method, as Heinlein does not.

Sturgeon does not divorce scientific intelligence from human feelings. He evaluates his protagonists less by the quality of their ideas (though this is significantly high) than by the quality of their social orientation: the bad are isolated or selfish, while the good stand for solutions that support society. For instance, the scientist in "Microcosmic God" is both self-centered and self-isolated from society. He disdains and refuses to help his own society, and his treatment of his "neoterics" seems abominable if viewed as anything other than a metaphor for a mechanistic, uncaring universe. (Given the communication between creator and creature and the final dependence of creator on creature, any such metaphoric connection is difficult to maintain.) In "Memorial," the scientist feels forced to work outside of and hidden from society; although he aims his work at effecting desirable social change, this is prevented by his alienation. In "The Wages of Synergy" (1953), the scientist suffers for letting his work cut him off from his dangerously warlike (contemporary) society, and that society benefits from his return, although he must destroy his work to do so. The "scientist" in "The Touch of Your Hand" (1953), in contrast, is completely oriented within a cooperative society, and his apparently disruptive work successfully supports it.

THE SOCIETY

To examine the societies that each author presents, we must not only see each one through the protagonists' eyes; we must also look at the expectations the authors hold for these societies. Here we discover a contrast as radical as that between their heroes.

Heinlein's genius at presenting a society as the extrapolation of new technologies in a context of familiar social characteristics, showing details through action and consequence, has often been praised.[7] He almost always sets up his plot by creating tension between a hierarchical, rigidly conservative, violence-prone, "bossy" society and a hero who deeply resents being "bossed." But Paul Carter shows that even within these authoritarian societies, Heinlein often displays an "expectantly utopian" mood (1977, 218). He may pose unbearable, even apparently insoluble social problems, but they improve rapidly, at least for the protagonist, who is plucked out of the dystopian society that forms the background of the story. The hero is either a member of "normal" society who is immediately removed from it into an elite group, or he is already a member of such an isolated and fortunate elite. The plot, of course, follows the hero into a world where all important problems get solved; the ability to "fix things properly" equates with "utopia."

Only once, in "Solution Unsatisfactory," does Heinlein explicitly admit that a solution imposed by force can become society's next problem.[8] Only once, in "Coventry" (1940), does Heinlein posit a radically changed society, and in that story he sets up a self-contradictory situation.[9] Although he claims that the background society is both flexible and humane, permitting and requiring each individual to exist as a responsible social creature—the protagonist is under arrest for failing in this precise regard—he shows a rigid society that has only two ways of dealing with a person who acts "antisocially": forcible rearrangement of the psyche or banishment. The hero "learns better" by discovering, while in "Coventry," that he gets more out of helping the elite who keep society running than from fighting them. His inflexibility reflects the "either-or" characteristics of the society.

Heinlein pictures his societies as resulting from economic, political, sociological, and psychological forces. His stories show the powerful regressive force of human nature in conflict with the powerful progressive force of a hero who seems like an idea in human form; the plot comes from their interaction. As a rule, the idea wins. But forces are not changed by such an interaction.[10] Heinlein does not assume that fundamental social change is possible.

In Sturgeon's early stories, his protagonists were very nearly as isolated and traditionally romantic as Heinlein's, but his focus changed. As he explained: "You can not write good fiction about ideas. You can only write good fiction about people."[11] His people are social creatures, and he works out their relation to society with care. While his societies are not often presented as elegantly as Heinlein's, they are more varied and self-consistent. Some look strange indeed, even anarchic, as in "The Skills of Xanadu" (1956). Some of them may seem repressive—Sturgeon frequently uses sexual metaphors to indicate this repression—but few are really unpleasant. (Exceptions include the society in "Granny Won't Knit" [1954], deliberately showing Sturgeon's most mechanical, least favored extrapolation.)

For Sturgeon, a change in society always is reflected in the characters, and change in the characters changes society as a whole. Sometimes this change arises positively from cultural development. If the change is instead engineered by a single character, it is presented as an ambiguous advance, as in "Unite and Conquer" (1948); as foolish, as in "Never Underestimate" (1952); or as disastrous, as in "Memorial" (1946). Sturgeon represents humans as existing in, not beside or in contest with, society. Society does not consist of hierarchical forces that can only be opposed by counterforce, but of people transacting, that is, of people who can change both themselves and each other. For Sturgeon, true progress comes not from competition but from cooperation.

BEFORE THE BOMB

Heinlein's most powerful "awful warning" stories were written before the atomic bomb was used and while the average American still considered atomic power merely a subject for "crazy science fiction stories." Two stories, "Blowups Happen" (1940) and "Solution Unsatisfactory" (1941), gave Heinlein a high reputation as a futurist and predictor, as John Campbell was delighted to remind his readers.

"Blowups Happen"

"Blowups Happen" dramatically demonstrates the dangers posed by a nuclear power plant that provides electricity to a large portion of the country. The various protagonists share responsibility for ensuring the safety of the pile and most of Nevada, Arizona, and Utah.[12] In the original version, the plant made power by a "uranium bomb"; the explanatory portion of the story was thoroughly rewritten to reflect technological developments when the story was included in the anthology *The Man Who Sold the Moon* (1950). The premise of this story depends upon an implicit trade-off between the opposing forces of public demand and public safety. People demand power. If the atomic plant is closed down, society may collapse (or relapse) into mass psychosis, and the "Crazy Years" will come again. (This telling argument the reader must take on faith, since no evidence is adduced.) If the only alternative to social breakdown involves operating the plant with inadequate safeguards, then the safety of a significant percentage of the population must take second place, especially since the public is kept ignorant of the danger.

Maintaining the stability of the pile is such a demanding job that even a slight mistake may lead to catastrophe. The highly trained operating personnel are aware of the danger. Moreover, they must work under the constant scrutiny of psychiatrists who expect them to become unstable, and many do. The strain increases when they learn that an accident could do more damage than merely killing everyone for hundreds of miles around; it could destroy the entire world. But the situation is saved when a space drive is developed as a spin-off of the research going on in the power plant, and the entire installation is moved into orbit, where an explosion will be "safe." Heinlein assumes that the technicians will function stably in space, though they will be in greater personal danger. Apparently they became "psychotic" not from fear of losing their own lives but from fear of killing their countrymen.[13]

"Solution Unsatisfactory"

"Solution Unsatisfactory," also written early in 1940, details the dangers of advanced research in wartime. It is unusual among Heinlein's stories in having a contemporary setting.[14] H. Bruce Franklin calls "Solution Unsatisfactory" the only story Heinlein wrote "that directly confronts the actual international situation emerging in those early years of World War II" (1980, 60). Alexei Panshin suggests that Heinlein wrote "Solution Unsatisfactory" because Campbell insisted on having stories about atomic war or atomic power for his magazine (1969, 24). Fortunately for Heinlein's reputation as a predictor, it was published before censorship of atomic subjects, before Pearl Harbor, and long before the bomb. Campbell may have suggested the situation addressed by "Solution Unsatisfactory"; it is certain that he suggested the title (see note 8).

The story begins with the "fortuitous" discovery by a gentle, humanitarian scientist of a radioactive "dust" with terrifying properties. Even though the United States is not involved in the World War under way in Europe,[15] she is unable to keep this dust from being conscripted as a weapon "too terrible to use." The dust is, of course, used—by the "non-combatant" United States—to enforce peace on the world. The only solution to continuous international crisis, "unsatisfactory" though it seems, is to establish a supranational control force armed with ethical considerations and the dust, led by the protagonist, now a reluctant though benevolent dictator.

Panshin calls "Solution Unsatisfactory" "more dramatized essay than story" (1969, 24). In *The Issue at Hand*, James Blish notes that Heinlein is one of the two science fiction writers who "have managed to get away with [the lecture technique] and make the reader like it" (1973, 90). In "On the Writing of Speculative Fiction," Heinlein agrees: " 'Solution Unsatisfactory' is a fictionalized essay, written as such" (1977, 202).

"Solution Unsatisfactory" is indeed a special kind of essay: a Machiavellian argument. Rather than explore a number of possible outcomes for the given problem, Heinlein presents one "solution," declares it the only feasible answer, and sets up his argument to prove it. Like Machiavelli, Heinlein has analyzed "human nature" and found it wanting. Unlike Machiavelli, he presents his conviction covertly. He does not openly say that "men are not good," but he shows the President worrying about his successors, who may be tempted (as he is not) to misuse the power inherent in the discovery of the "dust" as a weapon. He does not openly declare that democratic institutions, swayed by demands of the venal electorate, are incapable of dealing with the kind of absolute power that the World Commission must wield, but while he carefully gives opposition arguments to apparently worthy speakers (members of the Cabinet, for instance), he counters them all without effort and then creates circumstances that prove him right.[16]

Heinlein prepares his reader to discount even the most competent "liberal" opposition. Manning and the narrator criticize liberal thinking both directly and implicitly. Manning, the protagonist, is given the inherent virtues of a Heinlein hero: he is a military man who is also a member of the House of Representatives.[17] "Manning was no ordinary man. In him ordinary hard sense had been raised to the level of genius" (125). But most important, "though he was liberal, he was tough-minded, which most liberals aren't" (97).[18] Having taken his master's degree with a "brilliant thesis on the mathematical theories of atomic structure," Manning needs only to "bone up" on some information to organize a laboratory full of experts.

Sixth Column

Heinlein wrote *Sixth Column* (1941) from ideas supplied by John Campbell,[19] who anticipated war with Japan. It is set in the fairly near future, soon after "PanAsian" hordes overwhelm the United States. Only a supersecret group of scientists remains free. (The analogy to the Manhattan Project can only be seen in retrospect.) However, the story opens with apparent disaster: one of the physicists has developed a variation of an existing law of physics, but almost all of the group die in the first test of the "Ledbetter effect." The "effect," which can be "tuned" to affect only members of a given race, becomes an invincible weapon against the invading foe when the hero, an advertising man, ingeniously dresses his men up as members of a variant religious group so they can safely attack and defeat the PanAsians.[20]

Sixth Column is virtual fantasy, with a society shown as resentful but passive under PanAsian rule. But the realistic development, in "Solution Unsatisfactory," of an atomic superweapon that produces indiscriminate, long-lasting destruction and that requires constant supervision and absolute control while making such supervision and control virtually impossible under normal international conditions, depends entirely upon Heinlein's assumptions about society. Although the weapons could destroy all life in the world, no halfway measure is allowed or even seriously considered. No one protests. The radioactive dust defends a curiously apathetic society: we see neither popular agitation against nor enthusiasm for the weapon nor dismay at the socially disruptive measures (including the banning of all military and commercial air travel) taken to control it. Given a society composed of fallen humans, the only choice lies between control imposed by an elite (which will stultify progress) and chaos.

Moreover, when the "benevolent" dictator dies, who will watch the watchers? This problem persists in Heinlein's fiction, for since he continues to posit a society that is dangerous to itself, he must also posit some continued, powerful control to harness that danger. Even in "Coventry," the allegedly peaceful society has continually to guard itself both against antisocial citizens, who would apparently infect or at least distress the helpless body politic, and also against attack from those it has outlawed. In later "future history" stories, the supranational Patrol proposed as an "unsatisfactory solution" becomes the accepted method of control for humans unable to get along with each other. This problem also presents a tacit and persistent emotional ambiguity: "control" is precisely what a Heinlein hero must protest against, although we see him not protesting the Patrol but joining it.

"Microcosmic God"

Sturgeon's pre-Hiroshima stories deal rather conventionally with atomic power and atomic weapons. They are neither scientific nor predictive in their use of atomic power; they include it as a symbol either of future technology bordering on "magic" or of the political power that structures the uses of that technology. "A God in a Garden" (1939) simply mentions atomic power as something that naturally exists in an advanced society.

"Microcosmic God" (1941), one of Sturgeon's most famous stories, does not use the term "atomic power," though the implications are there. The hero is a scientist of powerful intellect, but an isolate by choice. He has never learned to enjoy or get along with people, so he finds a way to keep himself busy and happy alone, while creating the "neoterics," a tiny sentient race, who answer his "scientific" questions. They develop a way to unleash controlled but unlimited power. A greedy banker, who has grown rich while taking care of the scientist's economic needs, tries to control this power as a virtual dictator; the scientist becomes aware of the danger and barely manages to escape personal destruction while foiling the evil banker. In so doing, he cuts himself off even further from humanity, with unusual thoroughness. Only one kindred soul, a construction engineer, is trapped with him. And the isolate may return; the possibility is left open (and threatening).

"Artnan Process" (1941) deals explicitly with atomic energy, but uses it only as a metaphor to indicate both technological prowess and social control. The protagonists try to discover how aliens who have robbed humanity of its characteristic self-determination manage to provide the Earth with unlimited atomic power. This story shows Sturgeon at his most conventionally "science fictional," since his heroes are stereotypical cowboys humorously translated to outer space. But it is interesting to notice that the triumph of these conventional heroes, even in this "space Western" situation, should change the social context of an Earth that hardly shows in the story at all except as a topic for authorial discussion of its cooperation in its own enslavement.

"Killdozer!"

"Killdozer!" (1944) is a different kind of story entirely and demonstrates the ability to portray character development for which Sturgeon has become famous. A group of construction workers are left on a Pacific island after the War to build an airstrip. Their miniature society is depicted as friendly and generally cooperative. They disturb an alien weapon, buried for eons after the cataclysmic end of the war it was built to fight. This weapon is a nonphysical "force"; it animates a bulldozer and regains its original function: to kill.

The men must first convince themselves that this is really happening—that a machine has developed a bloodthirsty life of its own—and then try to counter the threat. The protagonist, a sensible and competent man, finally does understand something of the situation and with the help of a coworker kills the creature. The larger society never knows what it has escaped, since a fortuitously misguided test missile hits the island and destroys the evidence. Sturgeon does not make society or social change the focus of these early stories. Yet much of the impact of "Killdozer!" comes from the metaphoric connection between our society, the war it was then fighting, and the vanished society that created the ancient weapon: each fights against itself in a war that it may not survive.

THE BOMB AND AFTER

For a number of years after Hiroshima and Nagasaki, while many other authors agonized over the atomic scenario, Heinlein avoided it. The first stories he wrote after the hiatus from 1942 to 1947 due to his war-related work deal almost lyrically with an atomic future. As in "Blowups Happen," he assumes that familiarity with and demand for the marvels of atomic progress will encourage people to put up with "necessary" dangers. For example, in "The Green Hills of Earth" (1947), atomic engines are used in spaceships. The plot revolves around an emergency in which an expedient violation of safety rules causes these engines to leak radiation, and explosion is imminent. Only the hero dies to make a point about following regulations.

Heinlein was not complacent about either the danger or the possibility of atomic war. He claims to have written nine articles during this period that attempted to get people seriously to consider international inspection and control of atomic weapons, on the sensible supposition that what one country could invent, another could copy.[21] He has since published three of them in *Expanded Universe* (1980). These factual articles express his conviction that "the next war can destroy us utterly, as a nation—and World War III is staring us right in the face" (148). Combining emotional appeal with survival information, they are carefully researched, strongly written, and readable. But Heinlein was not able to find a suitable market for them,[22] nor did he use this dark vision as the background material for fiction, the mode of writing for which he was best known, and which he was most apt to sell. The science fiction magazines carried an abundance of "awful warning" stories during this period, but Heinlein had moved out of the science fiction market into magazines of wide circulation and large readership, like the *Saturday Evening Post*. This was the audience that he claims he most wanted to educate but did not reach. Instead, for this audience he domesticated atomic energy and downplayed the danger of atomic war.

In *Space Cadet* (1948), the Space Patrol regularly uses (and takes appropriate but not very stringent precautions with) both atomic engines in their ships and atomic bombs in orbit. The Patrol finds evidence that "Planet Lucifer," now represented only by fragments in the asteroid belt, once was a planet not only inhabited by "intelligent" life, but "disrupted by artificial nuclear explosion. In other words, they did it themselves" (161).[23] The implication is that Earth is lucky to have the Patrol to control human nature; "it has given the human race a hundred years of peace, and now there is no one left who remembers war."

"The Long Watch," published in the *American Legion Magazine* (1949), does use a form of the atomic scenario. Like *Space Cadet*, it is set in the fairly distant future where the military has ships that routinely patrol cis-lunar space and missile bases on the Moon. But the political situation sounds very contemporary: "The League of Nations had folded up; what would keep the United Nations from breaking up, too, and thus lead to another World War"? A fearful faction in the armed forces attempts a political coup. "It was not safe (so he said) to leave control of the world in political hands; power must be held by a scientifically selected group. In short—the Patrol" (211).

To control a situation in which no one has attacked anyone, these officers are willing to use atomic bombs against Earth for "demonstration purposes." Heinlein shows the military equating political solutions with capitulation: politicians compromise, and compromise is possibly dishonest and certainly weak. But a stubborn young Patrol officer refuses to alter the guidance systems on the bombs. His insistence on accepting personal responsibility for the consequences of military obedience seems to be one of the few cases in which science fiction takes the Nuremberg decisions into account. Unlike the protagonist of Chandler Davis's "To Still the Drums" (1946) he does not have to stand trial for his actions, however; he dies of radiation and becomes one of the immortal "Four" whose ethical standards inspire the Space Patrol in the juvenile novel *Space Cadet* (1948).[24] Implicit in this story is the assumption that society does not need to watch its watchers; the watchers will always include at least one hero who will sacrifice himself. Nor does "The Long Watch" teach the American Legion any of the urgent "lessons to the reader" included in Heinlein's unpublished essays.

"Gulf" (1949), another story set in the future, anticipates private control of superweapons by a few capitalist monsters who put selfish interests (not clearly spelled out; but in the atomic scenario, the enemy's reasons for aggression are rarely made explicit) above the welfare of the nation and indeed of all humanity. That the enormously wealthy and utterly evil Mrs. Keithley seems more like a mafiosa than a representative of godless communism is irrelevant; only a superheroic pair can save the world from her machinations once she steals the atomic secret.

In 1950, Heinlein rewrote "Blowups Happen" for inclusion in *The Man Who Sold the Moon* to reflect advances in nuclear power technology. He was also aware that once atomic weapons had been used in war, any war set in a realistic future had to take them into account. Consequently, in 1953 he rewrote "If This Goes On—" (1940), explaining the Cabal's failure to use atomic weapons so cleverly that he did not have to rewrite the battle scene:

> We weren't using atomic bombs for three reasons: we didn't have any; the United States was not known to have had any since the Johannesburg Treaty after World War III. We could not get any. . . . Lastly, we would not have used one if it had been laid in our laps. . . . an atom bomb, laid directly on the Palace, would certainly have killed around a hundred thousand or more of our fellow citizens in the surrounding city—and almost as certainly would not have killed the Prophet (122).

This concern for "fellow citizens" who might fall victim to the war parallels the change in their treatment in another way; in the 1940 version of the story, mass psychohypnotic techniques are used to recondition the people who otherwise would reject freedom and continue to accept the Prophet's dictatorial theocracy. In 1953, Heinlein has apparently noticed this as a contradiction in terms and no longer frees the minds of his citizens by force. But it is the newly free people of the first version that create the society that the protagonist of "Coventry" finds so utterly stultifying. For Heinlein, as for Campbell, a stable society is one in danger of devolution, and control (except of war) is its greatest danger. (Time has not altered Heinlein's convictions on this point. In *Friday* (1982), he posits a fragmented United States in which personal safety is constantly under attack, creating highly competent survivors. But the war that forms the pivotal action is not nuclear and later turns out to be "merely" the result of a power struggle among factions within a multiplanetary corporation.)

The two short stories dealing specifically with atomic war that appeared in the early fifties, when wholesale nuclear catastrophe seemed particularly imminent,[25] have little to do with solving or even facing the international situation.[26] "The Year of the Jackpot" (1952) posits a concatenation of cycles that causes lunatic behavior all over the world, including public nudity by "decent" young women and the atom bombing and invasion of the United States by Russia. The prescient protagonist has cleverly secluded himself in the wilderness with his love, however, so we hear of this invasion, which breaks up U.S. society and destroys the government, only through news broadcasts. The protagonist needs only to mention casually that he killed a few enemy soldiers to assure us that the United States has defended itself competently. But the end is inevitable. As predicted by the cycles, it comes not from invasion, anarchy, nuclear fallout, or war, but from the sun going nova.

"Project Nightmare"

In 1953, a year in which both the United States and Russia tested their H-bombs, Heinlein published "Project Nightmare." Assuming that the enemy will inevitably attack us, he invents supermen to oppose superweapons.[27] In this story, a squad of psychic "operators" telepathically capable of locating and controlling atomic reactions saves the nation from atomic devices planted in various American cities to force the government to capitulate.[28] They can choose whether to excite or to damp subatomic emissions. The psychic operators are already on a military base and have just proven their efficacy when the threat develops. They are immediately given full responsibility for dealing with it[29] and manage to save all but one American city (its loss is the fault of a bumbling bureaucrat who does not understand the needs of these special people). Once the country is safe, they cheerfully agree to the President's suggestion that they set off all of Russia's stockpiled weapons in retaliation. No one mentions the danger to the world created by fallout from this retaliatory action.[30] Like "The Long Watch," "Project Nightmare" expresses in fiction Heinlein's conviction that diplomacy equals capitulation.

Heinlein's next stories dealing with atomic weapons assume that the contemporary danger of atomic war has been handled. In the juvenile novel, *Have Space Suit—Will Travel* (1958), some powerful (possibly atomic) energy is possessed by benevolent aliens who take it upon themselves to decide whether humanity should be allowed to continue to exist now that it has space-travel capability, or if its irredeemably violent nature will endanger all the worlds—a tacitly megalomaniacal consideration, but one that Heinlein frequently employs. The magnificently solipsistic " 'All You Zombies—' " (1959) may pose a kind of answer to this question. It takes place in an undescribed (but apparently quite familiar) future, after an atomic war has miraculously been prevented by the time-traveling protagonist and his group.

Starship Troopers

Throughout this period, Heinlein openly expressed his fear of nuclear attack by Russia and demanded a high level of government preparedness to meet the threat. In 1958, he was outraged by the ad taken out by the "National Committee for a Sane Nuclear Policy" advocating limitations on nuclear weapons testing. At his own expense, he published a full-page newspaper advertisement entitled "Who Are the Heirs of Patrick Henry?" that denounced the group as Communist-inspired and called on patriotic citizens to resist such arrant defeatism. In *Expanded Universe*, he claims that he then put aside his other work to write *Starship Troopers* to convey the same message (396).

Starship Troopers (1959) seems a paean to political strength through military preparedness; but Heinlein again avoids any reference to the contemporary situation. He sets the tale in the distant future, when all differences with Russia have long been resolved, though we do not find out how. In this new world, there is a "Federation"—perhaps a world government—that is constituted "rationally." To be able to vote or hold office, citizens, male or female, must have served in the "Federal Service," a systemwide military force. (This Service is obligated to take in and find a place for every volunteer. Heinlein claims that the vast majority of these pre-citizens never see combat; in the book, we are shown no one who sees anything else.) This Federation apparently formed where the forces of moral decay, equated with anarchy and symbolized by the irresponsibility of the average citizen, which undermined democratic institutions, met some unspecified resistance to such weakness.

As H. Bruce Franklin notes, "Social collapse came in the form of moral collapse" (1980, 114).

Frank Tucker argues that "the veterans-only government . . . is considered efficacious because all those admitted to citizenship have, in the service, placed group welfare ahead of their personal advantage; they have at least made some sacrifices for the nation," so "this system would indeed coordinate privileges with responsibility in a significant way" (1978, 187–88). But the new social system functions mainly as a plot device to get Juan Rico into the Mobile Infantry.

We are told that this service will make him, like all other volunteers, fit for as well as able to exercise the privileges of citizenship. We are supposed to assume that the world is run by a strong representative government. What we see is a superbly equipped and trained military force that invades alien planets for no apparent reason (as in the opening action) and reacts quickly and effectively to attack from aliens (as in the concluding action); we never see it controlled by an elected government. We do not even see anyone vote.[31] Rico will become a citizen only after he is discharged (honorably) from the service, after the war, if he lives that long. The Federal Reserve, a much enlarged version of the supranational force created in "Solution Unsatisfactory" and developed in *Space Cadet*, is explicitly not a "mass conscript army called up . . . to defend democracy" but a "superelite force designed to fight the permanent wars necessary to fulfill Earth's manifest destiny in the galaxy," as Franklin states (1980, 115). The Federation seems committed to a policy of interplanetary expansion, possibly amounting to colonialism; war may become a permanent way of life.

Heinlein posits both planet-busting and hand-held atomic weapons as a matter of course for the Mobile Infantry. In this novel, the apparent danger comes not from man's inability to get along with different national versions of himself, the source of Heinlein's real-life distress, but from utterly inhuman insectoid aliens, with whom Earth makes contact as it expands its hegemony throughout the Galaxy.[32] If the aliens are intended to represent Russia and its dangerous "monolithic" ideology, the message is again diluted by its alienation from real time and real life.

"August Sixth, 1945"

If Heinlein's post–1945 fiction became less predictive and more "utopian" in its treatment of the atomic scenario, the opposite is true of Sturgeon's fiction, which responded directly and passionately to Hiroshima. He wrote "August Sixth, 1945," a "poem" expressing both the fear and the sense of power he experienced from that event, while "the dust was still settling over Nagasaki."[33] It is a moving, if hastily written, gut-level response to a thrilling yet terrifying experience of history. In this, Sturgeon was responding to the fact of the atomic bomb in very much the same manner that many other Americans did—with great ambivalence.[34]

"Memorial"

Following this immediate reaction, Sturgeon paid serious fictional attention to the possibilities involved in the use of atomic weapons in war. "Memorial" (1946) chronicles the attempt by a scientist concerned with international instability to find a way to warn the world about the horrifying possibilities of atomic war. Since he was working on a peaceful use for atomic energy until shut down by the government, he has bombs on hand. Believing that a terrible Pit of active radiation will alert people to the dangers of nuclear war and make it unthinkable, he decides to explode one to set off an atomic pile safely away from civilization.[35] The result is, of course, quite the opposite. Under arrest, he sets off the bomb by a ruse, blowing up himself, his friend, and the officials the friend has enlisted to stop him, but he does not manage to let anyone else know what is going on. (This may be hard for the reader to remember, for the story begins and ends with a clear, almost lyrical explanation of the scientist's intentions, but—at the scientist's own demand—that information is never made public.) The country assumes that it is under attack. It retaliates.[36] The First Nuclear War is followed by the Second. After that, there is the Mutant's War, which no humans survive. In a devastated world, the Pit continues to pour out deadly radioactivity, just as the scientist expected it to.

In this tragedy, the protagonist tries to alter events by imposing his vision on society by scientific means. The means are effective; his Pit does all he expects it to and more. Yet his humane intent is frustrated by his withdrawal from society (even though he felt compelled to remove himself from a society that rejected his ideas) and his monomaniac conviction of absolute rightness, of a special election to save the world from nuclear war. While election means success for a Heinlein hero, for a Sturgeon protagonist it indicates obsession. The greater the power such a person wields, the greater the danger he poses, even if his cause is pure.

"Thunder and Roses"

"Thunder and Roses" (1947), another justifiably famous story, uses the standard atomic scenario with a twist. War is already under way as the story opens. The analogy to Pearl Harbor is obvious; the United States has been hit "from both sides" without warning and without the opportunity to use its own nuclear weapons in retaliation. Now the whole hemisphere is poisoned; the protagonist, a soldier, knows that he is already dying of radiation. No matter who "wins" the war, Pete and his friends will not live to see the "victory." Soldiers are going mad or committing suicide. Then a helicopter arrives carrying Starr Anthim, a famous entertainer. Pete, who has long been in love with her, discovers with rage and grief that she, too, is dying; in fact, she is so ill that it is hard to understand how or why she has made the trip.

She explains that the United States still has usable nuclear missiles, and that his base may contain the last functional controls for firing them. She is trying to find and deactivate these controls, for the only effect these weapons can now have is to further poison the Earth. Even those in charge of national policy before the war failed to realize how many bombs each enemy country had; as Starr tells the soldiers, "There has been so much secrecy. . . . They have killed us, and they have ruined themselves. As for us—we are not blameless, either. . . . But what we must do is hard. We must die—without striking back" (124). No living thing anywhere could possibly survive the radiation from a retaliatory strike. She convinces Pete (who has already stumbled on the secret room containing the controls) that vengeance and patriotism must be put into a wider context, one that includes the whole human race. Tragically, to destroy the controls, Pete must kill his only surviving friend.

In "Memorial," we see society only through the embittered speech of the scientist and his relationship with his dilettante writer friend, but even so, its salvation is his major aim. His attempt fails terribly. In "Thunder and Roses," Pete's relationship to society is detailed through his concern for his friends and his willingness to sacrifice even friendship for the possible future of all humanity. The tenuous possibility of human survival remains, the gift of an ordinary young man who transcends his own death and the death of all he loves: " 'You'll have your chance,' he said into the far future. 'And by heaven, you'd better make good.'

After that he just waited" (133).

Sturgeon has said that he wrote "Thunder and Roses" at the same time that he wrote "August Sixth, 1945," and that "it is, historically, the very first post-atomic doom story that was written after Hiroshima."[37] Over the next several years, he wrote a number of stories that dealt either specifically or inferentially with the dangers of atomic war. These include "Prodigy" (1949), a short story about mutant children; "Unite and Conquer" (1948); "Granny Won't Knit" (1954); and his novel *Venus Plus X* (1960). In "Unite and Conquer," Sturgeon examines the same problem Heinlein dealt with in "Solution Unsatisfactory": the military use of scientific discovery. Everything the protagonist, a genius, invents becomes a new and more deadly weapon, until in desperation he creates a weapon so frightening that all Earth must unite against it:

an alien invasion. Only his brother (an army officer) guesses what he is up to and tries to intervene. Unlike Heinlein's hero in "The Long Watch," Sturgeon's scientist, having saved humanity, survives his deed and must face the legal consequences.

"Granny Won't Knit"

"Granny Won't Knit" takes place hundreds of years after humanity almost wiped itself out by atomic war. Only a few people survived, in South Africa. The emotional sterility of the postholocaust society is metaphorically embodied in sexual rigidity. The society is still so traumatized that having achieved a technologically enhanced worldwide peace, it now refuses new technology. In fact, it has become "utopia," resisting change of any sort. Sturgeon shows his dislike for this by making the society mechanical. It rejects normal life processes: people hide in geometrical clothing; they eat rapidly and shamefully, by themselves, in the "flower shop," a sort of closet where they also excrete. Swear words include "blossom" and "petals."[38] The Father is an autocrat, the "mam" a shadow at his feet. Every person has a place in society, indicated by age and title, and is expected to stay in it. Marriage is arranged. Even reproduction is controlled: each family can have two children, one boy and one girl, apparently placed in the family after proper conditioning.

"Granny Won't Knit" is a tale of reversal: life is denied, but what is covered up is not only sexuality (as in our society), but also human individuality and spontaneity in favor of mechanical motion and form. Roan Walsh has been fully conditioned. At thirty, he has no independence or self-determination, only ambition. If he can ever impress his father, the Private, he may be given a partnership in the family business and, perhaps, a wife. But he meets a "may" (a girl) who acts with startling freedom (she bares not only her hands, but also her arms and feet!) and falls in love with her.

With her, he "dreams" of a green world, outside the protected, identical, mechanized cities, which are all instantly accessible by "transplat," a matter-transmitting platform. In this green world, people eat and work and play together and touch grass with their bare feet. Somehow Roan has no trouble in accepting his dream and the possibility of a freer life as real; what he cannot accept is the idea of a new and more powerful transmitting device, for he has been "conditioned" against new technology. But his "Granny," who invented the transplat in the first place, and who now despises the social rigidity it helped emplace, has devised a way of breaking the static society they proudly call "Stasis" to save humanity from itself.[39] She tells him:

> Stasis is the end product of a lot of history. Human beings had clobbered themselves up so much for so long, they developed what you might call a racial

phobia against insecurity. When they finally got the chance—the transplat—they locked themselves up tight with it. That isn't what the transplat was for, originally. It was supposed to disperse humanity over the globe again, after centuries of huddling. *Hah*!

About the time they started deep conditioning in the creches, walling each defenseless new generation off from new thoughts, new places, new ways of life, a few of us started to fear for humanity. Stasis was the first human culture to try to make new ideas impossible. I think it might have been humanity's first eternal culture. I really do. But I think it would also have been humanity's worst one. (166–167)

A different kind of reversal is found in the hint that since the entire society is now unified by custom and the transplat, it will not again develop the antagonisms that led it to destroy itself before.

"Never Underestimate"

Sturgeon often connects sexual conflict with atomic war. In "Never Underestimate" (1952), the priggish protagonist unilaterally determines that women have too much power over men after discovering that his wife, whom he had assumed to be completely under his control, uses sexual attractiveness and social rewards to influence his actions, and that other women share this ability; in other words, he notices that women are holding their own in the war between the sexes. (This "war" is entirely the product of his egomania; his wife treats him quite lovingly, if somewhat patronizingly.) His pride is hurt. Without consulting anyone, he sets out to modify female sexuality, using a chemical spread by an atomic test explosion. He succeeds in modifying human sexual patterns, though not in the way he expected. And the women, somewhat amused, set out to make the best of the new situation as they did the old. This story is a humorous reversal on the unilateral attempt to control war through terror in "Memorial," as "The Wages of Synergy" (1953) is a dark comment on the feasibility of controlling scientific discoveries by some supervening agency, the idea that Heinlein explored in "Solution Unsatisfactory."

"The Wages of Synergy"

"The Wages of Synergy" is a variant of "the knowledge too dangerous to know" story. It is also a marvelous, though complicated, pun. When Paul thundered at the Romans that "the wages of sin is death" (Rom. 6:32), he was referring explicitly to sins of the flesh. But what is "synergy"? Killilea, a steroid chemist, explains to his wife Prue:

Chemistry is a strange country where sometimes the whole is greater than the sum of its parts, if you put the right parts on top. When one reaction finishes with *blue*, and another reaction finishes with *hot*, and you put the end products together and the result is bluer and hotter than the blue one and the hot one before, that's synergy. (55)

The story opens with a clearly sinful situation: a man dies in the act of intercourse, and since the woman runs away rather than calling for help, we understand that their liaison is illicit. We should see her as a "bad" woman. We are not permitted this simplistic assumption, however. Her husband values her; he has abandoned his scientific research and has been searching for her for more than a year. But this, too, is less simple than it seems. Killilea did not just leave his work; he destroyed it utterly, in revulsion, notes and all, leaving (he hopes) no trace of his technique or even of his area of inquiry, for the product of his experiment is a hormone derivative that—without any warning symptoms—kills men at the moment of orgasm.

Prue did not leave Killy because she was "bad," or "bored," or even "tempted." She left because his work left no room for her. She could live happily with Killy while he did joyful, creative work; "important" work drove her away. Now she refuses to return to him, not because she no longer loves him, not because either she or he is "ashamed" of her, but because it could kill him, and she will not take that chance. Prue is a woman who also symbolizes the life force, the loving instinct, the true intuition of humankind. It is she who works out the distinction between morals and ethics the forms the heart of the story's action: ethics form "the survival patterns of the individual within the group, toward the end of group survival," as opposed to morals, "the pattern of survival within the group," or conformation with group expectations (which may not even have survival value, as well as being not at all ethical) (61).

This distinction is crucially important to the story. Mankind seems to be about to get its act together, "toward the end of group survival," by creating an Ethical Science Board whose purpose is "to establish a genuine ethic for science, right across the board; to study the possible end effects on humanity of any progress in any science" (49–50). This board would have two effects: it might curtail work with highly dangerous implications (the kind of work that Killilea has been doing, for instance); it might also provide cross-fertilization of ideas, synergizing the work done by its own members. Moreover, any board with the power to say "stop" to some scientific endeavor would also have the power to direct (or even to pervert) research.

The distinction is even more important to the reader on a deeper level, for only on this basis can we judge the actions Killy and Prue take to locate and stop the man who has stolen Killy's secret and used it to kill selected scientists—those few men capable of directing the Ethical Science Board on which so much depends in a world "where men can soberly plan the use of such a thing as an H-bomb" (57).

Once Killilea understands how these men died, he can understand his own danger. More than that, he can visualize the result if his biological poison is widely distributed:

> You see, it would do more than kill men and put their women through the hell you already know. It would throw a city, a whole nation, a culture, into an unthinkable madness. You know the number of pitiful sicknesses that are traced to frustration. Who would dare to relieve frustration with a ghostly killer like that loose in the land?... In a week there would be suicides and mutilations; in two they would start to murder their women to get them out of sight. And all the while no man would truly know whether the sleeping devil lay within him or not. He'd feel it stir and murmur whether it was there or not. (57–58)

In this case, the wages of synergy is worse than death. The very nature of man can naturally be used against him.

The "super poison" has vital metaphoric resonances. It comes from the human body, a concentrated byproduct of the reproductive act. Used as a weapon, it will sever humanity not only from its sexuality, but also from its descendents. It stands as a powerful metaphor for atomic war, which perverts or destroys the germ plasm. But Sturgeon's point is social: the protagonists of this story are ethical. Prue has not "cheated" on Killilea; she is not owned by him, so she "steals" nothing from him. He loves her utterly, trusts and seeks her, not because he is being faithful to some idea of fidelity, but because he lives that way. Together they synergize both a solution to their crisis and a way of life that is "bluer and hotter" than anything they can create alone. Their relationship stands as a model for a healthy society: if people truly act ethically (rather than morally), the result will transform society. This can be seen in little in the care Prue takes for the man who nearly killed Killy, and in large in Killy's care to preserve the world from his own work. Sturgeon shows that the twin drives of life-enhancing "ethics" and death-dealing "morality" are two sides of the same human coin. Prue's ability creatively to violate various "moral" ways society uses to destroy itself demonstrates Sturgeon's optimism about humanity. Here the wages of synergy is social health.

"The Skills of Xanadu"

A reversal of the "repel the invaders" plot occurs in "The Skills of Xanadu" (1956). Xanadu, an Edenic postholocaust planet, is apparently ripe for conquest by an equally human but more aggressive world, represented by a "scout" who comes to plan the invasion. The entire society of Xanadu, fully aware of the intentions of the invader, mobilizes peacefully. They share with him their advanced technology (much of which he finds intolerable), until their invisible superiority tricks him into stealing a sample of their "power belt," which he takes home with him, reproduces, and distributes. Only then does he discover that all who wear the belt become part of the greater unity of humankind, and that in this unity, invasion and conquest make no sense at all.[40]

Farnham's Freehold

Despite Heinlein's frequently expressed concern with atomic war, he did not write a novel dealing with atomic war as it could occur today until 1964. *Farnham's Freehold* employs the atomic scenario in its purest form. It begins realistically enough: a wealthy and sensible man provides a really effective bomb shelter for himself and his family. In it, they survive an apparently devastating atomic attack. (We are not told, nor do we need to be, who bombs whom or why.) They emerge from this shelter not into postnuclear holocaust, but into a "green world" reminiscent of Thoreau's Walden, in which each man must hoe his own beans and make do with what comes to hand. (Plenty does; Farnham's shelter is stocked better than Robinson Crusoe's ship.)

This green world ceases to seem Edenic, however, when the Farnham group is discovered by one of the rulers of this time-and-place: a cultured black cannibal overlord, who treats them as property. This is favored treatment, for here whites are worse than slaves; they are animals.[41] Although the master seems somewhat partial to his prehistoric captives, Farnham feels that their only hope for freedom and dignity is to escape back into their own time, arriving just before bombs fall, and to change the situation enough to avert (or at least to miss) this intolerable future.

Farnham himself is the capable man, "the man who knows how," and the virile father of several of the other characters.[42] His family, however, is decadent.[43] His wife is a selfish, helpless alcoholic; his son, a "mother's boy," permits himself to be castrated in order to enjoy the benefits of the luxurious yet repulsive society into which they have fallen, even while his father works to get them out of it. His lovely daughter is even less capable, since she cannot fulfill the basic "female" role and dies in childbirth. In spite of setbacks—losing son, daughter, and wife (who enters a harem)—Farnham fathers another set of children on his daughter's best friend, returns through time, and takes up a life of free enterprise and self-help in postholocaust America. Like a good pioneer, he does it alone. As Franklin notes:

> The isolation of Hugh Farnham and his dependents is downright eerie. The only voice they hear from the world of the 1960's in each of the alternative

scenarios is a radio message warning of the nuclear attack. Their only direct contact with that contemporary world comes in the form of the hydrogen bombs dropped on them. Knocked loose from their historical time, they enter a world in which all the people and objects of their world have been utterly wiped out. Even when they return to the present from the nightmare world of the future, the world they enter is also deserted, with not a soul to be seen in the city, except for those huddled together in Farnham's own house. (1980, 154)

Despite its recurring violence and primitive conditions, we may infer that Heinlein prefers rugged postholocaust America to either the decadent "green world" of the future or the prewar world in which Farnham was just another slightly overage, unhappily married man. Farnham now has the opportunity to prove himself both Superman and a modern, self-made Job.

Venus Plus X

In contrast, Sturgeon's novel of atomic war, *Venus Plus X* (1960), is explicitly about human contact. As he has in other works, Sturgeon explores the possibility that the "natural" dichotomies we express in sex may lead inevitably (and be an inevitable result of) wider interpersonal conflicts. The Ledom are hermaphroditic. They are also genuine scientists. Faced with conflicting hypotheses—that "homo sap." would or would not accept them if their existence were known—they devise and carry out a critical experiment. They allow a "human," Charlie Johns, to explore their world. He finds it both beautiful and challenging. They have solved the problems of interpersonal strife and, consequently, of intraspecies war. Throughout the book, as Ledom society is contrasted with an average, "normal" family, the Ledom seem far more humane and happier. But when Charlie is told their "secret," he is appalled and tries to destroy all that he had first admired. He claims that he could stand it if the Ledom were the victims of some natural mutation, but they deliberately create themselves so. The Ledom see Charlie's reaction as representative of humanity's and reluctantly remain hidden as war begins: "Suddenly the sky blazed; the stars were gone. . . . The sky began to shimmer, then to sparkle. 'Oh, pretty!' cried Froure. 'Fallout,' said Philos. 'They're at it again, the idiots.' They began to wait" (158–159).

One can hardly help noticing the resonance with the end of "Thunder and Roses" or the difference in situation. In the earlier story, Pete has no way of knowing if anyone will actually survive; he only knows that survivors stand a better chance from his sacrifice. The Ledom, created to survive while "homo sap." destroys itself, need only wait; but they would vastly prefer sharing their love and their knowledge with humans to prevent a global war.

THE CONTRASTING VISION

Communication

Sturgeon and Heinlein frequently use paranormal modes of communication in their fictions, but they do so in very different ways and for different purposes. Heinlein posits an inherent human capability for telepathy in a number of his stories, some of them frankly fantasy, such as "Lost Legacy" (1941; variant title "Lost Legion"), but also in others more securely embedded in the science fiction tradition, such as *Beyond This Horizon* (1942), and *Time for the Stars* (1956). Telepathy is posited as a "lost ability" of the human race, and one that can be cultivated by certain people under certain conditions: in "Gulf" by people of very high IQ who learn a special language,[44] and in "Lost Legacy" by a group of specialists so intelligent that they have almost guessed the human "secret" even without the help of the real elite who have hidden, more or less immortally, in Mt. Shasta.[45] In other stories, it signifies the danger that the gifted few find themselves in when struggling against the forces of unreason. They need a more-than-human light to hold back the coming dark. But always beneficial telepathy is described as fully under human control. The communicator can hang up the mental "telephone" at will.[46]

Heinlein never shows what society would look like if full, telepathic communication were a normal part of human life, though in "Lost Legacy" he shows that it is not sufficiently powerful to prevent human nature from fragmenting and destroying society. For Heinlein, the better the system of communication, the more it tends to remove people from ordinary society (already seen as "subnormal" in interest, skills, and activity) and to create a superior group.[47] Sometimes he assigns this kind of special communicative ability to especially powerful aliens, both friendly and unfriendly. His Martians have it; in *Red Planet* (1949, a juvenile novel), *Double Star* (1956), and *Stranger in a Strange Land* (1961), the Martians are portrayed not only as telepathic but also as unemotional, logical, intellectually superior, and not much concerned with humans, though they are potentially dangerous.[48]

Communication without control is very dangerous for Heinlein. The "Little People" in *Methuselah's Children* (1941) form a homogeneous group, without individual identity. Despite this drawback, Little People are presented as attractive; they have made technological advances and are very comfortable—and immortal. They are thus seductively dangerous. When a human joins them, each one "becomes" her and she "becomes" each one; there is no residual self or remaining unmerged identity. Heinlein presents this option of immortality at the price of individuality as inhuman and destructive. Heinlein has always been fascinated by immortality, but he wants it on his own terms.[49] His eponymous hero Lazarus Long does it right: he is "the man who knows how," competent in all areas of life, including extreme natural longevity; Long is repelled by the Little People. Even to achieve immortality, allowing one's ego to be subsumed in some group is unacceptable.

The Puppet Masters

The Puppet Masters (1951) can be read as Heinlein's representation of the cold war, a struggle for men's minds. It is set in a future when man has established colonies throughout the solar system. The parasitic aliens who land, take over, and wreak havoc are virtually unstoppable; they can put any human completely under their mental control. The repulsive "slugs" reproduce by fission so as to take over more and more humans; they require hosts on which to live and breed, but they do not create a symbiotic (mutually beneficial) relationship with them. A "ridden" human is not only deprived of will but is also prevented from dealing with his most basic physical needs unless the alien permits him to do so. Consequently, conquered populations become sick, starved, and feeble; this does not, apparently, bother the aliens much, as they can always find other hosts.[50]

The hero—a trained, secret government agent of incredible ability (closely related to the hero of "Gulf" but engagingly boyish and naive)—is captured and escapes several times; he is one of the few who establish an adversary relationship with the aliens instead of either avoiding them by luck or being enslaved by them. This closely knit, yet antagonistic relationship between man and alien reflects the relationship between the intelligence group to which the hero belongs and "ignorant" society. As usual, the elite know what is going on and what to do, but must use force or trickery to make even the government believe them (see Franklin 1980, 34). As the novel progresses, we find that, although "the man in the street" is frightened and shaken, and dress codes get drastically revised, "human nature" and the way society "works" remain quite unchanged.

This is not true for the hero, who experiences capture by a slug. His mind is completely open to the alien, who controls him physically as well as mentally; he cannot hang up the phone. Not only does he lose free will, but the experience is shown as rape. Despite his revulsion, he allows himself to be "ridden" again rather than allowing his wife to substitute for him. The slugs "ride" humans in order to control them and in order to "conjugate" (significantly, the hero has a hard time recognizing the sexual aspect of this procedure, preferring to believe that the slugs are having a "conference"); information and genetic material get exchanged simultaneously.

Using information gathered from the hero's sacrifice, the humans destroy the aliens by infecting them with a disease fatal to humans in nine days and to aliens in four.[51] Once the aliens die, medical teams save as many people as possible. Nor is Heinlein content with merely saving Earth from the enemy. Uncharacteristically, he allows his hero to experience real anger at the aliens. Then, more characteristically, he displaces this anger and assigns it to the race as a whole. Having wiped out the aliens on Earth, the hero and his group prepare to attack them on their home planet, feeling "exhilarated" because "the free men" are coming to deal "*Death and Destruction*!" (175).

Where Heinlein uses paranormal communication as a metaphor for control, Sturgeon posits it as a medium of healing and improved social relations. Sturgeon shows human beings as capable of loving, supportive relationships. He also sees how frequently relationships founder over misunderstandings or incomplete communications. On a broader scale, he sees society as the transmitter of human culture and thus both as a positive force for human growth and as the source of human frustration, inhibition, and misery. Lack of communication brings disaster: "Memorial" and "Thunder and Roses" show the danger of shutting oneself (or one's country) off from the rest of humanity. The disconnected communication among the crew in "The Pod in the Barrier" (1957) not only drives the plot but also stands as an effective metaphor connecting the human condition with the isolation the alien Lunae have imposed on themselves. When the Lunae make paranormal contact with humans, it marks the end of their war against the universe and the beginning of friendship. The better the communication the more "human" and effective society can become.

In some stories—"The Traveling Crag" (1951), for example—Sturgeon explicitly demands that "will" or "reason" solve emotional or social malfunctions. But what he demonstrates in these situations is that improved communication, both with other humans and with the "self," leads to psychological release from the fixation with "bad" feelings and fear. This is made especially clear in "The [Widget], the [Wadget], and Boff" (1955), where the aliens discuss freeing their human friends' "reason" from "unreasonable" repressions. The return to "sanity" of the various characters and the conditions under which they experience this freedom to act "rationally," however, demonstrate no application of "will." Instead, people experience emotional release resulting in healthy self-appreciation and self-expression accompanied by improved social relationships, love, and joy. Sturgeon's inner awareness is truer than his explanation.

Unlike Heinlein, Sturgeon rarely envisions telepathy as a skill possessed only by the elite. Except in *More Than Human* (1953), he employs it as a kind of full-group communication. It makes possible the sharing of abilities as well as of needs, and also the community of effort that permits both full participation in the group and full development of individual ability. This is the opposite of Heinlein's concept of a "group mind" in *Methuselah's Children*, where people melt into the mass. Heinlein presents the loss of "self" as a terrible sacrifice; Sturgeon does not consider it at all a necessary corollary to full communication. Sturgeon's communal group mind does not overwhelm. As he shows in *The Cosmic Rape* (1958; expanded from "To Marry Medusa," also 1958), participants become more themselves, rather than less:

> Your memory, and his and his, and hers over the horizon's shoulder—all your memories are mine. More: your personal orientation in the framework of your own experiences, your I-in-the-past, is also mine. More: your skills remain your own (is great music made less for being shared?) but your sensitivity to your special subject is mine now, and your pride in your excellence is mine now. More: though bound to the organism, Mankind, as never before, I am I as never before. When Man has demands on me, I am totally dedicated to Man's purpose. Otherwise, within the wide, wide limits of mankind's best interests, I am as never before a free agent; I am I to a greater degree, and with less obstruction from within and without, than ever before possible. For gone, gone altogether are individual man's hosts of pests and devils, which in strange combinations have plagued us all in the past: the They-don't-want-me devil, the Suppose-they-find-out devil, the twin imps of They-are-lying-to-me and They-are-trying-to-cheat-me; gone, gone is I'm-afraid-to-try, and They-won't-let-me, and I-couldn't-be-loved-if-they-knew. . . .
>
> In short, it was abruptly possible for mankind to live with itself in health. (142–143)

The emphasis is less on information (though that, too, is shared) than on emotional openness. In *The Cosmic Rape*, when humans gain the ability to combine into a "hive mind," they not only defeat "Medusa" but also enable a lost child to find her way to safety, while the entire world rejoices with and for her. This is not achieved without cost. Defeating the alien invasion takes the life of at least one unhappy child who throws himself into the alien's machinery; the human collective has that grief to live with as well.

This openness eliminates the fears that lead to divisiveness, hatred, and war among mankind, strengthening rather than weakening society. As in *Venus Plus X*, "The Skills of Xanadu," and other stories, society becomes "whole" in a wholly self-satisfying way. It also becomes wholly capable of defending itself from aggression without feeling forced to resort to the violence it has forsworn. In "The Skills of Xanadu," the society simply shares its communications technology with the aggressor, thus automatically converting "them" to "us," a true example of the Golden Rule; in *The Cosmic Rape*, it merges with the "Medusa," creating a greater unity "full of wonder, full of worship" (155).

One story in which paranormal communication seems strangely limited is *More Than Human* (1953). (This famous story skims the atomic scenario: what is the "magic" device that Lone has applied to Prodd's ancient truck? What could the army have done with it, had Hap been allowed to discover it?) Here, communication allows a group of subnormal but also paranormal people to live and grow into a powerful ethical force. "To blesh" is far more than "to receive information." It transmits all the needs and emotions that connect them as well. Society need not fear the result, however, since Hap becomes the "heart," the ethical center of the group. This permits them to join a greater community, and hope remains that the few "more-than-human" entities who welcome the newcomer will continue to grow in number.

For Sturgeon, genuine communication reveals the inherent goodness in people while permitting both acceptance and healing of the incomplete or unhappy. As a metaphor, it emphasizes the oneness of humanity. Where Heinlein's elite is marked by its supernormal communication, Sturgeon's supernormal communication includes everybody; we are all elite. His telepathy encompasses all spectra of experience and claims it as "human."

The Aliens, Ourselves

For both Sturgeon and Heinlein, aliens often serve as the "other," the emotional opposite of man, the mirror that reflects what the writer believes to be "truly human." The wider the emotional range a writer can envision, the better able he is to convince a reader of the validity of his characters' emotions. If, however, there is a substantial part of his own experience that he has repressed or denied as being his own emotion or action, the only way he can portray it—and then without deep understanding or conviction—is to project it upon some "outside" character, the "enemy." As many psychologists have pointed out, aliens often figure as the part of "ourselves" that we wish to deny or repress and that we project into others.[52]

Heinlein creates two very different kinds of aliens: those he approves of and those he does not. In each, the pattern of projection is clear. Aliens he likes embody all the characteristics that he feels characterize "man" at his best: intelligence, logic, longevity (or relative immortality), power over nature and circumstances, and close (but rarely demonstrative) social relations. This description fits the "Martians" he invented in *Red Planet* (1949) and continued to use in *Double Star* (1956) and *Stranger in a Strange Land* (1961), as well as the Venusian "dragons" in *Between Planets* (1951) and the "Mother Thing" in *Have Space Suit—Will Travel*.[53] Heinlein describes these aliens inventively, making the physical characteristics plausible. Quite realistically, he shows that humans may have difficulty adjusting to them. Sometimes these aliens pose an unintended threat to humans simply because they have other, conflicting concerns; sometimes they develop a long-term fear of humanity as a supplanting race; but they are not presented as menacing simply because they "are" that way (see note 48).

But Heinlein also creates another group of aliens in his fiction. These are portrayed as intent on wiping out humanity, either on Earth, as in *The Puppet Masters*, or in space, as in *Starship Troopers*. The more dangerous they are, the more they revolt us physically, like the "slugs" in *The Puppet Masters* or "wormface" in *Have Space Suit—Will Travel*. In *Starship Troopers*, the insectoids of the "Hive" are shown to be a far more formidable enemy than the humanoid "skinnies." Group minds are dangerous and unknowable; humans cannot develop treaties with the "Hive" the way they did with the "skinnies" whose planet they have invaded. As in *The Puppet Masters*, the Troopers feel compelled to wipe out the dangerous aliens entirely. In *Have Space Suit—Will Travel*, the verdict of the galactic trial "rotates" the wormfaces' planet out of normal space without its sun. This drive utterly to eliminate the "enemy" functions as a psychological denial of sharing any of the "evil" characteristics projected onto the aliens. We find exactly the opposite effect with the "good" aliens, on whom admirable characteristics are projected; in this case, ordinary human society is portrayed as lacking most of these desirable traits.

For Sturgeon, however, invading aliens usually are either actively or inadvertently benevolent.[54] In "Rule of Three" and "Make Room for Me" (both 1951), aliens who group in threes, a problem when they are forced to inhabit Terrestrials whose sexual and social units are normally binary, set off a radical redisposition of human society, in the first by accident, in the second by design. In "The Traveling Crag" (1951), the aliens are actively helpful. In "The [Widget], the [Wadget], and Boff," (1955), the aliens may originally have come merely as observers but have become fond of humans and intervene to release at least a few of them from the emotional and psychological blocks that inhibit their full effectiveness and normal levels of self-preservation. The result is that these humans become potentially able not only to save themselves but also to pass their new capabilities to their race and culture.

In "To Marry Medusa" and *The Cosmic Rape* (both 1958), the "Medusa" does not intend evil for mankind, though it may seem to. Since it has never met an intelligent race that did not possess a group mind, it sets out to take over and "recombine" the individual humans for their own good. Under the influence of powerful alien technology, humanity does find a unified consciousness; then it joins the greater consciousness, but is not subsumed by it. As he does in "The [Widget], the [Wadget], and Boff," Sturgeon expresses the benefits of the new consciousness largely through sexual metaphor. Inhibited, self-righteous, unhappy people become joyous participants in sexual experience and in society. In only two stories, "The Sky Was Full of Ships" (1947) and "Beware the Fury" (1954), do the aliens seem genuinely evil.

For Heinlein, any diminution of ego equates with "losing control." He avoids emotional extremes. His protagonist may love (or at least like someone well enough to engage in sex, which amounts to about the same thing for Heinlein), but he rarely hates. If he gets really angry, as Kip does during his trial in *Have Space Suit—Will Travel*, the outburst is shown as childish, but the result is unexpectedly fortunate, as his anger somehow gives him control in an otherwise uncontrollable situation.[55] But a threat to his self-control, particularly a threat to control of himself expressed in his sexuality, can elicit genuine terror expressed as rage, as we see in the two novels with the most terrifying, cold-blooded, and destructive aliens: *The Puppet Masters* and *Starship Troopers*. Even so, these aliens, on whom Heinlein has projected the limits of his fear and loathing, are opposed only by an elite group of united, passionately committed, and angry humans; the rest of humanity appears helplessly passive.

Sturgeon's characters can lose control if that seems appropriate; they can love passionately, hate deeply, fear terribly, and generally express the gamut of human emotions. Since Sturgeon's aliens, like his humans, show a wide emotional range, we may infer that Sturgeon integrates and accepts the range of emotions and states available to humans and portrays them through aliens when that seems most useful.[56] This gives him extreme freedom in his choice of protagonists and plots. James Blish finds "Sturgeon's work . . . charged with highly personal emotion" (1973, 43). This emotional freedom has given Sturgeon the reputation of an artist among science fiction writers, but it sometimes results in stories that seem to lose resolution in the complications of the situation.[57] It also makes him somewhat threatening to those expecting no more than a traditionally logical and emotionally restrained literature.[58]

To emphasize Sturgeon's emotional range is not to imply that Heinlein creates stiff, unbelievable "cardboard" characters; indeed, many are extremely attractive. But they are *characteristic*, and very often they are simplified. Heinlein shows people acting in ways that are easy for the reader to identify and empathize with and that do not often call up strong emotions. Indeed, some of his popularity may have come from his careful refusal to exceed emotional limits in creating characters, while creatively exceeding limits in his extrapolation of technology and social development.

SUMMARY

We find a striking contrast here: the Heinlein hero, popular, powerful, and capable as he is, and coming as he does from a society in apparent need of thoroughgoing change, is not often shown as able to create this change or even as interested in doing so. He wants only to save the world so things work for him; when his own condition is significantly improved (and this often takes place away from the social situation that appeared to motivate him in the first place), he rarely even attempts to improve the condition of society as a whole. If he does, the change is not portrayed as fundamental. Indeed, given Heinlein's concept of society, he cannot change it. It is subject to impersonal forces beyond human control. Moreover, society itself does not desire or deserve such change. In the Heinlein universe, "human nature" and social forces naturally and inevitably cause recurring wars.[59]

The Sturgeon hero does not usually expect to save the world. He interacts with his society to do his best for it and for himself. If he does try single-handedly to save the world, he is often shown as making a tragic mistake, even in stories where the salvation seems effective, like "Unite and Conquer." For unlike the hierarchical societies of Heinlein, those that Sturgeon envisions as ideal have all members in full communication, acting in full cooperation one with another. This cooperation does not, as in some utopian visions, lead to stasis or stagnation; rather, the society provides full happiness for everyone, with creative people sharing their creativity and those whose contribution is to work with the ideas of others having those ideas available at all times. Sturgeon moves his protagonist more intimately into society, as Heinlein moves him out, but both want the end to be an ideal associating, signified by the metaphor of full communication. While Heinlein often uses relative isolation as a reward for excellence, Sturgeon uses it as his closest metaphoric approach to hell.[60]

The explicit contrasts between possibilities for human social transacting that show up when we compare Sturgeon's assumptions with Heinlein's also give us some insight into what we may call the "American myth" of society. Heinlein accepts the popular assumptions, tacitly treating society as a "thing" constructed by interacting forces and less than the sum of its human parts. Sturgeon explicitly treats society as made up of valuable and salvageable humans, even while he criticizes it; as society is currently structured, its human components find themselves isolated, alienated, and unhappy. He accepts the possibility of altering this intolerable condition by exploring the methods by which such alteration might take place. That neither Heinlein nor Sturgeon can envision salvation for humanity without some drastic realignment of society or of human nature is clear. Heinlein insists that a superforce must be applied to control the "wild animal," man. This will not eliminate war, which he does not consider possible, but may postpone it as long as possible.[61]

In contrast to Heinlein's "optimism," which foresees a cycle of recurring catastrophes narrowly averted, Sturgeon's position seems radical, but more genuinely optimistic. He shows that humanity can destroy itself utterly, but that an alternative is possible: openness and true expression of humanness can give even the least gifted and competent person the opportunity to participate in a radical change that fully affects society. Although his message is not only fictional but often cast in fantastic terms, Sturgeon searches for ways to organize society so as to eliminate the fundamental causes of atomic war.

Heinlein finds the need to save society obvious and the problems identifiable. As he repeats in *The Puppet Masters* and *Starship Troopers*, the danger to mankind comes not from intraspecies warfare—man's inhumanity—but from powerful, alien, utterly "inhuman" forces (including aggression and sexuality) that must be opposed by force. The solution is equally obvious: society can be saved from these forces only by a strong or unusually gifted human or group of humans who can act to save society only if removed from that society. His metaphor of change usually appears as a new force or weapon. Sturgeon's view is quite the opposite. He is much less sure that anyone knows what needs to be done to save society, aside from improved intraspecies and communication and emotional openness. He feels that changes are possible and that they may be initiated by unlikely people. Moreover, as they occur in individuals, these changes will affect society as a whole. The process is transactional and can only take place among people engaged in social intercourse; his metaphors are frequently sexual.

The contrast between the assumptions of Heinlein and Sturgeon can be stated in existential terms. Heinlein divides all humanity into two groups. He projects qualities he esteems on his hero—intelligence, energy, health, emotional control, and enormous good fortune—while tacitly denying those qualities to the rest of the human race.[62] These are the hopeless masses who must be saved from some external threat by the elect, with or without their consent. But they cannot change their nature and will certainly get into trouble again. As before, they will be unable either to counter the threat themselves or to see that they had any role in creating it. What else can you expect from fundamentally weak people like us? he seems to ask. Heinlein thus operates from existential shame.

Sturgeon assumes that people are fundamentally competent and caring, but that they often prevent their own effectiveness by artificial separation and culturally imposed rigidities. This attitude implies their ability to change. Furthermore, Sturgeon assumes that when people change, those they come in contact with will necessarily change in response: he recognizes the transactional aspects of human behavior. Sturgeon thus operates from existential guilt and takes responsibility for it.

Heinlein usually writes about situations that are both more "realistic" and more limited in scope than those used by Sturgeon. He refuses both annihilation and the millennium. Other "people" may destroy their worlds, as he implies in "Blowups Happen" and *Space Cadet*, but this seems to be no more than a warning to our elite so they can maintain a "safe" status quo. Alien invaders, as in *The Puppet Masters* and *Starship Troopers*, cannot do humanity any permanent damage. *Farnham's Freehold*, although a dark vision, does not hint at the possibility of the end of humanity as a species. Heinlein sees no need to explain how or why humanity survives, though he does suggest that we may end our white-dominated (Northern Hemisphere) civilization. (Note that Heinlein also suggests that even this modest reversal of the status quo may again be reversed by Farnham's successful time travel.) He approves of Farnham, who rejects tenderness for sentimentality, and whose sex life leads to procreation, not cannibalism. He exhibits good American values: entrepreneurship, technological inventiveness, aggressive defensiveness, and patriotism. Thus he proves himself the "natural" heir to a long tradition, the one that led to the war that started the story and that gives promise of more wars in the future.[63]

Sturgeon looks carefully at both sides as well as at the middle of the nuclear scenario. He can envision humanity's self-generated genocide as well as its radical salvation, and he can envision that salvation as due to man's own efforts, to his having either avoided or survived atomic disaster. He can also imagine ways for humanity to utilize its own saving human capabilities to work out a truly satisfying social system that does not rely either on imposed force or on supernormal heroics to save itself. In connection with the atomic scenario, the one plot he does not favor is Heinlein's favorite: "human nature" forcing humanity to repeat the same errors and to experience recurring wars. Sturgeon's ability to look at the whole spectrum of possibility is similar to his ability to put "himself" into a wide variety of protagonists. The ability to envision and come to emotional terms with wholesale disaster—as in "Memorial" or "Thunder and Roses"—permits Sturgeon the freedom to search for inventive, radical solutions to the problem of war, as in *The Cosmic Rape* or *Venus Plus X*. Sturgeon was not successful in supplanting the popular assumptions that Heinlein and a majority of other science fiction writers so ably reinforced. Yet Sturgeon, rather than Heinlein, seems most powerfully to move science fiction beyond the simple didacticism of its origins towards the more complex, ambiguous, uncertain view of "reality" that we now expect from mature fiction and from "real life."

STORIES BY ROBERT A. HEINLEIN

Title	Date	Publisher
"Misfit"	1939, Nov.	*Astounding Science Fiction*
"If This Goes On—"	1940, Feb.–Mar.	*Astounding Science Fiction*
"Let There Be Light"	1940, May	*Super Science Stories*
"Coventry"	1940, July	*Astounding Science Fiction*
"Blowups Happen"	1940, Sep.	*Astounding Science Fiction*
Sixth Column	1941, Jan.–Mar.	*Astounding Science Fiction*
"Solution Unsatisfactory"	1941, May	*Astounding Science Fiction*
"Lost Legacy"	1941, Nov.	*Super Science Stories*
"The Green Hills of Earth"	1947, Feb. 8	*Saturday Evening Post*
Space Cadet	1948	Scribner's
"Gulf"	1949, Nov.–Dec.	*Astounding Science Fiction*
"The Long Watch"	1949, Dec.	*American Legion Magazine*
Between Planets	1951	Scribner's
The Puppet Masters	1951	Doubleday
"The Year of the Jackpot"	1952, Mar.	*Galaxy Science Fiction*
"Project Nightmare"	1953, April	*Amazing Stories*
Have Space Suit—Will Travel	1958	Scribner's
" 'All You Zombies—' "	1959, Mar.	*Fantasy and Science Fiction*
Starship Troopers	1959	Putnam
Farnham's Freehold	1964	Putnam

STORIES BY THEODORE STURGEON

Title	Date	Publisher
"A God in a Garden"	1939, Oct.	*Unknown*

"Microcosmic God"	1941, Apr.	*Astounding Science Fiction*
"Artnan Process"	1941, June	*Astounding Science Fiction*
"The Purple Light"	1941, June	*Astounding Science Fiction*
"Killdozer!"	1944, Nov.	*Astounding Science Fiction*
"August Sixth, 1945"	1945, Dec.	*Astounding Science Fiction*
"Memorial"	1946, Apr.	*Astounding Science Fiction*
"The Sky Was Full of Ships"	1947, June	*Thrilling Wonder Stories*
"Thunder and Roses"	1947, Nov.	*Astounding Science Fiction*
"There Is No Defense"	1948, Feb.	*Astounding Science Fiction*
"Unite and Conquer"	1948, Oct.	*Astounding Science Fiction*
"Farewell to Eden"	1949	Dell
"Prodigy"	1949, Apr.	*Astounding Science Fiction*
"Rule of Three"	1951, Jan.	*Galaxy Science Fiction*
"Make Room for Me"	1951, May	*Fantastic Adventures*
"The Traveling Crag"	1951, July	*Fantastic Adventures*
"Never Underestimate"	1952, Mar.	*If*
More Than Human	1953	Farrar; Ballantine
"The Wages of Synergy"	1953, Aug.	*Startling Stories*
"The Touch of Your Hand"	1953, Sep.	*Galaxy Science Fiction*
"Beware the Fury" ["Extrapolation"]	1954, Apr.	*Fantastic Stories*
"Granny Won't Knit"	1954, May	*Galaxy Science Fiction*
"The [Widget], the [Wadget], and Boff"	1955, Nov.–Dec.	*Fantasy and Science Fiction*
"The Skills of Xanadu"	1956, July	*Galaxy Science Fiction*
"The Pod in the Barrier"	1957, Sep.	*Galaxy Science Fiction*
"To Marry Medusa"	1958, Aug.	*Galaxy Science Fiction*
The Cosmic Rape	1958	Dell
Venus Plus X	1960	Pyramid

NOTES

1. The stories included here represent about 26 percent of Heinlein's body of work published between 1939 and 1965, and about 22 percent of Sturgeon's. Sturgeon wrote more short works and fewer novels than Heinlein did. Sturgeon published a total of 129 science fiction stories and 6 novels, not counting anthologies of previously published stories. (This total does not include his mystery and Western fiction or the 40 or so nonfantasy works he wrote for and published in *McClure's*, 1937–38, according to Sam Moskowitz in "Theodore Sturgeon: No More Than Human," *Amazing Fact and Science Fiction Stories*, February 1962, 31.) Heinlein produced 53 stories and 27 novels (not counting anthologies of previously published stories).

2. See Heinlein's Forward in *Expanded Universe: The New Worlds of Robert A. Heinlein* (New York: Ace, 1980), 145–47, and the three articles that follow.

3. This ironic blindness is even more noticeable since the character of Dr. Karst is developed on the person of Dr. Lise Meitner, who escaped from Germany in 1939. She had worked on nuclear fission. The factual Dr. Meitner must have been less of an "innocent" than the fictional Dr. Karst but would not have supported the pathos of the situation as well.

4. Robert A. Heinlein, "On the Writing of Speculative Fiction," 199–202, and "Science Fiction: Its Nature, Faults and Virtues," 4, both in *Turning Points*, ed. Damon Knight (New York: Harper and Row, 1977).

5. "To Marry Medusa" (1958) was expanded in the same year and published as *The Cosmic Rape*. They are counted as one story.

6. The protagonist of "To Marry Medusa" is not normal, but is competent; he has survived rather ingeniously (if uncomfortably) to adulthood.

7. Note, however, how often the extrapolated "problem" in Heinlein's society must be explained to the hero. Heinlein is very good at making the setting explain itself; he is less subtle in presenting lessons he wants the reader to learn about how the setting got that way. See especially *Sixth Column*, *The Puppet Masters*, "Gulf," and *Starship Troopers*.

8. The narrator of "Solution Unsatisfactory" discusses the protagonist's unhappy situation: hated and feared, yet responding to the demands of duty, he must somehow force an unwilling world to yield to his benign authority for its own self-preservation. But we should note that the title of this story, often cited to show Heinlein's distress at the situation, was provided not by Heinlein, but by the editor of *Astounding Science Fiction*, John Campbell. Heinlein, writing as "Anson MacDonald," had titled the story "Foreign Policy." (See *Astounding Science Fiction*, April 1941, 69.)

9. "Coventry" is a sequel to " 'If This Goes On—' " (both 1940). The society proposed in "Coventry" is the result of a revolution against a theocracy imposed upon the United States by a fundamentalist religious group. This revolution is achieved by force of arms and (in the original version) by psychological "readjustment" of a large segment of the population.

10. As H. Bruce Franklin comments in *Robert A. Heinlein: America as Science Fiction* (Oxford: Oxford University Press, 1980), Heinlein consistently sees only two "alternatives [for society]: either the elite (the *good* elite) saves the day,

which obviously contradicts democratic principles . . . or society succumbs to the ignorance and folly of the masses of common people. His concept of revolutionary social change imagines something created *by* an elite *for* the benefit of the people, usually quite temporarily. He seems incapable of believing that progressive social change could come through the development of the productive forces and consequent action by the exploited classes themselves" (34).

11. Theodore Sturgeon, Foreword to *Sturgeon Is Alive and Well . . .* (New York: Putnam, 1971), 11.

12. Heinlein accurately predicted the U.S. atomic test grounds.

13. It seems unfair to label the accurate perception of great danger a "psychosis," a term that implies an irrational apprehension or conviction of victimization. In Heinlein's context, however, it is metaphorically if not psychiatrically accurate. Technology may kill you, but it is not "out to get you." It represents progress and, as such, is automatically good. Fearing it, even fearing your own death from it, can thus be seen as an "irrational" condition.

14. This is also true for *Sixth Column*, another "Campbell" story.

15. Campbell's comments on future issues in the "In Times to Come" column, *Astounding Science Fiction*, November 1939, strengthen the presumption that Heinlein is working out a Campbell idea:

> This is the first issue of Astounding to be finally assembled since Europe lost its temper. . . .
>
> May we hope that attempts to release the unimaginable energy locked in uranium atoms, on a useful scale, remain complete and unmitigated failures until such time as the family fight in Europe is concluded? (78)

16. Heinlein seems to be trying out tactics here, like the "voice of moderation" who dies before he becomes inconvenient. He will repeat these tactics in later works such as " 'If This Goes On—' " as revised, and *The Moon Is a Harsh Mistress*. He also creates phrases that he becomes fond of and repeats both in his fiction and his factual articles, like his description of a liberal as one who knows water runs downhill but hopes it won't reach the bottom.

17. Manning thus succeeds in two fields that Heinlein tried without success.

18. Heinlein is not enamored of politicians, as a rule, and often has some pretty harsh things to say about military men; but when they are good, they are very very good. These qualifications establish Manning as a practical man: the "man who knows how" (see note 10).

19. Heinlein claims in *Expanded Universe* that it was hard work for him to write from Campbell's ideas: "I had to reslant it to remove racist aspects of the original story line. And I didn't really believe the pseudoscientific rationale of Campbell's three spectra—so I worked especially hard to make it sound realistic" (93). He "removes racist aspects" by including a "good Jap"—a Nisei who sacrifices himself for his country, as does the Japanese aviator in Meek's "The Red Peril."

20. "Solution Unsatisfactory" and *Sixth Column* reflect older patterns: fear of the "Yellow Peril" and use of a secret weapon to enforce Pax Americana on the world. Each new generation must explore the old plots in its own way, and here the old master suggested the plots.

21. H. Bruce Franklin observes that "Robert Heinlein was not the only one

having recurring fantasies about nuclear bombs raining on American cities in a sneak attack. This was and is a national nightmare in the only country in the world that has ever actually used nuclear bombs, a country that had launched sneak attacks not on military targets but on the civilian population of two major cities" (*Robert A. Heinlein*, 156). Note that Sturgeon also projects this fearful nuclear scenario in "Thunder and Roses," where the United States is the victim of a sneak attack by not one but two "enemy" nations.

22. In *Expanded Universe*, Heinlein claims that he "wrote nine articles intended to shed light on the post-Hiroshima age" but was "up against some heavy tonnage," so they went unpublished. This "heavy tonnage" consisted of conservative, comforting reassurance from highly placed military experts to the effect that atomic war was impossible. "The old sailors want wooden ships, the old soldiers want horse cavalry" (145–46). He gives no dates for the writing of the three articles included in this volume: "The Last Days of The United States," "How to Be a Survivor," and "Pie from the Sky," nor did he respond to my letter of inquiry. Internal evidence suggests that they were written before Russia exploded its atomic bomb in 1949.

23. Note the similarity of this conclusion to that of Captain Harrington in "Blowups Happen." He warns the engineers of potential errors in the mathematics by which they run the atomic plant, claiming that the Moon might once have been inhabited by sentient beings who blew away their atmosphere with an atomic explosion.

24. This apparent back-formation shows how carefully Heinlein makes his "future history" consistent.

25. The "clock" on the cover of the *Bulletin of the Atomic Scientists* that "tells the world what [nuclear] time it is" registered two or three minutes to midnight during this period. We were as close, they felt, to imminent disaster then as at any time since 1947, when the clock first appeared on the *Bulletin* cover showing seven minutes to midnight.

26. *The Puppet Masters* (1951), which does not explicitly operate from the atomic scenario, will be discussed later.

27. Heinlein does not always make his "superman" a young, handsome, Aryan male. He is particularly fond of superbly capable little old ladies; his paranormal heroes also include a sickly youngster and several social misfits like Andrew Jackson Libby in "Misfit" (1939). In this regard, Heinlein and Sturgeon reflect similar tastes in characters. See, for example, Sturgeon's "Granny Won't Knit," *More Than Human*, and *The Cosmic Rape*.

28. The possibility of smuggling atomic devices into the "wide-open" United States rather than delivering them by missile, airplane, or submarine was specifically mentioned in the Franck Report and much feared during this period. See, for example, Philip Wylie's *The Smuggled Atom Bomb* (1951, in the *Saturday Evening Post*) and James Blish's "One-Shot" (1955).

29. Worthy of note here as a plot device is the ready adoption by the military of such an unconventional "weapon," although Heinlein has often criticized the conservatism of the military and its reliance on yesterday's weapons to fight tomorrow's war (see note 22).

30. Heinlein knows about radiation illness, as he shows in "Solution Unsatisfactory," but in later fiction he seems blithely to ignore the danger from any-

thing less than fatal doses of fallout. He tacitly denies that every move we make to "control" the international situation with atomic weapons puts "us" in as much danger as it does "them." (In 1958 he campaigned to continue nuclear testing when it endangered the same Southwest he threatened fictionally in "Blowups Happen.") Contrast Sturgeon's depiction of radiation poisoning in "Thunder and Roses" (1947).

31. Heinlein has received much criticism on this novel and has written an impassioned rebuttal aimed at those who cannot properly read the simple declarative English sentence and thus have misunderstand his message. This defense is included with the reprint of "Who Are the Heirs of Patrick Henry? Stand Up and Be Counted!" in *Expanded Universe*, 396–402. Unfortunately, Heinlein does not discuss how society decays sufficiently to require the Draconian measures shown in the book, whether through Communist infiltration and influence, as suggested by his "Patrick Henry" advertisement, or through democratic ignorance and decadence, as suggested in his rebuttal, or some combination of the two. (The implication seems to be that if you can understand what happened, you don't need to be told; if you need to be told, you wouldn't understand anyway.)

32. The situation in this novel thus repeats one that Heinlein had already imagined in *The Puppet Masters*, which will be discussed later. The difference is that in the earlier book, the aliens came to Earth; Earth did not go to them.

33. Until recently, this work had not been included in any Sturgeon bibliography. It appeared in the letters to the editor column in the first issue of *Astounding Science Fiction* that could possibly have printed it, December 1945. The quotation is from a telephone conversation between Sturgeon and the author, June 6, 1983.

34. See Paul Boyer, *By the Bomb's Early Light* (New York: Pantheon, 1985).

35. The idea of exploding the bomb in a deserted area reflects Sturgeon's awareness both of the nature of atomic testing and of the Franck Report's recommendation to drop a "demonstration" bomb on an uninhabited Japanese island in an attempt to force an early surrender while avoiding massive loss of life.

36. Note the similarity between this plot and Ridenour's in "Pilot Lights of the Apocalypse." It also shows another aspect of Campbell's warnings in his *Astounding Science Fiction* editorials: that an atomic war is entirely possible, even if no one knows who initiates the attack.

37. Quoted from a telephone conversation between Sturgeon and the author.

38. One problem with this story arises when the protagonist enters a "decorator shop" and buys flowers for his grandmother. Properly extending the metaphor would have precluded this—and the protagonist's immediate delight in the "green world" of his "dream" as well.

39. Note that although Heinlein formally advocates a government run by women, in his stories he often shows women as incompetent, selfish, cowardly escapists. Sturgeon does not lecture about equality of the sexes; he simply shows it in action. Here, women are less thoroughly conditioned than are men. Both physiologically and emotionally, they are the logical humans to create a new world. Granny's creation merely happens to require technological rather than physiological fertility.

40. This unity, though achieved by technology, resembles that at the end of "To Marry Medusa."

41. Apparently, the nuclear war that precipitated Hugh Farnham and his family into the far future spared only the blacks of darkest Africa; they have repopulated the world, enslaving or eating any whites they happened to find. White males who achieve even limited authority in this world pay for it with their testes and their thumbs, thus becoming human oxen. Heinlein is attempting a sexual reference here as well as a social one. (Note that Heinlein apparently concurs with Sturgeon's assumption about the location where humans may survive in "Granny Won't Knit," a much earlier story.)

42. It should be noted that Heinlein begins, about 1961, to employ explicit sexual situations in his writing. He felt that the country was beginning to relax its strictures on sexuality and was fully vindicated by the response to *Stranger in a Strange Land* (1961). (See *Expanded Universe*, 403.) Unlike Sturgeon, he uses sex situationally rather than metaphorically. Moreover, these situations seem oriented less to social integration and more to personal satisfaction than anything in Sturgeon's work. They approach soft porn in intent and effect.

43. Farnham's family stands as a tacit indictment of Farnham himself. Their problems are ascribed to socioeconomic forces, but neither wife nor son changes under the new conditions.

44. Compare this situation with that in *Stranger in a Strange Land* (1961).

45. In "Lost Legacy," the loss of telepathic power symbolizes the Fall of Man, who forfeits his right to godlikeness when he shows selfishness, pride, and competitiveness.

46. For Heinlein, telepathy provides a tremendous advantage for the user, although he does posit some psychological drawbacks in *Time for the Stars* (1956). His psi-users never suffer the kinds of psychological damage envisioned by Alfred Bester in *The Demolished Man* (1953), by Poul Anderson in "Journeys End" (1957), or by Robert Silverberg in *Dying Inside* (1972), because they control their telepathy. Nor does Heinlein explain why humanity has evolved away from such a useful ability.

47. The isolating quality of a special ability like telepathy is also a crucial part of the fictions by Bester, Silverberg, and Anderson cited in note 46. In Silverberg's *Dying Inside*, for example, the protagonist is not only bitterly unhappy and isolated from society, but can feel himself as human only as and to the extent that he loses the telepathic talent with which he was born. In contrast, Heinlein seems to show this isolation of the elite as reward, not as punishment (see note 10).

48. This is particularly true in *Stranger in a Strange Land*, where the Martians teach Valentine Michael Smith their magically potent language and manner of thought and permit him to return to Earth. These aliens are fully telepathic, but remain individuals who are often shown as withdrawing into meditative solitude for eons. Their social life is undescribed, but it seems mentally close (at the individual's option) and physically solitary. They can withdraw from telepathic contact at will. It is made clear that they have tremendous power; they both can and probably will attempt to destroy Earth some day. On the other hand, since Smith has taught his special language and the ability it confers to other humans, by the time the Martians get around to it, they may not be able to.

49. Heinlein's first story, "Life-Line" (1939), involved a man who knew when people (including himself) would die; the narrator in "Solution Unsatisfactory" wonders, as he writes the story to pass time while he dies of radiation poisoning, whether or not there is something to the idea of life after death. As Heinlein ages, more of his fiction includes speculation on longevity, personality survival after death, and immortality.

50. Heinlein, who feared the Russian ability to extend its hegemony without provoking war, may be commenting on conditions in Russia and its satellites.

51. Thus the aliens are destroyed in much the same way that some American Indian tribes were. Instead of being given smallpox-infected blankets, they are exposed to a deadly disease deliberately given to their hosts.

52. "A projection is a trait, attitude, feeling, or bit of behavior which actually belongs to your own personality but is not experienced as such; instead, it is attributed to objects or persons in the environment and then experienced as directed *toward* you by them instead of the other way around. The projector, unaware, for instance, that he is rejecting others, believes that they are rejecting him; or, unaware of his tendencies to approach others sexually, feels that they make sexual approaches to him" (Frederick S. Perls et al., *Gestalt Therapy* (New York: Julian Press, 1951), 212.) Projecting is especially noticeable in Heinlein's fiction, since he limits the range of feelings and actions he permits both his society and his protagonists so severely and projects both his fears and his desires so obviously upon "alien" enemies.

53. Note the contrast between aliens in *Have Space Suit—Will Travel*: the "bad" one emanates pure evil, is probably a cannibal, and is considered a menace by other aliens, while the "Mother Thing" not only acts good, she "feels good" to the young protagonists as well.

54. Sometimes they are not even alien; see "Unite and Conquer."

55. As George Slusser, *The Classic Years of Robert A. Heinlein* notes, a similar courtroom scene occurs in *Farnham's Freehold*, with a surprisingly similar result (56).

56. Note the number of times he deals with homosexuality by imputing it to aliens rather than to humans, as in "The World Well Lost (1953)," "Affair With a Green Monkey (1957)," and so on.

57. It also results in stories that become popular after society as a whole has caught up to the ideas Sturgeon was presenting—see, for example, "The World Well Lost" (1953), which caused quite a furor when first published, and "If All Men Were Brothers, Would You Let One Marry Your Sister?" (1967).

58. James Blish, "Theodore Sturgeon's Macrocosm," in the *Magazine of Fantasy and Science Fiction*, September 1962, 43.

59. "Heinlein still subscribes to a rather naive theory—'you can't change human nature.' And his concept of human nature . . . seems to include pugnacity, sensuality, and sentimentality in extremes." Robert Bloch, "Imagination and Modern Social Criticism," in *The Science Fiction Novel*, ed. Basil Davenport (Chicago: Advent, 1959), 112.

60. Note that in "Memorial" and in "Microcosmic God," the protagonists have voluntarily cut themselves off from society. In this, they approach the sin of Satan—instead of challenging God, they have challenged the constructive

unity of society—and have chosen their punishment, which is to be appropriately isolated or destroyed.

61. Heinlein, "The Third Millennium Opens," in *Expanded Universe*, 382.

62. Note that psychologists find nothing wrong with projection; used awarely, it allows people to understand others, to empathize, and to cooperate. When it operates unawarely, however, it can be pathological. The projector believes that he knows how people really are, while failing to see that he is projecting aspects of himself on them. He also refuses to admit the existence of those qualities in himself that he fears, like tenderness for a "he-man." Thus he must perceive all such threats as external to himself; he literally cannot see them as a natural part of his being.

63. Compare Heinlein's use of time travel to save Farnham and his group from an undesired future with that employed in Asimov's *The End of Eternity* (1955).

8

Humans and History

Told of Hiroshima by a reporter, Einstein (who was sailing at Saranac Lake) said, shaking his head,

> "Ach! The world is not ready for it!" . . . Within a year after Hiroshima, Einstein assumed an active role as spokesman for scientists who were worried about the bomb. "The unleashed power of the atom has changed everything except our modes of thinking," he asserted, "and we thus drift toward unparalleled catastrophe."[1]

What Einstein called "unparalleled catastrophe" we now call nuclear holocaust. Since then, we have moved no further from ground zero, and our actions show that all our effort has not altered our modes of thinking. How we act depends on the way we see our predicament, and that depends upon our assumption that history reflects human nature and that human nature is essentially fixed.

The traditional Judeo-Christian view of history is linear. It begins when

God created man, giving humans dominion over Eden. When we ate of the Tree of the Knowledge of Good and Evil, we claimed both free will and the responsibility to choose the values we live by as we create a community in the wilderness. Apocalypse will reinstate God's values and bring the millennium for the redeemed. This pattern is assumed in works like *The Man Who Ended War* and *The Vanishing Fleets*, with the millennium introduced by the Pax Americana.

The secular view of history is cyclical and entropic. It begins when we ate of the Tree of Scientific Knowledge, a fruit that we assume to be objective and value-free. It gives us control over the wilderness but dismisses values as being dictated by unalterable human nature. Since that nature is naturally aggressive, and since knowledge inevitably leads to improved weapons, Armageddon is unavoidable. Apocalypse is imminent, nuclear, self-imposed, nonredemptive, and not followed by the millennium, for this view admits no new, redeeming possibilities.

These views cannot be reconciled, but the function of myth is not to reconcile contradictions but to provide a logical model capable of overcoming them.[2] As we give fictional reality to our assumptions, we create a symbolic structure in which contradictions seem to vanish because we become blind to them. We can thus see war as the inevitable result of unalterable human nature. We structure history to validate this assumption; it shows recurrent, ever more destructive wars, punctuated by periods of prehostility designated as peace.[3] Even while we explore this in our fiction, we restate and reconfirm the assumptions that keep the cycle in place.

Contemporary writers have no trouble picturing Armageddon[4] but do not show it as followed by a thousand years of love and peace enjoyed by a redeemed elect. Instead, they either explore ways to control human nature and thus continue the (temporary) avoidance of nuclear holocaust, or they show a secular Armageddon that leaves survivors (if any) in a degraded Eden where unredeemed human nature will continue the downward spiral. In *The Sense of an Ending*, Frank Kermode argues that although we may fear the end, a figure for our own death, we who live in the middle of history need to see it in order to see the whole pattern (1966, 7). The way we see the end affects the way we live as well as the way we die, an insight that forms the major premise of Jonathan Schell's *The Fate of the Earth* (1982).

In "The Remaking of Zero," Gary Wolfe summarizes the organization of most end-of-the-world fiction as showing "five large stages of action":

> (1) the experience or discovery of the cataclysm; (2) the journey through the wasteland created by the cataclysm; (3) settlement and establishment of a new community; (4) the re-emergence of the wilderness as antagonist; and (5) a final,

decisive battle or struggle to determine which values shall prevail in the new world. (1983, 8)

To refuse an ending is to refuse pattern and purpose, a kind of psychological suicide. Our fiction thus defeats the very need to make sense of life that it is designed to satisfy, and we circle ground zero without hope and without resolution.

WAR PREVENTED

Many of the fictions we have looked at assume that humans must struggle to progress, and that solving problems may create a world in which struggle, and thus human progress, ends forever. But this assumption, tacitly continued in the nuclear age, runs counter to observed reality: after nuclear Armageddon, struggle must take place in a poisoned biosphere, in a world bereft of its Edenic potential. We now solve our problems or die. Social evolution cannot compete with environmental devolution.

To avoid this impasse, some authors provide a kind of plot "magic" (technological or otherwise) that intervenes before humanity wipes itself out, as in Rog Phillips's "Atom War" (1946), John D. MacDonald's *Ballroom of the Skies* (1952), Theodore Sturgeon's "Granny Won't Knit," (1954), and Robert A. Heinlein's *Farnham's Freehold* (1964). Others, assuming that human nature can only make things worse, bring alien cavalry over the hill. Still others assume that the current sociopolitical solution, mutual assured destruction (MAD), will continue indefinitely.

Peace Imposed

Peace may be maintained, at least temporarily, by the intervention of superhumanly benevolent and self-sacrificing scientists. Usually they intervene by inaction, withholding dangerous knowledge from the less capable and less stable populace who might misuse it. As the scientist argues in Charles Willard Diffin's "The Power and the Glory" (1930), atomic power could bring great good, but people might misuse it. The benefits of atomic energy are withheld along with the dangers, and peace is imposed by ignorance.

If the scientists are greedy instead of benevolent, peace may seem even more ambiguous. Vernor Vinge's *The Peace War* (1984) shows the effect of an antiwar weapon in dictatorial hands. When an atomic war is stopped by technology that locks every atomic explosion safely in a time-suspending "bobble," one might expect that peace and progress would result. Instead, the Peace Authority bans vehicles, power-intensive work, and all biological research, even to cure war-related diseases.

Still, people feel grateful; "The Peace has meant the end of sovereign nations and their control of technologies that could kill us all" (179). After the Peacers win the war, they continue to bobble any resistance to their authority, but many resist anyway. Once power is returned to the people, the world can reorganize and try again for peaceful contests, like space travel. (This echo of the Kuttners' "Tomorrow and Tomorrow" and "The Fairy Chessmen" may be no accident; science fiction often reflects itself.)

Since human beings cannot achieve peace unaided, some authors provide a quasi-human superrace like van Vogt's Slans to do the job. David Palmer's *Emergence* (1984) introduces a superrace, not created by atomic war but uniquely equipped to survive it and the plague that follows. These new humans spend very little time enjoying the earth they inherit, however, and quite a lot in fighting each other over now-irrelevant political issues.

Other authors bring in aliens, projecting on them either the qualities they most admire and thus find lacking in humans, or the ones they most fear and thus deny in humans. Some aliens quarantine us for our misdeeds, as in Graham Doar's "The Outer Limit" (1949), or threaten to destroy us as a danger to them, as does the tribunal in Heinlein's *Have Space Suit—Will Travel* (1958).[5] Some aliens come as angels of God, providing warring humanity one more chance to prove itself worthy of salvation, as in Frank Quattrocchi's "The Sword" (1953) and Mack Reynolds's "The Galactic Ghost" (1954). Philip Wylie's "The Answer" (1955) is far more ambiguous; how many angelic messengers can we kill before Someone gets truly upset?

Aliens can be enigmatic, as in Robert Spencer Carr's "Morning Star" (1947) and "Nightmare at Dawn" (1949), Horace Gold's "At the Post" (1953), and Ralph Williams's "Business as Usual, during Alterations" (1958), and the result of their intervention will depend upon the response of humanity. Some aliens who come to help humanity are repulsed by the people they contact, as in Mack Reynolds's "Isolationist" (1950). Sometimes, as in Jack Williamson's "With Folded Hands" (1947), alien control seems entirely too complete. That the humanoids have been constructed by humans to control destructive human impulses makes them even more alien, but no more helpful to humanity.

Even if aliens come to conquer, they may still be good for us, for they provide a target for our "natural" belligerence that does not result in international war. Instead, humanity unites against the invading forces and finds a new unity that it does not lose when the aliens are defeated.[6] The atomic scenario is merely played out with different teams—our world against theirs—as shown in Theodore Sturgeon's "There Is No Defense" (1948), or they may expose human malfeasance while doing minimal damage to Earth, as in Robert Crane's *Hero's Walk* (1954).

However peace arrives, it seems a temporary visitor. An imposed peace may become the next cause of conflict. The struggle that superraces go through to establish dominance so they can enforce peace, as in van Vogt's *Slan* (1940) and the Kuttners' *Mutant* (1953), implies (as Gordon Dickson's "Childe Cycle"[7] states explicitly) that the new race will self-destruct as well. Thus even an end that seems desirable leaves us unsure of its permanence or even of its plausibility.

MAD Forever

Mutual assured destruction may seem to be the safest international position that humans can realistically hope to achieve. We see it as an unstable but familiar and provably survivable condition. We naturally counter force with force, preparation with preparation, weapon with weapon, and provocation with provocation, as does our opponent; thus even while the opposing forces remain equal, the situation becomes more and more dangerous. A. E. van Vogt's cycle of "Weapon Shops" stories shows a society locked in MAD: the power of the Empire seems permanently balked by the magical weapons sold by the Shops to members of a static, repressed, backward, and superstitious society. Without the Weapon Shops, these people would obviously be mere serfs. Even with them, they seem to accrue no improvement in economic or political conditions.

The hope of MAD is a balance of power that ensures peace. This hope is expressed in Jack Williamson's "The Equalizer" (1947), where the ultimate power source provides everyone with absolute equality in weapons. This capability actually enhances cooperation and progress and eliminates war. In the Kuttners' *Mutant* and "Tomorrow and Tomorrow," on the other hand, the fact that everyone has atomic weapons is used to keep everyone fearful and passive.

Gully Foyle in Alfred Bester's *The Stars My Destination* (1956) creatively uses knowledge as power. By telling the common people about it and its danger, he rips the veil of secrecy that surrounds "pyrE" and permits the elite of the world to play power politics with everyone's life. Although the establishment tries to kill him as he speeds around the world spreading the word, Foyle—who has raised himself from the "common" by sheer determination—insists that people accept responsibility for themselves and their future. The opposed powers must then operate from full disclosure rather than from secrecy and planned deviousness; in a sense, all sides have become equally well armed with a weapon that actually might avert war.

But most fiction assumes that in the "real world," as in Kris Neville's "Cold War" (1949) and James Blish's "To Pay the Piper" (1956), the balance of power works in secret and leads only to madness and escalated conflict. As David Duncan shows in *Dark Dominion* (1954), destabilizing the balance of power, by putting an armed satellite in orbit, for example, may bring on the very war that the new weapon was designed to prevent. But if we lock ourselves in permanent political conflict, the situation will escalate, while "we" become more and more mechanical and more and more like "them" until, as shown by Joseph Kelleam's "Rust" (1939) and Bernard Wolfe's *Limbo* (1952), no difference exists between sides except the color of the uniform.

Even moving to a new world is not likely to solve the problems that create the need for mutual assured destruction. In Frederik Pohl's *JEM* (1979), the three great power blocs of Earth each send an expedition to a newly discovered, barely explored planet. Each expedition has the responsibility of representing its side and of outdoing and (if possible) defeating the other two. No cooperation is officially permitted among them, though it sometimes occurs when necessary. Each side finds an ally in one of the three semisentient, native races, normally held in ecological balance, and uses them against each other. As the inevitable war on Earth puts the settlers on their own, the absurd, suicidal war on JEM almost destroys the human settlement. Nobody wins, especially not the natives, who wind up in virtual slavery to the surviving humans.

A status quo of peace imposed by superior force or alien guile is little different from that of mutual assured destruction. The more effective the control, the more we will contest it or risk losing our humanity. Without war to prove our human strength of purpose, we might not even be able to recognize ourselves. Yet if atomic war should occur, we may not be here to recognize. In a very real sense, peace imposed by force or by an unstable balance of power provides no resolution to our scenario. It is a way of maintaining ambiguity, of refusing an ending.

WAR PRESENTED

In many stories, the actual advent of hostilities comes almost as a relief. We expect it and live in anticipation of it, as does the family in Tenn's "Generation of Noah" (1951). Once hostilities commence, the waiting is over, and a new kind of life begins.[8] As Wendell Johnson remarks in *Verbal Man*, "Peace on earth is an ideal to which we contribute generous ceremonial tribute, though not without uneasiness over its disquieting promise of no more fighting" (1956, 60). War provides our necessary punishment, the externalization of our internal war, and a chance to start anew, if anything is left to start from.

In the literature of atomic Armageddon, the first stages of action generally follow a similar pattern. The cataclysm is more commonly discovered than experienced; mushroom clouds appear on the horizon, not in the protagonist's front yard. Pat Frank's *Alas, Babylon* (1959) is typical:

the world is bombed, but not the protagonist and his friends. Even in Philip Wylie's *Tomorrow!* (1954) and Martin Caidin's *The Long Night* (1956), where the bombing of civilians forms the whole plot, the war itself seems remote. The enemy is invisible, and aside from radiation deaths, the towns might as easily have been leveled by an earthquake, a tornado, or a fire. Those books that most clearly outline military objectives and procedures, like Leonard Engel and Emanuel A. Piller's *World Aflame* (1947) and Lt. Col. Robert B. Rigg's *War—1974* (1958), do not seem like novels, but like dispatches from the front. Yet even these stories do not present a decisive battle that determines new values for a new world. The old ones will have to do.

Biocide

Some stories show only the first of Wolfe's stages of action, the discovery of the cataclysm. These stories represent records left by the victim of extinction, written or told while dying, reflecting our assumption that no weapon is as well designed to extinguish all life on earth as is the atomic bomb. Authors who end their tales with biocide have a peculiar problem convincing readers that they, along with the characters in the story, have been extinguished. Some forgo the attempt and use irony. Commenting on the consequences of our political fragmentation, Emery Balint in *Don't Inhale It*! (1949) and E. B. White in "The Morning of the Day They Did It" (1950) blow the world to pieces. Their stories are warning metaphors, not awful warnings. The narrators seem to get along quite well with what is left. The Kuttners' vision of Earth as a blackened cinder in *Fury* (1947), on the other hand, is pure extrapolation; the possibility was seriously considered.

Kurt Vonnegut attacks Armageddon with despairing humor in *Cat's Cradle* (1963), destroying life not with fire but with Ice–9, its complete opposite, as Robert Frost suggests.[9] Developed by a scientist partly responsible for the atomic bomb, it is willed by him to his children, not all of whom seem very responsible; eventually, it gets loose. Ice–9 is contagious. It not only freezes anything it touches, it causes that to freeze whatever it touches, and so on. As the narrator learns to live with his past in the living present, the present freezes permanently.

The vision of war beyond logic or hope of resolution is made especially real in "Flying Dutchman" (1956) by Ward Moore. Automatic bases send out unmanned bombers to avoid automatic defense systems in order to bomb cities "which had long since become finely pulverized rubble." Men who automated every aspect of war planned that "the war would go on until victory was won," no matter how civilians quailed or armies died. "The Flying Dutchman flew toward the country of the enemy, a defeated country whose armies had been annihilated and whose people had perished," over "the earth, that dead planet, upon which no living thing had been for a long, long time" (25).

Mordecai Roshwald mechanizes humanity and desertifies the planet, killing all living things, in *Level 7* (1959). His soldiers seem like robots as they march underground: they accept exchanging their names for numbers; they mechanically follow orders; they survive beyond the death of the surface of Earth from the "safety" of an underground bunker, but soon run down, poisoned by their own power source. (We may note here that no one in the underground army asserts his humanity by protesting or refusing to push a button. Responsibility under the Nuremberg decisions is not even considered.)

In *The Last Day* (1959), Helen Clarkson also shows the end of life on Earth, this time from the viewpoint of an innocent victim. Quietly, in the words of a woman who cherishes birdsong and sleep, she shows in the death of insects the final extinction of all life, even of the plants that seem to survive the narrator.

Although Jonathan Schell's *The Fate of the Earth* (1982) makes the same point from a fully documented and logical though emotional position, Clarkson's poignant story seems somehow more telling, but neither can avoid the tacit assumption the reader must make: "Of course someone survives. I'm reading it." Stories that extinguish life on Earth serve as awful warnings, but they refuse millennium and thus do not create new assumptions that may help us change our modes of thinking.

The Wasteland Wins

Various authors suggest that mankind, having violated his responsibility to take care of the Earth, will wipe himself out but leave room for some other life form—dogs, or perhaps ants—to become sentient. In Lester del Rey's "The Faithful" (1938), mutated dogs obediently help Man kill himself, dropping "tiny atomic bombs . . . on all that was Man's, who had made my race what it was. For man had told me I must fight" (9). Roshwald's unquestioning soldiers in *Level 7* are on a par with the faithful dogs; they destroy their birthright because they have been told to do so. There is some hope for the dogs, since they take responsibility for their actions and truly repent. On the other hand, Frederik Pohl's "Let the Ants Try" (1949) does not show ants as an improvement over man.

Although scientific evidence for "nuclear winter" has only been gathered in the past several years, such results of atomic war are not new in science fiction. Malcolm Jameson posited the possibility when he suggested using atomic weapons to divert ocean currents and freeze all of Eurasia in "Eviction by Isotherm" (1937). In "Tomorrow's Children" (1947), Poul Anderson and F. N. Waldrop's characters call it "*Fimbul-*

winter" and recognize that it comes from "dust, colloidal dust of the bombs, suspended in the atmosphere and cutting down the solar constant by a deadly percent or two." Though it seems like "the doom of the prophecy," the protagonist refuses it: "But no, we're surviving. Though maybe not as men . . ." (68).

William Tenn's "The Liberation of Earth" (1953) is a graphic experience of bare survival in a degraded environment. The narrator commands his audience to "suck air and grab clusters" while they listen to "the story of our liberation" (56). Caught in the middle of a great interstellar war, Earth has been persuaded to take sides first with one alien race and then the other. In every battle for its own "liberation," Earth suffers, and there is always another battle. Now little air, food, and water remain. "Suck air, grab clusters, and hear. . . . *we have been about as thoroughly liberated as it is possible for a race and a planet to be!*" (75).

In "Darwinian Pool Room" (1950), Isaac Asimov suggests that man has usurped the task of the Creator with his various machines, and that the Creator will allow them in their turn to usurp man's place. Other writers graphically portray the mechanical servants of science as continuing their assigned tasks long after man is dead. The surviving war robots in Kelleam's "Rust," having killed all men, discover that they miss humans and try unsuccessfully to reconstruct one. Philip K. Dick's "Second Variety" (1953) shows much more "human" and vicious robots; we have little hope that they will feel remorse. Not only do they seek out and kill humans, they also destroy other robots. If they inherit the earth, they will fight among themselves to glory in their triumph. Dick argues that when man acts mechanically, the result is aggression and conquest, and that man acts mechanically much of the time. His "Impostor" (1953), "Jon's World" (1954), and "Autofac" (1955) all explore this theme.

David Bunch's *Moderan* (1971)[10] implies that reliance on the mechanical is the only means to safety and efficiency in a world that includes atomic war. He extends artificiality beyond the prostheses of Wolfe's *Limbo* (which were intended to avert war), and shows human voluntarily transmuting themselves into war robots. Each hides in his own castle, gleefully bombing his neighbors and feeling annoyed when they bomb him. These stories assume that humans have qualities separable from themselves that somehow prevent or pervert full humanity, that these bad qualities are much stronger than any good ones can be, and that they will inevitably result in war.

Some authors recognize the death-wish that appears to underlie much atomic war fiction by showing humans deliberately hastening apocalypse. In Robert Sheckley's "The Battle" (1954), man anticipates Armageddon and attacks Satan in his stronghold. Although religious workers want to fight, they are turned down by the military in favor of competent robots. Nearly defeated, the robots are aided by the Lord Himself and taken bodily to heaven, while the people who have delegated their inheritance are left behind. Here, man's fondness for mechanical salvation prevents him from reaching heaven. James Blish's "After Such Knowledge" trilogy, including *A Case of Conscience* (1953, 1959), *Black Easter* (1968) and *The Day After Judgment* (1971), examines the relationship of religion and power through the metaphor of atomic war. In the last books, Satan is deliberately loosed on earth with startling, though ambiguous, results. In "The Big Flash" (1969), Norman Spinrad combines our apparent death-wish with our fascination with atomic holocaust. A rock group called the "Four Horsemen" take the country by storm; their music and their special effects combine to demand a union with death. In an orgasmic climax, the military men watching the show race to push their nuclear buttons. The story, which has been counting down from days to seconds, ends (as does its world) in "THE BIG FLASH" (259).

The Journey

If humans survive to make it, the journey through the wasteland created by the cataclysm is, as Wolfe notes, "often one of the most important elements in post-holocaust fiction" (1983, 10). Robert Crane's *Hero's Walk* (1954) and Alfred Coppel's *Dark December* (1960) are virtually all journey. The journey may be an attempt to reunite families, as in *Hero's Walk, Dark December*, and Pat Frank's *Alas, Babylon*, or, as in Leigh Brackett's *The Long Tomorrow* (1955), it may explore new frontiers while looking for a better society and other survivors. The condition of the wasteland determines if a new community and set of values can exist in the postholocaust world.

Whitley Streiber and James Kunetka's *Warday and the Journey Onward* (1984) records a journey through a realistically damaged United States—if we assume that atomic war is not intended really to invade or destroy us. Kunetka, who carefully describes his experience during the first few days after the bombs go off, quotes a newspaper headline, "NUCLEAR ATTACK BY AT LEAST THREE MISSILES DEVASTATES CITY" (20), but does not then (or later) say who bombed whom or for what reason. The two authors make pilgrimage through the remaining United States, some of it now foreign territory and some receiving foreign aid, but they do not show it as conquered. In the atomic scenario, this is not unusual.

THE POSTWAR COMMUNITY

If the postholocaust biosphere will support a new community, available resources and the nature of the people who survive will determine what it will look like. When the fertility of the Earth itself is damaged, as Isaac Asimov shows in *Pebble in the Sky* (1950), a reduced population can barely feed itself, and people are euthanized on their sixtieth birthday or when they can no longer work, whichever comes first. Some people spy on each other to make sure no one is using up "their" resources; others volunteer for "the Sixty" early so they can die with their mate. Poor, despised, and without much hope, they still have plenty of pride and plenty of vindictiveness.

The small community organized by the survivors in *Alas, Babylon* emphasizes self-sufficiency and mutual protection; by the end of the book, some effort at social community has begun, but the main thrust of the story is that of survival. In the wilderness, danger comes from wild things and man's inability to cope, an inability that seems the natural result of city living. Many stories reinforce the message: living in the city when the bombs fall is fatal. Judith Merril's *Shadow on the Hearth* (1950), Philip Wylie's *Tomorrow!* (1954), and Richard Foster's *The Rest Must Die* (1959) vividly present the horrors of the city in war. "Dance of the Dead" by Richard Matheson (1954) shows the fatalistic and self-destructive hedonism that may follow.

Cities are obviously dangerous targets, while small rural communities are safe, at least from bombs, as we see in the Kuttners' *Mutant* (1953), Leigh Brackett's *The Long Tomorrow* (1955), C. M. Kornbluth's *Not This August* (1955), Clyde B. Clason's *Ark of Venus* (1955), Pat Frank's *Alas, Babylon* (1959), and Ray Bradbury's "The Highway" (1950).[11] But they offer no protection against a degraded environment. Extrapolated futures that show the effects of social and ecological devolution include "So Shall Ye Reap!" by Rog Phillips (1947), "Shark Ship" by C. M. Kornbluth (1953), and *The Hills Were Liars* by Riley Hughes (1955). Communities that manage to survive under such conditions have few concerns beyond survival.

Community life after nuclear war is often portrayed as hierarchical, conservative, illiterate, and intellectually stultifying, but it rarely exhibits the standard social and sexual prejudices. Tribes are often sexually egalitarian or even women-dominated, as Francis Flagg and Nelson Bond describe. *Alas, Babylon* shows women as contributing vitally to the new community, but the most important contributions come from blacks, once house servants (and generally disregarded), who have basic knowledge that the more urban and civilized whites lack. Prejudice is shown as counterproductive.

But even very small communities may not be safe. In Robert Abernathy's "Heirs Apparent" (1954), after collecting enough people laboriously to regain cooperative community life on a village level, an American soldier stranded in Russia and his Russian comrades are captured and swept away by nomads who fear that even that much of a settlement will bring more bombs, and darkness falls again. Assumptions about the safety and sanity of small communities scattered in an idyllic countryside stem only partly from our conscious knowledge of nuclear war. They come much more deeply from our mythic past.

The "Safe" Frontier

Setting a postholocaust future in a familiar, demonstrably survivable past subtly assures us of survival. The American frontier achieves mythic importance in science fiction as the destination sought by space travelers (often to re-create a "lost Earth") and as the "safe haven" for the survivors of a civilized holocaust, sometimes furnished with renegade looters in lieu of Indians.

When the wilderness represents the millennium, it is romanticized, a new frontier. If a new and healthy society is to grow from the dead past, it is expected to remain in the wilderness, as do the couples in Sherwood Springer's "No Land of Nod" (1952), Damon Knight's "The Last Word" (1957), and William Sambrot's "A Son of Eve" (1959), rather than to urbanize. This wilderness is clearly biblical, as the titles indicate; Knight's story even has the surviving couple taunt Satan with their victory and get away with it. To be doubly sure of success, the new society should spring from tested stock, a newly anointed Adam and Eve.

If the wilderness is not Edenic, it is at least friendly. As Andre Norton's *Star Man's Son* (1952) competently seeks the secret of his tribe's history, he must avoid enemies from other quasi-Indian groups, but he finds the wilderness as friendly as any Western desert can be. Only in the radiation-polluted cities is he menaced by devolved, animal-like mutants. But it is in the city that the secrets he is looking for are kept; the City is both the sanctuary of the Beast and the repository of Knowledge.

Towns must remain small to be safe. In *Mutant*, any town that grows large enough to achieve a concentration of power is "dusted off" by its "civilized" neighbors as a preventive measure. Technology flourishes, nonetheless, and the danger of adding to the level of ionizing radiation in the environment is considered unimportant beside the need to control dangers before they occur. A similar self-imposed restriction limits the size of communities in Leigh Brackett's *The Long Tomorrow*.

People who live in a degraded world may themselves suffer degradation, as Ward Moore shows in two unsettling commentaries on survivalism, "Lot" (1953) and "Lot's Daughter" (1954). At first, "Lot" seems a fairly competent and foresighted father who has made plans and laid in supplies against the much-feared day of holocaust. When the first warnings sound, he (virtually alone among his neighbors) knows what to do: he gets his family and necessary supplies into the car and heads for a mountain hideaway in which he expects to outlive the destruction.

As he drives away from Los Angeles, however, he is gradually revealed as a weak tyrant, unable to handle the emotional demands of wife and son (admittedly unpleasant characters) and incestuously attracted to his nubile daughter. He takes advantage of his wife's stupidity and ignorance and his son's gullibility and self-centeredness to get rid of them so he can retreat safely to the hills with his daughter.

The sequel, "Lot's Daughter," shows Lot not only as weak but as unprepared for the long haul. Guilty of laziness, stupidity, and incest, he hides in the mountains long after the known need has passed and long after his supplies have given out. The wilderness is undamaged, but he does not know how to make use of it. His daughter, now the mother of his child, has learned some survival tricks, but she too is ignorant. But others survive; when the daughter finds truck tracks on a long-deserted road, she tricks her father as he tricked her mother and leaves him to care for himself and his get. Although she has matured in the "innocent" wilderness, she has learned, from having been treated unethically herself, to treat others the same way. Whether or not we see the daughter as "savage," we cannot see her as "noble." "Lot" and "Lot's Daughter" challenge popular assumptions about survival in the wilderness.

So does Wilson Tucker's *The Long Loud Silence* (1952), where an unpleasant but highly skilled soldier survives nicely in the quarantined area of the United States following an atomic attack. Rejecting various opportunities for community living, he manages to satisfy all his needs and (in an unpublished ending) some of his perversions as well.[12]

Walter Tevis's *Mockingbird* (1981) shows the wilderness as inhospitable, but the degraded and mechanical city as even more dangerous. Whether or not this world has been ravaged by nuclear war (as the underground shelter of Maugre suggests), it has certainly been ravaged by fear of such a war. Men have made robots in their own image and then repudiated their humane responsibility. The last of the ruling robots wants only to die, but cannot kill himself; only a human could kill him, but he is systematically wiping out humanity by tampering with reproduction, a metaphonic reminder of the effects of the bomb. The robot, a victim of his own ignorance and blindness, is simultaneously defeated and granted his dearest wish by two humans—a man who has taught himself the forbidden art of reading while learning the true meaning of humanity from the woman, and the woman herself, now pregnant with his child. Together they abandon the dying city for the unknown (but welcoming) wilderness.

The Ambivalent City

The cycle of empire and decadence is the cycle of the city: a period of growth and concentration of wealth and technological power, followed inexorably by luxury, ease, and decay. Like the underground tunnels that simultaneously protect and confine the survivors of nuclear war, the city is seen both as a womb and a tomb. We invent vicious metaphorical descriptions for the city: it strangles, it smothers, it feeds on itself. To us, the city symbolizes "old Europe" that Americans fled from, the culture that corrupts, that limits freedom and enforces cooperation.

In our fictions, we give evidence of disliking our own urban society to the point of desiring its destruction. We would like the world to be magically restructured for our personal benefit. In Wolfe's *Limbo*, Martine marvels at how cleanly the H-bombs destroyed the old slums, allowing a new city to be born. Subconsciously, we may agree: the devastation is dreadful, but the chance to rebuild on a wholly new model seems exhilarating, almost worth it, as "Omega" urges in the Kuttners' "Tomorrow and Tomorrow" (1947). Perhaps in the "new city" we shall be as "new men," full of all the virtues that we now lack.

This peculiarly American ambivalence toward our own culture remains unresolved. We distrust ourselves. If we cannot get along with ourselves, we surely cannot get along with others, and most of the "others" are in the city. If they should all be destroyed, a large part of the world will die; but we cannot be entirely sure that we shall miss them. As John D. MacDonald suggests in "Trojan Horse Laugh" (1949), concentrations of people are dangerous. Their emotions are catching.

One method of controlling the city is to cover it with a dome, simultaneously protecting it from outside influence and enabling the continuous monitoring of the population. In Arthur Leo Zagat's "Slaves of the Lamp" (1946) emotions are controlled by Lampmen working in a "Peace Dome." Lampmen believe that human nature cannot be changed and that this nature is erratic at best and warlike at worst. Natlane, a Lampman, hopes to create a rational super race; this makes his supervisor very nervous. To retain control the supervisor replaces the trained Lampmen with his own people, and nuclear war promptly breaks out. When the situation is stabilized, the various leaders agree that "each of us was bent on saving the world *in his own way*—which is good. What was bad was that we all wanted to save the world *only* in our own ways." This does not mean that ordinary humans will be allowed to work out their own destinies, however. Despite Natlane's good intentions, the domed cities will remain under the Lampmen's control.

Underground cities seem merely a natural extension of the bomb shelters that every American city was supposed to equip itself with, but Philip K. Dick carries this to extremes in *The Penultimate Truth* (1964), an elaboration of the idea presented in "The Defenders" (1953): the humans kept safe underground are at the mercy of the machines working and fighting above them. If the machines choose to lie about conditions on the surface, humans may be trapped below forever. (Fortunately, Dick's machines are occasionally benevolent.)

Fritz Leiber's short story "The Moon Is Green" (1952) shows us just one evening in the dreary life of a couple forced to live deep underground to avoid the radiation that has made the "outdoors" deadly. The eventual madness and escape of the wife not only from her claustrophobic quarters but also from forced marriage with an insensitive, egotistical man she despises—those women able to breed must bear, since most cannot—says more about the consequences of such "living" than could long pages of psychological description. We know nothing of the circumstances that drove these unhappy survivors underground, no details of the war. Yet we know it all; the "atomic scenario" has played itself out, and death rules this wilderness.

The underground retreats sought by (or forced upon) the survivors of nuclear holocaust metaphorically describe the worst features of the city. They are crowded, dark, technologically dependent, complicated, confining; eventually they become tombs. In Daniel Galouye's *Dark Universe* (1961) the cities are not only underground but absolutely without light, a literal representation of ignorance. Yet leaving them for the sunlight is, as Plato noted, almost unbearably painful.

Sometimes people come out of the bomb shelter to find themselves alone. The few survivors of the deep shelter in Bruce Ariss's *Full Circle* (1963) are met by Amerindians who reconstituted their culture after the war, but they find no other living humans. David Palmer's *Emergence* (1984) presents a young superwoman with what amounts to a world of her own, peopled by a few other extraordinary youngsters, mutants like herself. Sometimes elimination of humanity is the aim rather than the result; M. J. Engh's *Arslan* (1976) uses the threat of nuclear war to destroy urban life, throwing the survivors on their pioneer resources. But we soon find that this is only the opening move in a more sinister plan, one that depends upon fragmentation and lack of communication to divide and destroy.

Richard Matheson describes the person most apt to remain sane in the loneliness of postholocaust urban America in "Pattern for Survival" (1955): Richard Allen Shaggley, who writes a lyrical science fiction love story every morning, mails it (with himself as mailman) to an editor named Rick, who excitedly puts it through to R. A., the publisher, having ordered Shaggley paid by check from his destroyed office. R. A. laughs and cries over the story and sends it at once to Dick Allen, the linotypist, who sets it that afternoon and gets it out in time for Shaggley to buy it (from himself) on his way home. Shaggley reads it before he goes to bed to dream of mushroom clouds and wakes in the morning to write a new story. In an insane situation, the only sane reaction is insanity.

The Wasteland Again

The wasteland is the enemy of community. Margaret St. Clair's "Quis Custodiet . . . ?" (1948) and Fritz Leiber's "Night of the Long Knives" (1960) are laid in a future where people must live in an area much like a violently radioactive Death Valley. In this desert, people live alone, not daring to trust anyone else, or they gather in small bands, barely able to scavenge their own survival and fiercely protect their territory. Although technology remains, community seems to have vanished.

Harlan Ellison's "A Boy and His Dog" (1969)[13] shows that community dies from either living out war or hiding from it. Safe in their underground shelters, the now-sterile middle class tries to pretend that nothing is really wrong. Aboveground in the (possibly radioactive) wasteland, young men battle each other for food and sex. Some combine into gangs, while others hunt with telepathic dogs. But these young men systematically destroy what little remains alive in their territory; while the undergrounders force reproduction on their young women, the abovegrounders fight for the few they find. (In the movie version, which Ellison denies writing, they also kill them.) In neither situation is life apt to continue, even though Vic eventually feeds to his injured dog the girl sent aboveground to trap and use him sexually. Both groups are settling for short-term solutions to a long-term problem. These stories end not with a new society but with an uninhabitable world, or at least one in which no further human action is possible.

Sexual sterility leads to the ultimate wasteland. Judith Merril's "That Only a Mother" (1948) takes place during a prolonged atomic war and deals with teratogenic mutations: the hopeful young mother who tells the story delivers a precocious but phocomelic infant whose deformity she refuses to recognize. A gender-based conflict then arises, since the father sees only his daughter's physical abnormalities while the mother sees only her superior abilities and charm. The story ends with the unresolved question: will the father kill his child? If he does, his act stands as evidence of the end of human reproduction in a damaged world.

Margaret St. Clair's "The Hole in the Moon" (1952) presents a postatomic junkyard world. Women have been infected with a disease that coarsens them and makes them avid for sex, but does not kill them. The disease is deadly to males, however. The protagonist simultaneously desires and fears sexual contact; he repulses a "dream woman" who seems healthy. Then, in drunken despair, he calls in an obviously infected woman, ironically assuring her that he will not hurt her.

Women see themselves as particularly victimized by a postnuclear war future.[14] Reproduction—life itself—is the issue, and men, with their mutilated intra- and interpersonal skills, are not expected to handle it well. Maggie may be mad in "That Only a Mother," but she will not destroy the bright girl-child that represents the only future remaining to the race; her perfectionist husband, whose war work exposes him to radiation, probably will. In a world without a future, without even an unblemished moon, Margaret St. Clair declares that the sex act will be fatal, not fulfilling.

Some women looked into the future and found none: "The Hole in the Moon" gives little hope for a viable future, while Helen Clarkson's *The Last Day* (1959) offers no hope of survival whatever. M. J. Engh's *Arslan* (1976) posits a future destroyed through nuclear blackmail by a gnostic idealist who conquers the world only so he can sterilize the human race. The nearly twenty years that pass between these books is significant, since the hiatus spans the inception of the women's liberation movement. It also marks the end of stories by women set in unself-consciously patriarchal societies, the beginning of stories showing overt domination or elimination of one sex by the other, and the connection of nuclear war and sexual slavery as metaphors showing the ultimate denial of life.

In Suzy McKee Charnas's *Walk to the End of the World* (1974), women (called "fems") are blamed by the men for the destruction of prewar society and are treated so badly that they would have to rise several degrees to approach slavery. But the men's Holdfast, like the rest of the world, has been devastated by radiation; food is often hard to come by, and one man plans to breed fems for food. Alldera, a fem trained to carry messages, escapes to seek help for her fellows as the men's wars apparently destroy Holdfast.

The sequel, *Motherlines* (1978), shows only a tenuous hope of survival in the wilderness. Two groups of women live on the plains: the Riding Women, who live and reproduce entirely without men, and the Free Fems, who hope to liberate the fems of the Holdfast. Neither group seems truly viable; the Riding Women cannot initiate new lines but can reproduce, while the fems can neither breed without men nor live with men of Holdfast, if any remain. The world may die of projected guilt and anger.

Kate Wilhelm's *Where Late the Sweet Birds Sang* (1976) shows worldwide ecological disaster, not political intransigence, as the cause of nuclear war. The combination destroys human fertility. Anticipating this possibility, a small group clones itself. When only mutually dependent groups of clones remain, they find themselves poorly equipped to survive in a wilderness that demands creative initiative. One naturally conceived child learns survival skills, kidnaps some of the fertile women (kept by the clones as brainwashed, isolated breeders), and starts his own colony. Some years later, he returns to find the valley deserted; his now-healthy group may contain all that is left of humanity. No artificial substitute for humanity can inherit this earth.

Pamela Sargent's *The Shore of Women* (1986) reverses the situation in Charnas's *Walk to the End of the World*. Here, the women have maintained technology and live in comfortable walled cities scattered across North America. All men are locked out in the wilderness, where they live in primitive fashion by hunting and by raiding other bands. If small bands of men begin to group together, the women kill them. The story follows a girl thrown out of the city and recounts her love affair with a man (city women reproduce by tricking men out of sperm and enjoy physical love only with each other), the natural birth of her daughter, and her subversion of the religion that maintains the status quo, though she does not topple it.

In each of these works, women see a society organized along hierarchical lines, generally resisting change. Whether the society is dominated by men or by women, it is run by the few for the few, and the maintenance of control seems a paramount concern. But long-term survival depends upon two factors: peace and procreation. These require living cooperatively with our world and ourselves, a process most powerfully represented in fiction by the sexual relationship between men and women.[15] If that relationship is destroyed—by infertility, by sexual domination, or by separation of the sexes—then the human race has committed suicide by entropy, no matter what shape the political and social world may be in.

CYCLES OF HISTORY

The Dark Ages, which saw the birth of science from the womb of superstition and the consolidation of the city as a center of knowledge and power, like the American frontier, is a period of mythic importance and the setting for many stories. Frank Kermode reminds us that "apocalyptic types—empire, decadence and renovation, progress and catastrophe—are fed by history and underlie our ways of making sense of the world from where we stand"; we need them to make sense of post-holocaust society (1966, 29). Implicit in this structure lie the values that such religious communities held during the so-called "Dark Ages": they were benevolent, authoritarian, cooperative, walled centers within which received knowledge was conserved by those who, by and large, remained ignorant of its use.

Fritz Leiber's *Gather, Darkness!* (1943) posits a return to medievalism in which only power-hungry "monks" retain scientific knowledge. The stories that became Walter M. Miller's *A Canticle for Leibowitz* also remain safely rooted in history. The monastery setting for Miller's "Canticle for Leibowitz" (1955) is medieval, while his "And the Light Is Risen" (1956) is set in a second Industrial Revolution and the "The Last Canticle" (1957) is an entirely contemporary and familiar-sounding time. Robert Silverberg's *The 13th Immortal* (1957) contrasts a medieval world whose people seem curiously contemporary with a simultaneously existing technological utopia locked safely away from unscientific tampering. Isaac Asimov is partial to empire; his *Pebble in the Sky* (1950) replays the problems Rome had governing Judea, with "Earthie scum" acting as Maccabees, while his *Foundation* stories re-create Britain's problems with various colonies, including the American. In every case, history is rewritten to reassure us that holocaust is not the end of the world. But all stories that recover a mythic past tacitly depend upon a cyclical view of history: what has been will be again.

Even *A Canticle for Leibowitz* refuses Apocalypse; though he organizes it on a religious pattern, Miller presents only cycles of self-destruction. As the nations of the distant future rage at each other, each blaming the other for breaking the nuclear faith, Dom Zerchi, Abbot of Leibowitz Abbey, still hopes for peace, but is disturbed by the knowing smile on the lips of the ancient called Lazarus, who has seen it all before. In spite of the hopes of the monks, in spite of the optimism of the politicians who organize a cease-fire, the war begins, each side "retaliating" against the other, each apparently surprised by the vigor and desperation of such retaliation, each escalating the combat. The end is annihilation of Earth as the chosen monks put a few children into a spaceship. No millennium follows the Armageddon on Earth, nor is it likely on a new world. In a cyclical mythology, a new world means only the opportunity to repeat the same mistakes.

Bernard Wolfe's *Limbo* also follows this cyclical pattern, but with a difference. World War III has caused men to control those parts of human experience they have labeled "bad" or "dangerous" by physical amputation. This allows them to feel "safe from their own feelings. . . . But by attempting to amputate anger, men succeed in eliminating love," and another war begins.[16] *Limbo* completes all five of Gary Wolfe's stages. Martine discovers the catastrophe, journeys to Mandunga Island and then back to what is left of the United States, finds the new (amputated) society, battles the new (technological) wilderness of rejected emotion, and discovers new, redemptive values. He thus enters the final battle armed with acceptance of human experience and recognition of human interrelatedness. We do not see how this battle comes out, but we can believe that with this positive value system he may win and move away from the cycle of war.

CIRCLING GROUND ZERO

Most nuclear fiction stops before it plays out the five stages of action. Some get no further than the discovery of the cataclysm, like Rog Phillips's "Atom War." In some, the wilderness becomes the "final solution" when no life can exist in it, as we see in Roshwald's *Level 7* and Clarkson's *The Last Day*. Some dismiss man and create a nonhuman "new community," as in Clifford Simak's *City* (1944) and Kelleam's "Rust." Some, like Tenn's "The Liberation of Earth," show the planet as so damaged that little life can exist on it, and we question whether the storytellers are still human. Other writers collapse time with the blast, as does Edmond Hamilton in *City at World's End* (1951) and Robert A. Heinlein in *Farnham's Freehold* (1964).

Either a wilderness without humans or a magical arrival at the end of time denies the possibility of renewal, as does the actual end of life on earth; the reemergence of the wilderness as antagonist implies that some fruitful resolution can be found. But it is the final struggle for abiding value, the most important part of the five-stage action, that is most often refused or truncated. Maintaining the status quo, whether it be war or peace, inhibits or puts off true resolution. Mutual assured destruction can no more bring the millennium than can peace enforced by an elite or war continued after life and logic are dead.

The assumption that holds these modes of thinking in place devalues and rejects parts of human living, immobilizing the repudiated activities and driving out of awareness the feelings and perceptions that accompany them, a process we call control. Our fiction shows us that we believe the result of this control will be inevitable conflict within each individual, necessarily expressed in conflict among people and between cultures. The technological changes we make during our journey through the wilderness and in our new societies will make no difference unless and until we find new, positive values to live by. We can identify our values by examining what we spend the most time, effort, and attention on. History and fiction agree that this is war, not peace. We will fight for peace but do not live it. We have no picture of peace, because it is a negative condition. Even the dictionary agrees: peace is defined as "1. The absence of war or other hostilities" or "3. Freedom from quarrels and disagreement; harmonious relations."[17] We cannot do peace. In a story, all people can do is not-war, and that stops the progress of the plot. War may be hell, but it is at least interesting. In the "battle of life," peace is not a victory; it is an epitaph.

We may tacitly accept these assumptions or we may resist them, but in neither case do we invent anything to replace them. We truncate ourselves and our stories to conform to a pattern of crisis that remains fixed and unchanging (though the details of crisis change, the pattern does not); refusing an ending, we tacitly value entropy, a conviction that things must get worse. Therefore we feel safe only with changes that truly make no difference. This assumption forms the basis for those fictions that predict war continuing forever, without meaning and without resolution. C. M. Kornbluth's "The Luckiest Man in Denv" (1952) shows this especially clearly: given a chance to stop the senseless war between Denv and Ellay (two cities that now represent the whole remaining culture of the United States), all the protagonist can think of is his own advancement. He betrays the peacemaker, sabotages the negotiations, and continues the war that gives him a job and an identity.

The atomic scenario makes our assumptions "real" even while it helps hide them in cultural familiarity. Caught in our contradictory assumptions about ourselves and our history, we feel helpless to act. Living in existential shame, we feel victimized by our world and explain it away rather than modeling it as a process we can participate in. Living in existential guilt, we assume that we know how to "win" against ourselves. Our fiction grows from these cultural assumptions, organizes our experiences, and helps to mold them. In fiction, we reflect and illuminate our history; through it, we may also find ways to alter our assumptions. What we can envision, we act upon. What we cannot remains impossible, leaving us refusing the end—and any hope of escaping ground zero.

NOTES

1. New York *Times, Hiroshima Plus 20* (New York: Delacorte Press, 1965), 22.

2. Claude Lévi-Strauss, *Structural Anthropology*, trans. Claire Jacobsen and Brooke Grundfest Schoepf (New York: Basic Books, 1963), 229.

3. Peace as "a state of permanent pre-hostility," a "joking" Pentagon euphemism, was reported in *SANE News*, January 1985, 8.

4. As previously noted, this specific term has frequently been used in nuclear war fictions, beginning long before 1945.

5. Imputing this concern to aliens implies that humans are more powerful than they, or at least more dangerous. Heinlein is very fond of the idea and uses it frequently.

6. Note the iconoclastic change Ursula Le Guin makes on this assumption in *The Lathe of Heaven*.

7. Considered Dickson's most impressive work, the "Childe Cycle" comprises a sequence of stories still in progress. It begins with *Necromancer* (1962) and continues with the Dorsai stories and *The Final Encyclopedia* (1984). When finished, it will begin in the historical past and span the present to reach the already depicted future. Although these stories avoid the nuclear war scenario, they tacitly assume that humans will continue to fight with each other or die.

8. Tenn remarks that when he wrote this story in 1949, it was rejected "across the board by the general-fiction magazines" as "a shade too fantastic." After its publication in a minor science fiction magazine, *Suspense*, it was rejected by a movie producer as "far too prosaic for today's audiences." Tenn's "Note" preceding the stories in his *The Wooden Star* (New York: Ballantine. 1968), 9.

9. Vonnegut often takes on topics that move him to silence; the gallant helplessness of humanity at war cannot be described, but in *Slaughterhouse Five*,

his refrain, "so it goes," becomes an expression of pain beyond words, while in *Galápagos* (1985) his "humans" become happy only by being released from their humanity. Robert Frost, "Fire and Ice."

10. *Moderan* collects stories published between 1959 and 1970, more or less novelized by a frame and explanation.

11. Bradbury usually expects people to run towards, not away from, the dangerous city in case of nuclear war; see, for example, *The Martian Chronicles* (1950).

12. See Gary Wolfe's comments in "The Remaking of Zero," in *The End of the World*, ed. Eric S. Rabkin, Martin H. Greenberg, and Joseph D. Olander (Carbondale: Southern Illinois University Press, 1983), 10.

13. In his public lectures, Ellison says that he wrote this story to protest the escalation of the Vietnam war.

14. I have identified sixteen specifically postnuclear holocaust stories written by women: Leigh Brackett's *The Long Tomorrow*, Suzy McKee Charnas's *Walk to the End of the World* and *Motherlines*, Carol Emshwiller's "Day at the Beach," Ursula Le Guin's *The Lathe of Heaven*, Vonda McIntyre's *The Exile Waiting* and *Dreamsnake*, Judith Merril's "That Only a Mother," Andre Norton's *Star Man's Son*, Margaret St. Clair's "Quis Custodiet . . . ?" and "The Hole in the Moon," Pamela Sargent's *The Shore of Women*, Susan Weston's *Children of the Light*, and Kate Wilhelm's *Where Late the Sweet Birds Sang*. Ten of these stories show hierarchical social structure, six posit sexual bondage and/or separation of the sexes, twelve show little or no chance for long-term human reproduction, and twelve show little or no chance for peace.

15. Theodore Sturgeon's work also combines nuclear war with sexual dysfunction to portray our cultural condition. He is one of the very few male authors to do so.

16. Martha Bartter, "Nuclear Holocaust as Urban Renewal," *Science-Fiction Studies* 39 (1986): 155. The use of "man" here is not sexist, since women in *Limbo* are not permitted "Immob."

17. *American Heritage Dictionary*, 2nd college ed. (1982).

PART III

LEAVING GROUND ZERO

9

New Assumptions

Our definition for science fiction includes three major points: a portrayal of technological change; consideration of the danger this change poses to the world or to the human race; and representation of the ability of humans to alter themselves and their society in response to that change. The definition is thus transactional: humans both cause and respond to change. Science fiction has long identified nuclear war as our most dangerous technological change, and few would deny that world and race are in danger. What most nuclear science fiction fails to show is that humans can respond to that threat in any way other than as aggressors or as victims.

Traditionally, we have assumed that change is effected either by Superman or by Frankenstein, never by "ordinary people." We have also failed to see these roles as opposite sides of the same character, motivated by the same impulses: to do good, and to do it by taking and maintaining control of the situation. Neither of these roles allows choice either for the hero or for society. The hero must control or fail—both himself and those he has undertaken to serve; the society must passively be saved while remaining a victim of the natural forces that initiated the crisis. But this success often results in failure for the rest of the world. Even if Superman wins, the rest of us lose. We sacrifice autonomy and flexibility when we demand that salvation come from outside.

Successful control usually results in one or the other of two unpleasant outcomes: evasion or rebellion. Neither Superman nor Frankenstein seems able to effect the kind of change we need in a world where nuclear annihilation threatens the entire world culture. We can no longer rely on heroes who impose solutions upon us from outside our social fabric. But we need some myth to follow, some model on which to predicate our actions, some patterned assumptions to live out; and we find them most effectively in our fiction.

Looking at science fiction as it has extrapolated the nuclear war scenario, we can see that it has faithfully anticipated the ways in which we have acted and continues to predict a future from which we can choose only grim, grimmer, or grimmest outcomes. We can also see that fiction creates a scenario that people follow simply because it has become the normal, logical thing to do; scientists, for instance, may play out some role not because events force them to but because their assumptions match the role. We can also see that these assumptions follow the patterns established in our culture, and that authors like Theodore Sturgeon who fail to reinforce the familiar patterns sometimes have problems, both in writing and in selling their work. There is much extrapolation but little speculation in nuclear war fiction, and even less creative speculation about human behavior as it manifests itself in politics and war.

But one of the most important products of science fiction is the sociological thought experiment. John Campbell proposed this as vital to the health of our society when he noted that we accept the inevitability of technological change but often ignore the need to plan or at least to think seriously about the nature of this change. He points out that some changes can be tested experimentally, but others cannot: for instance, "an interesting idea that happens to involve the annihilation of the planet Earth. The old method of trial and error comes to a point where it is no longer usable—the point where one more error means no more trials."[1] Considering atomic war in fiction is the only way we can experiment with it safely. We have been doing so for almost a hundred years and have succeeded only in envisioning greater and greater danger.

It is not that we lack prescient predictors. In *Robert A. Heinlein*, H. Bruce Franklin discusses Heinlein's visions of atomic war, beginning with sneak attack and continuing with the hero surviving against all odds in the wilderness; but he argues that although Heinlein characteristically uses them, we also see at a glance that none of these visions is the exclusive property of Robert Heinlein. All were, and perhaps still are, endemic in America at least from the early 1950's on. Heinlein's spectacular popular success is closely tied to his extraordinary ability to project the fantasies of his audience. (1980, 155–56)[2]

If grim and accurate "awful warnings" failed to avert escalation to atomic weapons in World War II, what dark visions like Heinlein's have accomplished since is open to debate. Certainly we have not had another atomic war. Equally certainly we have not abandoned Ground Zero. Perhaps Campbell was wrong in assuming that fictional "thought experiments" could provide the basis for changed sociocultural behavior in more or less the same way that Einstein's *Gedankenexperimente* already had. Or perhaps we have been doing something wrong.

We may be asking fiction to do the wrong thing. Frightening people has rarely changed their behavior, and as the Kuttners demonstrate in "Tomorrow and Tomorrow," rigid controls can make unavoidable the very situation they were set up to avoid. Nor will speculation serve our need; in dealing with the historical world, fantasy that falsifies what we know about human nature will have no more positive effect than will horror fiction. But our examination of nuclear war fiction has shown some surprising contradictions and blind spots, about which we can do nothing until we are able to see them.

Instead of a new weapon or improved technology, we may need fiction to envision new assumptions to live from. We lack a positive vision to work towards. We lack heroes able to work *in* as well as *on* society. Our assumptions about war include some values we might prefer not to recognize that we hold; our assumptions about peace make it seem unsuitable for fiction. Fiction needs a plot; a good plot needs tension, which war automatically provides and peace does not.[3]

Peace is defined as the absence of war. Inactivity is bound to be boring, and stories that no one reads can change nothing. But science fiction stories, as *Gedankenexperimente*, can try out new assumptions about what humans do and how they transact with the society they create. Some, like Bernard Wolfe's *Limbo* and Ursula K. Le Guin's *The Lathe of Heaven*, assume the transactionality of human behavior and show some things that we have been doing wrong. Others look at our human history and ask what we have been doing right. Altered assumptions lead to altered actions, and noticing what works is often more useful than finding fault with what does not.

In Susan B. Weston's *Children of the Light* (1985), a concerned and informed young man of today is thrown forward to a lifetime after holocaust. He brings technological knowledge and information that he cannot share with the people there and tacit assumptions that he must notice and change. The people do not even know what the atomic war was, much less what it was all about. But as they struggle to live and reproduce in their tainted environment, they have formed a caring society without dominance, based on ability and cooperation. Faced with destruction by madness, disease, sterility, and hunger, these people trust and care for each other. Their society is contrasted with two others, one that rejects reality and seeks victims for its anger and one that tries to enforce rigid social control. Given a choice, a woman from the rigid, hierarchical society joins their group, becoming warmly human as she transacts in new ways; the young man not only "grows up" but is shown as making a real difference to the people around him as he does.[4]

David Brin demonstrates people's innate needs for cooperation in *The Postman* (1985). While many writers have explored results of the communications breakdown that would result from a nuclear exchange, Brin explores the real power of its symbolic restoration. A man stripped by robbers takes the first clothes he finds—from a long-dead postman—and finds himself enjoying the privileges and carrying out the duties of his uniform, much to his surprise. Communication opposes the brutal "human nature" we deplore (embodied in the Holnists). That such a peaceful function can survive the battle against ego, power struggle, and Holnist violence evokes something we can all recognize in ourselves: we humans can take responsibility for ourselves and our actions, for our communications, and for our cooperation, changing ourselves and our world as we do so. Dealing with such responsibility is not easy, nor is it dull. Creating a way of living where everybody wins is a continuing challenge.

James P. Hogan's *Voyage from Yesteryear* (1982) contrasts two societies fictionally removed to space. One looks uncomfortably familiar, with a system of rewards and punishments based on money, status, and shame imposed by a rigid hierarchy. This group, fleeing an Earth on its way to nuclear war, lands on Chiron, a planet inhabited by another, equally human culture. This one seems startlingly unfamiliar until we recognize that Hogan has applied basic psychology to it. Biofabricated from digitally recorded DNA codes and raised by robots, the people demonstrate creativity, energy, integrity, and responsibility. Rather than punishing anyone for misbehavior, they give each other powerful emotional rewards when they do well. The result is a delightful group of friendly, enthusiastic, cooperative, joyful young people, whose example soon entices some of the less rigid members of the newly arrived group to join them.

But the spaceship culture has atomic weapons, economic power, and experience in making recalcitrant groups toe the line. It applies standard colonizing tactics, claiming territory, passing restrictive laws, and demanding cooperation without giving any in return. The Chironians cheerfully permit the new people to run their own society just as they please, but refuse to participate. They are soon seen as a threat by the spaceship's leaders, despite their apparent weakness and peaceful behavior, because so many people are choosing to join them. The Chironians are much too busy with their own affairs to waste time on dominance or aggression, but they are not weak, and they certainly are not boring. Hogan does a remarkable job of showing how behavior and experience change transactionally for those who try the new ways, and how the group changes as they join it.

These stories embody creative assumptions about human nature and the cultures that humans construct together, made real in our imagination and presented for our consideration. Each presents alternatives that move away from war not by controlling or denying it but by admitting war as a possibility and transcending it. Each demonstrates behavior that we might call "peaceful" but that looks like vigorous action. As *Gedankenexperimente*, they stand ready for testing in our own experience if we so choose.

Rather than assuming it to be merely not-war, we can develop a positive set of criteria for peace and play with it in fiction. We can make it real for ourselves, imagining what it might be like to live out those assumptions. It should not be boring. Peace is the zeal of the creator encouraged to create, the lover encouraged to love, the builder to build, and the changer to change without internal conflict or external restrictions beyond those required by natural circumstance. It is the freedom to be oneself and to glory in it, neither compelled to imitate nor to rebel against some ideal model. It is life and growth and sharing the surprise of being, of accepting fear but not the fear of fear, while enjoying both love and the love of love. It is the fostering of the next generation to independence without envy or resentment. It is the wonder of companionship and the challenging comfort of cooperation; permission to speak the thoughts that come from the heart and that can be discovered in solitude as well as in company—all of them—the joy and rage and pain and grief and glee of living. It is the full acceptance of our threefold relationship as a time-binding species: inheritors of the past, contributors to the present, and trustees for the future.[5] When such a vision becomes a common assumption in our fiction, and thus readily available for our everyday living, we can forever abandon the zero-sum game of the atomic scenario.

NOTES

1. John W. Campbell, Jr., "The Place of Science Fiction," in *Modern Science Fiction: Its Meaning and Its Future*, ed. Reginald Bretnor, 2nd ed. (Chicago: Advent, 1979), 16.

2. That this vision of survival against all odds is still widely celebrated is made clear by the popularity of movies like *Rambo* and many "men's adventure" stories where the hero saves society by killing most of it. The resurgence of this literature is discussed by Paul Brians in "Red Holocaust: The Atomic Conquest of the West," *Extrapolation* 28, no. 4 (1987): 319–29.

3. Two science fiction writers with whom I discussed this problem came up with the same response, independently and at different times. Theodore Sturgeon (in 1983) and Lois McMaster Bujold (in 1986) each objected initially to the idea of structuring a story plot around peace on the grounds that if nothing was happening in the story, no one would read it. Each gave the idea some thought and reconsidered.

4. It is instructive to notice how often a writer who overtly posits the nurture model for the protagonist of a bildungsroman tacitly denies it elsewhere. While the focal character learns from experience, most of the other characters adamantly refuse to. This usually advances the plot, but the fact that so many writers assume this as a fact of life shows how strongly the nature model fits our cultural assumptions.

5. This is suggested by Alfred Korzybski, *Manhood of Humanity*, 2nd ed. (Lakerville, Conn.: International Non-Aristotelian Library Publishing Co., 1950), 59–60.

Bibliography

FICTION

Abernathy, Robert. "Heirs Apparent." *Magazine of Fantasy and Science Fiction*, June 1954, 4–12.

———. "When the Rockets Come." *Astounding Science-Fiction*, March 1945, 158–76.

Ackerman, Forrest J. "The Mute Question." *Other Worlds*, September 1950. Reprinted in *Adventures in Tomorrow*, edited by Kendall Foster Crossen. New York: Greenberg, 1951, 32–33.

Ahern, Jerry. *The Survivalist Number One: Total War*. New York: Zebra, 1981.

Alpert, Hollis. "The Simian Problem." *Magazine of Fantasy and Science Fiction*, July 1960. Reprinted in *17 X Infinity*, edited by Groff Conklin. New York: Dell, 1963, 10–19.

Alvarez, John. *See* del Rey, Lester.

Anderson, Poul. "Details." *Worlds of IF*, October 1956. Reprinted in *7 Conquests*. London: Collier, 1969, 117–39.

———. "The Helping Hand." *Astounding Science-Fiction*, May 1950. Reprinted in *The Stars Around Us*, edited by Robert Hoskins. New York: Signet, 1970, 139–65.

———. "Inside Straight." *Magazine of Fantasy and Science Fiction*, August 1955. Reprinted in *7 Conquests*. London: Collier, 1969, 93–116.

———. "Journeys End." *Magazine of Fantasy and Science Fiction*, February 1957. Reprinted in *A Science Fiction Argosy*, edited by Damon Knight. New York: Simon and Schuster, 1972, 633–41.

———. *Twilight World*. New York: Torquil, 1961.

———. "Wildcat." *Magazine of Fantasy and Science Fiction*, November 1958. Reprinted in *7 Conquests*. London: Collier, 1969, 39–71.

Anderson, Poul and F. N. Waldrop. "Tomorrow's Children." *Astounding Science-Fiction*, March 1947, 56–79. Reprinted as first part of *Twilight World*. New York: Torquil, 1961.

Ariss, Bruce. *Full Circle*. New York: Avalon, 1963.

Asher, Marty. *Shelter*. New York: Arbor, 1986.

Asimov, Isaac. "Darwinian Pool Room." *Galaxy Science Fiction*, October 1950. Reprinted in *The End of Summer: Science Fiction of the Fifties*, edited by Barry Malzberg and Bill Pronzini. New York: Ace, 1979, 15–24.

———. *The End of Eternity*. Garden City, N.Y.: Doubleday, 1955. Reprinted New York: Signet/NAL, 1958.

———. *The Foundation Trilogy: Three Classics of Science Fiction*. Garden City, N.Y.: Doubleday, nd. Contains *Foundation* (1951), *Foundation and Empire* (1952), and *Second Foundation* (1953).

———. "The Pause." In *Time to Come*, edited by August Derleth. New York: Farrar, Straus and Young, 1954. Reprinted New York: Berkley, 1958, 55–67.

———. *Pebble in the Sky*. Garden City, N.Y.: Doubleday, 1950.

Balint, Emery. *Don't Inhale It!* New York: Gaer, 1949.

Bates, Harry and Desmond Winter Hall. "A Scientist Rises." *Astounding Stories*, November 1932. Reprinted in *Gosh! Wow! Sense of Wonder Science Fiction*, edited by Forrest J. Ackerman. New York: Bantam, 1981, 555–61.

Benét, Stephen Vincent. "The Place of the Gods." *Saturday Evening Post*, July 31, 1937. Reprinted as "By the Waters of Babylon" in *Twenty-five Short Stories by Stephen Vincent Benét*. Garden City, N.Y.: Sun Dial, 1943, 3–20.

Berriault, Gina. *The Descent*. New York: Athenaeum, 1960.

Bester, Alfred. "Adam and No Eve." *Astounding Science-Fiction*, September 1941. Reprinted in *Isaac Asimov Presents the Great Science Fiction Stories Volume 3, 1941*, edited by Isaac Asimov and Martin H. Greenberg. New York: DAW, 1980, 237–50.

———. *The Demolished Man*. Chicago: Shasta, 1953.

———. "Disappearing Act." *Star Science Fiction Stories No. 2*, edited by Frederik Pohl. New York: Ballantine, 1953, 1–21.

———. "The Push of a Finger." *Astounding Science-Fiction*, May 1942. Reprinted in *Isaac Asimov Presents the Great Science Fiction Stories Volume 4, 1942*, edited by Isaac Asimov and Martin H. Greenberg. New York: DAW, 1980, 110–49.

———. "The Stars My Destination." *Galaxy Science Fiction*, October 1956-January 1957. Reprinted as *The Stars My Destination*. New York: Signet/NAL, 1957.

Binder, Otto as Gordon A. Giles. "The Atom Smasher." *Amazing Stories*, October 1938, 30–41.

Blish, James. *Black Easter*. Garden City, N.Y.: Doubleday, 1968.

———. "The Box." *Thrilling Wonder Stories*, April 1949. Reprinted in *Omnibus of Science Fiction*, edited by Groff Conklin. New York: Crown, 1952, 117–32.

———. "A Case of Conscience." *If: Worlds of Science Fiction*, September 1953. Reprinted in *Best SF: Science Fiction Stories*, edited by Edmund Crispin. London: Faber, 1955, 299–365.

———. *A Case of Conscience*. New York: Ballantine, 1958.

———. *The Day after Judgment*. Garden City, N.Y.: Doubleday, 1971.

———. "One-Shot." *Astounding Science-Fiction*, August 1955. Reprinted in *So Close to Home*. New York: Ballantine, 1961, 27–38.

———. "Sponge Dive." *Infinity Science Fiction*, June 1956. Reprinted in *So Close to Home*. New York: Ballantine, 1961, 14–26.

———. "To Pay the Piper." *Worlds of If*, February 1956. Reprinted in *Galactic Cluster*. New York: Signet, 1959, 74–88.

Bloch, Robert. "The Past Master." *Bluebook Magazine*, January 1955. Reprinted in *The Best of Robert Bloch*. New York: Ballantine, 1977, 113–40.

Bond, Nelson. "The Judging of the Priestess." *Fantastic Adventures*, April 1940, 42–59.

———. "Magic City." *Astounding Science-Fiction*, February 1941, 9–36.

———. "The Priestess Who Rebelled." *Amazing Stories*, October 1939. Reprinted as "Pilgrimage" in *Isaac Asimov Presents the Great Science Fiction Stories Volume 1, 1939*, edited by Isaac Asimov and Martin H. Greenberg. New York: DAW, 1979, 332–52.

Bone, J. F. "Triggerman." *Astounding Science-Fiction*, December, 1958. Reprinted in *Prologue to Analog*, edited by John W. Campbell. Garden City, N.Y.: Doubleday, 1962, 206–18.

Brackett, Leigh. *The Long Tomorrow*. New York: Ace, 1955.

Bradbury, Ray. "The Highway." *Copy*, Spring 1950. Reprinted in *The Illustrated Man*. New York: Bantam, 1952, 39–52.

———. *The Martian Chronicles*. Garden City, N.Y.: Doubleday, 1950.

———. "The Naming of Names." *Thrilling Wonder Stories*, August 1949. Reprinted in *Best from Startling Stories*, edited by Samuel Mines. New York: Holt, 1953, 115–33.

Brennan, Frederick Hazlitt. *One of Our H Bombs Is Missing*. New York: Fawcett, 1955.

Brin, David. *The Postman*. New York: Bantam, 1985.

Brown, Fredric. "The Waveries." *Astounding Science-Fiction*, January 1945. Reprinted in *Connoisseur's Science Fiction*, edited by Tom Boardman. Harmondsworth, Middlesex, England: Penguin, 1964. Reprinted 1976, 210–34.

———. "The Weapon." *Astounding Science-Fiction*, April 1951. Reprinted in *Omnibus of Science Fiction*, edited by Groff Conklin. New York: Crown, 1952, 483–85.

Buck, Pearl S. *Command the Morning*. New York: John Day, 1959.

Bunch, David R. *Moderan*. New York: Avon, 1971.

Caidin, Martin. *The Long Night*. New York: Dodd, Mead, 1956.

Campbell, John W., Jr. as Don A. Stuart. "Atomic Power." *Astounding Stories*, December 1934, 88–97.

———, as Don A. Stuart. "Blindness." *Astounding Stories*, March 1935. Reprinted in *The Best of John W. Campbell*, edited by Lester del Rey. Garden City, N.Y.: Nelson Doubleday, 1976, 107–21.

———, as Don A. Stuart. "The Cloak of Aesir." *Astounding Science-Fiction*, March 1939. Reprinted in *Isaac Asimov Presents the Great Science Fiction Stories Volume 1, 1939*, edited by Isaac Asimov and Martin Harry Greenberg. New York: DAW, 1979, 56–102.

———, as Don A. Stuart. "Forgetfulness." *Astounding Stories*, June 1937. Reprinted in *The Cloak of Aesir*. New York: Lancer, 1972, 15–46.

———, as Don A. Stuart. "Frictional Losses." *Astounding Stories*, July 1936. Reprinted in *Who Goes There?* Chicago: Shasta, 1948, 96–126.

———, as Don A. Stuart. "The Invaders." *Astounding Stories*, June 1935, 54–67.

———. "The Last Evolution." *Amazing Stories*, August 1932. Reprinted in *The Best of John W. Campbell*, edited by Lester del Rey. Garden City, N.Y.: Nelson Doubleday, 1976, 7–23.

———, as Don A. Stuart. "The Machine." *Astounding Stories*, February 1935. Reprinted in *The Best of Science Fiction*, edited by Groff Conklin. New York: Bonanza, 1946, 460–74.

———, as Don A. Stuart. "Out of Night." *Astounding Stories*, October 1937. Reprinted in *The Best of John W. Campbell*, edited by Lester del Rey. Garden City, N.Y.: Nelson Doubleday, 1976, 164–200.

———. *The Planeteers*. New York: Ace Double, 1966.

———, as Don A. Stuart. "Rebellion." *Astounding Stories*, August 1935. Reprinted in *The Cloak of Aesir*. New York: Lancer, 1972, 115–150.

———, as Don A. Stuart. "Twilight." *Astounding Stories*, November 1934. Reprinted in *The Road to Science Fiction*, vol. 2, edited by James Gunn. New York: Mentor/NAL, 1979, 267–86.

———. "Uncertainty." *Amazing Stories*, October-November 1936. Reprinted as *The Ultimate Weapon*. New York: Ace Double, 1966.

———. "When the Atoms Failed." *Amazing Stories*, January 1930, 911–25, 975.

Carr, Robert Spencer. "Morning Star." *Saturday Evening Post*, December 6, 1947. Reprinted in *Beyond Infinity*. New York: Dell, 1951, 87–128.

———. "Mutation." In *Beyond Infinity*. New York: Dell, 1951, 209–23.

———. "Nightmare at Dawn." *Saturday Evening Post*, September 24, 1949. Reprinted as "Those Men from Mars" in *Beyond Infinity*. New York: Dell, 1951, 131–206.

Cartmill, Cleve. "Deadline." *Astounding Science-Fiction*, October 1944. Reprinted in *The Best of Science Fiction*, edited by Groff Conklin. New York: Crown, 1946, 67–88.

———. "Overthrow." *Astounding Science-Fiction*, November 1942. Reprinted in *Journey to Infinity*, edited by Martin Greenberg. New York: Gnome, 1951, 259–311.

———. "With Flaming Swords." *Astounding Science-Fiction*, September 1942. Reprinted in *A Treasury of Science Fiction*, edited by Groff Conklin. New York: Crown, 1948, 201–33.

Casewit, Curtis W. *The Peacemakers*. New York: Avalon, 1960.

Chandler, A. Bertram. "False Dawn." *Astounding Science-Fiction*, October 1946, 126–58.
Charnas, Suzy McKee. *Motherlines*. New York: Berkley, 1978.
———. *Walk to the End of the World*. New York: Ballantine, 1974.
Clark, Walter van Tilburg. "The Portable Phonograph." 1941. Reprinted in *Adventures in Tomorrow*, edited by Kendall Foster Crossen. New York: Greenberg, 1951, 34–40.
Clarkson, Helen. *The Last Day: A Novel of the Day After Tomorrow*. New York: Dodd, Mead, 1959.
Clason, Clyde B. *Ark of Venus*. New York: Knopf, 1955.
Coon, Horace C. *43,000 Years Later*. New York: Signet, 1958.
Coppel, Alfred. *Dark December*. New York: Fawcett, 1960.
Corley, Edwin. *The Jesus Factor*. New York: Paperback, 1971.
Courtney, Robert. *See* Robinson, Frank M.
Crane, Robert [pseudonym of Bernard Glemser]. *Hero's Walk*. New York: Ballantine, 1954.
Davis, Chandler. "The Nightmare." *Astounding Science-Fiction*, May 1946, 7–24.
———. "To Still the Drums." *Astounding Science-Fiction*, October 1946, 159–72.
De Camp, L. Sprague. "The Blue Giraffe." *Astounding Science-Fiction*, August 1939. Reprinted in *Isaac Asimov's Presents the Great Science Fiction Stories Volume 1, 1939*, edited by Isaac Asimov and Martin H. Greenberg. New York: DAW, 1979, 248–71.
———. "Judgment Day." *Astounding Science-Fiction*, August 1955. Reprinted in *A Science Fiction Argosy*, edited by Damon Knight. New York: Simon & Schuster, 1972, 616–32.
Delany, Samuel. *Dhalgren*. New York: Bantam, 1974.
———. *Stars in My Pocket Like Grains of Sand*. New York: Bantam, 1985.
Del Rey, Lester. "The Faithful." *Astounding Science-Fiction*, April 1938. Reprinted in *Early del Rey*. Garden City, N.Y.: Doubleday, 1975, 7–16.
———, as John Alvarez. "Fifth Freedom." *Astounding Science-Fiction*, May 1943. Reprinted in *Early del Rey*. Garden City, N.Y.: Doubleday, 1975, 328–38.
———. "For I Am a Jealous People." *Star Short Novels*, edited by Frederik Pohl. New York: Ballantine, 1954. Reprinted in *The Best of Lester del Rey*. New York: Ballantine, 1978: 197–242.
———. "Into Thy Hands." *Astounding Science-Fiction*, August 1945. Reprinted in *Analog: Writer's Choice*. Analog Anthology #5, edited by Stanley Schmidt. New York: Davis, 1982, 123–38.
———. "Nerves." *Astounding Science-Fiction*, September 1942. Reprinted in *Adventures in Time and Space*, edited by Raymond J. Healy and J. Francis McComas. New York: Ballantine, 1974, 46–114.
———. *Nerves*. New York: Ballantine, 1956.
———. "Reincarnate." *Astounding Science-Fiction*, April 1940. Reprinted in *Early del Rey*. Garden City, N.Y.: Doubleday, 1975, 150–77.
———. "The Smallest God." *Astounding Science-Fiction*, January 1940. Reprinted in *Early del Rey*. Garden City, N.Y.: Doubleday, 1975, 60–93.
———. "The Stars Look Down." *Astounding Science-Fiction*, August 1940. Reprinted in *Early del Rey*. Garden City, N.Y.: Doubleday, 1975, 94–129.

———. "Whom the Gods Love." *Astounding Science-Fiction*, June 1943. Reprinted in *Early del Rey*. Garden City, N.Y.: Doubleday, 1975, 341–50.

Dick, Philip K. "Autofac." *Galaxy Science Fiction*, November 1955. Reprinted in *Beyond Control*, edited by Robert Silverberg. New York: Dell, 1974, 48–82.

———. "The Defenders." *Galaxy Science Fiction*, January 1953, 4–28.

———. "Foster, You're Dead." *Star Science Fiction Stories 3*, edited by Frederik Pohl. New York: Ballantine, 1954, 64–85.

———. "Impostor." *Astounding Science-Fiction*, June 1953. Reprinted in *Dark Stars*, edited by Robert Silverberg. New York: Ballantine, 1969, 121–36.

———. "Jon's World." In *Time to Come*, edited by August Derleth. New York: Farrar Straus and Young, 1954, 102–36.

———. *The Penultimate Truth*. New York: Belmont, 1964.

———. "Second Variety." *Space Science Fiction*, May, 1953. Reprinted as "Claws" in *Best of Philip K. Dick*. New York: Ballantine, 1977, 17–66.

Dickson, Gordon R. *The Final Encyclopedia*. New York: Tor, 1984.

———. *Three to Dorsai!* Garden City, N.Y.: Doubleday, 1975. Contains *Necromancer* (1962) *Tactics of Mistake* (1971), and "Dorsai!" (1952).

Diffin, Charles Willard. "The Power and the Glory." *Astounding Stories of Super Science*, July 1930. Reprinted in *The History of the Science Fiction Magazine* vol. 1, edited by Michael Ashley. Chicago: Henry Regnery, 1974, 99–106.

Doar, Graham. "The Outer Limit." *Saturday Evening Post*, December 24, 1949. Reprinted in *The Classic Book of Science Fiction*, edited by Groff Conklin. New York: Bonanza, 1982, 226–34.

DuBois, Theodora. *Solution T–25*. Garden City, N.Y.: Doubleday, 1951.

Duncan, David. *Dark Dominion*. New York: Ballantine, 1954.

Ellis, Edward S. *The Steam Man of the Prairies*. New York: American Novels Publishing Co., 1868.

Ellison, Harlan. "A Boy and His Dog." *New Worlds*, April 1969. Reprinted in *The Beast That Shouted Love at the Heart of the World*. New York: Signet, 1974, 217–54.

Emshwiller, Carol. "Day at the Beach." *Magazine of Fantasy and Science Fiction*, August 1959. Reprinted in *The Best of the Best*, edited by Judith Merril. New York: Delacorte, 1967, 274–84.

Engel, Leonard and Emanuel A. Piller. *World Aflame: the Russian–American War of 1950*. New York: Dial, 1947.

Engh, M[ary] J[ane]. *Arslan*. New York: Warner, 1976. Reprinted New York: Arbor, 1987.

Farmer, Philip Jose. "The God Business." *Beyond Fantasy Fiction*, March 1954. Reprinted in *The Classic Philip Jose Farmer 1952–1964*, edited by Martin H. Greenberg. New York: Crown, 1984, 43–109.

Flagg, Francis [pseudonym of George Henry Weiss]. "After Armageddon." *Wonder Stories*, September 1932, 341–45, 375. Reprinted in *Startling Stories*, Fall 1946, 72–80.

Foster, Richard. *The Rest Must Die*. New York: Gold Medal, 1959.

Frank, Pat [pseudonym of Harry Hart Frank]. *Alas, Babylon*. New York: Harper, 1959. Reprinted New York: Bantam, 1981.

———. *Forbidden Area*. Philadelphia: Lippincott, 1956.

———. *Mr. Adam*. Philadelphia: Lippincott, 1956.

Friborg, Albert Compton. "Careless Love." *Magazine of Fantasy & Science Fiction*,

July 1954. Reprinted as "Pushbutton Passion" in *Best from Fantasy & Science Fiction Fourth Series*, edited by Anthony Boucher. Garden City, N.Y.: Doubleday, 1955, 159–81.

Gallun, Raymond Z. "Atomic Fire." *Amazing Stories*, April 1931, 64–9.

———. "Magician of Dream Valley." *Astounding Science-Fiction*, October 1938, 12–22.

Galouye, Daniel F[rancis]. *Dark Universe*. New York: Bantam, 1961.

Gernsback, Hugo. *Ralph 124C 41+*, 2nd ed. New York: Fawcett Crest, 1958.

Giesy, J[ohn] U. *All for His Country*. Frank A. Munsey, 1914. Reprinted. New York: Macaulay, 1915.

Godfrey, Hollis. *The Man Who Ended War*. Boston: Little, Brown, 1908.

Gold, H[orace] L. "At the Post." *Galaxy Science Fiction*, October 1953. Reprinted in *The Old Die Rich and Other Science Fiction Stories*. New York: Crown, 1955, 157–93.

Gunn, James. "The Boy with Five Fingers." *Startling Stories*, January 1953, 58–60.

———. *This Fortress World*. New York: Gnome, 1955. Reprinted New York: Berkley, 1979.

Hale, Stephen G. "The Laughing Death." *Amazing Stories*, April 1931, 42–57, 90.

———. "Worlds Adrift." *Amazing Stories*, May 1932, 158–79, 183–84.

Hamilton, Edmond. *City at World's End*. New York: Frederick Fell, 1951.

———. "Devolution." *Amazing Stories*, December 1936. Reprinted in *Before the Golden Age*, edited by Isaac Asimov. Garden City, N.Y.: Doubleday, 1974, 796–809.

———. "The Man Who Evolved." *Wonder Stories*, April 1931. Reprinted in *Before the Golden Age*, edited by Isaac Asimov. Garden City, N.Y.: Doubleday, 1974, 23–38.

Hawkins, Willard. "The Dwindling Sphere." *Astounding Science-Fiction*, March 1940. Reprinted in *Isaac Asimov Presents the Great Science Fiction Stories, Volume 2, 1940*, edited by Isaac Asimov and Martin H. Greenberg. New York: DAW, 1979, 13–29.

Heinlein, Robert A[nson]. " 'All You Zombies—' " *Magazine of Fantasy & Science Fiction*, March 1959. Reprinted in *6 X H*. New York: Pyramid, 1961, 126–37.

———. *Between Planets*. New York: Scribner's, 1951.

———. *Beyond This Horizon*. Reading, PA: Fantasy Press, 1942.

———. "Blowups Happen." *Astounding Science-Fiction*, September 1940. Reprinted, revised, in *The Man Who Sold the Moon*. Chicago: Shasta, 1950. Reprinted, New York: Signet, 1951, 213–67.

———. "Coventry." *Astounding Science-Fiction*, July 1940. Reprinted in *The Past Through Tomorrow*. New York: Putnam, 1967, 471–508.

———. *The Day After Tomorrow*. New York: Signet, 1951. Reprint of *Sixth Column*, 1941.

———. *Double Star*. Garden City, N.Y.: Doubleday, 1956.

———. *Expanded Universe: The New Worlds of Robert A. Heinlein*. New York: Ace, 1980.

———. *Farnham's Freehold*. New York: Putnam, 1964.

———. *Friday*. New York: Holt, 1982.

———. "The Green Hills of Earth." *Saturday Evening Post*, February 8, 1947.

Reprinted in *The Past Through Tomorrow*. New York: Putnam, 1967, 294–302.

———. "Gulf." *Astounding Science-Fiction*, November–December 1949. Reprinted in *Assignment in Eternity*. New York: Signet, 1953, 7–67.

———. *Have Space Suit—Will Travel*. New York: Scribner's, 1958.

———. " 'If This Goes On—' " *Astounding Science-Fiction*. February–March 1940. Reprinted, revised, in *Revolt in 2100*. Chicago: Shasta, 1953. Reprinted, New York: Signet, 1954, 11–129.

———, as Lyle Monroe. " 'Let There Be Light.' " *Super Science Stories*. May 1940. Reprinted in *The Man Who Sold the Moon*. New York: Signet, 1951, 1–19.

———. "Life-Line." *Astounding Science-Fiction*, August 1939. Reprinted in *The Past Through Tomorrow*. New York: Putnam, 1967, 15–29.

———. "The Long Watch." *American Legion Magazine*. December 1949. Reprinted in *The Past Through Tomorrow*. New York: Putnam, 1967, 211–22.

———. "Lost Legacy." Reprint of "Lost Legion." In *Assignment in Eternity*. New York: Signet, 1953, 96–170.

———, as Lyle Monroe. "Lost Legion." *Super Science Stories*, November 1941. Reprinted as "Lost Legacy" in *Assignment in Eternity*. New York: Signet, 1953, 96–170.

———. *Methuselah's Children*. *Astounding Science-Fiction*, July–September 1941. Reprinted Hicksville, N.Y.: Gnome, 1958.

———. "Misfit." *Astounding Science-Fiction*, November 1939. Reprinted in *The Past Through Tomorrow*. New York: Putnam, 1967, 509–25.

———. *The Moon Is a Harsh Mistress*. *Worlds of If*, 1965–66. Reprint, revised. New York: Putnam, 1966; New York: Bantam, 1968.

———. "Project Nightmare." *Amazing Stories*, April 1953. Reprinted in *The Menace from Earth*. New York: Signet, 1963, 158–78.

———. *The Puppet Masters*. *Galaxy Science Fiction*, September–November 1951. Reprint. Garden City, N.Y.: Doubleday, 1951.

———. *Red Planet*. New York: Scribner's, 1949.

———, as Anson MacDonald. *Sixth Column*. *Astounding Science-Fiction*, January–March 1941. Reprint. New York: Gnome, 1949. Reprinted as *The Day After Tomorrow*. New York: Signet, 1951.

———, as Anson MacDonald. "Solution Unsatisfactory." *Astounding Science-Fiction*, May 1941. Reprinted in *Expanded Universe: The New Worlds of Robert A. Heinlein*. New York: Ace, 1980, 92–144.

———. *Space Cadet*. New York: Scribner's, 1948.

———. *Starship Troopers*. As "Starship Soldier" in *Fantasy & Science Fiction*, October–November 1959. New York: Putnam, 1959.

———. *Stranger in a Strange Land*. New York: Putnam, 1961.

———. *Time for the Stars*. New York: Scribner's, 1956.

———. "The Year of the Jackpot." *Galaxy Science Fiction*, March 1952. Reprinted in *The Menace from Earth*. New York: Signet, 1959, 7–38.

Herbert, Frank. "Cease Fire." *Astounding Science-Fiction*, January 1958. Reprinted in *A Century of Science Fiction*, edited by Damon Knight. New York: Simon & Schuster, 1962, 331–50.

Hogan, James P. *Voyage From Yesteryear*. New York: Ballantine, 1982.

Hughes, Riley. *The Hills Were Liars*. Milwaukee: Bruce, 1955.

Hunter, E. Waldo. *See* Sturgeon, Theodore.

Ing, Dean. *Pulling Through*. New York: Ace, 1983.

Jameson, Malcolm. *Atomic Bomb*. Reprint of "The Giant Atom." Hollywood: Bond-Charteris, 1945.

———. "Eviction by Isotherm." *Astounding Science-Fiction*, August 1937, 134–40.

———. "The Giant Atom." *Startling Stories*, Winter 1944.

Jenkins, Will F. *The Murder of the U.S.A.* New York: Crown, 1946.

Jones, Alice Eleanor. "Created He Them." *Fantasy and Science Fiction*, June 1955. Reprinted in *The Best from Fantasy and Science Fiction Fifth Series*, edited by Anthony Boucher. New York: Ace, 1956, 123–34.

Jones, Raymond F. "The Person from Porlock." *Astounding Science-Fiction*, August 1947. Reprinted in *A Treasury of Science Fiction*, edited by Groff Conklin. New York: Crown, 1948, 268–86.

———. *Renaissance. Astounding Science-Fiction*, July–October 1944. Reprint. New York: Gnome, 1951.

———. "A Stone and a Spear." *Galaxy Science Fiction*, December 1950. Reprinted in *Omnibus of Science Fiction*, edited by Groff Conklin. New York: Crown, 1952, 419–35.

Kelleam, Joseph E. "The Eagles Gather." *Astounding Science-Fiction*, April 1942, 93–97.

———. "Rust." *Astounding Science-Fiction*, October 1939. Reprinted in *Isaac Asimov Presents the Great Science Fiction Stories Volume 1, 1939*, edited by Isaac Asimov and Martin Harry Greenberg. New York: DAW, 1979, 353–62.

Keller, David H. M.D. "The Revolt of the Pedestrians." *Amazing Stories*, February 1928. Reprinted in *The Road to Science Fiction #2: From Wells to Heinlein*, edited by James Gunn. New York: Mentor/NAL, 1979, 169–97.

Kline, Otis Adelbert. "The Man From the Moon." *Amazing Stories*, October 1930, 646–57.

Knight, Damon. "The Last Word." *Satellite Science Fiction*, February 1957. Reprinted in *The Best of Damon Knight*. Garden City, N.Y.: Doubleday, 1976, 171–78.

Kornbluth, C[yril] M. "The Altar at Midnight." *Galaxy Science Fiction*, November 1952. Reprinted in *The End of Summer*, edited by Barry Malzberg and Bill Pronzini. New York: Ace, 1979, 151–60.

———. "Gomez." *New Worlds*, February 1955. Reprinted in *The Best of C. M. Kornbluth*, edited by Frederik Pohl. Garden City, N.Y.: Doubleday, 1976, 105–29.

———. "The Luckiest Man in Denv." *Galaxy Science Fiction*, June 1952. Reprinted in *The Best of C. M. Kornbluth*, edited by Frederik Pohl. Garden City, N.Y.: Doubleday, 1976, 70–82.

———. "The Mindworm." *Worlds Beyond*, December 1950. Reprinted in *The Best of C. M. Kornbluth*, edited by Frederik Pohl. Garden City, N.Y.: Doubleday, 1976, 176–89.

———. *Not This August*. Garden City, N.Y.: Doubleday, 1955.

———. "Shark Ship." *Vanguard Science Fiction*, June 1953. Reprinted in *The Best of C. M. Kornbluth*, edited by Frederik Pohl. Garden City, N.Y.: Doubleday, 1976, 208–39.

———. "Two Dooms." *Venture Science Fiction*, July, 1958. Reprinted in *The Best of C. M. Kornbluth*, edited by Frederik Pohl. Garden City, N.Y.: Doubleday, 1976, 264–310.

———. "The Words of Guru" *Stirring Science Stories*, June 1941. Reprinted in *The Best of C. M. Kornbluth*, edited by Frederik Pohl. Garden City, N.Y.: Doubleday, 1976, 9–16.

Kuttner, Henry. *Mutant*. New York: Ballantine, 1953.

———. *Fury*. New York: Grosset & Dunlap, 1950.

Kuttner, Henry and C[atherine] L. Moore as Lewis Padgett. "Beggars in Velvet." *Astounding Science-Fiction*, December 1945, 7–46. Reprinted in *Mutant* by Henry Kuttner. New York: Ballantine, 1953, 105–50.

———, as Lawrence O'Donnell. "Clash by Night." *Astounding Science-Fiction*, March 1943. Reprinted in *The Astounding Science-Fiction Anthology*, edited by John W. Campbell. New York: Simon & Schuster, 1952, 160–212.

———, as Lewis Padgett. "The Fairy Chessmen." *Astounding Science-Fiction*, January 1946, 7–45; February 1946, 122–76.

———, as Lawrence O'Donnell. "Fury." *Astounding Science-Fiction*, May 1947, 6–49; June 1947, 103–62; July 1947, 105–45.

———, as Lewis Padgett. "Humpty Dumpty." *Astounding Science-Fiction*, September 1953, 47–84. Reprinted in *Mutant* by Henry Kuttner. New York: Ballantine, 1953, 150–90.

———, as Lewis Padgett. "The Lion and the Unicorn." *Astounding Science-Fiction*, August 1945, 144–78. Reprinted in *Mutant* by Henry Kuttner. New York: Ballantine, 1953, 69–104.

———, as Lewis Padgett. "The Piper's Son." *Astounding Science-Fiction*, February 1945, 6–28. Reprinted in *Mutant* by Henry Kuttner. New York: Ballantine, 1953, 7–34.

———, as Lewis Padgett. "Three Blind Mice." *Astounding Science-Fiction*, June 1945, 68–97. Reprinted in *Mutant* by Henry Kuttner. New York: Ballantine, 1953, 35–68.

———, as Lewis Padgett. "Tomorrow and Tomorrow." *Astounding Science-Fiction*, January 1947, 6–56; February 1947, 140–77.

Le Guin, Ursula K. *The Lathe of Heaven*. New York: Avon, 1971.

Leiber, Fritz. *The Big Time*. *Galaxy Science Fiction*, March–April 1958. Reprint. New York: Ace, 1961.

———. "Gather, Darkness!" *Astounding Science-Fiction*, May–July 1943.

———. *Gather, Darkness!* New York: Pellegrini & Cudahy, 1950.

———. "The Last Letter." *Galaxy Science Fiction*, June 1958. Reprinted in *A Pail of Air*. New York: Ballantine, 1964, 132–44.

———. "The Moon Is Green." *Galaxy Science Fiction*, April 1952, 89–104.

———. "Night of the Long Knives." *Amazing Stories*, January 1960. Reprinted as "The Wolf Pair" in *The Night of the Wolf*. New York: Ballantine, 1966, 56–137.

Leinster, Murray [pseudonym of William Fitzgerald Jenkins]. "First Contact." *Astounding Science-Fiction*, May 1945. Reprinted in *The Astounding Science-Fiction Anthology*, edited by John W. Campbell, Jr. New York: Simon & Schuster, 1952, 218–46.

———. "The Power Planet." *Amazing Stories*, June 1931. Reprinted in *Avon Fantasy Reader* no. 1, February 1947, 7–44.

———. "Proxima Centauri." *Astounding Science-Fiction*, March 1935. Reprinted in *The Road to Science Fiction #2: from Wells to Heinlein*, edited by James Gunn. New York: Mentor/NAL, 1979, 290–338.
———. "West Wind." *Astounding Science-Fiction*, March 1948, 77–107.
MacDonald, Anson. *See* Heinlein, Robert A.
MacDonald, John D[ann]. *Ballroom of the Skies*. New York: Greenberg, 1952.
———. "A Child Is Crying." *Thrilling Wonder Stories*, December 1948. Reprinted in *The Science Fiction Galaxy*, edited by Groff Conklin. New York: Permabooks, 1950, 115–30.
———. "Trojan Horse Laugh." *Astounding Science-Fiction*, August 1949. Reprinted in *Dimension 4*, edited by Groff Conklin. New York: Pyramid, 1964, 58–102.
Masters, Dexter. *The Accident*. New York: Knopf, 1955.
Matheson, Richard. "Dance of the Dead." *Star Science Fiction Stories no. 3*, edited by Frederik Pohl. New York: Ballantine, 1954, 114–29.
———. "Pattern for Survival." *Magazine of Fantasy and Science Fiction*, May 1955. Reprinted in *The Best From Fantasy and Science Fiction Fifth Series*, edited by Anthony Boucher. New York: Ace, 1956, 219–22.
McIntyre, Vonda N. *Dreamsnake*. Boston: Houghton Mifflin, 1978.
———. *The Exile Waiting*. New York: Fawcett, 1975.
Meek, Captain S[terner St.] P[aul], U.S.A. "Awlo of Ulm." *Amazing Stories*, September 1931. Reprinted in *Before the Golden Age*, edited by Isaac Asimov. Garden City, N.Y.: Doubleday, 1974, 86–142.
———. "The Red Peril." *Amazing Stories*, September 1929, 486–503, 521.
———. "Submicroscopic." *Amazing Stories*, August 1931, 390–401. Reprinted in *Before the Golden Age*, edited by Isaac Asimov. Garden City, N.Y.: Doubleday, 1974, 61–85.
Merril, Judith. *Shadow on the Hearth*. Garden City, N.Y.: Doubleday, 1950.
———. "That Only a Mother." *Astounding Science-Fiction*, June 1948. Reprinted in *The Road to Science Fiction* vol. 3, edited by James Gunn. New York: Mentor/NAL, 1979, 143–52.
Michel, John B., and Robert W. Lowndes. "The Inheritors." *Future Fantasy and Science Fiction*, October 1942, 55–69.
Miller, P. Schuyler. "The Atom Smasher." *Amazing Stories*, January 1934, 127–30.
Miller, Walter M[ichael] Jr. "And the Light Is Risen." *Fantasy and Science Fiction*, August 1956. Reprinted, revised in *A Canticle for Leibowitz*. New York: Lippincott, 1959.
———. "A Canticle for Leibowitz." *Fantasy and Science Fiction*, April 1955. Reprinted in *The Magazine of Fantasy and Science Fiction: A 30-Year Retrospective*, edited by Edward L. Ferman. Garden City, N.Y.: Doubleday, 1980, 85–105. Reprinted, revised in *A Canticle for Leibowitz*. New York: Lippincott, 1959.
———. *A Canticle for Leibowitz*. New York: Lippincott, 1959. New York: Bantam, 1961.
———. "The Last Canticle." *Fantasy and Science Fiction*, February 1957. Reprinted, revised in *A Canticle for Leibowitz*. New York: Lippincott, 1959.
Monroe, Lyle. *See* Heinlein, Robert A.

Moore, Ward. *Bring the Jubilee*. New York: Avon, 1955.

———. "Flying Dutchman." *Fantasy & Science Fiction*, September 1956. Reprinted in *Adventures in Tomorrow*, edited by Kendall Foster Crossen. New York: Corwin, 1951, 21–25.

———. *Greener Than You Think*. New York: Ballantine, 1947.

———. "Lot." *Fantasy and Science Fiction*, May 1953. Reprinted in *Best From Fantasy and Science Fiction, Third Series*, edited by Anthony Boucher and J. Francis McComas. Garden City, N.Y.: Doubleday, 1954, 100–130.

———. "Lot's Daughter." *Fantasy and Science Fiction*, October 1954, 3–27.

Nathanson, Isaac R. "The World Aflame." *Amazing Stories*, January 1935, 44–87.

Neville, Kris. "Cold War." *Astounding Science-Fiction*, October 1949. Reprinted in *The Astounding Science-Fiction Anthology*, edited by John W. Campbell, Jr. New York: Simon & Schuster, 1952, 404–14.

Norton, Andre. *Star Man's Son*. New York: Ace, 1952. Reprinted as *Daybreak 2250 A.D.* New York: DAW, 1954.

Norton, Roy. *The Vanishing Fleets*. New York: D. Appleton, 1908.

Nowlan, Philip Francis. "The Airlords of Han." *Amazing Stories the Magazine of Scientifiction*, March 1929, 1106–36. Reprinted, revised, in *Armageddon 2419 A.D.* New York: Ace, 1978.

———. "Armageddon 2419 A.D." *Amazing Stories the Magazine of Scientifiction*, August 1928, 422–49. Reprinted, revised, in *Armageddon 2419 A.D.* New York: Ace, 1978.

Noyes, Pierrepont B. *Gentlemen: You Are Mad!*. New York: Baxter Freres, 1946. Reprint of *The Pallid Giant: a tale of yesterday and tomorrow*. Old Tappan, N.J.: Fleming H. Revell, 1927.

O'Donnell, Lawrence. *See* Kuttner, Henry and C. L. Moore.

Oliver, Chad [pseudonym of Symmes Chadwick Oliver]. "The Life Game." *Thrilling Wonder Stories*, June 1953, 108–22.

Orlovsky, V. "The Revolt of the Atoms." *Amazing Stories*. April 1929, 6–17, 37.

Padgett, Lewis. *See* Kuttner, Henry and C. L. Moore.

Palmer, David R. *Emergence*. New York: Bantam, 1984.

Phillips, Rog [pseudonym of Roger Phillips Graham]. "Atom War." *Amazing Stories*, May 1946, 74–91.

———. "The Mutants." *Amazing Stories*, July 1946, 41–69.

———. "So Shall Ye Reap!" *Amazing Stories*, August 1947, 8–43, 101–55.

Piper, H. Beam. "The Answer." *Fantastic Universe*, December 1959, 4–12.

———. "Day of the Moron." *Astounding Science-Fiction*, September 1951. Reprinted in *The Worlds of H. Beam Piper*, edited by John F. Carr. New York: Ace Books, 1983, 199–231.

———. "Time and Time Again." *Astounding Science-Fiction*. April 1947, 27–48.

———. "Uller Uprising." In *The Petrified Planet* by Fletcher Pratt, H. Beam Piper and Judith Merril. New York: Twayne, 1952, 75–196.

Pohl, Frederik. *JEM*. New York: St. Martin's, 1979.

———. "Let the Ants Try." *Planet Stories*, Winter 1949. Reprinted in *Mutants*, edited by Robert Silverberg. Nashville, Tenn.: Thomas Nelson, 1977, 49–60.

———. "The Wizards of Pung's Corners." *Galaxy Science Fiction*, October 1958.

Reprinted in *Connoisseur's Science Fiction*, edited by Tom Boardman. Harmondsworth, Middlesex, England: Penguin, 1964, 33–63.

Quattrocchi, Frank. "The Sword." *Worlds of If*, March 1953. Reprinted in *The Spear of Mars*, edited by Reginald Bretnor. New York: Ace, 1980, 40–100.

Rein, Harold. *Few Were Left*. New York: Day, 1955.

Reynolds, Mack. "The Galactic Ghost." *Planet Stories*, March 1954. Reprinted as "Last Warning." In *Compounded Interests*. Boston: NESFA, 1983, 51–60.

———. "Isolationist." *Fantastic Adventures*, April 1950. Reprinted in *The Classic Book of Science Fiction*, edited by Groff Conklin. New York: Bonanza, 1982, 177–82.

Ridenour, Dr. Louis N. "Pilot Lights of the Apocalypse." *Fortune Magazine*, Jan. 1946. Reprinted in *Great Science Fiction by Scientists*, edited by Groff Conklin. New York: Collier, 1962, 279–88.

Rigg, Lt. Col. Robert B. *War—1974*. Harrisburg, Pa.: Military, 1958.

Robinson, Frank M. as Robert Courtney. "One Thousand Miles Up." *Science Stories*, April 1954, 88–101.

Roshwald, Mordecai. *Level 7*. New York: McGraw-Hill, 1959.

Rousseau, Victor [pseudonym for Victor R. Emanuel]. "The Atom Smasher." *Astounding Stories of Super-Science*, May 1930, 234–76.

St. Clair, Margaret as Idris Seabright. "The Hole in the Moon." *Fantasy and Science Fiction*, February 1952. Reprinted in *The Best From Fantasy and Science Fiction*, edited by Anthony Boucher and J. Frances McComas. Boston: Little, Brown, 1953, 93–100.

———. "Quis Custodiet . . . ?" *Startling Stories*, July, 1948. Reprinted in *The Science Fiction Galaxy*, edited by Groff Conklin. New York: Permabooks, 1950, 131–43.

Sambrot, William. "Deadly Decision." *Extension*, 1958. Reprinted in *Island of Fear*. New York: Permabooks, 1963, 115–28.

———. "A Son of Eve." *MR. Magazine*, 1959. Reprinted in *Island of Fear*. New York: Permabooks, 1963, 160–66.

Sargent, Pamela. *The Shore of Women*. New York: Crown, 1986.

Schachner, Nat. "City of the Corporate Mind." *Astounding Science-Fiction*, December 1939.

———. "Emissaries of Space." *Wonder Stories Quarterly*, Fall 1932, 6–59.

———. "Past, Present, and Future." *Astounding Stories*, September 1937. Reprinted in *Before the Golden Age*, edited by Isaac Asimov. Garden City, N.Y.: Doubleday, 1974, 843–77.

———. "The Time Impostor." *Astounding Stories*, March 1934.

———. "The World Gone Mad." *Amazing Stories*, October 1935, 122–35.

Seabright, Idris. *See* St. Clair, Margaret.

Sheckley, Robert. "The Battle." *If: Worlds of Science Fiction*, September 1954. Reprinted in *Citizen in Space*. New York: Ace, 1978, 194–200.

Shelley, Mary. *Frankenstein, or, the Modern Prometheus*. 1818.

Sherred, T. L. "E for Effort." *Astounding Science-Fiction*, May 1947. Reprinted in *The Astounding Science-Fiction Anthology*, edited by John W. Campbell, Jr. New York: Simon & Schuster, 1952, 280–325.

Shiras, Wilmar H. *Children of the Atom*. Garden City, N.Y.: Doubleday, 1953.

Silverberg, Robert. *Dying Inside*. New York: Ballantine, 1973.

———. *The 13th Immortal*. New York: Ace D223, 1957.

Simak, Clifford D. "City." *Astounding Science-Fiction*, May 1944. Reprinted in *The Best of Science Fiction*, edited by Groff Conklin. New York: Crown, 1946, 476–96. In *City*. New York: Ace, 1981, 13–43.

———. "Lobby." *Astounding Science-Fiction*, April 1944. Reprinted in *The Best of Science Fiction*, edited by Groff Conklin. New York: Crown, 1946, 89–102.

Smith, Carmichael [pseudonym of Paul Myron Anthony Linebarger]. *Atomsk*. New York: Duell, Sloan and Pearce, 1949.

Smith, E[dward] E[lmer] Ph.D. *The Skylark of Space*. *Amazing Stories*, August–October 1928. Reprinted, revised. New York: Pyramid Books, 1958.

———. *Triplanetary*. *Amazing*, January–April 1934.

Spinrad, Norman. "The Big Flash." In *Orbit 5*, edited by Damon Knight. New York: G. P. Putnam's, 1969. Reprinted in *The Star-Spangled Future*. New York: Ace, 1979, 227–59.

Spohr, Carl W. "The Final War." *Wonder Stories*, March 1932, 1110–29, 1187–89. April 1932, 1266–86.

Springer, Sherwood. "No Land of Nod." *Thrilling Wonder Stories*, December 1952. Reprinted in *Best from Startling Stories*, edited by Samuel Mines. New York: Holt, 1953, 135–61.

Stewart, George R. *Earth Abides*. New York: Houghton Mifflin, 1949.

Stewart, Will. *See* Williamson, Jack.

Stockton, Frank. *The Great War Syndicate*. New York: Dodd, Mead, 1889.

Streiber, Whitley, and James Kunetka. *Warday and the Journey Onward*. New York: Holt, Rinehart and Winston, 1984.

Stuart, Don A. *See* Campbell, John W., Jr.

Sturgeon, Theodore. "Affair With a Green Monkey." *Venture*, May 1957, 121–30.

———. "Artnan Process." *Astounding Science-Fiction*, June 1941, 50–68. Reprinted in *Starshine*. New York: Pyramid, 1966, 49–78.

———. "August Sixth, 1945." in "Brass Tacks." *Astounding Science-Fiction*, December 1945, 176–78.

———. "Beware the Fury." *Fantastic*, April 1954, 74–94, 129. Reprinted as "Extrapolation" in *Sturgeon in Orbit*. New York: Pyramid, 1964, 9–35.

———. *The Cosmic Rape*. New York: Dell, 1958.

———. "Excalibur and the Atom." *Fantastic Adventures*, August 1951: 8–51.

———. "Farewell to Eden." In *Invasion from Mars: Interplanetary Stories*, edited by Orson Welles. New York: Dell, 1949, 165–180.

———. "A God in a Garden." *Unknown*, October 1939, 75–84.

———. "Granny Won't Knit." *Galaxy Science Fiction*, May 1954, 6–61.

———. "If All Men Were Brothers, Would You Let One Marry Your Sister?" In *Dangerous Visions*, edited by Harlan Ellison. Garden City, N.Y.: Doubleday, 1967, 344–89.

———. "Killdozer!" *Astounding Science-Fiction*, November 1944, 7–63. Reprinted in *Aliens 4*. New York: Avon, 1959, 5–74.

———. "Make Room for Me." *Fantastic Adventures*, May 1951, 48–65. Reprinted in *Sturgeon in Orbit*. New York: Pyramid, 1964, 80–104.

———. "Memorial." *Astounding Science-Fiction*, April 1946, 158–69. Reprinted in *The Worlds of Theodore Sturgeon*. New York: Ace, 1972, 380–98.

———. "Microcosmic God." *Astounding Science-Fiction*, April 1941, 46–68. Reprinted in *The Science Fiction Hall of Fame*, edited by Robert Silverberg. Garden City, N.Y.: Doubleday, 1970, 87–111.

———. *More Than Human*. New York: Farrar, Straus and Young, 1953. New York: Ballantine, 1953.

———. "Never Underestimate." *If Worlds of Science Fiction*, March 1952, 99–113. Reprinted in *Omnibus of Science Fiction*, edited by Groff Conklin. New York: Crown, 1952, 65–78.

———. "The Pod in the Barrier." *Galaxy Science Fiction*, September 1954, 8–47. Reprinted as "The Pod and the Barrier" in *Starshine*. New York: Pyramid, 1966, 103–48.

———. "Prodigy." *Astounding Science-Fiction*, April 1949, 71–80. Reprinted in *Caviar*. New York: Ballantine, 1955, 77–88.

——— as "E. Waldo Hunter." "The Purple Light." *Astounding Science-Fiction*, June 1941, 117–21.

———. "Rule of Three." *Galaxy Science Fiction*, January 1951, 74–107. Reprinted in *The Stars Are the Styx*. New York: Dell, 1979, 37–74.

———. "The Skills of Xanadu." *Galaxy Science Fiction*, July 1956, 116–143. Reprinted in *The Worlds of Theodore Sturgeon*. New York: Ace, 1972, 3–38.

———. "The Sky Was Full of Ships." *Thrilling Wonder Stories*, June 1947, 55–60. Reprinted in *The Worlds of Theodore Sturgeon*. New York: Ace, 1972, 254–68.

———. "There Is No Defense." *Astounding Science-Fiction*, February 1948, 7–45. Reprinted in *The Worlds of Theodore Sturgeon*. New York: Ace, 1972, 39–100.

———. "Thunder and Roses." *Astounding Science-Fiction*, November 1947, 76–96. Reprinted in *The Astounding Science-Fiction Anthology*, edited by John W. Campbell. New York: Simon & Schuster, 1952, 351–70.

———. "To Marry Medusa." *Galaxy Science Fiction*, August 1958, 4–62. Reprinted in *The Cosmic Rape and "To Marry Medusa"*. Boston: Gregg, 1977, 161–231.

———. "The Touch of Your Hand." *Galaxy Science Fiction*, September 1953, 4–47. Reprinted in *Visions and Venturers*. New York: Dell, 1978, 201–58.

———. "The Traveling Crag." *Fantastic Adventures*, July 1951, 100–121. Reprinted in *Visions and Venturers*. New York: Dell, 1978, 261–300.

———. "Unite and Conquer." *Astounding Science-Fiction*, October 1948, 63–90. Reprinted in *A Way Home*. New York: Pyramid, 1956, 9–41.

———. *Venus Plus X*. New York: Pyramid, 1960.

———. "The Wages of Synergy." *Startling Stories*, August 1953, 84–112. Reprinted in *Sturgeon in Orbit*. New York: Pyramid, 1964, 36–79.

———. "The [Widget], the [Wadget], and Boff." *Fantasy & Science Fiction*, November 1955, 3–38; December 1955, 94–126. Reprinted in *A Treasury of Great Science Fiction* vol. 1, edited by Anthony Boucher. Garden City, N.Y.: Doubleday, 1959, 308–69.

———. "The World Well Lost." *Universe*, June 1953, 16–33, 123.

Szilard, Leo. "Report on Grand Central Terminal." *University of Chicago Magazine*,

June 1942. Reprinted in *Great Science Fiction by Scientists*, edited by Groff Conklin. New York: Collier, 1962, 289–96.

Taine, John [pseud. for Eric Temple Bell]. *Seeds of Life. Amazing Stories Quarterly*, Fall 1931. Reprinted, New York: Dover, 1966.

Temple, William F. "The Four-Sided Triangle." *Amazing Stories*, November 1939. Reprinted in *Isaac Asimov Presents the Great Science Fiction Stories Volume 1, 1939*, edited by Isaac Asimov and Martin H. Greenberg. New York: DAW, 1979, 363–84.

Tenn, William. [pseudonym for Philip Klass]. "Brooklyn Project." *Planet Stories*, Fall 1948. Reprinted in *17 X Infinity*, edited by Groff Conklin. New York: Dell, 1963, 263–72.

———. "Generation of Noah." *Suspense*, Spring 1951. Reprinted in *The Wooden Star*. New York: Ballantine, 1968, 73–94.

———. "The Liberation of Earth." *Future Science Fiction*, May 1953. Reprinted in *Of All Possible Worlds*. New York: Ballantine, 1955, 56–75.

———. "Null–P." In *Worlds Beyond*, January 1950. Reprinted in *The Wooden Star*. New York: Ballantine, 1968, 57–72.

———. "The Sickness." *Infinity Science Fiction*, November 1955. Reprinted in *Time in Advance*. New York: Bantam, 1958, 77–101.

Tevis, Walter. *Mockingbird*. New York: Bantam, 1981.

Thackara, James. *America's Children*. London: Chatto and Windus, 1984.

Train, Arthur, and Robert Williams Wood. *The Man Who Rocked the Earth*. Garden City, N.Y.: Doubleday, Page, 1915.

Tucker, [Arthur] Wilson. *The Long Loud Silence*. New York: Rinehart, 1952.

Van Vogt, A[lfred] E[lton]. *Empire of the Atom*. New York: Timescape/Pocket, 1983.

———. "The Seesaw." *Astounding Science-Fiction*, July 1941, 60–74.

———. *Slan. Astounding Science-Fiction*. September–December 1940. Reprinted, revised in *Triad: Three Complete Science Fiction Novels*. New York: Simon & Schuster, 1962, 371–527.

———. "The Weapon Makers." *Astounding Science-Fiction*, February 1943.

———. "The Weapon Shops of Isher." *Thrilling Wonder Stories*, February 1949. Reprinted in *A Treasury of Great Science Fiction*, vol. 1, edited by Anthony Boucher. Garden City, N.Y.: Doubleday, 1959, 413–527.

———. *The Weapon Shops of Isher*. New York: Greenberg, 1951.

———. "The Weapon Shop." *Astounding Science-Fiction*, December 1942. Reprinted in *Adventures in Time and Space*, edited by Raymond J. Healy and J. Francis McComas. New York: Ballantine, 1974, 741–88.

———. *World of Null-A. Astounding Science-Fiction*, August–October 1945. Reprinted. New York: Simon and Schuster, 1948. Also in *Triad: Three Complete Science Fiction Novels*. New York: Simon & Schuster, 1962, 7–186.

Verne, Jules. *Twenty Thousand Leagues Under the Sea*. Boston: George M. Smith, 1873.

Vinge, Vernor. *The Peace War*. New York: Bluejay, 1984.

Vonnegut, Kurt, Jr. *Cat's Cradle*. New York: Dell, 1963.

———. *Galápagos*. New York: Dell, 1985.

———. "Harrison Bergeron." *Magazine of Fantasy and Science Fiction*, October 1961. Reprinted in *The Road to Science Fiction #3: from Heinlein to Here*, edited by James Gunn. New York: Mentor/NAL, 1979, 316–22.

———. *Slaughterhouse-Five or the Children's Crusade*. New York: Delacorte, 1969.
Wandrei, Donald. "The Atom-Smasher." *Astounding Stories*, April 1934: 85–86.
———. "Colossus." *Astounding Stories*, January 1934. Reprinted in *Before the Golden Age*, edited by Isaac Asimov. Garden City: Doubleday, 1974, 423–59.
Wells, H. G. *The World Set Free*. New York: E. P. Dutton, 1914.
Weston, Susan B. *Children of the Light*. New York: St. Martin's, 1985.
White, E. B. "The Morning of the Day They Did It." *The New Yorker*, February 25, 1950. Reprinted in *Past, Present, and Future Perfect*, edited by Jack C. Wolfe and Gregory Fitz Gerald. Greenwich, Conn.: Fawcett, 1971, 131–50.
Wilhelm, Kate. *Where Late the Sweet Birds Sang*. New York: Harper, 1976.
Williams, Nick Boddie. *The Atom Curtain*. New York: Ace Double, 1956.
Williams, Ralph. "Business as Usual, During Alterations." *Astounding Science-Fiction*, August 1960. Reprinted in *Prologue to Analog*, edited by John W. Campbell. Garden City, N.Y.: Doubleday, 1962, 230–58.
Williamson, Jack. "Backlash." *Astounding Science-Fiction*, July 1941, 148–62.
———, as Will Stewart. "Collision Orbit." *Astounding Science-Fiction*, July 1942, 80–106.
———. "The Equalizer." *Astounding Science-Fiction*, March 1947, 6–55.
———. "Hindsight." *Astounding Science-Fiction*, May 1940. Reprinted in *The Astounding Science-Fiction Anthology*, edited by John W. Campbell, Jr. New York: Simon and Schuster, 1952, 43–59.
———. *The Humanoids*. New York: Lancer, 1969.
———. *The Legion of Space*. *Astounding Science-Fiction*, April–September 1934. Reading PA: Fantasy Press, 1947. Reprinted in *Three From the Legion*. Garden City, N.Y.: Doubleday, nd, 5–179.
———. *The Legion of Time*. *Astounding Science-Fiction*, May–July 1938. Reading PA: Fantasy Press, 1952.
———, as Will Stewart. "Minus Sign." *Astounding Science-Fiction*, November 1942, 43–79.
———, as Will Stewart. "Opposites—React!" *Astounding Science-Fiction*, January 1943, 9–33; February 1943, 95–129.
———, as Will Stewart. "Seetee Shock." *Astounding Science-Fiction*, February 1949, 8–49; March 1949, 114–52; April 1949, 105–45.
———. "With Folded Hands." *Astounding Science-Fiction*, July 1947, 6–45. Reprinted in *The Road to Science Fiction #2: From Wells to Heinlein*, edited by James Gunn. New York: Mentor/NAL, 1979, 367–410.
Wolfe, Bernard. *Limbo*. New York: Random House, 1952.
Wouk, Herman. "The 'Lomokome' Papers." *Collier's*, February 1956. Reprinted *The "Lomokome" Papers*. New York: Pocket, 1968.
Wright, S. Fowler. "Obviously Suicide." *Suspense*, Spring 1951. Reprinted in *Beyond the End of Time*, edited by Frederik Pohl. Garden City, N.Y.: Permabooks, 1952, 321–34.
Wylie, Philip. "The Answer." *Saturday Evening Post*, May 7, 1955. Reprint. *The Answer*. New York: Rinehart, 1956.
———. "Blunder." *Collier's*, February 12, 1946. Reprinted in *Strange Ports of Call*,

edited by August Derleth. New York: Pellegrini and Cudahy, 1948, 145–62.
———. "The Paradise Crater." *Bluebook Magazine*, October 1945, 2–27.
———. *The Smuggled Atom Bomb. Saturday Evening Post*, August 4 to September 1, 1951. Reprint. New York: Avon, 1951.
———. *Tomorrow!*. New York: Rinehart, 1954.
Zagat, Arthur Leo. "Slaves of the Lamp." *Astounding Science-Fiction*, August 1946, 7–45; September 1946, 141–78.

NONFICTION

Ackerman, Forrest J., ed. *Gosh! Wow! (Sense of Wonder) Science Fiction*. New York: Bantam, 1981.
Allen, Francis R., Hornell Hart, Delbert C. Miller, William F. Ogburn, and Meyer F. Nimkoff. *Technology and Social Change*. New York: Appleton-Century-Crofts, 1957.
Allen, Thomas B. *War Games*. New York: McGraw-Hill, 1987.
Amrine, Michael. *The Great Decision: The Secret History of the Atomic Bomb*. New York: Putnam, 1959.
Asimov, Isaac. "Social Science Fiction." In *Modern Science Fiction, Its Meaning and Its Future*, edited by Reginald Bretnor. 2nd ed. New York: Coward McCann, 1979, 158–96.
Bailyn, Bernard, David Brion Davis, David Herbert Donald, John L. Thomas, Robert H. Wiebe, and Gordon S. Wood. *The Great Republic*. Boston: Little, Brown, 1977.
Barber, Bernard and Walter Hirsch, eds. *The Sociology of Science*. New York: Free Press of Glencoe, 1962.
Barron, Arthur S. "Why Do Scientists Read Science Fiction?" *Bulletin of the Atomic Scientists* 13, no. 2 (February 1957): 62–65, 70.
Bartter, Martha A. "Nuclear Holocaust as Urban Renewal." *Science Fiction Studies* 39 (1986): 148–58.
Beardslee, David C. and Donald D. O'Dowd. "The College-Student Image of the Scientist." *Science* 133 (March 31, 1961): 997–1001. Reprinted in *The Sociology of Science*, edited by Bernard Barber and Walter Hirsch. New York: Free Press of Glencoe, 1962, 247–58.
Ben-Aaron, Diana. "Rethinking the Legacy of Los Alamos." "MIT Reporter" Column in *Technology Review*, July 1985, 24–25.
Berger, Albert I. "Nuclear Energy, Science Fiction's Metaphor of Power." *Science-Fiction Studies* 18 (1979): 121–28.
Berger, Morroe. *Real and Imagined Worlds The Novel and Social Science*. Cambridge, Mass.: Harvard University Press, 1977.
Bliss, James, as William Atheling, Jr. *The Issue at Hand*, 2nd ed. Chicago: Advent 1973.
———. "Theodore Sturgeon's Macrocosm." In *Magazine of Fantasy and Science Fiction*, September 1962, 42–45.
Bloch, Robert. "Imagination and Modern Social Criticism." In *The Science Fiction Novel*, edited by Basil Davenport. Chicago: Advent, 1959.

Boyer, Paul. *By the Bomb's Early Light: American Thought and Culture at the Dawn of the Atomic Age*. New York: Pantheon, 1985.

Bradley, David. *No Place to Hide*. Boston: Little, Brown, 1948.

Bretnor, Reginald, ed. *Modern Science Fiction: Its Meaning and Its Future*, 2nd ed. Chicago: Advent, 1979.

———. *Science Fiction, Today and Tomorrow*. New York: Harper, 1974.

Brians, Paul. *Nuclear Holocausts: Atomic War in Fiction, 1895–1984*. Kent, Ohio: Kent State University Press, 1987.

———. "Nuclear War in Science Fiction, 1945–59." *Science-Fiction Studies* 34 (1984): 253–63.

———. "Red Holocaust: The Atomic Conquest of the West." *Extrapolation* 28 no. 4 (1987): 319–29.

Bruffee, Ken. "Social Construction, Language, and the Authority of Text." *College English* 48 no. 8 (1986): 773–90.

Budrys, Algis. "Non-Literary Influence on Science Fiction (An Essay)." Drumm Booklet no. 9. Polk City, Iowa: Drumm, 1983.

Burroway, Janet. *Writing Fiction A Guide to Narrative Craft*, 2nd ed. Boston: Little, Brown, 1987.

Campbell, John W., Jr. *The Atomic Story*. New York: Holt, 1947.

———. "Concerning the Atomic War." Editorial in *Astounding Science-Fiction*, March 1946, 5, 178.

———. Introduction to *The Man Who Sold the Moon* by Robert A. Heinlein. New York: Signet/NAL, 1951, vii–xi.

———. "The Place of Science Fiction." In *Modern Science Fiction: Its Meaning and Its Future*, edited by Reginald Bretnor. 2nd ed. Chicago: Advent, 1979, 3–22.

———. "Unsane Behavior." Editorial in *Astounding Science-Fiction*, March 1953, 6–7.

Carter, Paul A. *The Creation of Tomorrow: Fifty Years of Magazine Science Fiction*. New York: Columbia University Press, 1977.

Ceadel, Martin. "Popular Fiction and the Next War." In *Class, Culture, and Social Change*, edited by Frank Gloversmith. Sussex: Harvester Press, 1980, 161–84.

Clarke, I[gnatius] F[rederick]. *Voices Prophesying War 1763–1984*. London: Oxford University Press, 1966.

Coblentz, Stanton A. *From Arrow to Atom Bomb: The Psychological History of War*. New York: Beechhurst, 1953.

Contento, William, comp. *Index to Science Fiction Anthologies and Collections*. 2 vols. Boston: Hall, 1978.

Day, Donald B., comp. *Index to the Science Fiction Magazines 1926–1950*. Portland, Ore.: Perri Press, 1952.

Del Rey, Lester. *Early del Rey*. Garden City, N.Y.: Doubleday, 1975.

———. "The Three Careers of John W. Campbell." In *The Best of John W. Campbell*, edited by Lester del Rey. Garden City, N.Y.: Doubleday, 1976, 1–6.

Dietz, David. *Atomic Energy in the Coming Era*. New York: Dodd, Mead, 1945.

Diskin, Lahna. *Theodore Sturgeon*. Starmont Reader's Guide, no. 7. Mercer Island, Wash.: Starmont House, 1981.

———. *Theodore Sturgeon, A Primary and Secondary Bibliography*. Boston: Hall, 1980.

Dowling, David. *Fictions of Nuclear Disaster*. London: Macmillan, 1987.

Franklin, H. Bruce. *Robert A. Heinlein: America as Science Fiction*. Oxford: Oxford University Press, 1980.

———. "Strange Scenarios: Science Fiction, the Theory of Alienation, and the Nuclear Gods." *Science Fiction Studies* 39 (July 1986): 117–28.

Fromm, Erich. *May Man Prevail? An Inquiry into the Facts and Fictions of Foreign Policy*. Garden City, N.Y.: Anchor/Doubleday, 1964.

Frye, Northrop. *Anatomy of Criticism: Four Essays*. Princeton: Princeton University Press, 1957.

Fuller, John G. *The Day We Bombed Utah: American's Most Lethal Secret*. New York: New American Library, 1984.

Furnas, C. C. *The Next Hundred Years: The Unfinished Business of Science*. New York: Blue Ribbon Books, 1936.

Fussell, Paul. *The Great War and Modern Memory*. New York: Oxford University Press, 1975.

Geduld, Carolyn. *Bernard Wolfe*. TUSAS 211. New York: Twayne, 1972.

Gernsback, Hugo, F. R. S. "A New Sort of Magazine." *Amazing Stories: The Magazine of Scientification* 1, no. 1 (April 1926): 3.

Groueff, Stephane. *Manhattan Project: The Untold Story of the Making of the Atomic Bomb*. Boston: Little, Brown, 1967.

Gunn, James. *Alternate Worlds: the Illustrated History of Science Fiction*. Englewood Cliffs, N.J.: Prentice-Hall, 1975.

———. *The Road to Science Fiction: From Gilgamesh to Wells*. New York: Mentor/NAL, 1977.

Hall, Edward T. *Beyond Culture*. Garden City, N.Y.: Anchor/Doubleday, 1977.

———. *The Silent Language*. Garden City, N.Y.: Anchor/Doubleday, 1973.

Hall, Harry S. "Scientists and Politicians." *Bulletin of the Atomic Scientists*, February, 1956. Reprinted in *The Sociology of Science*, edited by Bernard Barber and Walter Hirsch. New York: Free Press of Glencoe, 1962, 269–87.

Heinlein, Robert A[nson]. Forward to "The Last Days of the United States." In *Expanded Universe: The New Worlds of Robert A. Heinlein*. New York: Ace Books, 1980, 145–47.

———. "On the Writing of Speculative Fiction." In *Turning Points: Essays on the Art of Science Fiction*, edited by Damon Knight. New York: Harper & Row, 1977, 199–204.

———. "Science Fiction: Its Nature, Faults and Virtues." In *Turning Points: Essays on the Art of Science Fiction*, edited by Damon Knight. New York: Harper & Row, 1977, 3–28.

Hersey, John. *Hiroshima*. New York: Knopf, 1946.

Hilgartner, C. A. "How to Abolish War." *International Language Reporter* XV: 54 (1969): 1, 7–24.

———. "Some Traditional Assumings Underlying Western Indo-European Languages: Unstated, Unexamined, and Untenable." *General Semantics Bulletin* 44/45, 1977–78: 132–53.

Hilgartner, Stephen, Richard C. Bell, and Rory O'Connor. *Nukespeak: Nuclear Language, Visions, and Mindset*. San Francisco: Sierra Club, 1982.

Hirsch, Walter. "The Image of the Scientist in Science Fiction: A Content Analysis." *American Journal of Sociology* 63 (1958): 506–12.

Johnson, Wendell. *Verbal Man: The Enchantment of Words*. New York: Collier, 1956.

Kermode, Frank. *The Sense of an Ending*. London: Oxford University Press, 1966.

Keyser, Cassius Jackson. "Korzybski's Concept of Man." In *Manhood of Humanity*, by Alfred Korzybski. 2nd ed. Lakeville, Conn: International Non-Aristotelian Library Publishing Co., 1950.

Knight, Damon. *The Futurians*. New York: John Day, 1977.

———, ed. *Turning Points: Essays on the Art of Science Fiction*. New York: Harper and Row, 1977.

Korzybski, Alfred. *Manhood of Humanity*. 2nd ed. Lakeville, Conn.: International Non-Aristotelian Library Publishing Co., 1950.

Krutch, Joseph Wood. *Human Nature and the Human Condition*. New York: Random House, 1959.

———. *The Modern Temper*. New York: Harcourt, Brace, 1929.

Kuhn, Thomas S. *The Essential Tension: Selected Studies in Scientific Tradition and Change*. Chicago: University of Chicago Press, 1977.

———. *The Structure of Scientific Revolutions*. 2nd ed. Chicago: University of Chicago Press, 1970.

Lakoff, George and Mark Johnson. *Metaphors We Live By*. Chicago: University of Chicago Press, 1980.

Lasch, Christopher. *The New Radicalism in America (1889–1963): The Intellectual as a Social Type*. New York: Knopf, 1965.

Laurence, William L. *Dawn over Zero: The Story of the Atomic Bomb*. New York: Knopf, 1946.

Lévi-Strauss, Claude. *Structural Anthropology*. Translated by Claire Jacobson and Brooke Grundfest Schoepf. New York: Basic Books, 1963.

Manhoff, Robert Karl. "The Silencer." *ETC.: A Review of General Semantics* 41 (Summer 1984): 152–59.

Maslow, A. H. *Motivation and Personality*. New York: Harper, 1954.

Mead, Margaret, and Rhoda Métraux. "The Image of the Scientist among High-School Students: A Pilot Study." *Science* 126, no. 3270 (August 20, 1957): 384–90. Reprinted in *The Sociology of Science*, edited by Bernard Barber and Walter Hirsch. New York: Free Press of Glencoe, 1962, 230–46.

Menger, Lucy. *Theodore Sturgeon*. New York: Frederick Ungar, 1981.

Merril, Judith. Introduction to *SF, The Best of the Best*, edited by Judith Merril. New York: Delacorte, 1967, 1–7.

Montagu, Ashley. *The Biosocial Nature of Man*. New York: Grove, 1956.

Morison, Samuel Eliot. *The Oxford History of the American People*. New York: Oxford University Press, 1965.

Moskowitz, Samuel. "Fantasy and Science Fiction by Theodore Sturgeon." *Magazine of Fantasy and Science Fiction*, September 1962, 55–61.

———. *Seekers of Tomorrow: Masters of Modern Science Fiction*. Westport, Conn.: Hyperion Press, 1966.

———. "Theodore Sturgeon: No More Than Human." *Amazing Fact and Science Fiction Stories*, February 1962, 27–39.

Moskowitz, Samuel, and Robert Madle. "Did Science Fiction Predict Atomic Energy?" *Science Fiction Quarterly*, November 1952, 81–88.

New York *Times*. *Hiroshima Plus 20*. New York: Delacorte Press, 1965.

Noyes, Pierrepont Burt. *While Europe Waits for Peace; describing the progress of economic and political demoralization in Europe during the year of American hesitation*. New York: Macmillan, 1921.

O'Neill, John J. *Almighty Atom: The Real Story of Atomic Energy*. New York: Ives Washburn, 1945.

Panshin, Alexei. *Heinlein in Dimension*. Chicago: Advent, 1969.

Parrinder, Patrick. "Utopia and Meta-Utopia in H. G. Wells." *Science-Fiction Studies* 36 (July 1985): 115–28.

Peirce, Charles S. *The Essential Writings*. Edited by Edward C. Moore. New York: Harper, 1972.

Perls, Frederick S., Ralph Hefferline, and Paul Goodman. *Gestalt Therapy Excitement and Growth in the Human Personality*. New York: Julian Press, 1951.

Pocket BOOKS. *The Atomic Age Opens*. Montreal: Pocket Books, 1945.

Pohl, Frederik. "The Publishing of Science Fiction." In *Science Fiction, Today and Tomorrow*, edited by Reginald Bretnor. New York: Harper, 1974: 17–44.

———. *The Way the Future Was: A Memoir*. New York: Ballantine, 1978.

Rhodes, Richard. *The Making of the Atomic Bomb*. New York: Simon and Schuster, 1986.

Rockwell, Joan. *Fact in Fiction: The Use of Literature in the Systematic Study of Society*. London: Routledge and Kegan Paul, 1974.

Sapir, Edward. *Language*. New York: Harcourt, Brace, 1949.

Schell, Jonathan. *The Fate of the Earth*. New York: Knopf, 1982.

Scholes, Robert. *Textual Power: Literary Theory and the Teaching of English*. New Haven: Yale University Press, 1985.

Scholes, Robert, and Eric S. Rabkin. *Science Fiction: History, Science, Vision*. New York: Oxford University Press, 1977.

Slusser, George. *The Classic Years of Robert A. Heinlein*. The Milford Series, Popular Writers of Today, vol. 11. San Bernardino, Calif.: Borgo Press, 1977.

Smythe, Henry De Wolf. *Atomic Energy for Military Purposes*. Princeton: Princeton University Press, 1946.

Strauss, Erwin S., comp. *The MIT Science Fiction Society's Index to the S-F Magazines, 1951–1965*. Cambridge, Mass.: MIT Science Fiction Society, 1966.

Sturgeon, Theodore. Foreword to *Sturgeon Is Alive and Well. . . .* New York: Putnam, 1971, 9–12.

———. Telephone interview. June 6, 1983. Reproduced with permission in *Symbol to Scenario: the Atomic Bomb in American Science Fiction, 1930–1960* by Martha A. Bartter, 385–86. Diss. University of Rochester, 1986.

Superman from the Thirties to the Eighties. New York: Crown Publishers, 1983.

Suvin, Darko. *Metamorphoses of Science Fiction*. New Haven: Yale University Press, 1979.

Tuchman, Barbara W. *The Guns of August*. New York: Macmillan, 1962.

Tucker, Frank H. "Major Political and Social Elements in Heinlein's Fiction." In *Robert A. Heinlein*, edited by Joseph D. Olander and Martin Harry Greenberg. Writers of the 21st Century. New York: Taplinger, 1978, 172–93.

Van Tassel, Eric. "Remembrance." *Fellowship* 50, nos. 7–8 (July–August 1984): 31.

Vygotsky, Lev. *Thought and Language*. Translated by Eugenia Hanfmann and Gertrude Vakar. Cambridge, Mass.: the M.I.T. Press, 1962.

Weinbaum, Stanley G. "An Autobiographical Sketch." *Fantasy Magazine*, June 1935. Reprinted in *Gosh! Wow! (Sense of Wonder) Science Fiction*, edited by Forrest J. Ackerman. New York: Bantam, 1981, 384–85.

Whorf, Benjamin Lee. *Language, Thought and Reality*, edited by John B. Carrol. New York: Wiley, 1956.

Williamson, Jack. *Wonder's Child: My Life in Science Fiction*. New York: Bluejay, 1984.

Wilson, Robert O. *Sociobiology: The New Synthesis*. Cambridge, Mass.: Belknap, 1975.

Wolfe, Gary K. *Critical Terms for Science Fiction and Fantasy: A Glossary and Guide to Scholarship*. Westport, Conn.: Greenwood Press, 1986.

———. "The Remaking of Zero: Beginning at the End." In *The End of the World*, edited by Eric S. Rabkin, Martin H. Greenberg and Joseph D. Olander. Carbondale: Southern Illinois University Press, 1983, 1–19.

Index

About the Author

MARTHA A. BARTTER is a member of the English Department of the Ohio State University at Marion. A former book reviewer for the Gannett Rochester newspapers, she has written several articles on science fiction and is currently working on a novel.